New Approaches to Welfare Theory

Edited by
Glenn Drover
Patrick Kerans

Edward Elgar

Published by Edward Elgar Publishing Limited
Gower House
Croft Road
Aldershot
Hants GU11 3HR
England

Edward Elgar Publishing Company
Old Post Road
Brookfield
Vermont 05036
U.S.A.

British Library Cataloguing in Publication Data

New Approaches to Welfare Theory: Making
and Sorting Claims
    I. Drover, Glenn II. Kerans, Patrick
    361.6

ISBN 1 85278 881 X (cloth)
      1 85278 981 6 (paperback)

Printed in Great Britain at the University Press, Cambridge

Contents

List of Contributors

Michael Bach is a research consultant on Public Policy and Disability at the Roeher Institute, Toronto, and is Assistant Professor (Part-time) in the Faculty of Environmental Studies at York University, Ontario.

Ota de Leonardis is Professor of Sociology at University of Milan

David Donaldson, Professor of Economics at University of British Columbia, works in social choice theory and welfare economics.

Len Doyal taught moral and political theory at Middlesex University for over twenty years and is now Senior Lecturer in Medical Ethics at the London and St. Bartholomew's Hospital Medical College.

Glenn Drover is Professor at the School of Social Work, University of British Columbia.

Ian Gough is Reader in Social Policy at the University of Manchester.

Derek Hum is Professor of Economics and Fellow of St. John's College, University of Manitoba.

Lesley A. Jacobs is Assistant Professor of Philosophy and Social Science at York University in Toronto.

Jane Jenson teaches in the Département de science politique of the Université de Montréal.

Bill Jordan, after 20 years in practice as a social worker, and teaching on training courses for social workers at Exeter University, is currently Principal Lecturer in Social Work at Huddersfield University.

Patrick Kerans is Professor at the Maritime School of Social Work, Dalhousie University, Halifax, Nova Scotia.

Henri Lustiger-Thaler teaches social theory and urban sociology at Concordia University in Montreal.

Ronald Melchers is Associate Professor of Criminology at the University of Ottawa where he teaches public policy and research.

Allan Moscovitch teaches social welfare policy in the School of Social Work, Carleton University, Ottawa.

Claus Offe is Professor of Political Science and Sociology and co-director at the Centre for Social Policy Research, University of Bremen.

Gillian Pascall is Lecturer in Social Policy in the School of Social Studies, University of Nottingham.

Peter Penz teaches in Environmental of Studies at York University.

Raymond Plant, Professor of Politics, Southampton University, is Opposition spokesperson on Home Affairs in the House of Lords.

Janice L. Ristock is Coordinator of the Women's Studies Program and Assistant Professor at the University of Manitoba.

Alan Scott teaches in the School of Economic and Social Studies, University of East Anglia.

Eric Shragge teaches social policy and community organization at the School of Social Work, McGill University.

Dorothy E. Smith is Professor of Sociology at the Ontario Institute for Studies in Education at the University of Toronto.

Kate Soper is Senior Lecturer in Philosophy at the University of North London.

Tim Stainton is Assistant Professor of Social Work at McGill University, specializing in disability and philosophy and social welfare.

Deborah Stienstra teaches politics at the University of Winnipeg, Manitoba, and researches women's international organizing.

In addition to the contributors to this volume, the following people participated in the seminar where these papers were presented.

Nancy Fraser is Professor of Philosophy at Northwestern University, Evanston, Illinois

Kathryn McCannell is Associate Professor in the School of Social Work at the University of British Columbia.

Gerald de Montigny is Supervisor of Undergraduate Studies at the School of Social Work, Carleton University, Ottawa.

Raymond Morrow is Professor of Sociology at the University of Alberta.

Gillian Walker is Director of the School of Social Work, Carleton University, Ottawa.

Introduction

This book grew out of a seminar held in Aylmer, Quebec, September 24–8, 1992. It is the product of a group of international scholars invited to the seminar to share their insights into the meaning and dynamics of claims-making in modern society. The seminar was interdisciplinary in focus including academics from economics, political science, philosophy, psychology, sociology, social work and women's studies.

Since the collapse of the Fordist paradigm — or what has been more generally called the Keynesian consensus — in the 1970s, social policy has been at an impasse (Myles 1988). While there have been interesting developments in welfare theory, notably in international political economy and in philosophy, they have shed little light on strategic questions with respect to the impasse. It seemed to us, however, that there were important studies on exactly these strategic questions in the sociology of social action, in the feminist literature, and in critical social theory. On the basis of an exploratory essay, which eventually became Chapter 1 of this volume, we invited a variety of scholars to help us work through some of the problems and implications of an approach to welfare from the perspective of social action.

THE SEMINAR

In that paper, we characterized the major tension in welfare theory to be that between 'thin' and 'thick' notions of need. However, while the relationship between these two notions and indeed the usefulness of the distinction were discussed at length during the seminar, no-one in their subsequent reflections on the seminar named this tension as a principal issue. Participants spoke instead of the tension between 'universalist' and 'particularist' approaches to welfare even though the language they used to speak of the tension varied somewhat because of their diverse academic background. Kate Soper, a philosopher, spoke of a

> definite sense of focus on the central tensions of welfare theory, and it was very interesting to have the respective strengths and limitations of *universalist* versus *difference* approaches illuminated from such a wide range of perspectives.

Ota de Leonardis, a sociologist, dealt with this same tension, in both her paper and her comment on the seminar, by contrasting a 'basic capabilities' approach to welfare with that of abstract rights:

> On the one hand, a capabilities approach puts the emphasis on individual or group needs and the corresponding inequalities, but it does not go on from there to derive any objective or decisive definition of needs upon which to work out interpretations or policies for the good of those individuals or groups. Conversely, this perspective implies a subject who is the bearer of rights, but these have a status different from the formal abstract rights of the traditional guarantee system: these are rights to the resources needed by each person to exercise his/her own basic capabilities.

Alan Scott, also a sociologist, made two important points about the distinction by linking the debate about welfare to practice and middle-range theorizing:

> The most striking division was between universalizing approaches and those which started from practice and attempted middle-range theorizing. The universalizing approaches were not confined to philosophy but included sociology and economics.

These observations, in our mind, are interconnected. If one brackets the moral dimension which is implied by the term 'welfare', and begins with actual practice within the parameters of action theory, one can pursue the investigations which are the subject of many of the chapters in this volume. However, if one is to characterize the overall project as welfare theory, then one must eventually deal with how the findings of the social scientific inquiries relate to philosophic reflections about the moral dimension of welfare. To speak of 'moral dimension' has usually meant, because of the influence of Kant, reversibility of standpoint, which issues in universalizability: a person has achieved a moral point of view only when s/he has examined the question from another's standpoint and can safely say that any other person would reasonably have to agree. However, this position has been attacked — first by Hegel and latterly by the communitarians — as too individualistic and formalistic. Though we do not think of ourselves as philosophers, our seemingly innocent suggestion to approach welfare questions from the point of view of social action landed us in the middle of one of the central philosophical disputes of our time.

Bill Jordan, a social worker, set the tension in perhaps its most comprehensive context:

> The seminar discussions tended to be polarized between abstract analyses in terms of universal yet individuated needs and distributional justice and praxis-based analyses of diversified autonomy among emerging social groups and movements.

A praxis-based approach to welfare notes as a matter of fact that claims are made by groups. Given technical capabilities of the powerful in modern society to manipulate and restrain people's sense of themselves, it is only (we will argue) from groups characterized by mutual respect and recognition that claims can be made which will challenge hegemonic order. It is only in such groups that people can learn to name their aspirations and needs and on that basis make claims. In the end a theory must deal with the welfare of individuals; but to begin there is to leave out an essential element in the understanding of the social process of making and responding to claims.

Henri Lustiger-Thaler, a sociologist, also characterized the tension from that perspective.

> My own sense is that much social movement theory has been seduced by the diversity of claims lodged in the increasingly impossible arena of the political, where identity concerns are played out as a form of cultural praxis. The problematic hiatus for social movement theories is between the widening sphere of values and politics. The importance of the seminar for me was to see a similar problematic addressed in terms (and languages) not often used by the social movement theories more interested in establishing a theory of action than a theory of needs.
>
> In brief, I think that there is much work to do, not only for the welfare theorist here but for the social movement theorist as well. The most important part of this seminar, certainly for me, was in bringing together these two disciplines.

But he was not alone in this characterization of the problem. Deborah Stienstra, a political scientist, queried the value of even making a distinction between theory and practice:

> At times the conference broke down into those who dealt with theory and those who discussed practice....This was a surprising element of the conference to me partially since I have a difficult time separating the two approaches so neatly.

Her observation was reinforced by Janice Ristock, a psychologist who, from a feminist perspective, remarked not only on the unnecessary, and possibly unhelpful, divide between theory and practice, but also on the linear method of presentation and discussion of the seminar which highlighted some aspects of welfare while ignoring or downplaying others. One way she suggested of bridging the gap was by starting theory from a specific location.

> Why were we focusing on autonomy, claims and independence? What about empowerment and interdependence? I recognize that many of these issues reflect the difficulties of doing interdisciplinary work — how do we find a common language? But I do think that feminism has at least emphasized the need to locate ourselves in our work as a place to begin when working through and with issues of diversity and difference.

Kathryn McCannell, also a psychologist and a feminist, put the same issue somewhat differently. For her the divide between theory and practice was unsatisfactory, both personally and professionally. It reinforced a language of exclusion rather than inclusion, of essentialism rather than of plurality, of disembodied talk rather than body talk. Instead for her

> The recurring themes were interdependence and diversity. I kept feeling/thinking we were stuck in a paradigm with blinders. How does an almost entirely white group of people so 'schooled' in one way of thinking see beyond its borders to conceptualize 'new parameters'.

In his assessment of the seminar, Derek Hum, an economist, raised concerns about the lack of attention to important everyday issues like race, religion, or culture, as well as a propensity to focus almost exclusively on the demand side of claimsmaking.

> Many commented on the need to recognize the broader concept of 'work', in particular the naming of need or the construction of a narrative to utter a credible claim for entitlement that lies outside the narrow confines of market paid work....For me, most of this reduced to the familiar (legitimate) refrain of the social work position of claimsmaking as 'mere asking' without regard to specifying the resources that are needed.

Peter Penz, also an economist, also elaborated on the tensions between practice and theory by stressing the need for more consideration of institutional parameters and materiality. He remarked that there was

> a dimension missing. On the one hand, we focused on the ethical dimension of social welfare, and, on the other, on discourse closer to the ground. Between the two of them, however, it seemed sometimes as though only thought matters. The actual economic and structural pressures seemed to be neglected.... Nor was there any focus on social welfare in the context of global economic restructuring....Are we becoming so postmodern that the material base not only loses its causal primacy, but loses its causal significance entirely?

It is clear from these observations that simply to begin with action theory, as we proposed, and to note the radical pluralism entailed in the variety of value-frames which groups develop as they come to articulate their aspirations and claims, is insufficient for a welfare theory. One cannot assume that claimsmaking is progressive and not raise the philosophic question of the grounds for evaluating a group as progressive. That means that the claim of a group in the name of the welfare of its own members must be morally evaluated, and the grounds of that evaluation must be specified.

While we had originally focused on 'thin' and 'thick' notions of need, after the searching discussion at the seminar, we see the distinction as one which, while helpful, led to differences which could be resolved — or indeed clarified — only if one broached the 'universalist-particularist' problem directly.

Ensuing from the discussion, there was some agreement on thin and thick need. For instance, there seemed no dissent from the proposition that a thin notion made reference to the right, a thick notion to the good. During the seminar, Nancy Fraser,[1] a philosopher who first used the thin–thick word pair with relation to need (Fraser 1989), suggested that a thick notion takes for granted the legitimacy of need as a distributive criterion; to elaborate a thin notion was to argue against those who do not believe that need constitutes a privileged basis of distribution. Offe, a sociologist, read this relationship at a practical level, asking which of these two sets of concerns, in today's conjuncture, is more contested, more precarious, more central in political discourse. However, Ian Gough, a political economist, seemed to read it at a theoretical level, when he said that he could accept the thick notion of need if it 'played a component role' within the thin notion. He also argued that the two notions should be treated dichotomously, while others insisted that thin and thick formed a continuum.

Thus, what seemed a consensus around the thin–thick word pair was actually concealing a serious disagreement. Behind Gough's position on need — reflected in Doyal's response to Soper (*infra*) — was a position on the relation between a descriptive account and a normative evaluation of claims: since 'need' is a notion with moral weight, and since a moral notion must be objective, a mere description of claims ought not to include the notion of need. Admittedly, by using 'need' in both senses, we had been trying to make the argument that a different understanding of the objectivity of moral notions, and hence of the relationship between moral notions and empirical description, should obtain. It now seems that it would have been far clearer to make that argument directly rather than try to hang it, so to speak, on the notion of need. The concerns which were raised at the seminar advanced considerably our thinking which is outlined at the beginning of this volume. To respond to those concerns and to address what we consider to be some of their theoretical implications, we return to a discussion of universalist and particularist perspectives of welfare in an Afterword. At the core of the tension between universalism and particularism, theory and practice, is, as we see it, the essential dilemma of how one sorts claims.

THE BOOK

The first chapter outlines our initial approach, which is to examine the claims which groups — especially groups of marginalized people — make against various institutions in the name of their own well-being. In the first chapter, we explore: 1) the difficulty which groups experience in articulating their aspirations, needs and claims; 2) the structured institutional responses to those claims; and 3) the dynamics of claimsmaking, especially the applicability of the notions of social action and collective action. Tim Stainton, in his comment,[2] recasts our approach by delineating three discursive realms — that of a thin theory of the good, that of decisional distance, and that of everyday life — by exploring briefly the relations among them.

The next four contributions focus on the problems of establishing the moral justifiability of claims. Over the past two hundred years, there have been two approaches to this problem, the consequentialist approach of utilitarianism and the principled consensual approach of contractarianism. All of our contributors explore the contractarian approach within a broad discourse of rights; one commentator affirms the merits of utilitarianism. Raymond Plant reviews the arguments rejecting a qualitative difference between civil rights and welfare rights. He also explores more recent arguments, which state that reception of state aid destroys one's self-respect in a culture which sets up independence as a norm. Lesley Jacobs provides a possible framework to understand the ethical dimension of claims. Responses to claims, he suggests, cannot be morally neutral, but can and should raise questions about how valuable are the goals and form of life implied by a claim. His concern is to create theoretical space for a theory of differential provision in order to achieve equality of life prospects. Kate Soper highlights the pitfalls for welfare theory in opting either for a universalist (thin) or a particularist (thick) theory of need by examining the weaknesses of both positions. Len Doyal's comment defends universalist theory.

The second set of papers deal with the constraining and enabling effects of social structures on claimsmaking; the various excluding and filtering institutional responses, rooted in structural patterns of inequality and oppression; and the interaction between claimsmakers and those who act in the name of hegemonic order as well as other claimsmakers. Because of the centrality of market norms in the institutional sorting of welfare claims, we have placed the chapters on economic institutions first. Ian Gough combines the findings from his book with Doyal on a theoretically grounded and operational definition of universal need with an analysis of institutional economics, to discuss which economic system fits best with the demands of procedural and material need satisfiers. He comes to the controversial conclusion that, apart from market socialism (which he does not discuss) corporatist systems may meet needs more adequately than other forms of market provision. Peter Penz, in response, challenges Gough's consensual approach, in light of the achievements of the communist regime of West Bengal in tackling poverty. Taking quite a different tack, Derek Hum highlights some of the discursive measures which economic institutions deploy through the practices of economists to defend and even mask extant power imbalances. David Donaldson, however, suggests that it is not only discourse which is at issue in understanding welfare questions but poor welfare economics. He shows that Pareto-optimality is neutral with respect to various distributive options. Because of the weakness of Paretianism, his own preference is an enriched utilitarianism.

The two following papers explore the interaction of claimsmakers with political institutions, each exploring citizenship as contested terrain. Starting with the tension between the equality connoted by citizenship and the dependence of women within the family, Gillian Pascall explores the implications of a politics of difference with respect to needs, rights and duties. An important contribution in her analysis are the different models she elaborates for understanding the reciprocity between rights and duties, in the light of women's experience of inequality. Jane Jenson examines the relation between citizens and the state in a different way by arguing that traditional dualities of inclusion–exclusion, which entail universal rights attaching to each individual, have been effectively challenged by a series of subcommunities in the Canadian context. For them, universally applicable individual rights are inherently unsatisfactory even if they are politically useful. Ronald Melchers explores the judicial system of the state both as resource and as constraint, arguing that the claims made against it are primarily for new identities. While the courts and police are engaged in the 'social production of crime', social actors make claims that the social meaning of various actions be redefined, in light of their own experience and problems.

We have next grouped those papers whose primary focus is on the interactions between social groups and institutional patterns. Henri Lustiger-Thaler and Eric Shragge attempt to sort a variety of interrelations between the local state and groups which have provided alternate social services and community economic development. They argue that the matrix of social rights is basically conflictual, since '...formal democracy is incapable of revealing its own inequalities, thereby consistently nurturing negativity' in the form of social movements, and that the conflict takes two basic forms, the demand for rights of inclusion within a political system and for counter-rights directed towards institutional transformation. Alan Scott argues that while the distinction they make is useful it cannot be thought of as categorical, but should be seen as between ideal types which are variable over time. Ota de Leonardis, in her paper, concentrates on the empirical point made by Lustiger-Thaler and Shragge. She notes that while there is a general dismantling of much of the protection associated with the welfare state, a new rights discourse has become established which enables groups to define their needs and to cease being 'passive recipients of institutional interventions', and become 'active, competent and also conflictual partners in the decisions that affect them.' Since this new relationship also opens the way for a politics of difference, she argues that welfare theory should turn away from the universal notion of need to Sen's notion of capabilities, which more readily grounds a politics of difference.

Michael Bach analyses a claim made by a young man before a court that, despite his profound mental and physical disabilities, he should be entitled to live outside an institution. While Bach uses postmodern conceptual tools, such as narrative and its relation to an emerging, fragmented self, his analysis explores the interrelations between personal knowledge of the particularity and abstract knowledge of universal norms. Bill Jordan, reporting from professional experience and a major qualitative research project, suggests that the practices of resistance by the weak do not encompass the articulation of oppositional discourse or (to use Lustiger-Thaler's and Shragge's word) the framing of counter-rights. While ostensibly accepting the dominant discourse and articulating their experience within its terms, according to Jordan, the powerless develop alternate interpretations in order to express and explain their deviance. He argues that the artful practices of the weak are not only strategic (in giving them symbolic space to resist) but are interactional in motivation: dominator and dominated have an interest in saving each other's face; this consideration overrides even the requirements of justice. While Allan Moscovitch has some questions about the generalizability of lessons drawn from Jordan's samples, he nonetheless agrees that, in his experience as the chair and coordinator of a legislative review of a social assistance programme, recipients by and large accept the publicly defined rules governing them. In contrast to Jordan, Janice Ristock reports on her research among members of feminist collectives providing alternate social services. She concludes that, despite the pressure to conform to 'mainstream' values and organizational norms, they succeed in keeping their organizational practices in conformity with their ideology. Despite tensions, they are able both to provide social services and work for social change. She outlines the main characteristics of feminist, alternative service: the empowerment of clients; the respect of clients' choices; an ethic of care; survival in the face of oppression. Deborah Stienstra comments that while Ristock has given a rich and nuanced account of feminist social service collectives, she overdraws the tension between mainstream and collectives.

We asked two eminent sociologists, Dorothy Smith and Claus Offe, each to give us their overview of the papers and the discussions at the seminar. Their concluding remarks are sharply contrasting statements of the two perspectives on welfare theory which emerged in a variety of guises during the three-day discussion, namely the 'universalist' and 'particularist'. Drawing on the notion of standpoint (with which she is often associated), Smith argues that it is altogether too easy for theorists to occlude important realities and motivations of everyday life. She locates people's everyday quest for welfare in 'life support economies' and suggests that welfare theory should examine the ways in which people resist the interference by capitalist institutions in their life support economy. Offe's theme is the political probability of an acceptance of claims. He suggests that this probability will vary inversely with three factors: the costliness of the resources demanded, the social distance between claimsmakers and those who will bear the costs, and the moral separation of the rights demanded from burdens accepted by the individual claimsmakers. Thus he argues that social homogeneity can be expected to correlate with a strong welfare state (as in the case of Sweden), and questions the 'romanticizing celebration of particularistic identities.'

In our Afterword, we try to clear up some difficulties with our approach, which seem to have arisen largely from a lack of clarity in our earlier formulations. However, the major point of the Afterword is to return to the question of universalism and particularism in respect of the moral dimensions of welfare. We also think that a reading of the book will show that each contributor is striving to give an account of welfare claims which encompasses both the particularity of the claims and a broad, universally accepted set of discursive norms which will enable the claimsmakers and respondents to engage in contestation and negotiation. What separates contributors is the attempt to specify the relation between the two. Those in this volume who lean to universalism argue that universal moral norms ought to set the frame for the variety of claims, and provide criteria both for settling the differences and setting the limits *a priori* of responsible differences. Those with a particularist approach place more emphasis on the politics of difference. Our sense, however, is that most contributions actually explore claimsmaking either implicitly or explicitly as a dialectical relationship between the universal norms which supply the cultural matrices whereby situations are interpreted, and the particularities of people's experience. This dialectical relationship, we conclude in the Afterword, may be best characterized as a hermeneutic circle.

ACKNOWLEDGEMENTS

We wish first to acknowledge the support of Sandra Chatterton, Program Consultant and Dr David Thornton, Director, at National Welfare Grants, in the federal department of Health and Welfare Canada, the source of funding for the seminar and this book. Secondly, we thank the participants of the seminar, who were enormously disciplined, even-tempered and hard working. The contributors to this volume have been equally cooperative and punctual in meeting deadlines. Marion Kerans was especially helpful in organizing the seminar. Elizabeth Eve has done wonders as editorial assistant. Aside from participants and contributors and organizers, however, several people have been extremely important from the beginning, with their encouragement, their criticisms and their pointing to implications of our approach which we had not seen: Nancy Fraser in Chicago; Deborah Stienstra in Winnipeg; Michael Bach and Peter Penz in Toronto; David Braybrooke, Jeanne Fay and Michael Welton in Halifax; Ron Melchers and Allan Moscovitch in Ottawa; Peter Taylor-Gooby in Canterbury; and Iain Marrs in Vancouver. We are also fortunate to have been able to work in close collaboration on a cognate project with David Hay, Michael Clague and Michael Goldberg of the Social Planning and Research Council of British Columbia, with Deborah Rutman and Andrew Armitage of the University of Victoria, and with Marcia Rioux, Leon Muszynski and Michael Bach of the Roeher Institute in Toronto. Most importantly we are deeply grateful for the encouragement and support of our spouses, Eleanor and Marion.

NOTES

1   The paper which Nancy Fraser and Linda Gordon contributed to the seminar 'A Genealogy of Dependence' could, unfortunately, not be included in this volume for copyright reasons. It will appear in *Signs* in 1993.

2   The papers were not read at the seminar; a commentator introduced each one. Some comments were incorporated into chapters; some were expanded into chapters themselves; others could not be revised because of time constraints. The comments are found at the end of this book.

FRAMEWORK

1. New Approaches to Welfare Theory: Foundations

Glenn Drover and Patrick Kerans

Theories of human well-being or welfare have been fraught with many difficulties.[1] To overcome these difficulties, we are proposing an approach to welfare which is rooted in the notion of social action (Dawe 1978; Hassard and Pym 1990; Honneth and Joas 1988), specifically focusing on claimsmaking.[2] Other distinctive features of the approach are the following: 1) we root the notion of need in the process of claimsmaking as it emerges from everyday practice;[3] 2) we go beyond theories of the political economy of the state both by considering other axes of oppression besides class and by recognizing that welfare claims are made against institutions other than the state; and 3) we move beyond the debate on social movements around resource mobilization and identity to focus on organization and goals within a context of social action.

1. ALTERNATIVE APPROACHES

Modern notions of welfare or well-being have been stimulated by important developments in economics and the social sciences that began with the rise of utilitarianism (Barry 1990; Goodin 1988; Pinker 1979; Plant 1991a; Weale 1978). Essential to classical utilitarianism (Bentham 1982) is the idea that individual well-being or welfare is tied to human happiness and that public policies should be judged right or wrong to the extent that they achieve the greatest happiness of the greatest number. Inherent in the utilitarian notion of well-being is an ineradicable element of subjectivism since ultimately, as subsequent debate has shown, whether happiness is defined as pleasure and the absence of pain or preference and choice, the inevitable measure of utility is individual sensation or individual consumption. What welfare economics has done in large measure (Culyer 1973) is to take these utilitarian assumptions as given (although utility increasingly has been weakened to mean little more than a ranking of preferred alternatives and an embargo has been placed on interpersonal comparisons) and postulate that the maximization of social welfare is realized through a process of exchange when one person can be made better off (by his or her own definition) while others are made no worse off (a Pareto optimum). From that assumption, it is a short jump to the central theorems of welfare economics and the optimal conditions of market provision.

Modern welfare ethical theories have broadened the scope of well-being beyond simple preference utilitarianism to more sophisticated versions based on enjoyment, accomplishment, personal relations, liberty, health, security, and meaningful work (Griffin 1986; Hahnel and Albert 1990; Sumner 1992). However, because of its welfarist consequentialism (Sen 1979, 1987c p.39), utilitarianism is inadequate as a definitional base for well-being on four accounts. First, it focuses on the benevolence involved in ameliorating states of affairs rather than on agency (Williams 1985). Second, while well-being is postulated to be tied to individual preferences, the question of the autonomy of individual preferences is begged. Third, because the manipulability of preferences is ignored, the social processes required to make autonomous claims and to settle those claims justly have also been ignored. Finally, utilitarianism, even in its expanded version, cannot conceptualize the maximization of welfare except as a summation of individual well-being (Sen and Williams (eds) 1982). While contractarianism goes beyond utilitarianism in positing rights as having intrinsic rather than instrumental value (Dworkin 1977; Walzer 1983; Rawls 1971), it is beset by the weakness of assuming an 'unencumbered self'; thus it postulates fictitious processes which are meant to lay bare the rational demands of a just distribution. The contractarian approach asks whether claims are based on right while our approach focuses on the social meaning of claimsmaking. In examining the question of social meaning, we are closer to feminists than communitarians since we emphasize not the cultural distinctiveness of claims, but the hegemonic context.

A needs-based approach to well-being cuts across these various approaches. It rests on an objective and universal notion of need with determinate content and with 'moral weight', which can thereby command universal assent as the basis of the non-market allocation of resources. Thus, need is said to become the objective basis for persons having a right to goods that has priority over the market demand which others might have over that same good (Braybrooke 1987).

The objective notion of need has been developed in contradistinction to notions such as preference or want. Need on this view refers not to instinctual drives nor indeed to any motivation for action, but to the objective preconditions required for a person to attain a goal (Doyal and Gough 1991 pp.50–55). Key to this argument is that a lack of the requisite precondition will issue in harm, which is the source of the moral weight of need. A subjective assessment of the ensuing harm is insufficient to establish need; an objective determination is required (Plant 1991a pp.190–92). Thus an expert is often — and in principle — in a better position to assess need than the subject (Kerans 1993). On the left[4] it is clear who have been considered the experts: those with the theoretical overview of the exploitative conditions of workers' lives, caused by a regime of capital accumulation, are in a position to impute to the workers what their true, long-term needs are.[5]

Whatever the philosophic strengths of a needs-based approach to well-being, from a social action viewpoint the implication that need is in principle best known by experts is a difficulty. Even those who have developed this approach admit the danger of paternalism and officiousness, of 'arrogant and pernicious elitism' (Penz 1987 p.17; Braybrooke 1987 p.14). Right-wing critics of the welfare state since Pareto have pounced on this weakness of need-as-known-by-experts, insisting that it gives rise to the 'despotism of experts' and rejecting the very notion of needs (Flew 1981; Gaylin et al. 1978). On the left, neo-marxist debates around the state, focusing on the dependency created by welfare programmes, implicitly criticized the notion of need. While they ascribe this dependency to the role of the welfare state as the reinforcer of the unequal market relations, we find it more parsimonious to say simply that dependency is forced on people when an expert — whether a vanguard party, a policy maker or a social worker — has the authority to tell them what they really need (London Edinburgh Weekend Return Group 1980; Jessop 1982; Offe 1984).

Our concern is that posing the question of needs in this way has presupposed that the question of welfare is primarily about the distribution of resources (Young 1990a pp.15–38); we will argue, instead, that welfare or well-being entails three stakes: identity, resources and relationships, especially caring relationships (Baines 1991; Kymlicka 1990; Allen 1987; Tronto 1987). The following sketch of a new approach to social welfare examines the problematic of social identity from the viewpoint of the duality of claimsmaking; the implication for resource distribution is the background to our discussion of institutional order; and the dynamics of effective claimsmaking pursues the question of relationships.

2. THE DUALITY OF CLAIMSMAKING

We start our discussion of the duality of claimsmaking by focusing on the notion of the development of human capacities since much of the politics — and indeed much of the theory — of the welfare state has not broken past the assumption that people are infinite consumers of utilities (Macpherson 1973 pp.34–5; Elster 1985 p.83). There are a variety of implications which stem from the latter assumption, the primary being that welfare has been associated with the non-market allocation of essentially scarce resources. While we have no wish to minimize the real scarcities facing communities, we nonetheless consider the definitional scarcity which arises from the assumption of the infinite consumer to be one which skews all subsequent debate about welfare. It might be objected that 'infinite consumer' doesn't actually mean that everyone wants to consume everything, only that neither a government nor a theoretician is entitled to limit in any way what a consumer can legitimately desire. But even this weaker reading of the assumption skews the debate about welfare, since it delegitimizes the ethical aspects of questions such as redistribution and leaves no moral demands on the subject. Furthermore, there is a stronger reading of the assumption, namely that the social order which is built upon it gives rise to a structured system of needs which is characterized by acquisitiveness and competitiveness (Heller 1976 pp.62, 96).

There are at least two particular implications of the shift to a notion of welfare based on the development of human capacities. The first is that which Block names the shift from compensatory welfare to empowering welfare (1987 pp.31–2). Welfare as the reallocation of resources gives rise to a deficit model of the welfare state: those who fall below some agreed-upon community standard — for instance a poverty line — are construed as deficient and should be compensated by the rest of us who are its beneficiaries.[6] Welfare as the development of human capacities, by contrast, is empowering. It implies that society is not divided into those who can cope and those who are deficient; rather, everyone requires the help of others in order to develop. The second implication flows from the first. Welfare as empowerment entails a profound diversity or pluralism in people's understanding of their needs and therefore of their welfare. What is central is the struggle over the interpretation of needs.

In line with the latter idea, there are two levels at which the development of human capacities can be understood, both of which lead to an understanding of the diversity of human needing. Benhabib distinguishes between self-actualization and self-determination (1986a p.340). Self-actualization points to the range of capacities which people seek to develop: motor skills of a wide variety, aesthetic sensibilities and competencies, conceptual and linguistic competencies — the list could be extended indefinitely. One way to account for the uniqueness of each person's path to self-development or self-actualization is to point to the infinite variety of those competencies and their combinations. But the second level, of self-determination, is equally important in grasping the true diversity of human needing and of welfare. The human capacity for self-determination is grounded in critical reflection which enables people to understand who they really are by developing a genuine autobiographical narrative. Once this is accomplished, people are in a position to grasp which of their needs are genuine and should be struggled for in a claimsmaking process (Fay 1987 ch. 8).

Self-actualization and self-determination do not imply that social welfare should simply be equated with independence. The association of well-being and personal development with individuality, separation, and autonomy may be, at best, a reading of the behavioural development of men in western society, and at worst, a distortion of reality for everyone. Personal self-realization is dependent upon the recognition and respect accorded a person by others. Accordingly, a reflection on welfare must be stripped entirely of that methodological individualism which assumes atomistic individuals, fully formed as subjects, in a position to make rational decisions.

In recent years, the individualistic bias inherent in theories of human development has been countered by feminist psychologists among others (Chodorow 1978; Gilligan 1982; Jordan et al. (eds) 1991; Miller 1986). The buried message in such theories is that people cannot flourish, cannot be autonomous, unless they first disconnect from others in order to form a separated sense of themselves as persons. Conventionally, therefore, human development or maturity is defined as a process of disconnection, objectivity and individuation in which intimacy, relatedness and empathy are seen as threats to autonomy, agency and self-determination unless they are kept in check. In contrast to this view, a theory of development based on interdependence proceeds along quite another path in which separation and individuation are replaced by relationship and differentiation.

Thus welfare is grasped as a dynamic process, which one might call 'well-seeking', in which human worth is grounded in increasing levels of personal and institutional complexity within which bonds of attachment and affection are integral parts of relationships. What is key here is not the necessity of interaction and interdependence for economic and personal survival, which everyone will immediately recognize and publicly acknowledge (Mansbridge (ed.) 1990), but the centrality of relationships for the full development of tolerance, consideration and mutual adaptation, as well as our capacity to identify who we are in the crowd. Those who are aware of their interdependence are least wary of the stranger in their midst.

There are at least four reasons why the development of human capacities is grounded in sociality, through relationships with others. First, autonomy, self-determination or critical consciousness, is available to people only linguistically, and language is a social product. Claimsmaking involves creative, critical uses of language — but the prerequisite basic linguistic competence is a social gift. This social relatedness of self and language has been central in the hermeneutic and structuralist tradition and is now widely acknowledged in the social sciences.

Second, the development of capacities, and the articulation of claims, take place within a frame of values. As people advance in self-actualization and self-determination, they choose to develop those capacities which emerge as important within the value constellation with which they identify. This seems to be a fairly concrete way to speak of 'constitutive goods', a phrase much used by Taylor and other communitarians (Taylor 1989; Sandel 1982). But, as those philosophers argue, a person develops an autobiographical narrative around the core meaning of the constitutive good to which she commits herself only within a community of like-minded persons who also are committed to that good.

The third reason is that only through others can individuals receive the basic recognition which arises both from the empathetic care which others show and from the comprehension they show with respect to the constituent values of personal autobiographies. Without the encouragement which comes from that recognition, people cannot embark on the difficult venture of developing a critically self-aware autobiography (Honneth 1990).

The fourth reason relates to the moral dimension of claimsmaking. Since claims made in the name of enhanced welfare are based on the articulation of needs, those claims constitute a political struggle around the interpretation of need. What saves a theory of welfare which takes claimsmaking as its starting point from being simply an account of a struggle over interests is that a group can articulate needs which are universalizable, hence 'true' in the sense that in an ideal speech situation there can be common consensus. But this does not just require the capacity of self-reflection, whereby a subject articulates an abstract need, a kind of lowest common denominator. To admit that is to deny the importance of the development of uniquely personal capacities as central to the notion of welfare. It requires as well a capacity to take the standpoint of another, to savour the differences and then to be able to bridge that difference with apt communication (Benhabib 1986a pp.330–43). Autonomy, then, is not independence; it depends upon mutual recognition and communicative competence. Autonomy — and by implication welfare — requires a reciprocity which goes beyond formal reciprocity, whereby each recognizes the other as equally an agent, hence the bearer of rights. It requires mutuality (Gould 1988 p.292), or complementary reciprocity, the recognition of the other as different.

From the essential sociality of claimsmaking there emerges a duality of welfare. On the one hand, welfare bespeaks autonomy. If the individual can achieve personal self-realization, growth and autonomy only within and with the support of community, then human welfare depends upon community, upon stable, satisfactory social order. From this point of view, talk of welfare is talk of justice, of universality. On the other hand, welfare bespeaks emancipation. As people develop their uniquely personal capacities, they will experience new dissatisfactions, articulate new needs and make new claims in a never-ending process. They rarely, if ever, experience the social order as completely satisfactory. Reflection on this basic duality discloses a series of dialectical tensions, in at least three dimensions: between the self and society, between justice and the good life, and between a 'thin' and a 'thick' understanding of need. The tensions are both irresolvable and creative. Only in conceptualizing the dialectical tensions can an adequate understanding of welfare be attained.

(i) Agency and Structure

The basic tension is between agency and structure, or self and community. Each person is born and educated into a relatively stable social order. The inequalities contained in such an order, whether they are along the axis of class, race, nationality or gender, are — to the extent that the order is indeed stable — legitimated. Whether the warrants for the inequality are internal or external to the society itself, they will — again, to the extent that the order is stable — be accepted as legitimate by members, even by those who are put at a disadvantage. However, the very stability which seems a necessary condition to the process of personal autonomy also constitutes a constraint, particularly among members of subgroups who experience inequality as subordination.

Essentially, the quest for autonomy can be construed as the quest to narrate one's genuine autobiography, to be the judge with respect to the meaning and coherence of one's life, to secure one's own identity. But it is always only a quest. Because of the unintended consequences of actions and the uncontrollable variety of interpretations of individual actions on the part of others, one's narrative is never complete, never wholly in one's own control, never definitively 'genuine'.

Pursuing the question of identity sheds light on the inescapable tension between agency and structure. One's autobiographical narrative relies on the social gift of language; by that very token, the linguistic structures will tend to delineate and contain a person's or a group's social identity. To put the matter in structuralist terms, if the hegemonic order of meaning has not been differentiated in a way to accommodate the social identity of a claimsmaker, then the claimsmaker will have to embark on a struggle simply to make the claim public. There might well be a word or set of words to designate the group (often a stigmatizing word: welfare mothers, unwed mothers), but the idioms, the vocabulary and the paradigms of argument required for the group's own interpretation of the meaning and dignity of their lives to be generally recognized have not yet been articulated within the hegemonic discursive order (Fraser 1989 pp.154–65).

Much recent literature on new social movements concentrates on the reflexivity with which these groups struggle to establish new rules of public discourse, such that their new identity is recognized. Thus, the political struggles which arise from such claims are not simply conflicts over who will control economic and social resources; they are also 'over the power to give meaning to the world by defining legitimate participants, issues, alternatives and alliances.' (Jenson 1989a p.74). People will consider they are adequately represented if not only their interests (in the traditional sense of that phrase) but their identity — who they are, what they aspire to, what their values are — is also represented. Politics is a struggle for identity as well as for resources.

Inasmuch as welfare is towards emancipation, at the heart of claimsmaking is a critical movement away from structural norms. On the other hand, structures and institutions are experienced not only as constraining (with the resultant requirement that claims be critical) but also as enabling. A sociological reflection on welfare is an analysis of people's experience of structures in all institutional contexts, from the most private and domestic institution (the family) through a variety of voluntary organizations where most claims are articulated, to the most public and bureaucratic institutions. Some aspects of each will be experienced as enabling, others as constraining.

For this reason, we read Habermas' distinction between lifeworld and system as counterfactual and ethical; as such it is enormously illuminating. It is, however, somewhat misleading to equate 'lifeworld' with particular sorts of experiences, such as 'the everyday', or with a kind of institution, such as family or the intimate sphere. As Fraser has argued, the patterns of the intimate sphere (so often associated with everyday life) are themselves characterized by relations of domination and subordination (1989 pp.131–4). Furthermore, the value of universality, which is at the heart of Kantian respect, characterizes the public sphere. Perhaps it is clearer to speak of hegemonic patterns, which, when internalized, structure relationships in both the public and the most intimate spheres of our lives. A critical shift is required to break the constraining, hegemonic patterns. Contributing to that critical shift are both publicly affirmed ideals such as universality or equality, and private, affect-laden recognition and affirmation of the person.

(ii) Justice and the Good Life

Ethically, the tension is between the right and the good, between justice and the good life. Because the individual is related to another at every step of the process towards the realization of welfare, each individual is equally the bearer of rights with respect to that community. In this sense, universality is the heart of justice. Herein lies the classic liberal distinction between the public and the private. Justice is properly dealt with in the public realm; the public authority is both guided by and imposes canons of justice. The good life, on the other hand, can be pursued in the private sphere, where individuals are free to adopt their own conception of the good. Because the resultant pluralism, which opens up the social space within which the good life is pursued, is merely abstract and formal, the liberal distinction between public and private is, from the viewpoint of welfare theory, unsatisfactory.

Universal rights and the resultant equality are rooted in the respect due to an abstract, generalized, 'disembedded and disembodied' other. The universalism that is achieved in such a scheme is 'substitutionalist' rather than 'interactive', that is, some paradigmatic case of the human as such is presupposed (generally white, male, propertied adults), and people who define themselves or are socially defined in other ways are understood as lacking (Benhabib 1986b pp.405–6).

Because every individual is dependent upon another for self-realization, each must be socially recognized as the subject of a set of rights which are universally applicable. However, while this is a necessary condition for welfare, it is not sufficient. Each individual, in order to begin the process of self-realization, requires personal affirmation within a sphere of intimacy or friendship. Thus, justice must be complemented by a recognition of human caring because as Tronto puts it (1987), an ethic of caring contrasts development of moral dispositions with an understanding of moral principles, particularity of response with universal applicability, and attending to relationships with attending to rights and fairness. A reflection on welfare cannot rest content with the received distinction between the right and the good, nor that between public and private. Welfare claims emerge out of dissatisfactions experienced in the private sphere, but are articulated by groups who care, and who, by achieving solidarity, are able to name their needs, hence to translate their private dissatisfactions into public issues.

(iii) Thin and Thick Needs

The third tension relates to need. While there have been a variety of ways of talking about the ambiguity of need,[7] the 'thin–thick' word pair suggested by Fraser (1989 pp.161–87) is helpful, largely because it evokes a continuous spectrum rather than a dichotomy. This is important, because the two approaches are interdependent and complementary rather than oppositional.[8]

A 'thin' notion of need is abstract, objective and universal. It has been the commonly developed notion largely because, since at least as far back as Marx's formulation of the needs principle, it has served as a constitutive criterion for distributive justice (Miller 1976 pp.24–31; Benn and Peters 1959 pp.107–54). Somewhat more broadly put, the 'thin' notion has been developed to show that need has 'moral weight', that it implies an obligation on the part of others to meet it, hence it provides the moral foundation for the non-market allocation of resources (Penz 1986; Doyal and Gough 1991).

There are two reasons for insisting on the universality of need. The deontological tradition since Kant has argued that, in order for need to carry moral weight it must be universalizable. Furthermore, needs must be universal — that is, broader than and prior to social formations — if unmet need is to serve as the base for a moral critique of social formations (Geras 1983, 1985). A need is universal if it is rooted in the human physical constitution or flows from general obligations imposed by basic social roles (Braybrooke 1987 pp.46–8). The 'thin' notion of need, it is argued, must be objective in order to avoid relativism (Doyal and Gough 1991).

By contrast, a thick understanding of need is rooted in an attempt to understand the cultural context in which people name their needs (Fraser 1989; Geertz 1973). It relies on interpretive methods to grasp the full particularity of the meaning of social action generally and of need in particular in its everyday context. If welfare is to be understood in the context of people's quest for the development of their human capacities, then the notion of need as that upon which claims for welfare are based, requires such an interpretive reading, at least as a complement to the thin reading.

The development of capacities leads to a notion of 'the self-expanding process of needs creation, whereby the satisfaction of one need gives rise to another.' (Elster 1985 p.71). This in turn gives rise to the Marxian notion of persons 'rich in needs', who, the more they meet their needs, discover further needs, needs which are more evidently personal and incommensurate with those of others (Heller 1976; Feher and Heller 1977; Galtung 1980). To deal with this incommensurability in such wise that it does not simply appear as fragmentation is to develop a theory which accounts for 'meaningful differentiation' (Taylor 1979 pp.114–16). In traditional societies, conceptions of cosmic order and organic analogies gave a meaning to differences between social groups but also gave them all a sense of unity. The Enlightenment put paid to any hope of a consensus with respect to cosmic order. The resulting pluralism — the Enlightenment's most important legacy — is, as Taylor insists, a 'net epistemic gain' (Taylor 1989 p.313). The net gain should be maximized by cutting the loss involved, namely that entailed in the abstract formality which has characterized a liberal understanding of pluralism.

Liberal pluralism has rested on the distinction between the right and the good. Public authority is both guided by and imposes canons of justice; on the other hand, it does not impose any conception of the good upon individuals' private lives, where they are free to pursue their own form of the good life. The formal understanding of pluralism has created a social space for what Weber saw to be the overwhelming power of bureaucratic, instrumental rationality (Taylor 1989 p.340). On the other hand, 'thin' theories of justice have developed an irrefutable argument with respect to universality implicated in the recognition of the dignity and worthiness of the abstract generalized other.

The purpose of a thick, interpretive approach is critical rather than prescriptive, i.e., to point to the 'ideological limits of universalistic discourse – the unthought, the unseen and the unheard in such theories.' (Benhabib 1986b pp.415–16) This can only happen within a framework which is dialogical, where those without power are heard out as carefully as any other (Fraser 1989). A thick notion of need, therefore, focuses on the politics of need interpretation, since it foresees that claims arising from the particularities of everyday experience, hence incommensurate with other claims, will be contested.

3. INSTITUTIONAL ORDER

The limits of possible responses to claims are either outright acceptance or rejection. In most instances, however, claims are neither accepted as they are originally made nor are they rejected outright. In fact, the only clear examples of outright rejection are the death or exile of the claimants. These extreme measures are taken in such a way that not only are the claimants definitively removed from the community, but their claims are utterly discredited. Hence the death is usually either brutal or public or both.[9]

Because the essential purpose of response is to preserve the hegemonic order, claims which do not advocate or require changes in that order — for instance, claims made by elements of the dominant group — will rarely be challenged or reframed. People remain members of the dominant group because they interiorize the values and norms which legitimate the prerogatives and power of the hegemonic group. Nor will it be in their interest to challenge those values and norms. By contrast, the claims of a subordinate group will usually challenge the hegemonic order in one way or another. It is perhaps helpful in this respect to distinguish between the quantitative aspect of a claim — that is, the demand for a reallocation of resources — and the qualitative aspect, which refers to the grounds on which the claim is made. The latter usually implies a demand for a new social identity.

To the extent that claims are not fully and satisfactorily met, they are marginalized. By this we mean that while important elements of claims are rejected — especially the grounds for the claim — the response to the claim is designed to keep the claimant a subordinate member of society. One way to marginalize is to render the 'rebelliousness' ineffective by keeping onlookers quiescent. A second way is through stigmatization (Pinker 1971 pp.170–76). To stigmatize the claimant means to grant a moderated amount of the resources claimed, but to grant it in such a way as to demean the claimant, to reinforce their identity as subordinate. A third level of marginalization is institutionalization. It is an intensification of stigma. At a personal level, institutions lead to a loss of roles, a stripping of possessions, isolation, and psychological displacement (Goffman 1961). A fourth way is punishment. At this level, the purpose of the action is not to aid the recipient but to preserve institutional order.

Preservation of institutional order, and compliance with processes of marginalization, are procured largely through public compliance with the dominant values and discourse of a society. From the standpoint of welfare, the basic values or 'promises' of modernity are equality and autonomy. Institutional actors supplement those promises, but make them explicitly conditional on the acceptance of role expectations. While institutions transcend a single individual or claimant, they very much reflect patterns of human interaction as well as discursive and recursive practices. Analysing institutional arrangements thus means studying the ways in which they are grounded in the social action of actors as well as the structural dimensions which impinge differentially upon them, particularly relations of domination, legitimation and signification (Giddens 1984).

In pre-modern societies, relations of domination and subordination were usually associated with extra-social warrants; for instance, there was thought to be a religious warrant for the subjection of women to their husbands or fathers. However, a hallmark of power in modernity is the general acceptance of rationalized institutional arrangements which give an aura of detachment and objectivity which suggest that they mediate social claims while at the same time assuring predictability and stability over time and place. Weber initially identified bureaucratic order with rationalization in industrial society and the extension of power from sovereignty to governmentality (Weber 1968 ch. 3). More recently, Foucault (1977, 1980) has suggested that the important shift is not so much from sovereign power to a logic of government or welfare statism but to a pervasive model of power which through law uses techniques of discipline to structure the social locations within which individuals act. Domination, therefore, is not just or even primarily about the state but the expert management of social practices through the assignment of 'identity, roles, social stigma, norms, and meaning' (Luke 1990 p.243). To understand the constraints placed upon claims in modern society, analysis necessarily involves an examination of the way power is exercised in social networks, a consideration of the heterogeneity rather than the homogeneity of political form, an evaluation of how individuals are created as subjects and constituted as objects of power relations, and an understanding of the association of power and knowledge in the creation of 'truth' (Pavlich 1992).

Inequality is more than a class phenomenon. Gender, race and other axes of inequality influence the degree of division in society differently from class, and while the inegalitarian possession and control of material resources is usually associated with class, the influence of gender and race is also substantive. Welfare claims are about unsatisfactory stratification in all areas. Theoretically implicit in that assumption is not only a denial that the concentration of important welfare claims rests *a priori* on privileged agents, such as political parties or the working class, but also an acknowledgement that there is nothing inevitable about collective action. For the emergence of collective action directed against inequalities to occur, it is necessary to identify the conditions in which a relation of inequality becomes recognized as such and thereby is constituted into a site of struggle (Laclau and Mouffe 1985 p.153).

Thus, it is important to analyse those phenomena which constitute blocks to the recognition of inequality; that is, the structured patterns of inequality must be bolstered by structures of legitimation and signification. There are two aspects to this: the more difficult and interesting aspect is that the patterned inequality must be made acceptable to the subordinated persons if they are to remain quiescent; secondly, those who exercise effective domination will need plausible legitimating reasons. With respect to the latter, since equality is a generally accepted norm, existing inequalities must to some degree be justified and explained away. In terms of class, that has been achieved by securing a particular view of the sanctity of the individual and a theory of social choice which favours private property and private markets. One reason for this is that traditional welfare theories give high marks to those economic institutions which provide a close fit between the terms on which economic goods are made available and the relative preferences of people. Whereas utilitarianism justifies such economic institutions because they maximize welfare claims efficiently, contractarianism justifies them because they are compatible with individual liberty and satisfy distributive principles framed in an original position. The problem, however, is that traditional welfare theories disguise rather than clarify the fundamental flaws of old economic models by inadequately conceptualizing the labour process, externality effects, and endogenous preferences (Hahnel and Albert 1990). Moreover, as communitarians and feminists have shown, they also ignore significant cultural and relational determinants of well-being (Kymlicka 1990). Nevertheless, even if the legitimacy of the distributive logic of the market is undermined theoretically, it is only as the inconsistencies are increasingly experienced in everyday practice that new means of allocation which 'allow informed individual rationality to be fully consistent with social rationality' will be explored (Hahnel and Albert 1990 p.352). In terms of gender and race, inequality of treatment was, in the past, usually ascribed to 'real' inequalities, such as a deficiency in 'reason' which was claimed to call for a protective relationship rather than one of equality.

There are, of course, real limitations to possible responses to a claim, rooted in the inequalities of a given social order. From the perspective of claimants, therefore, the experience of structured inequality initially 'reflects the experience of being up against something, of limits to freedom, and also the experience of being able to operate by proxy, to produce results one's capacities would not allow.' (Connell 1987 p.92). The term structure, many modern sociologists insist (with Giddens the foremost among them) implies more than constraint. It refers also to the rules and resources on which knowledgeable agents can draw creatively to modify established social practices (Giddens 1984 p.9).

While functionalists located the difficulty in the fact that actors had internalized community values, Giddens, in counterposing the knowledgeable actor to the functionalist hypostatized society which acts purposefully to maintain its cohesion behind the backs of actors, locates social stability in routinization.[10] Knowledgeable agents reflexively monitor the flow of interaction with one another, are aware in a pragmatic way of the rules which constitute social life, and can use those rules to focus the resources at their disposal in order to make themselves understood and make effective demands on others (Giddens 1984 pp.15, 21, 90). Thus Giddens can reject the metaphor of structures as skeletons: structures are instantiated only in the interactions of actors. On the other hand, the continuity of daily life is not 'directly motivated' but assured in the routinization of practices. Routinization is possible because of 'predictable and caring routines established by caring parental figures' (Giddens 1984 p.50). To have established routines is to have developed a sense of the reliability of social systems, especially the expert institutions which manage modern society.[11]

Grand theorists such as Giddens, however, seem to develop their constructs on the basis of people who have framed their claims within the dominant discourse. We have, on the other hand, started our inquiry with the experience of those who experience the effects of institutions from the wrong end of axes of oppression — whether class, race, gender, age or any other. One of the key elements these various forms of oppression have in common is that dominant values and meanings are imposed on the everyday experiences of the oppressed (Hooker 1975; Smith 1987, 1990). As Bartky (1990 p.22) puts it when talking about the psychological oppression of women, it is 'to be weighed down in your mind; it is to have a harsh dominion exercised over your self-esteem.'

The categories which are socially mediated to oppressed people construe their experiences from the viewpoint of the oppressors; thus, their social self or standpoint, will be sharply at odds with self-esteem and a positive sense of themselves. Unless they resist, they are prone to directionless violence, often against themselves or against others like themselves. In fact, one of the dispiriting experiences of those who organize groups of oppressed people is the way they bring the linguistic baggage of oppression into the group, such that all the privileges of race, gender, class, age, ability etc. must be dealt with in order for people to find the real common ground — beyond easy rhetoric — which will enable them to resist the oppression which affects all members of the group.

But resistance is not enough; as bell hooks notes,

> The oppressed also create an oppositional worldview, a consciousness, an identity, a standpoint that exists not only as that struggle which also opposes dehumanization, but as that movement which enables creative, expansive self-actualization... In that vacant space after one has resisted there is still the necessity to become — to make oneself anew. (hooks 1991 p.15)

She adds that this process of becoming a subject involves 'coming to understand how the structures of domination work in one's own life'. Thus the purpose of claimsmaking to enhance welfare is 'the unlearning of unfreedom' and the establishment of new institutional and symbolic patterns.

Inequality is not stable without the oppression which engenders compliance and quiescence. The differential distribution of resources, life chances and options is accompanied by a differential distribution of wants, aspirations and needs (Thompson 1985 p.170). Thus an exploration of inegalitarian institutional responses leads to the structures of signification, the symbols embedded in institutionalized discourse. In doing so, we are not suggesting that the formal properties of discourse should be treated as a closed system or that primary attention should be given to ideology. Rather, we are recognizing that discourse and symbolization are themselves practices which are structurally related to other practices and to institutional realities. Welfare questions, in other words, are inevitably posed in discursive formations: the terms which are legitimized, the institutional forms which are promoted, and the parameters within which societal responses are positively evaluated. Foucault, for instance, has shown how discourse interacts with institutional processes to influence the form and functioning of specific practices (Gutting 1989 p.256) and how discourse influences not only what is accepted and praised, but also what is excluded from public attention through rules of exclusion, communication and ordering (Foucault 1972). Fraser adds that there can be a plurality of contending discourses and agents of discourse which depend upon multiple axes of power.[12]

Thompson (1985, 1990) suggests that ideology is the principal manner in which signification serves to sustain relations of domination, and that there are three central ways in which this occurs. First, it serves to cultivate a belief in existing institutions by appeals to rationality, tradition, or charisma. Secondly it operates by way of dissimulation in order to conceal, deny, or block relations of domination. Thirdly, it promotes reification by representing the transitory as permanent. Furthermore, since ideology is essentially about language and language is essentially about interpretation, then events, actions and expressions are constantly interpreted and understood by lay actors in everyday life, who routinely employ interpretative procedures in making sense of themselves and others. (Thompson 1990 p.133)

But since an interpretation is also an intervention, it makes a claim about something which may not be true for everyone or if it is true may be used to criticize the views of those whose interests are best served by existing institutional relations.[13] For these reasons, the struggle of claimsmakers is initially at the level of discourse even though it eventually must deal with legitimation and domination. All three can be illustrated by a brief examination of the principal institutions in which people stake their claims to welfare in modern society: the family, the market and the state.

(i) The Family

Because the family has been perceived as the focal point of human caring and consensual decision-making, it has been tightly connected with welfare. The idealization of the family as a symbol of welfare is so pervasive in fact that it is found as much in academic publications as it is in conservative-minded government reports (Moroney 1976; Dempsey 1981; Kamerman and Kahn 1981). Because it is assumed to be a source of interdependence and mutual care, the family as ideal is reinforced by a variety of social policies, such as social insurance, social assistance, tax policy, public health care (Hill and Bramley 1986 pp.119–20).

This ideal vision, which gives rise to a set of expectations connected with women's role (or legitimation structures), is both romantic and distorted (Eichler 1983; Dickson and Russell (eds) 1986; Zaretsky 1986). Patterns of inequality have been exacerbated by economic and policy changes which have led to the high participation of married women in the labour force and their shouldering a double duty. Thus, the family as an institution promises mutual care — as we have seen a necessary precondition for autonomous self-development — but on the condition that its members accept established gendered roles, thereby giving rise to the oppression of women and the distorted development of men.

In spite of the economic and social changes, and indeed in spite of the growing feminist critique of women's social location, the contemporary family is still largely constituted by a gender division which defines certain kinds of work as domestic, female and unpaid, while other kinds of work are public, male and paid. The gender division is particularly strong in childcare and household chores where polls show little substantive change in the role and weight of responsibility carried by women even though most of them work outside the household as much as men. Women are also called upon more frequently than men to care for the elderly and the sick (Pascall 1986; Connell 1987; Oakley 1974; Dickson and Russell (eds) 1986).

The patterned response of the modern family to welfare demands made upon it is rooted in patriarchy. This, in turn, suggests that the sexual division of labour is partly a consequence of the husbands' power to circumscribe their wives' situation, and partly a consequence of inegalitarian structures fed by market norms (Connell 1987). The link between the two is embedded in the structure of social organization, though patriarchy clearly transcends the bounds of capitalist societies. To say that the gender division in the family is based on the husbands' power, even in the case of those husbands whose class location would suggest that they have very little power in the conventional sense of that term, is to recognize that power is diffused throughout society in the everyday practices in which people are engaged, not just in the institutions of the state or the market.

(ii) The Market

Even though welfare and diswelfare are closely tied to the family, it seems safe to say that in capitalist societies the market is the central institution (Polanyi 1957 [1944]). That is, it provides the root symbols and the resultant norms, the acceptance of which leads to the unsatisfactory experience of inequality. The symbol system embedded in the market as central institution gives the basic promise of prosperity, that is, of the provision of the material preconditions necessary for equality and autonomy. However, it gives that promise under quite explicit conditions, namely that a person accept the roles of worker and consumer — or, in Macpherson's far clearer terms, that of possessive individual and infinite consumer of utilities.

This dual role is best explicated in utilitarian terms.[14] Utilitarians see humans as self-seeking agents who maximize their benefits from exchanges in the market. As agents who have access to appropriate information, consider available alternatives, and evaluate the costs involved, individuals determine for themselves and with others which choice will enhance their own well-being. Hence, an unhampered market is associated with the dual advantage of promoting efficient production and distribution based on self-interest while assuring the best institutional framework for welfare improvement. In general, the welfare claimant is viewed as someone who can or should maximize choice or preferences (Culyer 1973). Left to himself, he promotes his own welfare by maximizing utilities given constraints of talent, income and technology. When he makes claims outside the market, he is reminded of his own personal destiny in a free and democratic society.

The historical criticism of the constraints imposed by the market is perhaps best summed up in the notion of commodification. This notion has at least three implications. First, people are rendered dependent upon market rela-tions; despite the liberal insistence on the freedom exercised within the market, people are not free not to enter market relations. Thus all must assume the role of consumer; all needs are reduced to the abstract need for purchasing power and all needs are quantifiable. People must also adopt the role of producer. We would agree that people need to experience themselves as contributing to the community, for otherwise self-development could easily be construed as narcissistic. But once the market becomes the central institution and the norm of commodification becomes universalized, then a person's contribution is narrowed to that which the market recognizes — the paid job. The market norm tends to skew and narrow people's sense of their own welfare; even if they can successfully resist the internalization of that norm, the socially structured responses to their larger claims are dictated by that market norm. Secondly, as possessive individuals, people are expected to compete with one another. This a serious obstacle to claimsmaking, since it tends to keep people from forming groups to begin the process (Esping-Andersen 1990). Thirdly, workers' productive contributions have no meaning in themselves, but receive significance only from the overview which management provides. This aspect of commodification is probably best understood as a specific example of the more general Weberian notion of the rationalization of society, and the resultant power that a variety of experts tend to have over ordinary people. While the workplace has been contested terrain, especially around the issue of deskilling, it would seem that a key to feminist, peace and environmental groups is their challenge of the traditional legitimacy of experts.

(iii) The State

The modern state has become the ultimate guarantor of societal promises. Its own specific promise is that of civil peace, of stability; for this it must rationalize and stabilize power relations. It must also manage the crises which arise from the contradictions inherent in the promises of the other institutions. From the market emerges the contradiction that the state must assure both the accumulation of capital and the legitimacy of that process, largely through welfare measures. From the family emerge the crises that follow from the radical calling into question of the traditional liberal distinction between the public and the private.

Different theories of the state have attempted to explain the disruption of postwar efforts to stabilize power relations and secure capital accumulation. Structuralists tend to focus on the needs of capital or the capitalist system; instrumentalists usually concentrate on the role of labour and class actions or party politics. More recently, a number of theorists have used both structural and instrumental elements by focusing on institutional relations of power.

Offe does so by diagnosing initially the contradictions of the welfare state and subsequently by addressing deep-seated legitimation problems. The contradictions derive from the increasing necessity of the state to intrude not only in the economic but in the social life of capitalist societies. The extent to which it intervenes in the latter, especially in the form of decommodified goods and services, the more it paralyses the commodity form of value. Social intervention, however, is itself paralytic because on the one hand it raises expectations beyond the state's capacity to deliver while on other hand without that intervention, the legitimacy of private capital accumulation is undermined (Offe 1984).

What Offe does not address is the centrality of discourse in institutional relations. Jenson, in pursuing a regulation approach, sees discourse, or what she calls paradigm, essential to an understanding of social relations other than those which are predominantly economic. The regulation approach looks less at the totality of the state or formal relations of power and more at how social relations are stabilized through a set of practices and meanings associated with everyday life. Regulation then is not only about the state's role in balancing contradictory or destabilizing pressures but about the political struggles in and through which contradictions are addressed, collective identities constructed, and interests mobilized. From a political perspective, the significance of hegemonic paradigms is that they play a major role over and above relations of production in maintaining stability and that 'some power relations become visible while others are blurred into invisibility, because their meaning cannot be seized.' (Jenson 1989a pp.74–5). Which identities are recognized in the paradigm, and which emerge in contradistinction to it, require an analysis of social practices. Usually those interests which are not represented become most evident and most pressing in times of crisis.

The state, however, must manage more than the contradictions which emerge from the market. It must also manage the contradictions which cluster around the public/private dichotomy, especially as those affect women. The modern ideal has promised that the family — as the institution where intimacy is sanctioned — will be the location where people will experience mutual care. A serious aspect of those caring relationships of intimacy are intended to revolve around the care and upbringing of children. However, the family is implicated in the public project of a stabilized stratification (Parkin 1979). The family is central to stratification both in class and gender terms, because those who occupy privileged positions tend to provide the means for their own children to fill similar positions.

The family is also caught up in larger public processes because the traditional division of roles along gender lines with respect to reproduction is maintained and reinforced by the state. Many of the distributional tasks of the state are connected with reproduction. If, as Pascall notes, the production of things necessary to human survival has a fundamental bearing on consciousness and on social relations, a similar case can be made about the reproduction of people. Thus in the same way as production has become a substantial concern of public life, so has reproduction. (1986 p.24)

This is not to imply that reproductive relations are subordinate to productive processes, only that state activity cannot be understood in isolation from the incorporation of the reproductive sphere and women's work within the public sector. For instance, the state reconstitutes women's traditional work of nurturing and caring, and in so doing, tends to control women or subvert their interests. Because women are extensively employed by the state and because they have been active in promoting and shaping welfare services, they also have room to understand institutional, cultural and political sources of identity and change. This suggests that while the state is historically constituted as patriarchal, it may not be inherently patriarchal as the outcome of the political process is still open (Connell 1987). One current area of contestation, not surprisingly, is the division of labour within the state itself. While women form a large part of the public work force, they occupy disproportionately the lower rungs of the vocational ladder.

In short, the contradictions implicit in the liberal-modern promises em-bedded in key institutions such as the market and the family have spilled over to become political crises. As the state acts to manage those crises, it provokes another crisis: people experience the state's attempts to manage and control both in ever-wider areas of their lives and at more personal levels than ever before. These experiences sharpen rather than dull the sense that the promises of modernity are being broken. Offe sees the significance of the new social movements here, that they insist that the 'contradictions of advanced industrial society can no longer be meaningfully resolved through etatism, political regulation and the inclusion of ever more issues on the agendas of bureaucratic authorities.' (1987 p.64) In the terms of a theory of welfare claims, groups are not simply appealing to the state for a paternalistic redistribution of resources. Their claims imply — and often explicitly demand — a reformulation of their relationship to the state as well as to other key institutions, so that their well-being is enhanced.

4. CLAIMSMAKING PROCESS

Following on three assumptions we have made, that an understanding of human capacities is essential to the dynamic of welfare claims, that people learn to name their needs, both individually and collectively, and that claims are made, at the everyday level of experience, against institutions which confront claimants with patterned inequality and oppression, we turn to a closer examination of the claimsmaking process, and attempt to explain how people become critically aware of their needs through social action, and particularly through collective action. As people struggle to come to terms with their own biographies to articulate their aspirations, their needs become explosive with respect to the hegemonic order (Habermas 1975 p.78). Hence, they engage not only in a struggle for their own identity but also for the definition of the welfare of the whole. In order to understand this double *déroulement* of claimant to institution and claimant to claimant, we consider three further components of claimsmaking. The first is simply the dynamic, or what Touraine might call the stakes, of making claims public. The second is the centrality of social practices to the development of social identity. The third is the importance of consensual rationality to welfare claims.

(i) Making Claims Public

A theory of action implies the need to be agent, to strategize to establish one's identity, to bring about the articulation of needs and identity with the larger hegemonic order. The forum for the latter is the social, which means that while claims are made against institutions, and while political decisions with respect to resources are an essential stake, the claims are first sorted in the forum of 'discourse about people's needs, especially those which have broken out of domestic and /or economic spheres that earlier contained them as "private matters".' (Fraser 1989 p.6). This, in turn, implies a discourse which involves the claimant both in understanding the nature of the claim as a group process tied to certain assumptions, purposes, and expectations and also as a symbolically structured event constituted by its location within established beliefs and practices, values and norms.

Claimants organize themselves into groups in order to name their needs and to make their claims public. Because the design and everyday operation of institutions are an integral part of the overarching hegemonic legitimating institutional order, participants in a group process to articulate their needs will also have to recognize those hegemonic relations which result in their subordination and strategize to overcome them. Thus, when finally articulated by claimants, needs will be expressed inevitably as a criticism of the institutional order to which members of the group have been uncritically and submissively subjected and which has hitherto not recognized or deprived them of their needs. To the extent that their claim, and the needs on which the claim is based are not recognized, the hegemonic order of meaning has not been differentiated in a way to accommodate the social identity of the group. There might well be a word or a set of words to stigmatize the groups. The main point here is not where the group falls on the scale of stigmatization but the difficulty in interpreting their lives in ways that will be recognized and articulated with the hegemonic order. Thus, for their claim to be made public, to become part of public discourse, requires changes in that discourse.

Within the social, the claim will receive reactions, both by the hegemonic group and others. The hegemonic group is in a position to withhold legitimacy from the new claim. By contrast, other groups can be expected to scrutinize the claim in a relatively reasonable way — for instance, by comparing their own grounds for claiming resources with the new groups' grounds. In light of the filtering reactions of other groups, the new claim will be reframed. If the hegemonic group is successful in withholding all legitimacy from the new claim, then the claim will be reframed so that it presents no challenge to the existing institutional order. This could mean that the claimants receive some of the resources claimed; however, the grounds for the claim will have been totally rejected. The claimant group might, on the other hand, be even partially successful in establishing the legitimacy of its claim — that is, in shifting public discourse such that the social identity of the group and its newly articulated needs are at least partially recognized. The partial recognition will have been gained at the cost of reframing the claim, both by moderating the amount of resources claimed and by redefining the new identity of the claimant group such that its newly articulated needs are less of a challenge to the established institutional order.

The contestation of claims raises two additional points. First, as already noted, the struggle over the interpretation of people's needs, hence over the legitimacy of their social identity, is at the heart of politics (Fraser 1989 p.6). Secondly, the link between a claim and need as a moral basis for that claim is rationality. Competing claims should be rationally sorted and brought into line with a society's resources (Heller 1984 pp.138–9). On the other hand, to the extent that the institutional order is characterized by relations of domination and subordination, those competing claims will be sorted through the use of power, whereby manipulation and bias are marshalled to block a fair hearing for subordinate groups' claims.

The implications of rationality and equality for a critical group will differ depending on whether they are interacting with the dominant, hegemonic group or with another subordinate group. The very notion of domination implies that the hegemonic group is offending against the norm of equality and respect. Hence the strategies of a subordinate group with respect to the hegemonic group will be (at the levels of signification and legitimation) to expose the distortions, the use of manipulative power. In the face of domination, the subordinate group will attempt to gain countervailing power to force the dominant group to deal fairly and reasonably with them. The moderation of their claims is, then, forced on the subordinate group by considerations of strategy rather than equality.

On the other hand, in their relations with other subordinate groups, a group will moderate its claims primarily on grounds of reasonableness and equality. Since the self-actualization of the individual members of the group — those whose needs have been articulated and whose claims are being pressed — is the goal of the process, the process should be rational, and guided by the norm of equality. The self-actualization of one person cannot be pursued at the expense of the self-actualization of another. Each group will therefore want to formulate its claims such that they are complementary rather than competitive, differentiated rather than oppositional. This of course is also motivated by strategy, so that they are uniting against the domination of the hegemonic group, whose own strategy is often so to frame the question that subordinate groups are seen to be in competition with one another.

In summary, there is a filtering process in response to the public claim of a group. A goal of this process is to reject the public legitimacy of those aspects of a claim which call into question the established institutional order. The group itself, in the light of the filtering responses, will often reformulate its strategy in order to gain as much legitimacy as possible. On the other hand, if a group is successful in formulating its claims as complementary with other groups' claims, their concerted pressure might be successful in effecting a reformulation of public discourse and of the established institutional order.

(ii) Praxis

Claims are not only made public through the claimsmaking process but the identities of individual claimants are framed in a social context, through social practice. Human praxis contains two parts: a subjective element about which claimants think when they consider their needs and purposes, and an objective element when they confront a situation which has to be changed. The connecting link is the element of intention which is realized in the social. It is the ability of imagining that something can be different. Sartre claims that all human praxis is in some respects the negation, or satisfaction, of need, and that the struggle against need takes place in a condition of scarcity. Praxis therefore is a continuum of activity, a dialectic between project and fact, which at one end involves serial relationships and at the other a fusion of interests. At the serial end, of which market exchanges would be characteristic, the individual is in some respects free to negate need but does so at the expense of the 'other'. As Soper (1986) puts it, in 'the relations of "alterity" that derive from scarcity, each individual experiences the other as "one too many" — as a threat to his or her own survival and continued practice.' (pp.68–9).

The serial relationships imposed by scarcity cannot, according to Sartre, be avoided; they are as essential as they are real. But their outcome is 'pratico-inert', a humanly created passivity, materially grounded, in which personal choices are replaced by the choices of objects (Soper 1986). In contrast, groups help to fuse individuals into a single praxis, not only in the sense that an activity is common to all but also in a way in which the one and the other become a community rather than simply living side by side. This is not to suggest that a group has an organic life of its own, or its own laws of development, separate from the individuals who are a part of it. But it is to suggest that there is a triadic connection which enables the members of the group to interact with each other in ways which foster relationships that result not just from the necessities created by need but also become the means through which other people are a source of liberty and personal identity (Sartre 1976 pp.363–4).

Moreover, the notion that a group is not reducible to the behaviour of individual participants is psychologically as well as philosophically grounded. Psychologists associated with self-categorization theory lend credence to the complementary relationship of individual and social identity (Turner 1987; Tajfel 1981; Rosch and Lloyd (eds) 1978). Their 'basic hypothesis is a cognitive (or social-cognitive) elaboration of the nature of social identity as a higher order level of abstraction in the perception of self and others.' (Turner 1987 p.42). A second hypothesis is that the categorizations implicit in the notion of self-concept are themselves products of social activity. Essentially, this reinforces the view that social groups are what make cohesion, coopera-tion and influence likely. In a related theory, called social identity, the theme of cooperation is carried further in the exploration of intergroup, rather than intragroup, behaviour to look at the 'positive' aspects of discrimination in the absence of group conflicts of interest (Turner and Giles 1981). What the researchers have found to date is not conclusive but it is suggestive of the idea that identity is socially structured within the individual mind, and that its 'functioning provides group members with a shared psychological field, shared cognitive representations of themselves, their own identity, and the objective world in the form of shared social norms of fact and value.' (Turner 1987 p.207).

(iii) Collective Action

While welfare is realized in all forms of social action, collective action is a principal means by which, in modern society, cultural norms are contested and new claims asserted. Obvious examples of collective action which have been associated with welfare claims are the labour movement with respect to the development of the welfare state and the new social movements in the defence of civil society (Scott 1990; *Revue internationale d'action communautaire* 1983). From the standpoint of claimsmaking, the main advantage of such movements is that they break the culture of silence (Freire 1972, 1973) which envelopes the marginalized, and formulate new demands and new identities. To suggest, however that new social movements are instrumental in the development of social identities while older movements, like labour, are concerned about the distribution of resources does not imply that the significant difference between the two is that one is built on expressive forms of actions and the other on strategic. Most forms of collective action involve both to a greater or lesser degree.

Charles Tilly (1978, 1981) is associated with the view that collective action is variable depending upon circumstance. He focuses on the economic, organizational and ideological determinants of action as well as the characteristics of particular types of action, including disorder, disturbance, protest and rebellion. He shows that different types of action are called forth depending not so much upon the issue or the claim as upon the impact of the shift from local to national power. However, while he develops analytic categories to frame the different types of possible collective action — such as competitive, reactive and proactive claims — his primary focus is on the dynamics of resource mobilization. In contrast to this the identity paradigm has tended to highlight the reflexivity of the members of new social movements, their awareness of 'their capacity to create identities and of the power relations involved in their social construction.' (Cohen 1985 p.694). This aspect of collective action brings out, as Melucci (1983, 1985) shows, the social processes of identity formation, including the creation of societal norms, the contesting of structures of domination, the creation of symbolic forms of communication.

However, there is no need to construe these two approaches as mutually exclusive, nor is it an adequate approach, since neither alone explains the peculiarities of new welfare claims. Perhaps Touraine's language is sufficiently inclusive; he speaks of the capacity of social movements to contest control over what he calls the main cultural patterns of society — modes of knowledge, types of investment and ethical principles (Touraine 1981, 1985). Cohen (1985 pp.699–700) locates Touraine's importance in his emphasis on struggle in civil society rather than around the market or the state. He thereby highlights a range of social activities which until recently were relatively uncontested because they were considered as part of the private sphere or deeply embedded in the traditions and therefore the established institutions of society. This linkage of social movements with civil society, or what we called earlier 'the social', as the forum where claims are first sorted publicly is also associated with the characterization of social movements as anti-system movements (Arrighi et al. 1989), or as defences against the attempts to extend state control not only into new areas but also deeper into people's private lives (Offe 1987).

Two other aspects of social movements which are integral to the claimsmaking process are cognitive praxis and social inclusion. The conceptualization of social movements as cognitive praxis helps to bring together the instrumental and expressive as well as the normative and communicative dimensions of collective action. It emphasizes above all the idea that social movements are not only a challenge to established power but also a socially constructive force, a determinant of human knowledge.

The cognitive praxis of social movements is not just social drama; it is, we might say, the social action from where new knowledge originates. It is from, among other places, the cognitive praxis of social movements that science and ideology — as well as everyday knowledge — develop new perspectives (Eyerman and Jamison 1991 p.48).

Looking at social movements in this way highlights the way in which knowledge is a creature of collective process, a series of encounters between opponents, a linkage of new and old. But movements are more than promoters of new knowledge; they are also conveyors of political expectation, of social inclusion. By including subordinate or marginalized groups within the political process, they articulate the grievances and demands of those who have been excluded from the benefits typically available to dominant groups or from the processes of elite negotiation. At the same time, as Offe (1987) suggests, they are themselves subject to political intermediation. Hence, social movements are never simply integrationist (though that is a possible outcome); instead, they serve to thematize issues excluded from dominant discourse and political decision-making as well as having a potential for cultural transformation (Scott 1990).

One issue, however, which is not fully addressed by social movements literature is the significance of social integration based on communication and consensual rationality both in the process of creating group solidarity and in the making of welfare claims. We come back to the question raised earlier: how do members of a claimsmaking group come to share common goals or to have common interests? And how can they claim some legitimacy for their claims, that is, how can it be established that their claim is to enhance their welfare? The answer to both would appear to be best answered within the framework laid out by Habermas — through the uncoerced formation of a general will within a communicative community with a bias toward cooperation and a type of dialogue in which claims are subject to ongoing criticism (Rasmussen 1990; Roderick 1986). However, the potential for consensus-making dialogue, according to Habermas, presupposes a public space where the mechanisms of the state and the market (and their accompanying symbolic forms) have not, or have only partially, been able to penetrate — the most obvious examples being the life world or civil society. To the extent that these, in turn, are influenced by the relatively autonomous spheres of science, art and morality, there is increased potential for increased reflexivity regarding all dimensions of social action. And this is made possible because the dual structure of the institutions of civil society (domination and integration) means that the claims of newly emerging welfare groups can have a hearing, however limited. The law, for example, involves the protection of the individual, the freedom of association, and the right of deliberation unfettered by the exigencies of the market and the state, thereby guaranteeing the possibility of consensus making. At the same time, the law is increasingly used to enter into spaces that were previously outside legalistic regulation, thereby opening up areas for systematically distorted communication (Cohen 1985 pp.711–13). The same can be demonstrated with respect to the family as indeed with art and science. In the everyday world of practice, therefore, there is no guarantee, only constant struggle.

NOTES

1   It is difficult to know which word more to avoid. 'Welfare' has been almost irreparably contaminated both by utilitarian presuppositions and by the actual practices of the welfare state, which by the very design of its programmes creates the dependency which it ostensibly decries. On the other hand, 'welfare' does at least connote social provision as a necessary dimension of human well-being, while 'well-being' seems to evoke more the mobilization of internal resources.

2   Following Weber, we view action as social insofar as the individual attaches a subjective meaning to behaviour and takes account of the behaviour of others. Following Alan Dawe, we acknowledge that theorizing from a social action perspective focuses on a metaphor of conversation rather than closure, ambiguity rather than resolution. However, within these broad generalizations, we are closer to Freire and Honneth than Giddens or Berger and Luckmann in our attempt to integrate subjectivist and objectivist accounts of human welfare based on everyday practice and social struggle.

3   By this term we mean the ongoing struggle which people carry on in order to achieve their own sense of their lives, to set and meet their own goals. In this struggle they are both enabled and constrained by social forces.

4   Left functionalism has constituted an important variant of the needs-as-known-by-experts view. On this view, true need must be distinguished from false; people, interpellated as consumers, are duped into accepting as their needs what are really the interests of capital (Marcuse 1964; Springborg 1981 p.171). The experience of need and the act of consumption must be seen as moments in the process of the production and reproduction of capital, a fully integrated process which touches every aspect of people's lives, and which is dominated by the hegemonic class (Préteceille and Terrail 1985 pp.17,47; Préteceille 1975 pp.22–60; Fischer 1976; Baudrillard 1981 p.84).

5   We have found one author who puts the matter in just this way. In trying to clear ground for what she calls 'practical interests' — which seem remarkably close to what Fraser calls 'thick needs' — Molyneux (1985) concedes that 'strategic interests' are derived deductively from an analysis of patriarchal (or, for that matter, capitalist) society. She remarks that feminists often think of these latter as women's 'real' interests.

6   Titmus' original formulation was more benign; the whole thrust of his writing was to eliminate stigmatizing notions such as 'deficiency'. Our contention is that stigmatizing must be expected once the framework of welfare is compensatory.

7   Doyal and Gough (1984) spoke of a pluralist and a humanist approach to need; Soper (1981) of open and closed theories, rooted in cognitive and normative discourses; Weale (1983) of a positive and a normative approach; Penz (1987) distinguished between needs based on community standards and need as intrinsic to social justice. Doyal and Gough (1991) characterize the pluralist approach as 'relativist'; Penz and Soper call the other approach 'essentialist'.

8   On the one hand, Doyal and Gough (1991) argue persuasively that the relativist, pluralist talk of
     need presupposes universal norms. On the other hand, Wiggins (1985) especially argues
     convincingly that the notion of need, resting as it does on the inescapably culturally conditioned
     vision of human flourishing, is essentially contestable. In a subsequent edition, Wiggins (1987
     pp.314–18) returns to the point, arguing that essential contestability does not lead to relativism —
     in his words, there can nonetheless be a 'principled' discussion.
9   Indeed, the brutality is ritualistic in order to highlight the outrageousness of the claim. The
     symbolic importance of death is more important than the execution because it is intended as a
     message to the rest of society. The infrequent but much publicized executions in the United States
     serve much the same purpose today.
10   Giddens (1984 p.30). Giddens (1979 p.148): 'To mistake pragmatic/ironic/humorous, distanced
     participation in the routines of alienated labour for normative consensus, was one of the great
     errors of the orthodox academic sociology of the 1950s and 1960s.' He speaks also of 'calculative
     and manipulative attitudes' even though these may not be discursively conscious. See Giddens
     (1981 p.57).
11   Routines are made possible when actors have developed 'ontological security', that is, 'the
     confidence that most humans have in the continuity of their self-identity and in the constancy of
     the surrounding social and material environments of action.' Giddens (1990 p.92). The viability
     of modern society, he tells us, rests upon people's trust in abstract systems, 'especially trust in
     expert systems.' (p.83).
12   Fraser (1989 p.6). Fraser puts discourse at the centre of her analysis for three reasons. First, by
     focusing on the struggle over needs, she tries to counter the conventional view that needs are
     essentially and only about the distribution of satisfactions or preferences in a consumer-oriented
     society. Secondly, by linking ideas in the humanities and social sciences to larger political
     debates, she reframes the relationship between the cultural and social, the official and the
     unofficial. And thirdly, by emphasizing the plurality of discourse and multiple axes of power, she
     stresses the complexity of claimsmaking.
13   In the realm of discourse, feminism and environmentalism are clear examples of challenges to the
     prevailing ideology of modern society.
14   See Bentham (1982); Smith (1976); Barry (1990); Raphael (1990); Reisman (1976); Heilbroner
     (1986).There are of course differences in the brand of utilitarianism advocated by Smith and
     Bentham. Smith postulates, for example, that welfare results as an accidental by-product of the
     free flow of the market rather than through the structuring of the public good based upon a scale
     of observable identities. On the other hand, Smith's famous statement that it is not from 'the
     benevolence of the butcher, the brewer or the baker that we expect our dinner, but from their
     regard to their own interest' cannot be taken in isolation from the importance he attaches to moral
     sentiment as a major force for integration in society. In fact, at the heart of his book, *The Theory
     of Moral Sentiments,* is the assumption that sympathy (or identification) of one being for another
     is the basis of moral judgement and complementary to the self-interest or prudence of the
     economic person. Whereas, for Smith, sympathy produces one kind of social bond based on
     socializing attitudes associated with approbation, self-interest, as developed in *The Wealth of
     Nations,* generates a different bond or mutual dependence based on the division of labour. By
     rejecting a dichotomy between commerce and virtue, he describes a moral order that is based on
     the combined effect of the personal decision of individuals to do their duty and the self-correcting
     virtues of the market.
        In contrast to Smith, Bentham pours scorn on the idea that ethical values can be located in the
     concept of duty and makes possible the release of justice from its anchor in rule-following to a
     concern about the consequences of action for the individuals effected by the choices made in the
     market. For Bentham, therefore, the objective of society is the maximization of the sum total of
     utilities coupled with an assumption that the greatest happiness of the greatest number should also
     be the measure of right and wrong, whether in the area of welfare policy or in terms of individual
     action.The paradox of Bentham, however, is that while, unlike Smith, he provides a rationale for
     government intervention in the market in order to promote human welfare and formulates in a
     preliminary fashion the fundamental assumption that individuals are alike in their preferences
     and capabilities for enjoying the good life (an assumption which is used later by economists such
     as Pigou, Dalton, and Dobb to argue for a redistribution of income based on equality), he himself
     is a strong advocate of the *laissez-faire* economics which has become so closely associated with
     contemporary neo-conservative proponents like Friedman or Hayek.

For commentary on this chapter see page 267

PROBLEMS IN JUSTIFYING CLAIMS

2. Free Lunches Don't Nourish: Reflections on Entitlements and Citizenship

Raymond Plant

The quotation at the head of the paper is taken from Murray (1989), and it is part of the critique of the idea of welfare as a right or an entitlement to be found in his book. Critics of the rights approach to welfare have tended to take one of two alternative routes in attacking the idea that welfare is a right. The first is to concentrate on the idea of rights and to claim that the claim to welfare as a right is defective since the logic of rights is such that there can be no such rights. Welfare rights are an illusion, and a damaging one at that, because the idea of welfare as a right and an entitlement leads to all sorts of baleful consequences. The second line of attack is more recent and it involves the claim, partly empirical and partly conceptual, that the idea of a right to welfare makes fundamental errors about the nature of human beings and their essential capacities and powers. The idea of welfare rights should be resisted on this view not so much because the argument for their status as rights is defective, but because such supposed rights actually undermine some essential human characteristics, in particular self-respect and independence as well as motivations to achieve these things.

The main thrust of this paper will try to explain why I believe that this shift of ground has occurred and to assess the power of these arguments. I shall claim that this shift of ground has occurred among critics because the claim that welfare rights cannot be seen as genuine rights is unsustainable and therefore the critique of entitlements has to take a rather different form and one which invokes a quite rich, and needless to say, contested view of human nature and human capacities. I shall therefore begin by trying to show why the traditional approach of denying that welfare as a right cannot be sustained, and I shall then go on to discuss this new direction in the argument.

There are several reasons why critics of the right to welfare have rejected the idea that there can be genuine rights to resources such as income, health care and education. The first and in many ways the central one has to do with scarcity. In the critics' view, welfare rights are necessary claims to resources and in their view this marks a categorical difference between welfare rights and the civil and political rights which they favour. On this view, civil and political rights essentially entail corresponding duties of forbearance — that is to say 'I respect your civil right to freedom of speech by not interfering with it'; 'I respect your right to physical integrity by not assaulting you'; 'I respect your right to life by not killing you' and so forth. These rights are essentially rights to forbearance on the part of other people: to abstain from those actions which would in fact infringe on the rights in question. As such, two things follow for critics of social and welfare rights. The first is that civil and political rights are not asserted to scarce resources. Forbearance is costless: it is not something we can run out of. On the other hand welfare rights are asserted to scarce resources and we can clearly run out of them. The point at issue here has been rather well put by Fried:

> A positive right is a claim to do something — a share of material goods, or some particular good such as the attentions of a lawyer or a doctor, or perhaps the claim to a result like health or enlightenment — while a negative right is a right that something not be done to one, that some particular imposition be withheld. Positive rights are inevitably asserted to scarce goods, and consequently scarcity implies a limit to this claim. Negative rights, however, the rights not to be interfered with in forbidden ways, do not appear to have such natural, such inevitable limitations. If I am left alone, the commodity I obtain does not appear of its nature to be a scarce or limited one. How can we run out of people not harming each other, not lying to each other, leaving each other alone? (Fried 1978 p.110)

This argument has been fundamental to the critic and has led to the following two claims. The first is that there is a categorical difference between the two sorts of duties corresponding to civil and political rights and welfare rights respectively. In the case of civil rights these duties are duties of forbearance, not of the provision of resources. Since forbearances are costless the duties are categorical — they can always be performed, and as such are perfect duties. Welfare rights, however, imply positive duties to provide resources which are bound to be limited and therefore cannot be categorical and thus not amenable to being brought within the rubric of rights and the rule of the law. Secondly, it implies that there has to be some rationing principle for scarce resources to meet these claims as so-called rights. However, this rationing principle is likely to be of a utilitarian sort and therefore is likely to be incompatible with ideas about rights under which claims to resources are initially entered. In what sense are these genuine rights if there have to be some additional principles governing the allocation of resources, particularly if this principle is of a non-rights-based sort.

Indeed, critics, particularly those influenced by Hayek, argue that there cannot be a rational principle for such rationing at all. The reason for this is that it is argued that so-called welfare rights are based on ideas about needs and needs are intrinsically vague and open-ended in the potential demands which they represent. Take, for example, the need for health care: there is no clear limit to the resource demands to which such a need on the part of a specific individual might give rise. Once rights are based upon needs there is no clear limit to potential demand and because needs of different sorts, for example the needs of heart patients and kidney patients, or between different categories of needs, such as those in health compared to those in education, are incommensurable, there can be no rational basis for rationing between different sorts of needs. This means that resources are likely to be distributed according to discretion even where that discretion might be dressed up in terms of clinical or professional judgement (Gray 1984 p.73).

If discretion is to be avoided then positive rights have to be linked to some kind of view about the nature of social justice which will be concerned with the just apportionment of scarce resources. However, critics such as Hayek and Nozick argue that we do not in fact have either agreement about any pattern of just apportionment or social justice, because in a morally diverse society there can be no agreement about patterned principles of just apportionment (Hayek 1960) or there are deep philosophical objections to the idea of patterned principles of justice (Nozick 1974). It is in the highest degree unlikely therefore that discretion can be avoided on this view.

Needs as a basis for rights, on this view, should not be invoked as a principle for the distribution of resources, because if it is it will create unaccountable discretion at the heart of public policy. It is argued that we have no common, shared view of the nature or the priority of human needs and public policy should be protected against the arbitrary and discretionary power on the part of welfare bureaucrats which will follow from bringing into public policy a disputed view of needs, supposedly underpinning a conception of welfare rights. We shall need to come back to this when we look at the critic's claim, which will be discussed later, that a rights conception of welfare undercuts some essential human capacities and powers and we shall see how consistent they are in their approach to this issue since many of the critics of needs themselves bring into play quite a rich conception of human capabilities as a way of criticizing a rights- and needs-based approach to welfare.

It is assumed, in contrast, that civil and political rights are immune from this kind of discretionary power in relation to rationing just because they are not rights to scarce resources and the corresponding duties of forbearance are perfect duties and do not require rationing. It is also argued that civil and political rights do not make disputed assumptions about needs or any other sorts of human capacities.

Another way in which the argument about scarcity can be put would be to argue that scarcity implies that social and economic rights are not compossible, that is, they cannot be realized simultaneously by all right holders. However, if rights are not compossible, then it is claimed that there will have to be discretion exercised by the authorities in respect of whose rights are to be exercised at which time, and this again entrenches discretion at the heart of public policy; or there will have to be some non-rights-based rationing principle in regard to rights, such as a utilitarian principle of realizing those rights of that group of individuals which will maximize welfare. In the view of critics, such an approach either is incompatible with a rights-based approach; or some kind of rights-based prioritization in respect of rights will have to be constructed. In the view of critics, however, this is likely to be based on judgements about the urgency of the needs which underpin different sorts of rights, and, as we have seen, such an approach is regarded with scepticism by the critic just because we lack a consensus about the nature of needs, and judgements about urgency are bound to be subjective and discretionary.

It is further argued by critics of welfare rights that the core idea of rights is to protect individual freedom and autonomy, and these have to be construed in negative ways, as freedom from interference rather than freedom to do various things. Welfare rights are, however, in the view of the critic, based upon a false view of liberty as positive, as connected with ability and the associated resources which people need to do things. Civil and political rights as proscribing unjust interference are based upon a negative view of liberty whereas welfare rights as implying rights to resources are based upon the false view that liberty is the same thing as ability, which then requires resources for its exercise. This view of liberty underpinning welfare rights is regarded by the critic as defective in two main respects.

In the first place it is argued by critics like Hayek (1960) that there is a categorical difference between freedom and ability. Freedom is to be understood as the absence of intentional coercion and this is essentially negative and the rights associated with liberty are those which restrict coercion of one person by another. If freedom is understood in this way it is clearly different from ability. I am free to do all those things that I am not prevented by the intentional actions of others from doing. Whether I am able to do these things is quite a different question. No one is able to do all that they are free to do and this freedom and ability are two separate things. The political rub to this disjunction between freedom and ability is that poverty is not a restriction of freedom.

The second reason why the view of liberty underpinning welfare rights is disputed by the critic is that if liberty is assimilated to ability, then we need to have something which we have not got, namely an agreed view of those abilities which bear directly on liberty. It is argued, however, that in a morally diverse and pluralistic society we lack a consensus about what are the important human abilities since these must be related to goals and purposes which differ in a pluralistic society. This argument parallels the argument about needs which we considered earlier, namely, that in a morally diverse society we cannot expect agreement about the nature of human needs and abilities which crucially underpin positive conceptions of freedom which in turn underpin welfare rights. We shall return to this argument later in the paper since, as we shall see, the arguments of Murray (1984,1989), Mead (1985) and Novak et al. (1987) who are among the most forceful of contemporary critics of welfare rights, trade upon a rather rich and thick conception of human nature and human capacities.

From all of this it follows that while civil and political rights are legitimate because they are not constrained by scarcity and because they are underpinned by a negative conception of freedom, welfare rights are not legitimate: I do not owe positive duties to others other than those that arise out of explicit contract; another person holds a right against me that I should perform some duty or service if I have contracted with that person to provide it. There is however, no general welfare right to the resources of others since welfare rights cannot be understood as genuine rights — they are categorically different claims for the reasons I have stated.

It seems to me that while there are genuine civil and political rights and that these can be given some legitimate grounding, the arguments in favour of regarding welfare rights as categorically different from civil and political rights are in fact rather weak.

I shall consider the arguments about scarcity first since these underpin most of the critical case. There has been a standard response from the welfare rights perspective which its critics have not found persuasive. It is argued that in point of fact civil and political rights do require resources to protect them. A right not to be assaulted or coerced requires police, courts, prisons etc. to protect and enforce and that this involves resources just as much as welfare rights. However, the critic rejects this on conceptual or logical grounds. It is argued by the critic that this is a contingent feature of civil and political rights and is not of their essence, whereas the claim to resources is a logical feature of welfare rights. The point could be put informally in the following way. We could imagine a community of saints who always forbear from interference and coercion and that in such circumstances there would in fact be no need to protect civil and political rights by resource-based institutions such as the police, the courts etc. So, given that the argument of the critic is that there is a logical or categorical difference between the two different sorts of rights, this categorical distinction could still be preserved if it could be shown, as the critic thinks that it can, that the protection of civil and political rights is just a contingent feature of such rights and this is what, in their view, their counter example in fact does show. However, this can be doubted for two reasons.

The first reason is rather arcane but is based on the nature of the counter example of the community of saints. What the critic is relying on in this example is the counterfactual of a world without a scarcity of motivation to respect rights properly understood, that is to say, a world in which the motivation not to interfere, not to coerce etc. is not in short supply.[1] However, it is open to the welfare rights defender to conjecture another counterfactual world in which there was no scarcity of material goods, and therefore one in which the restrictions on welfare rights did not apply. It might be argued by the detached observer that there would be little point in talking about rights at all in either of these worlds and that is really the point, that in the world as we know it scarcity of both motivation and material goods is endemic and rights have to be understood in the world as we know it, rather than in some possible world of which we have no experience. Hence, civil and political rights too have to be considered against a real world background of scarcity in motivation and thus also have to include those resources which are involved in the protection of these rights.

The second reason why civil rights are as enmeshed in questions of scarcity as welfare rights has to do with another aspect of the critic's claim that the enforceability conditions of civil and political rights are a contingent feature of such rights while being a logical feature of welfare rights. It is very hard to see that this claim works because it is arguable that the idea of enforceability is logically connected to the idea of a right. People have all sorts of desires, interests, needs, demands, preferences and claims, but what marks out some of these as rights and therefore as having a special moral status is that we believe that a right gives rise to an enforceable moral duty on the part of the person, group or institution against whom the right is claimed. If enforceability were to be understood as a wholly contingent feature of rights then it would be difficult to provide some account of how those claims which come to be regarded as rights can be seen to differ from other sorts of claims which are not so dignified. It is the enforceability of those claims which makes them rights.

If enforceability is a necessary condition of something being regarded as a right then the conditions of enforceability are not a contingent feature of rights, but are central to them. Given that enforceability conditions are going to involve costs and resources, then the claim that welfare rights differ from real rights in this respect must be false. Of course it might be argued that the costs of enforcement will be less for civil and political rights than they are for welfare rights, but assuming that this is true, it makes a difference in degree not in kind. The distinction between negative and positive rights therefore becomes untenable if enforceability is taken as a defining criterion of a right because the enforceability conditions are a positive feature of negative rights.

Once this is accepted then we can see that in some practical respects the contrast between the negative nature of civil rights and the positive nature of welfare rights is wholly overdrawn. Critics have argued that welfare rights yield arbitrary discretionary power to those charged with the command of the resources to meet such rights. So, for example, there cannot be a general right to health because two people might at the same time need the services of a surgeon who can only treat one of them and the surgeon has to use discretion to decide whom to treat. However, if enforceability is a non-contingent feature of all rights then the same points apply equally well to civil rights. Take for example the role of the police force, which is part of the enforceability characteristics of civil rights. In the United Kingdom a chief constable has a general duty to provide a police service in the same way a health authority has a duty to provide medical services, but this does not yield an individually enforceable right to the services of a policeman at a specific time. The chief constable has the discretion as to how he will deploy his force and if the force decides not to investigate your burglary because it is not cost effective to do so, then this is as much an exercise of discretion as the surgeon deciding that it is not sensible to perform an operation. In the police case we do not believe that this example invalidates the whole idea that there should be civil rights and there is no reason why we should believe the same to be true of welfare rights. Of course, the radical critic might say that this shows that the whole language of rights is confused because there can in fact be no individually enforceable right to those positive services which will protect rights. However, dealing with this claim takes us outside the realms of this paper. All I am claiming here is that if we believe that there are civil rights then we have no good reason for thinking that these rights are categorically different from welfare rights. So the problem of either the discretionary or just apportionment of scarce resources will apply as much as they apply to positive rights.

These points apply equally well to the idea of compossibility of rights. If rights imply enforceability in order to distinguish them from other sorts of claims, then enforceable rights cannot be claimed simultaneously since there may not be the resources to protect rights claimed simultaneously. If the possession of a right implies the positive protection of that right then no rights can be compossible.

In the case of the enforceability conditions of civil and political rights, we are able to arrive at a negotiated political consensus about the level of resources which at a particular time seem to be necessary and reasonable to protect civil rights. Take for example the case of physical security: this is protected by a range of things from police forces to street lighting. It is possible to forge a consensus about what is needed at any point to protect civil rights in these sorts of respects. This consensus and the negotiations which lead to it are conducted against a background of scarcity and there is no reason of principle why, given a similar recognition of scarcity, it would not be possible to arrive at a similar consensus in respect of the funding and scope of welfare services to meet social and welfare rights. To be sure, the nature of the right does not specify the nature and scope of the provision to meet such rights, but exactly the same is true in respect of civil and political rights too.

As we saw earlier, the critic argues that freedom and ability are two different things. Freedom is the absence of coercion and not freedom to do things which would be positive freedom. Secondly, the critic argues that the positive freedom in the sense of ability is a moralized conception of liberty in that we would have to have an agreed conception of abilities to define that range of abilities which stand at the heart of free action, and this, the critic argues, we do not have in a pluralistic society. These arguments are, I believe, defective for these reasons.

It is difficult to believe that freedom and ability are two categorically distinct things because it can be argued that the generalized ability to do something is a necessary condition for any individual being free or unfree in relation to that thing. So, for example, if I asked whether people were free or unfree to sign cheques in AD 957 then most people would be inclined to say that the question did not make sense as there was no general ability to do it. Assessing whether someone is free or unfree to do something depends therefore on people in general being able to do what a specific individual is being diagnosed as being unfree to do. So if a general ability to do x is a necessary condition of someone being free or unfree to do x then it cannot be the case that freedom and ability are two different things.

The idea of ability also enters into the question of why we believe that liberty is valuable to us. If one were to ask the Hayekian negative libertarian why being free from coercion is valuable to us, then the most plausible answer would be that if I am free from coercion then, within that space within which I am not subject to the will of another, I am able to live a life shaped by my own interests and projects. However, this comes down to saying that liberty is valuable to me because of what I am able to do with it and therefore ability becomes part of the explanation of why we regard liberty as being valuable to us. As such there cannot be a categorical difference between freedom and ability.

The final reason why there cannot be a categorical difference has to do with the implausibility of the claim that the question of whether one society is freer than another depends on the quantitative judgement of how many coercive rules there are restricting action in one society rather than another. To take an example which is due to Taylor (1985 p.129), if I try to answer the question 'Was Britain in 1988 a freer country than Albania?' then, if I am a pure negative libertarian, this answer has to be quantitative — to do with the number, rather than the type of coercive rules in a society. It cannot have anything to do with the type of rules since this would imply a moralized conception of liberty which would have to do with human goals or purposes. Hence, it might be said that because Britain is a more complex society than Albania there are going to be far more rules, for example, governing traffic, or the conduct of financial business, than in Albania and it is quite possible that on a purely quantitative basis there are more rules limiting action than there are in Albania. However, few people would be convinced by this. Most people at this stage would be inclined to invoke some kind of standard about the type of rules in question. In the United Kingdom we can do things which are much more important and which were prevented in Albania, such as criticizing the government, or emigrating. This seems the most plausible response, but it does something which is contrary to the negative libertarians, that the idea of liberty should both be separated from ability and also that liberty should not be moralized by making it relative to human goals and purposes or to the pattern of human capabilities and desires.

These three counter-arguments tend to show that it is not in fact possible to produce an account of liberty which is disconnected from an account of abilities and some idea of the human capacities and powers which bear most directly on liberty. If this is so then the way is open to the welfare rights theorist to construct an argument to the effect that welfare rights protect a set of abilities and their associated resources which bear directly on liberty. They are concerned with the satisfaction of those basic needs or primary goods which are necessary conditions of any sort of free action. I shall not attempt this here as I have tried to do it elsewhere (Plant et al. 1980). The important point in this context, therefore, is that the idea that welfare rights depend upon a mistaken conception of liberty is itself mistaken.

The above points, I hope, weaken the arguments for the claim that there is a categorical distinction to be drawn between welfare and other sorts of rights, but in a sense they go further than this because they also weaken the idea that welfare rights, unlike other sorts of rights, depend upon a specific and contested account of human needs and abilities. If it can be shown, as I hope that I have shown, that the same is true of negative rights and negative liberties then this argument cannot be used uniquely to attack welfare rights. Indeed, the argument has recently come full circle because many of the most recent critics of welfare rights seem at least tacitly to agree that there is no future in trying to draw sharp conceptual distinctions which earlier critics tried to draw between civil and welfare rights and are now using a conception of the human good and human nature as a way of attacking welfare rights in that the assumption being made now is that while welfare rights may not be conceptually flawed, nevertheless they undermine certain important features of human need and weaken a central human ability, namely that of self-reliance and independence.

I have in mind here the arguments used by Murray (1984, 1989), Mead (1985), Novak et al. (1987) and Moon (1988). As we shall see the policy implications of these arguments are rather different in Murray as compared to the other authors, but they all share a common set of values in relation to human nature and human needs with which they criticize the idea of welfare rights. The issues at stake here have been put into the most acute philosophical context by Donald Moon.

As Moon points out, many of the issues at stake in this controversy can be found in the remarkable observations of Hegel about the nature of poverty and welfare to be found in *The Philosophy of Right*. However, I shall not discuss this as I have already considered these issues at some length elsewhere (Plant 1982). The issues have to do with whether the entitlement culture of the welfare state as theorized in the idea of welfare rights actually undermines the basis of self-respect as this is understood in western societies. Moon is not proposing some kind of universal theory of self-respect, only that the bases of self-respect as they are understood in western societies involve the ideas of independence and self-reliance and that this is being put at risk by a rights-based welfare state. The deep philosophical point here, which Hegel did much to theorize, is that rights protect some kind of antecedent moral status whereas self-respect is something that people have to achieve according to the norms of respect in a particular society. A rights-based approach to welfare ascribes rights to people in a rather static way because they share certain needs in common or because, as Gewirth has argued, they share in certain generic goods of agency (1977). This neglects a much richer, thicker and more particularized point that self-respect is not about common needs or generic needs, but rather about living in accordance with the norms and standards of human excellence in a particular society. The liberal defence of welfare rights neglects this much more particularized form of self-understanding and therefore does not address the question of how self-respect can be achieved within a welfare system. In western societies respect is earned by being independent, self-reliant, resourceful and self-motivating and yet to construe welfare as a right which one has and can claim, irrespective of whether one is exercising or trying to exercise these virtues, is likely to undermine the achievement of self-respect in these terms. It is in this sense that 'free lunches do not nourish', as Murray puts it. Entitlements and rights do not enhance self-respect, which is an achievement not based on an antecedent status.

The first thing to note is how far this argument is away from those we have met so far. Indeed Moon goes so far as to say that the case for welfare rights is well made on conceptual grounds. His argument against it, drawing upon his argument about human nature, is that welfare rights cannot nourish self-respect when understood in terms of independence and self-reliance, which have to be achieved by individuals through their own efforts. Secondly, it is worthwhile noting that compared with the earlier critics of welfare rights, these modern critics are quite happy to invoke moral categories and a conception of human excellence, although one that is seen as particularistic, that is to say relative to the values of particular societies. As we saw earlier, the first form of criticism of welfare rights drew quite heavily on the fact that welfare rights presupposed assumptions about a consensus over needs and abilities which they denied existed in contemporary societies. The critic argued that such a consensus does not exist. However, this new critique of welfare rights actually invokes a substantial level of agreement in society about morality, about the nature and basis of self-respect and about the motivations necessary to support it. To this extent there is common ground between the new critics of welfare rights and their defenders in that both accept that some conception of human capacities is central to arguments about welfare. They both reject the Hayek-inspired critique of welfare rights which depends partly, as we have seen, on invoking the idea that there is no social consensus about needs and about the abilities which bear most directly on liberty which has led people to defend welfare rights. The disagreement now is over a number of issues, some conceptual, some empirical, some a mixture of both.

Among the conceptual issues, two stand out. One is the conception of human nature and the analysis of self-respect as an achievement and not a prior status. In some respects the issues at stake here are those argued about one hundred and seventy years ago in Hegel's critique of Kant, who had seen personality as a basic status and deserving respect in terms which were not influenced by empirical consideration, such as the way of life of the individual. Respect was due to an individual and an individual has a duty to respect him or herself in terms of nonempirical characteristics, namely those of rational self-determination. This is a basic antecedent moral status which is not influenced by the empirical characteristics of persons and which is not modified by the fact that people may hold diverse moral views. Indeed in Gewirth's version of the argument, the generic conditions of agency, or what might be called basic needs, are precisely those conditions which are necessary to be a moral agent at all. For Hegel, however, self-consciousness and the respect to it is dynamic. It is to be achieved and acquired through struggle with the world and in community with others — it was not an antecedent nonempirical status as it was for Kant. Modern rights-based theories of both the welfare and civil sort tend to favour the Kantian side of this argument, that the status of being a person confers on that individual certain rights which are not fundamentally modified by the empirical character which the individual happens to develop. These features are independent of rights. The rights are not modified by the virtue or lack of it which the individual develops. The modern critics of welfare, however, want to emphasize the link between rights and entitlements and virtues.

This leads to the second theoretical point, namely the link that is forged between rights and entitlements and obligations. On the welfare rights view, a person has a right to basic resources whether he or she discharges the obligations which are seen to be at the basis of self-respect in a particular society. The new critics however argue that, in a sense, if there are to be entitlements then they should be conditional on discharging obligations which will lead to a growth in independence and self-reliance. Welfare rights at least are conditional on discharging obligations. These obligations are broadly, for example, for Mead and Novak of a workfare or learnfare sort. An entitlement to welfare is based upon being prepared to perform obligations in respect of the labour market, the justification of which in turn is based upon the idea that independence comes through being prepared either to work or to train for work.

This, however, leads to one possible line of criticism. As far as I am aware the modern critics of welfare do not wish to make the same argument in respect of civil and political rights. That is to say, they do not appear to want to say that people who fail to develop in accordance with those standards which define self-respect in western societies should lose their civil and political rights. This would indicate either an inconsistency in respect of civil and political rights, on the one hand, and welfare rights on the other; or it indicates that they do not really think that welfare rights are genuine rights at all. However, as we have seen, this claim is highly disputable and in any case, many of the new welfare critics have accepted that the categorical difference between the two sorts of rights cannot in fact be maintained. So, for example, Novak seems to accept the latter point while still arguing for an obligation- and virtue-based approach to welfare rights but not to civil and political rights and the same is true of Gray (n.d.) who accepts explicitly the claim that there is no categorical difference while at the same time arguing that welfare rights, particularly unemployment benefits, should be made dependent on undertaking training. This is not a constant position. If rights are conceptually all of a piece then one set cannot be made subject to the discharge of obligations when others are not.

This then leads to a further consideration which is more empirical. Given the assumption that the basis of self-respect in western societies is the achievement of independence, then I suspect that critics of welfare rights will respond to the above criticism in the following way. It will be claimed that civil and political rights can in fact be separated from the need to discharge obligations because such rights are essential to secure the kind of independence they want to see, whereas welfare rights, if they are treated as categorical and not conditional on discharge of obligations, actually undermine independence and create dependency. The reason for this is clearly stated in Mead, Murray and Novak. Welfare rights create dependency. The security of income detached from obligations to the labour market cuts people off from the discipline and self-respect that comes from work or training. Welfare rights create privatized and ill-disciplined individuals. They provide incentives which actually exacerbate the very problems which welfare rights were designed to solve. The prime need is to bring citizens back to a sense of the obligations of independent citizenship and this is to be done either by government-funded workfare or learnfare schemes, as argued by Novak and Mead, or by removing state benefits altogether for the able bodied, as in Murray, to force people onto the support of their friends, neighbours and communities in which they will be faced with peer pressure actually to do something for themselves to take them out of dependency. Some of these claims are empirical and not being an empirical social scientist I cannot adjudicate on the evidence which is adduced to support such claims. There are, however, a number of issues of principle which are central to these arguments which I believe are worth close attention.

The first is the claim that the unconditional civil rights do create a sense of independence whereas welfare rights do not. Civil rights give a sense of security and a firm base for independent citizenship, whereas welfare rights do not. This is certainly not the way in which welfare rights theorists have envisaged the issue. They have argued that the security given by a right to health care, education and basic income have in fact a similar function in giving a citizen a set of basic resources in which he or she is then able to act as an independent agent. As we saw earlier in the discussion of freedom, the aim has been to provide that set of resources which are the necessary conditions of independent action. The critic rejects this because in his view it is a claim which is not borne out by its effects. This is an empirical claim which can be investigated.

There is a second issue here which is partly one of the principle and partly bound up in empirical judgement. It is claimed that in our sort of society, independence is bound up with working for a living and therefore that obligations relating to welfare rights have to be based on getting people into work or training for work. However, this makes quite strong assumptions about the availability of work. Moon, for example, argues that if we were to move to an obligation-based view of welfare (as, for example, Bill Clinton has argued in his New Covenant proposals) then government has a duty to adopt economic policies which are likely to create employment. It would be inconsistent to insist that work is central to self-respect and that it should be part of the obligation of the citizen if government itself is pursuing policies which actually undermine the very value which is regarded as being at the heart of independent citizenship.

This leads to further considerations. The first is based on a judgement about the likely future of work in western societies. If we believe that there are economic policies which can lead us back to NAIRU levels of employment, then, assuming that other aspects of the critic's arguments are accepted, there might be an empirical basis for workfare or learnfare as a basis for welfare until such time as employment levels rise. If, however, one took the view that high levels of unemployment are likely to be with us indefinitely, then it seems to me that first of all workfare and learnfare are a cruel hoax — that people are going to have to perform obligations in respect of the labour market which are not likely to lead anywhere. This leads to the second point, which is much more fundamental: if the future of full employment looks bleak, should the state be taking the lead in insisting that the standard of self-respect and citizenship in society should be seen in terms of working for a living or training for work, rather than in taking a lead to help society to change its values in respect of the link between self-respect and work? It would be very demoralizing for there to be a kind of official endorsement of the view that self-respect comes from labour while at the same time being pessimistic about the future of work. If we take this pessimistic view (and this is again an empirical judgement), then there would still be a case for unconditional welfare rights even if one accepted the strictures of critics given that the alternative that they prefer is not in fact feasible.

The critic, such as Mead or Novak, although not Murray, would respond to this by arguing that if the prospects for employment are bleak, then government should become the employer of last resort. The aim is still to preserve the link between self-respect and work but that government rather than the labour market itself should secure employment by becoming the employer of last resort. This proposal in turn raises a number of questions. The first has to do with the size of government. Most of the critics of welfare rights come from the rank of the neo-liberal right who believe in limited government. However, make-work schemes, either provided directly by government or by government funding to non-governmental agencies, are likely to mean a considerable increase in the size of government and in public expenditure. Indeed, Mead's book (1985) is a defence of big government from a conservative rather than a neo-liberal perspective. Make-work schemes are going to be much more complex to create and administer compared with paying welfare benefits as an unconditional right. They are also likely to be much more expensive. These implications fit very uneasily with neo-liberal assumptions about limited government, taxation and the size of public expenditure.

There is, however, a deeper issue of principle. Remember that the whole of the argument of the critic of unconditional welfare rights is based on the link between independence, citizenship and work. It is argued that self-respect comes from getting a job and sticking with it. However, if a job is created by government or a government-funded agency for an unemployed person, is this likely to create a sense of personal satisfaction and self-respect for that person? It strikes me that there is all the difference in the world between arguing that self-respect comes from getting a job in the labour market and having a government-funded job created for you. It is far from clear to me that in the latter case there is much in the way of an increase in independence. Indeed, it might be argued that it is transferring dependency (assuming the empirical case that it exists under welfare rights) from the Department of Social Security to the Department of Employment. This point is well made by Jon Elster:

> Self esteem is undermined by the belief that one is parasitic on others. If true, this claim implies that highly and visibly subsidised work or make believe work ... is not a source of self esteem. The self esteem of people who are living on unemployment insurance may be damaged because they feel that they are being parasitic, but they would not be happier if they performed work that visibly was not paying its way. (Elster 1988)

On this view which seems to me to be wholly plausible, the link between self-esteem, which has been central to the new critique of welfare rights, cannot be established by workfare and learnfare schemes in which the government is the employer of last resort.

There is a further general issue about the nature of dependency which I believe is important, and is taken up in more detail by Fraser and Gordon (forthcoming) and that is the extent to which the idea of dependency is itself an ideological construction which puts more socially-based or structural ideas such as inequality off the agenda. I shall confine myself to just one point. The emphasis on dependency in respect of welfare recipients in modern society neglects the extent to which in a market economy we are all dependent on one another for the fulfilment of our needs. This idea is central in Adam Smith and is brought out very well by Hegel in the section 'The System of Needs' in *The Philosophy of Right*. The idea that I am an independent agent as a producer and consumer in the market in contrast to the dependence of the welfare recipient is a highly contentious reading of the nature of a market. I am only able to act as an independent person in the market because there is in fact a whole infrastructure of relationships on which I am dependent if I am to act. This is usually unexplicit from us, but nevertheless is still there and usually comes home to us only when it breaks down — when the telephone does not work, when the cleaner does not come, when the library is closed, when the taxi firm does not have a free cab, when the photocopier is broken. All these things which in the complex division of labour in a market society are undertaken by others form an infrastructure on which I depend as a producer in the market. On this basis, society is in Rawlsian terms a cooperative enterprise and we all depend on that cooperation. What matters then is that the terms of cooperation are fair between individuals and groups, rather than taking out of the scheme of social cooperation one particular aspect, namely independence, and abstracting this from the whole concatenation of relationships which form a market and elevating that into some kind of single moral touchstone. Once we see society as a scheme of social cooperation rather than as a set of atomistic independent individuals, then issues about the fairness and degree of equality between individuals are able to be put back on the agenda in a way which is blocked by emphasizing independence to the detriment of other ideas. At this point the social rights of citizenship and questions about the fair or just apportionment of scarce resources to meet the equal social rights of citizens finds its place again in political theory.

Overall therefore I remain unconvinced by the earlier and the more recent critique of welfare rights. The earlier approach assumed that welfare rights cannot be genuine. The latter approach tends to accept the untenability of this assumption but uses the arguments just discussed without having a very clear idea of the mechanism whereby self-esteem can be achieved in their obligation-based welfare system in which government has to be the ultimate employer. If one is a pessimist about the future of labour in western societies then the question that Moon (1988) poses to welfare rights theorists, if people hold the norm that they should be independent (in the sense of self-supporting), then how can the state provide them with the means of subsistence without violating their self-respect, applies equally well to the obligation-based view of welfare.

NOTES

1   Hillel Steiner, a prominent negative libertarian, made this point to me in conversation.

3. Realizing Equal Life Prospects: The Case for a Perfectionist Theory of Fair Shares

Lesley A. Jacobs

The most basic question of distributive justice asks what constitutes for each individual a fair share of the advantages of social life. Although many political philosophers now agree that in a democratic society a fair share of the advantages of social life is an equal share, the perennial issue among them is 'Equality of what?', for there are many possible accounts of what constitutes an equal share of those advantages (Sen 1982a pp.353–69). The point is that the nature of an individual's equal share is a function of one's views on the respect(s) in which individuals should be made equal. And there is widespread disagreement among egalitarians on this issue. What has emerged are a number of competing theories about how an equal share should be determined: equality of welfare, equality of resources, democratic equality, equal basic capabilities, equal opportunity for welfare, equal access to advantage.[1] This paper examines yet another such theory. This alternative theory (which I shall call *equal life prospects*) holds that each individual is entitled to an equal share of the opportunities available in a society to lead a valuable life. It denies that any opportunities which do not have the potential to contribute to the leading of a valuable life should count in the measurement of equal shares. Egalitarians should only be concerned with making people equal with respect to valuable life prospects. Certain ways of life are valuable and ought to be promoted through distributional equality. In other words, I reject the view that an egalitarian scheme of distribution should be neutral between particular ways of life and embrace instead the view that distributional equality should favour those ways of life that are valuable over those that are not. The assumption is not that there is one particular way of life that is valuable, but rather that there are a plurality of valuable ways of life.

Egalitarians have in recent years paid insufficient attention to the possibility of a perfectionist theory of distributional equality. While in many respects the statement of the theory of equal life prospects below is sketchy and brief, I hope nonetheless to show that for anyone who takes the realization of an egalitarian society seriously, the perfectionism maintained by that theory makes it a very attractive theory of fair shares. It has recently been suggested that a perfectionist theory of distributional equality that embraces value-pluralism is unlikely to differ significantly in practice from its counterparts which embrace neutrality (Arneson 1987 pp.526–7). I shall argue that the theory of equal life prospects offers an attractive and distinctive perspective on two issues that pose especially difficult problems for egalitarian schemes of distribution which seek to respect neutrality, the issue of how to distribute the pay-offs from natural endowments and the issue of how to compensate for handicaps.

1. EQUALITY AND NEUTRALITY

Liberal egalitarians have made the most valuable contribution to the recent debate over what constitutes a fair share of the advantages of social life. This contribution has been characterized by the widespread acceptance of two beliefs. The first belief is that a fair share requires in some sense an equal share. The second belief is that the determination of an equal share must respect what is now commonly called political neutrality — 'the idea that government should not seek to impose any way of life on individuals'.[2] The liberal egalitarian project can, then, be understood in terms of devising a theory of distributive justice which is consistent with these two beliefs (Alexander and Schwarzchild 1987 pp.85–110). The problem, in other words, is how to determine an equal share for each individual without favouring some ways of life over others.

Now, certainly the simplest way to approach this problem is to adopt a *subjectivist* approach to distributional equality (Scanlon 1975 pp.656–8; Arneson 1990 p.159). A subjectivist approach holds that the size of an individual's equal share of resources can be determined by the importance of those resources to the tastes and preferences of that particular individual. This theory — equality of welfare — says that individuals should be equal with respect to their individual welfare levels and that resources should be distributed among individuals so that no other scheme of distribution would leave them more equal in their preference satisfaction. It follows, on this view, that because some people might have very expensive preferences and others very inexpensive preferences, some people might enjoy many more resources than others in the name of distributional equality. Thus on a subjectivist approach no independent judgement of what is good for the individual has a role in determining the size or make-up of his or her share of the resources;[3] instead, his or her preferences and wants are taken as the sole determiner of that share. The attractiveness of this sort of approach to the determination of an equal share for the egalitarian liberal is that it appears to be consistent with neutrality because it does not seem to favour some ways of life over others.

Contemporary egalitarian liberals have by and large, however, been resistant to this type of subjectivist approach to distributional equality. Although their reasons for doing so are in fact complex and numerous,[4] the principal objection to this type of approach can be expressed by saying that it is not truly neutral between ways of life. By making every kind of life equally easy to lead, equality of welfare favours those who have expensive preferences over those who do not (Dworkin 1987 pp.30–31). It in effect rewards those with expensive tastes and penalizes those with less extravagant preferences.

The alternative to a subjectivist approach to distributional equality is an *objectivist* approach. Objectivist theories hold that the size of an individual's equal share of resources is determined to some degree independently of the importance of those resources to the satisfaction of the particular tastes and preferences of that individual. One variant is sometimes called *specific egalitarianism* (Tobin 1973 p.448; Weale 1983 ch.6). The aim of specific egalitarianism is to make people equal with respect to particular goods, such as health care, food, or housing, which are identified as especially valuable. A familiar social programme often motivated by specific egalitarianism is food stamps. Everyone should have at least a minimal level of food: the fact that food stamps cannot be exchanged for something which the beneficiary might prefer such as cigarettes reveals clearly the objectivist approach underlying this policy. The obvious difficulty liberal egalitarians have with specific egalitarianism is that, like equality of welfare, it appears to violate neutrality. This is because it seems inevitable that specific egalitarianism will favour some ways of life over others, in particular, those ways of life which make central the goods that a theory of specific egalitarianism identifies as important enough to equalize among individuals.

What are some objectivist alternatives to specific egalitarianism? For our purposes, it is sufficient to focus on the two theories of distributional equality that have dominated the liberal landscape, John Rawls' theory of democratic equality and Ronald Dworkin's equality of resources. I would like to make the somewhat controversial suggestion that although there are many very important differences between Rawls and Dworkin, their treatment of distributional equality works within the same basic framework.[5] Each approaches the determination of an equal share in a two-step manner. The first step is to assume a commitment to some version of equality of opportunity. That is to say, each is committed to the requirement that people with similar natural endowments and motivation are to have access to similar jobs, regardless of sex, racial origin or socio-economic background. The second step is to say that the pay-offs in terms of salaries and benefits from the realization of these opportunities are to be structured in a way that conforms with distributional equality. The rationale underlying this second step is that since the distribution of natural endowments among individuals is 'arbitrary from a moral point of view', the pay-offs from those endowments are to be treated as 'collective assets' that should be distributed in a fair and equitable manner (Rawls 1971 pp. 72–4 and 179). My analysis, then, assumes that Rawls and Dworkin differ principally over how to fill-in these two steps, not with the basic framework they set. It is also within this framework that I shall develop the alternative perfectionist theory of equal life prospects.

The two principles of justice advanced by John Rawls are well known:

> 1 Each person has an equal right to a fully adequate scheme of equal basic liberties which is compatible with a similar scheme of liberties for all.
> 2 Social and economic inequalities are to satisfy two conditions. First they must be attached to offices and positions open to all under conditions of fair equality of opportunity; and second, they must be to the greatest benefit of the least advantaged members of society. [6]

The second principle constitutes Rawls' answer to the question of how to determine an individual's fair share of the advantages of social life. And it of course conforms precisely to the framework identified above. The first condition — fair equality of opportunity — requires that 'those who are at the same level of talent and ability, and have the same willingness to use them, should have the same prospects of success regardless of their initial place in the social system, that is irrespective of the income class into which they are born.'[7] The second condition reflects Rawls' famous difference principle with its emphasis on the idea that 'injustice...is simply inequalities that are not to the benefit of all.'(Rawls 1971 p.62).

The objectivist dimension of Rawls' theory of distributional equality is found in his metric for measuring the inequalities that can be justified by the difference principle. At issue here is Rawls' account of social primary goods. The distinctive feature of primary goods is that they are goods which any person will require to further their particular way of life, regardless of the exact nature of that way of life. As Rawls puts it,

> Primary goods [are] things that every rational man is presumed to want. These goods normally have a use whatever a person's rational plan of life...[T]he assumption is that though men's rational plans do have different final ends, they nevertheless all require for their execution certain primary goods, natural and social. (Rawls 1971 pp.62, 93).

Social primary goods include rights and liberties, income and wealth, powers and opportunities, and the social bases of self-respect. Health and intelligence are examples of *natural* primary goods. From the perspective of a liberal egalitarian, the virtue of a theory such as Rawls' which measures equal shares in terms of social primary goods is that this determination of equal shares does not violate neutrality — no way of life is favoured over any other because primary goods are, by definition, instrumental for any way of life.[8]

The difference principle is only concerned with inequalities generated by some of the social primary goods. The background assumption is that assuming conformity to the first principle and fair equality of opportunity, rights, liberties, opportunities and the social basis of self-respect will be distributed equally among citizens.[9] It is principally powers, wealth and income that will be distributed unequally under a distributive scheme that conforms to Rawls' two principles: 'the primary social goods that vary in their distribution are the powers and prerogatives of authority, and income and wealth.' (Rawls 1971 p.93).

The claim that Ronald Dworkin's theory of equality of resources conforms to a framework very similar to Rawls' second principle of justice is controversial. So before I substantiate this claim, I shall outline the main elements of his theory.[10] The brilliance of Dworkin's theory is that while the size of each person's share is determined objectively, the particular make-up of each individual's share is determined by his or her own preference structure. At the core of Dworkin's theory is the distinction between an individual's personality and his or her circumstances. Among an individual's personality Dworkin includes features such as convictions, ambitions, tastes, and preferences. An individual's circumstances include his or her resources, talents and skills, and physical and mental capacities (Dworkin 1981b p.302, 1987 pp.18–19). On Dworkin's view, simply put, distributional equality requires that people be equal in their circumstances. And people can be said to be equal in their circumstances when the cost to other people of one person's life is equal to the cost of everyone else's. That cost (which Dworkin calls 'the opportunity cost of one's life') is to be measured by how valuable the resources and other elements of circumstances devoted to one person's life are to other people. Presumably, people will choose to do different things with their circumstances. These differences will reflect their personalities. One person might prefer to use his or her resources to produce something that others might utilize, someone else might prefer only to consume. The first person will in time come to have command over more resources than the second. But, on Dworkin's theory, this does not mean that they do not enjoy an equal share of resources. Provided that each is equal in the circumstances devoted to the whole of their lives, the differences resulting from differences in personality do not undermine their having equal shares. Equal shares can then be said to be *personality-sensitive* or, to use Dworkin's preferred expression, *ambition-sensitive*

(Dworkin 1981b pp.333, 338). And Dworkin's scheme for measuring equal shares can be said to respect neutrality precisely because it is ambition-sensitive. For, by being ambition-sensitive, it eliminates the possibility of some ways of life being favoured over others in the distribution of scarce resources.

While at first glance Dworkin's approach seems very different from Rawls', on closer inspection, especially given what he says about unequal natural endowments, the common ground becomes abundantly clear. Especially instructive here is the contrast Dworkin makes between equality of resources, on the one hand, and equality of opportunity and what he calls starting-gate theories, on the other. (Starting-gate theories hold that provided individuals with different talents start with equal amounts of external resources, any inequalities that might be generated through the exercise of those talents on those resources are just.[11]) What distinguishes equality of resources from these other theories is that it maintains that distributional equality is compromised when different incomes are rewarded purely on the grounds of differences in talents. But this point of distinction does not constitute a refutation of equality of opportunity; it merely suggests that like the Rawlsian approach the pay-offs that are generated by success under equality of opportunity should be distributed in a manner that treats everyone as equals. And indeed this appears to be precisely how Dworkin regards the issue:

> Notice that our analysis of the problem that differential talents presents to equality of resources calls for an income tax, rather than either a wealth or a consumption tax. If people begin with equal resources, then we wish to tax to adjust for different skills so far as these produce different income, because it is only in that way that they threaten equality of resources. (Dworkin 1981b p.312n9)

Everyone would have the opportunity to choose whatever occupation they wanted but they would have to bear the opportunity costs to others for doing so. In effect, then, this means that the distribution of careers and offices would track those with the talents to succeed in them; and this is, of course, the core idea of equality of opportunity.

The most important difference between Dworkin and Rawls is how they think the income generated by natural endowments under a scheme of equality of opportunity should be distributed.[12] While for Rawls it should be distributed in a manner that is to the greatest benefit of the least advantaged, for Dworkin it should be distributed in a manner that reflects the opportunity costs to everyone including the least advantaged. It is principally against these two theories — democratic equality and equality of resources — that I propose to develop my alternative theory of equal life prospects. Both of these theories have sought to respect neutrality in their measurement of an equal share. This strikes me as a mistake. The theory I shall defend rejects neutrality.

2. AN OVERVIEW OF THE THEORY

The theory of equal life prospects also takes an objectivist approach to distributional equality. But unlike the liberal egalitarian theories of Rawls and Dworkin, this objectivist approach is not supplemented by a commitment to political neutrality. Instead, equal life prospects endorses the view that certain ways of life should be favoured in the determination of equal shares and can thus be regarded as a *perfectionist* theory of distributional equality.[13]

Perhaps the most familiar perfectionist theory of fair shares is equality of self-realization. This is a theory which, in the recent controversy over Marx and justice, has been attributed to Marx.[14] The basic idea is that Marx held that everyone should lead equally valuable lives. What is significant for our purposes is that this view presupposes that only certain ways of life are valuable and that they ought to be promoted through distributional equality. In other words, equality of self-realization is incompatible with political neutrality.[15]

As a theory of fair shares, however, equality of self-realization has to be misconceived, for it has two serious flaws. First of all, it fails to recognize that it simply might not be possible to make everyone equal with respect to self-realization. The objection I am making here parallels one sometimes made that an individual can have a right to health, as opposed to a right to health care (see Buchanan 1984 pp.55–6). Although we certainly can finely control the distribution of health care, this is not the case with health itself — some people simply are going to be more unhealthy, no matter what other people do or give up. The second flaw arises from the fact that in conditions of moderate scarcity it is sometimes unreasonable, albeit still required by equality, to channel resources to one person when the consequent gains in self-realization will be only very marginal and the costs to others, in terms of lost opportunities for self-realization, very high (see Cohen 1989 p.911).

It follows, I believe, that we should be sceptical about the idea that a distributive scheme should seek to make people equal with respect to their self-realization.[16] A perfectionist theory of distributional equality should focus instead on the distribution of opportunities available to individuals to lead valuable lives. For our purposes, it is important to distinguish between two kinds of opportunities to lead a valuable life. On the one hand, there are opportunities upon which it is possible to build reasonable expectations of success.[17] These are what I mean by life prospects. The intended contrast is those opportunities (which might be described as life chances) that are so remote and improbable that it would be irrational to build expectations on them.

The theory of equal life prospects holds that it is precisely life prospects which ought to be distributed equally among individuals: each individual should enjoy an equal share of the life prospects available in a society to lead a valuable life. It follows, on this theory, that any opportunities which do not contribute to the leading of a valuable life do not count in the measurement of equal shares. The theory does not, then, require that people be made equal with respect to trivial or banal opportunities. It is not, for example, inconsistent with equal life prospects that some people have greater access to many — not all — of the consumer products on the market today. Nor does it seek to equalize the opportunities for repugnant choices, for those too do not contribute to leading a valuable life.[18] The underlying assumption, then, of the theory of equal life prospects is that those ways of life that are valuable and likely to be realized ought to be promoted through distributional equality.

Now, many people have reservations about any theory of political morality which adopts a perfectionist stand, for the fear is that what is being offered is a justification for the state acting as an instrument for imposing one particular way of life upon its citizens. But this fear is misplaced insofar as it does not recognize the diversity among objectivist approaches to distributional equality. The objectivist approach with which the theory of equal life prospects should be aligned is *value-pluralism*. Basically, value-pluralism says that there are many different and sometimes incompatible ways to lead a valuable life (see Raz 1986 pp.395–9, 403–4). Some people might realize themselves through work, others through social activities such as their church or philanthropy, and still others through activities such as growing flowers or writing poetry. Not only are all these different ways of life valuable, some of them are incompatible. It is, for example, impossible to lead a life of activity and a life of contemplation. What value-pluralism allows for is that all of these ways of life are valuable . The underlying belief is that these ways of life are valuable independently of whether or not people choose to live them; the fact that these different ways of life are valuable gives people reason to pursue them. Value-pluralism is, then, to be contrasted to what might be described as indiscriminate pluralism: the view that there are a wide range of ways of life that people might and do choose to lead. Indiscriminate pluralism might be a fact of political life in modern industrial societies but it does not have moral significance, from the point of view of the theory of equal life prospects.[19] Equal life prospects is a perfectionist doctrine because it combines the belief that there are a plurality of valuable ways of life — ways of life which have value independently of whether or not people choose to live them — with the belief that it is not self-defeating to promote these ways of life through a mechanism that distributes opportunities.

The emphasis I place on value-pluralism should, I hope, allay the fear that the theory of distributional equality advanced here seeks to reinforce one particular way of life as the only valuable means to self-realization. This point is reinforced by what I take to be a truism about leading a valuable life, namely, that self-direction is a necessary condition. People have to decide for themselves what sort of path they are going to follow in order for their particular way of life to be valuable. An egalitarian distributive scheme reflecting an objectivist concern for leading a valuable life can, therefore, only distribute 'life prospects'; to attempt anything more would be self-defeating. Equal life prospects is, then, perfectly compatible with the traditional array of liberal rights to basic liberties. Since it is these rights that are most often associated with the neutrality of the liberal state, the theory of distributional equality advanced here does not conflict with a restricted principle of political neutrality that only entails these rights. Moreover, even within the theory of equal life prospects there is some room for neutrality in the sense that given value-pluralism an egalitarian distributive scheme should be neutral between valuable life prospects; the only neutrality that I unequivocally reject is that a distributive mechanism should not favour valuable ways of life over debased or trivial ones.

With these considerations in mind, let me briefly outline the vision of an egalitarian society that drives the theory of equal life prospects. The assumption is that any such society would have a division of labour that would make it impossible for everyone to have the identical opportunities to lead a valuable life. Instead, within such a society there would be a diverse range of opportunities. The virtue of embracing, as I have, value-pluralism is that it allows for the possibility that people might have different but nevertheless equal life prospects. The character of an egalitarian society is not that everyone has the same valuable opportunities but rather that those opportunities be distributed to people in a way such that each person has command over a sufficient number to be able to be said to have life prospects equal to that of everyone else. Thus, while everyone enjoys some opportunities to lead a valuable life, they also would necessarily have forgone the enjoyment of others. The intended contrast is to contemporary (capitalist) society where it is generally the case that the most valuable opportunities are distributed among a small minority — those who have the most rewarding jobs are also the ones who typically enjoy exclusive holidays and own valuable land and rare goods.[20]

3. REALIZING EQUAL LIFE PROSPECTS

The focus for discussion in the rest of this paper is the issue of how the perfectionist ideal of equal life prospects can be realized. Which social and political institutions are best suited to achieve equal life prospects? My approach to this question involves a two-step analysis. First, I shall defend the controversial claim that economic markets should have a central place in the allocation of resources in an egalitarian society that embraces the ideal of equal life prospects. Then, I shall focus on two resource distribution problems — the issue of how to distribute the pay-offs from natural endowments and the issue of how to compensate for handicaps — that cannot be adequately addressed simply though a market mechanism.

Underlying this approach is the belief that it is not possible to think clearly about questions of distributive justice without confronting the problem of how any proposed ideal of distributive justice might be realized. This question is also taken seriously by Rawls and Dworkin. I shall argue that the question of realization reveals both the strengths and weaknesses of marrying an objectivist approach to distributional equality to political neutrality. The principal strength is the important place assigned to economic markets in the achievement of distributional equality. The principal weaknesses relate to how natural endowments are to be rewarded and how handicaps are to be compensated for. My defence of the theory of equal life prospects rests ultimately on the claim that only by adopting a perfectionist position on distributional equality is it possible to address adequately these two problems.

(i) The Importance of the Market

Distributive justice is essentially an issue of comparative justice; it is concerned fundamentally with comparisons between persons (Feinberg 1980 pp.265–306). For an egalitarian, this means that when we say that someone has an equal share of the advantages of social life, the basis for making this judgement necessarily involves reference to the share size of other individuals. How can we make this judgement? How can we determine that the valuable life prospects of one individual are equal to another individual? These are basic questions about the realization of equal life prospects that must be addressed. I argue here that economic markets are, in the first instance, the best way to determine when the life prospects of different individuals are equal and, therefore, that economic markets should have a primary role in the realization of equal life prospects.

Now, it is undeniable that the idea of assigning the market a primary role under a perfectionist theory of distributional equality goes against the current. Two reasons why this is so are especially worth mentioning. First of all, it is undeniable that, in general, egalitarians who have defended the importance of the market have been attracted to it because of its supposed neutrality.[21] Second, there is ironically a long tradition of objecting to markets on perfectionist grounds. Representative here is the Marxist view. As John Roemer has recently put it,

> Marxism has a tradition of arguing that capitalism is not conducive to self-realization — to creating people who are capable of fulfilling themselves in a meaningful sense. (Or, rather, capitalism allows this for only a small minority.) This is only partly because of the skewed distribution of wealth and the class system that markets bring about; it is also because the very process of organizing economic activity by use of private property, competition, and markets may instill in people values that stunt the development they otherwise could achieve. (Roemer 1989 p.153)

Roemer's point is that assuming the endogenity of preferences — the fact that personal preferences and values are shaped by one's environment — markets *cum* private property induce people to have certain preferences and hold certain values which are not conducive to self-realization. Thus, given my explicit rejection of neutrality, it is puzzling how my theory of equal life prospects can embrace markets.

My view is that the source of a lot of this puzzlement is confusion about the nature of markets and what it is about them that is important. I concur with the following explanation of what is a market offered by Joseph Carens:

> By 'market' (or 'market mechanism') I mean that individual economic units such as individuals and corporations generally make decisions about production and consumption on the basis of their own preferences rather than on the basis of directions from a central authority, that these individual economic units enter into exchange with other economic units, and that money is widely used as a medium of exchange. (Carens 1981 p.10)

In effect, then, market decisions are individual decisions. This means that when I say that markets under equal life prospects are to have the primary role in measuring valuable life prospects, the important contrast is to assigning that role to a centralized authority. (This is consistent with my attempt earlier to disassociate the theory of equal life prospects from authoritarian notions of political morality.)

The most fundamental feature of markets, in my view, is their pricing mechanism. Here I follow other egalitarians such as Rawls, Dworkin, and Hal Varian. As Varian puts it,

> The fundamental feature of the market mechanism is not private property but the price system. Within the market mechanism, prices serve two roles: an allocative role and a distributive role. The allocative function of prices is to indicate the scarcity value of goods and thereby reward the efficient use of resources. This is quite distinct from the distributive function which simply provides one way of distributing wealth among agents — namely, via permanent private ownership of the factor payments to property. It is perfectly possible to use prices for *allocation*, while basing *distribution* on factors other than the blind-chance assignment of initial endowments. (Varian 1975 pp.238–9)

Now, there are two pertinent points to be made here. The first is that it is my suspicion that the claim that markets hinder self-realization depends on an association between markets and the unequal private ownership of capital; it follows that if what is really distinctive of markets is their pricing mechanism, then this objection holds only against markets when they are used within an economy that allows for unequal private capital. The objection, in other words, is not against the use of markets *per se*. My second comment concerns the dual function of prices that Varian emphasizes. The *allocative* function of market prices is important because it offers us a way to determine the scarcity value of different goods and how to distribute them efficiently. The *distributive* function of the market pricing mechanism provides us with a way to determine the income to be received by individuals in return for what they contribute in terms of natural endowments and other forms of capital to production. It is my view that any institutional scheme which seeks to achieve distributional equality should assign the market pricing mechanism a primary role in the allocation of resources but seriously curtail the distributive role of markets.

Markets are most often defended on the grounds of their efficiency. That is to say, in contrast to centralized forms of allocation, the market is promising because through its pricing mechanism it is able to gather information about what people want and allocate resources in a manner that reflects this information. But, for those concerned with distributive justice, the market pricing mechanism is also attractive because it provides us with a metric for comparing the advantages of social life enjoyed by one individual to the advantages enjoyed by another. This is, in my view, the fundamental insight Ronald Dworkin has brought to bear on how we should think about distributional equality. And it seems to me that the market pricing mechanism is important for the realization of equal life prospects precisely because it allows us to make comparisons between the life prospects of different individuals. Assigning the market a primary role in the allocation of resources in an egalitarian society makes sense when value-pluralism is assumed because, on the one hand, it provides a forum for diverse but nonetheless valuable ways of life or to use John Stuart Mill's phrase 'experiments of living' and, on the other hand, it puts a price on these different ways of life which allows us to compare the societal costs of different opportunities that are available to different individuals.

On first appearance, the view I have just advanced may seem absurd. This is because, while it may be true that markets assess opportunities in terms of societal costs, this assessment is predicated on a rejection of the view of what counts as a valuable way of life according to the theory of equal life prospects. Markets assess opportunities from the perspective of wants or preferences. As Carens says, 'The market…is simply a mechanism which makes it possible for the community to indicate to people what productive activities they can engage in if they wish to help the community achieve its goals. Prices are

merely sources of information about what the community *wants* done.'
(Carens 1981 p.195, emphasis added). A market assessment would seem to
have moral significance only if what is wanted is what is valuable. And equal
life prospects assumes that certain ways of life are judged valuable, independently
of whether or not someone wants them. The strong inference that might be made
is that since the assessments made by markets of different ways of life are a
reflection of the preferences people express in markets and that those preferences ought not to be taken seriously for ethical purposes, then the allocation of
resources recommended by the market is of no significance to a theory of
distributional equality such as equal life prospects which is concerned with
distributing not simply opportunities but rather life prospects that are valuable.

However the problem with markets just noted is a difficulty not just for a
perfectionist theory of fair shares such as equal life prospects but is a problem
for any theory of distributional equality that adopts an objectivist approach. In
other words, markets are also problematic for theories such as Dworkin's that
marry an objectivist approach to political neutrality. Since Dworkin also
embraces the importance of markets for the same basic reason that I have, my
position is not so idiosyncratic as it might first appear.

The crux of the issue is whether or not preferences expressed in markets
ought to be taken seriously for ethical purposes. My embrace of the allocative
function of markets can only make sense if these preferences ought to be taken
seriously. The thesis that they ought not to be has been advanced by John
Bennett in an article criticizing Dworkin's reliance on markets in his theory of
equality of resources (Bennett 1985 pp.199–204). It is my view that Bennett
overstates the argument against the moral significance of preferences expressed in markets. Bennett's defence of his thesis is two-pronged. First of all,
he maintains that while the counterfactual claims made by economists about
the rationality and formation of our preference sets may be instructive for
analysing macro-economic phenomena, they undermine any normative value
that might be derived from such an analysis. To be frank, I find this criticism
baffling. Bennett's utter dismissal, without substantial argument, of the now
widely received view that formal methods derived from economics can
contribute to ethics seems hard to take seriously (see Broome 1991). His
second criticism, however, seems more to the point. In effect, he challenges
the idea that our purchases in a market indicate what is important to us on the
grounds that our purchases in markets are often based on impulse, ignorance,
or confusion. Now, certainly Bennett is right to say that we do sometimes buy
impulsively and so on; but in order to reach the strong conclusion he does, it
must be the case that our purchases in markets *never* indicate what is important
to us and this is a ridiculous claim. Instead, at most, what Bennett's argument
indicates is that preferences expressed in the market do not always indicate

what is important to us. This means only that we should not *always* take market preferences seriously from an ethical point of view.

The usefulness of markets for the measurement of valuable life prospects ultimately depends on an empirical issue, that is to say, whether what individuals think is valuable is a pretty good indicator of what really is of moral value. (It is important to note that treating this as an empirical issue is perfectly consistent with the perfectionism embraced earlier since it allows room for the possibility that we as individuals might be mistaken about what counts as a valuable way of life.) Tentatively, I am inclined to say that the degree to which individuals are good judges of what is a valuable way of life is significantly influenced by social and political institutions which have authority over them. This then suggests that a system of education that instils in citizens a sense of what are valuable ways of life is a necessary precondition for the complete realization of equal life prospects. But it is doubtful that this is enough. A strong argument can also be made for the proposition that this sense of judgement also requires political institutions that facilitate individuals actually participating in questions about what are the reasons for thinking that particular ways of life are valuable and making claims on behalf of those ways of life (Drover and Kerans *supra*).

So far, in terms of realization 'equal life prospects' has not differed significantly from Rawls' 'democratic equality' or Dworkin's 'equality of resources'. My defence of the allocative function of the market follows Dworkin's with its emphasis on the market as a device for comparing the heterogeneous resource bundles of different individuals. Rawls also defends the market, although principally on the grounds of efficiency and because it conforms to his principles of equal basic liberties and fair equality of opportunity. (Rawls solves the comparative justice issue through his notion of primary goods.[22])

The upshot of giving the market a primary role in the allocation of resources is that it implies some version of equality of opportunity. In effect, 'equal life prospects' accepts the requirement that people with similar natural endowments and motivation are to have access to the same offices and positions, regardless of sex, racial origin, or socio-economic background. Furthermore, like Rawls and Dworkin, I accept that the pay-offs in terms of salaries and benefits from success under equality of opportunity are to be structured in a way that conforms with distributional equality. Where 'equal life prospects' differs is on the issue of how specifically these pay-offs are to be distributed. I shall argue below that Rawls and Dworkin are too narrow in their focus on the pay-offs of being well endowed or handicapped. By focusing on the effects natural endowments and handicaps have on income, they miss the effects being well endowed or handicapped has on one's life prospects from a broader perspective. But in order to account for these effects within their theories of distributional equality, they must give up their general commitment to neutrality and adopt instead the sort of perfectionist approach taken by the theory of equal life prospects.

(ii) Pay-Offs from Natural Endowments

The market favours the well endowed over the less well endowed in the distribution of scarce resources. Under the analysis of the role of the market just offered, this reflects a flaw with the distributive function, as opposed to the allocative function of the market. From an egalitarian perspective, then, the distributive role of the market should be corrected to ensure a fairer distribution of scarce resources. Assuming a background system of equality of opportunity, egalitarians should be concerned with distributing the pay-offs that are generated by success under such an institution in a fashion that conforms with the demands of equality. If a distributive scheme, instead, allowed those pays-offs to be enjoyed by those who do well under equality of opportunity, such a scheme would simply amount to an equal opportunity to be unequal (Baker 1987 p.46).

Assuming an egalitarian perspective, the issue of how to distribute the pay-offs from natural endowments raises two distinct questions: (1) What exactly is the nature of the pay-offs that are generated by success under a scheme of equality of opportunity? (2) How should those pay-offs be distributed? With respect to (1), as I pointed out above, Dworkin and Rawls focus their concern principally on the income and wealth that is generated by natural endowments. They do, however, differ with regard to how they answer (2). For Rawls, income and wealth under a scheme of fair equality of opportunity is to be distributed in a manner that is to the greatest benefit of the least advantaged. For Dworkin, it is to be distributed in a manner that reflects the opportunity costs to everyone, not just the least advantaged. My view is that Rawls and Dworkin are both off the mark with regard to their answers to (2) because of their circumscribed answer to (1).

Under an institutionalized version of equality of opportunity, those who are well endowed have access to positions and offices that are not accessible to those who are less well endowed. This consequence of equality of opportunity would not be significant if the only differences between jobs are their correlated powers and prerogatives and the income they generate. But not all jobs are the same. Broadly speaking, it is possible to distinguish between two classes of jobs: (a) those jobs that have intrinsic value, that is to say, can have a constitutive role in the leading of a valuable life, and (b) those jobs that lack intrinsic value, that is to say, can only have an instrumental role in the leading of a valuable and meaningful life. While being a university teacher may be an example of a job that falls into class (a), collecting the garbage for the city may be an example of a job that falls into class (b). Given the division of labour inherent in modern industrial societies, it seems inevitable that some people are going to have jobs which fall into class (a), and others jobs which fall into class (b). Under equality of opportunity, many of the jobs that fall into class (a) will likely be accessible only to the well endowed. The relevant point is that the pay-offs from natural endowments are a matter not only of income and power but also offices and positions that can have a constitutive role in the leading of a valuable life.

If performing your job was the only way to lead a valuable life, the fact that some people will be doing jobs that lack intrinsic value would mean that everyone having equal life prospects would be impossible. But, as value pluralism emphasizes, there are many different and indeed incompatible ways to lead a valuable life. To make people equal in their life prospects requires, then, providing those who work in jobs in class (b) with access to certain valuable opportunities which are not open to those who work in jobs in class (a). A direct way to achieve this is by limiting certain valuable opportunities to those who work in class (b) jobs. An indirect approach might be to provide those who work in class (b) jobs with higher incomes or more leisure time. The idea underlying the indirect approach is that a higher income or more leisure time can translate into more life prospects outside the workplace.

The upshot of this analysis can be neatly summarized: although it is acceptable under a scheme of equality of opportunity to reward those with greater talents more jobs with intrinsic value, an egalitarian scheme of distribution must compensate those who do not work in these jobs with other opportunities not available to those who do. Probably the simplest way to institutionalize such a system would be to pay higher incomes to those in job class (b) than to those in job class (a). While the less well endowed might have to settle for class (b) jobs with higher incomes, under a scheme of equality of opportunity the well endowed would have the choice between performing jobs with intrinsic value or forsaking meaningful jobs for higher incomes which they could then use to further their prospects outside the workplace.

While what I have just outlined seems to flow logically from a concern for distributional equality, liberal egalitarians such as Rawls and Dworkin could not accommodate my analysis. The reason is that while both could accept the distinction I have drawn between jobs that have intrinsic value and those that do not, neither could mobilize this distinction in their theories of distributional equality without violating political neutrality. This indicates to me that a concern for distributional equality cannot be reconciled with a general commitment to neutrality. The theory of equal life prospects has no difficulty embracing the fact that differences in natural endowments are reflected not only in income differentials but also in access to jobs that can have a constitutive role in the leading of a valuable life.

(ii) Compensating for Handicaps

It is my intention here to make an argument about how to compensate for handicaps that parallels the one I have just made about the pay-offs from natural endowments. Intuitively, those with handicaps have an extra claim on resources in any egalitarian scheme of distribution. The challenge for a theory of equal shares is to give substance to this intuition. This concern cannot be captured by the effect of a handicap on a person's welfare or utility. We would not be inclined to say that because a person with a particular handicap is especially cheerful or happy, he or she therefore forgoes any claim to compensation he or she might otherwise have had (Sen 1984 p.318). Certain political philosophers such as Rawls simply put the issue aside, assuming that nobody in a well-ordered society has handicaps and then leave it open as to what sort of remedial treatment is necessary when handicaps do arise (Rawls 1982a p.168). Dworkin approaches handicaps in very much the same way that he approaches differences in natural endowments. (Recall that he includes both talents and physical and mental capacities among an individual's circumstances rather than a part of his or her personality.) That is to say, he reduces the egalitarian concern for those suffering from handicaps to the simple issue of how much effect handicaps have on income in a market economy.[23] I shall suggest here that such a narrow focus impoverishes the egalitarian intuition that we should be concerned with compensating the handicapped but that this narrow focus is inevitable, given Dworkin's commitment to political neutrality.

Handicaps are, in my view, disturbing for two distinct reasons. One reason is that they can have a detrimental effect on an individual's earning power. Another reason is that they can interfere with an individual leading a valuable life. A comprehensive egalitarian treatment of handicaps should try to mitigate for both of these effects of handicaps. This type of treatment flows easily from the theory of equal life prospects because the crux of it is captured by the idea that the basic aim of egalitarian social policy concerned with handicaps should be precisely to minimize the degree to which handicaps affect one's life prospects, whether this is directly or by reducing an individual's earning power.

This degree of comprehensiveness is difficult to achieve if one seeks to respect neutrality. How can we minimize the degree to which handicaps interfere with leading a valuable life without already knowing what is and what is not a handicap? How do we define a handicap?[24] When most of us think about handicaps, a general list comes to mind: physical impairments, mental dysfunctions, diseases, and so on. The problem with implementing any such list is that the inherent difficulties of compiling a complete list makes it inevitable that certain ways of life will be favoured over others. To avoid this problem, liberal egalitarians often respond by introducing a standard for identifying handicaps that seeks to respect neutrality. One such standard says that something is a handicap if the person who suffers from a particular mental or physical dysfunction wished (at some second-order level) that he or she did not. There are some immediate problems with using this approach to determine whether mental dysfunctions count as handicaps, but let us put those aside. It is undeniable that this approach works very well for certain tricky cases such as whether or not a desire for alcohol is a handicap. The relevant test would ask if the person who has the desire for alcohol wished that he or she did not. But I think it works less well in other, more basic cases. Consider the well-known example of the nineteenth-century philosopher Brentano who did not regret going blind because he felt that he was then better able to concentrate on deep philosophical problems. If we applied the test at hand, we would find that Brentano's blindness is not a handicap. But this is deeply counter-intuitive. Surely, it is a handicap; Brentano's lack of regret should not influence us in this judgement. Where his lack of regret should come into play, however, is in our consideration of what sort of remedial treatment his blindness warrants — it would be perverse to try to treat him in such a way that he can overcome his blindness.

The point just made about what to do about Brentano's blindness also has a bearing on the approach to compensating for handicaps I have endorsed. Regarding handicaps as a threat to equal life prospects does not entail a particular belief about what exactly egalitarians should do about handicaps. This is because of the complex reasons why handicaps pose a threat to the life prospects of those who suffer from them. Obviously, handicaps can diminish one's life prospects directly, but they also pose a threat partially because of the way in which those *without* handicaps regard those *with* handicaps. Certain social structures often reinforce this threat. These considerations cannot be remedied simply by providing handicapped individuals with additional resources. Instead, they raise an issue about the background conditions necessary for equality of opportunity in addition to the more formal procedural requirements that there not be explicit discrimination (see Fishkin 1983 pp.22–5).

4. CONCLUSION

The foregoing discussion illustrates that it is unfortunate that contemporary political philosophers working on the problem of what constitutes a fair share of the advantages of social life have ignored for the most part perfectionist approaches to distributional equality. It seems that only by adopting a perfectionist viewpoint is it possible to address certain fundamental issues that will inevitably arise in an egalitarian society that seeks to implement a scheme of equality of opportunity. While I have outlined certain basic tenets of an alternative perfectionist theory of fair shares, what I have called the theory of equal life prospects, the more specific features of such a theory remain to be explored.

Acknowledgements: I am grateful to G.A. Cohen, David Lloyd-Thomas, Colin MacLeod, Margaret Moore, Tom Pocklington, and Richard Vernon for valuable comments on earlier drafts of this paper. My research for this paper has benefited from a major research grant from the Social Sciences and Humanities Research Council of Canada.

NOTES

1   Notable contributions include Rawls (1971 esp. pp.65–90); Sen (1982a pp.353–69); Dworkin (1981a), (1981b); Rawls (1982b); Scanlon (1988 esp. pp.195–201); Arneson (1989, 1990); Cohen (1989).
2   Dworkin (1983 p.47). For our purposes, this rather simple definition of liberal neutrality is sufficient to make the contrast to the theory of equal life prospects. It should be noted that there is much debate on the exact formulation of the principle of neutrality. See, for example, Raz (1986 chs. 5–6); Mack (1988); Waldron (1989 pp.1098–1103, 1133–8); Kymlicka (1989a pp.883–6); De Marneffe (1990 pp.253–5).
3   This feature of subjectivist approaches to distributional equality is less apparent in more refined versions such as that defended by Richard Arneson. Arneson (1990) defends a view — equal opportunity for welfare — that makes central the idea of a 'hypothetical rational preference' which is a preference reflecting full information and full deliberative rationality (see pp.163–4). I am sceptical that it is possible to make sense of this idea without introducing an 'objectivist' standard into the determination of an equal share, despite Arneson's claim on p.170 that it does not. See a point to the same effect in Dworkin (1981a p.217).
4   See especially Dworkin (1981a). Arneson (1989, 1990) responds to a range of these criticisms.
5   For a similar treatment, see Roemer (1992 p.449).
6   Rawls (1982a p.5). This formulation reflects a slight refinement of Rawls (1971 pp.302–3).
7   Rawls (1971 p.73). Actually, there are some important ambiguities in Rawls' account of fair equality of opportunity. See the excellent discussion in Pogge (1989 ch.4), as well as Jacobs (forthcoming).
8   See Rawls (1988 p.259). Note that Rawls himself has serious reservations about the use of the term 'neutrality' to describe his position because of its ambiguity. The neutrality of primary goods has been frequently challenged. c.f. Alexander and Schwarzschild (1987 p.89).
9   My analysis here adopts the controversial thesis that for Rawls the social basis of self-respect can be met without the difference principle. See especially Rawls (1971 pp.84, 325, 329, 442). Pogge (1989) appears to reject this thesis on p.163.
10 I have critically examined Dworkin's equality of resources and its institutional implications in much more detail in chapter five of Jacobs (1993a).
11 Dworkin (1981b p.309). Dworkin's claim that such theories are incoherent has been refuted by Cohen (1986 pp.91–5).
12 I am taking issue, then, with those who maintain that the most important difference between the egalitarianism of Rawls and Dworkin has to do with the ambition-sensitive character of Dworkin's equality of resources. This is emphasized by, for example, Kymlicka (1990 pp.70–7). In my view, this ignores (a) Rawls' largely unexplored suggestion in, for example, Rawls (1988 p.257), that leisure be included among the social primary goods, and (b) Rawls' emphasise on motivation in his formulation of fair equality of opportunity as well as his suggestion that unlike natural endowments, motivation engendered by family or socio-economic background is not arbitrary from a moral point of view (see Rawls 1971 p.301).
13 My use of the term 'perfectionist' here is simply to denote theories which reject neutrality. I do not mean by it the view that there is only one valuable way of life. Nor do I use it in the very broad

way in which Joseph Raz uses it. For Raz, '"Perfectionism" is merely a term used to indicate that there is no fundamental principled inhibition on governments acting for any valid moral reason.' See Raz (1989 p.1230). My use is very similar to Arneson (1987 p.527n18).

14 Geras (1985). The claim that Marx himself was committed to equality is much debated. See for contrasting views, Wood (1986 pp.283–303), and Kymlicka (1989b pp.106–9).

15 A similar point is made by Roemer (1989 p.153). Actually, the issue is a bit more complicated than this. As Kymlicka points out, Marx was sceptical about the use of state institutions to promote equality. It follows that a state in Marx's communist state might not violate neutrality. But, as Kymlicka also argues, Marx's reasons for being sceptical of 'juridical equality' are misplaced. See Kymlicka (1989b pp.109–3.

16 For similar reasons, Peffer (1990) defends the right to equal access to the means of self-realization rather than the right to an equal amount of self-realization (see Peffer 1990 pp.131–2). Peffer believes that the means of self-realization can be captured by Rawls's index of social primary goods. But I think this fails to recognize the perfectionist implications of any theory of distributional equality where the measurement of equal shares reflects a concern with self-realization. The contrast between Peffer's equal access to self-realization and my theory of equal life prospects rests precisely on the explicit perfectionist character of the latter theory.

17 Equal opportunity on this understanding is, I suspect, a more demanding requirement than, for example, equal opportunity on Arneson's less stringent stipulation where 'An opportunity is a chance of getting a good if one seeks it.' See Arneson (1987 p.532n24, 1989 p.86).

18 In support of excluding repugnant opportunities in the measurement of equal shares, I have argued in Jacobs (1993b) that it is difficult to see how having the opportunity to do the morally wrong thing can provide grounds for redistribution.

19 This contrasts to Rawls' (1987) analysis of the problem of social justice.

20 In an important respect, the vision of an egalitarian society offered here bears resemblance to Michael Walzer's vision of a society free from what he calls dominance. See Walzer (1983 ch.1).

21 Dworkin is the clearest example: see Dworkin (1981b pp.283–90; 1985 p.195). For a discussion of the way in which markets are neutral between preferences, see O'Donnell (1989 pp.42–4). For a sceptical account, see Miller (1989 ch. 3).

22 The issue is trickier because Rawls' emphasis on wealth and money as a social primary good presupposes economic markets. In effect, then, a case could probably be made for saying that, like Dworkin, Rawls' solution to how you compare the advantages of social life enjoyed by one individual to the advantages enjoyed by another individual necessarily relies on the market pricing mechanism.

23 This reading of Dworkin differs from Alexander and Schwarzchild (1987 p.96). They maintain that Dworkin is committed to compensating the handicapped for more than simply reduced earning power. While I can find no textual evidence to support this, their conclusion is similar to mine and, therefore, this quibble is of no great consequence. Careful textual analysis that supports my reading can be found in Jacobs (1993a ch. 5:7).

24 The practical importance of this question is illustrated by the debate over whether pregnancy should be treated as a handicap or a unique condition. How this debate is resolved is important to social policy since it has a significant economic implications for women. At present, in Canada, for example, most pregnant women qualify under various maternal leave programmes for about 60% of their ordinary wage; if pregnancy was recognized as a temporary handicap and therefore if pregnancy leaves were covered by disability insurance, most women would receive 80% to 100% of their ordinary wages.

4. The Thick and Thin of Human Needing

Kate Soper

Why concern ourselves with a theory of needs in the context of social welfare?

One, rather obvious response is because 'need' everywhere figures in the discourse. Social welfare is about meeting needs, and claimants to it typically argue their case in the language of needs. Moreover, it is in terms of a provisioning of need that we have traditionally been invited to discriminate between the institutional services of the welfare state (the guarantor of essential goods against the relative needs–indifference of commodity society) and the offerings of the market (the accommodator of our desires and preferences). We may say, then, that welfare, whatever construction we may put on its purposes and achievements, has been standardly grounded in a logic of need, and drawn on its normative force or credentials. By talking of 'needs', welfare theory directs us to the fact that it deals not in desiderata, but in essentials, not in options, but in musts, not in what it would be nice to have but in what there is an obligation to provide.

Whether, however, this 'logic of obligation' is fully appreciated by all those who speak of 'needs' in a welfare context is rather doubtful. The concept of needs is, after all, notoriously loosely employed in other contexts and there is perhaps no reason to expect welfare talk to be any more punctilious than other discourse. But it certainly provides a starting point for discriminating between the two approaches to needs with which I shall here be primarily concerned: Glenn Drover and Patrick Kerans' defence of a 'thick' perspective (*supra*), and Len Doyal and Ian Gough's universalist theory (1991). For while Doyal and Gough wish to observe the logic of need as entailing rights to satisfaction, and for this reason cannot see how you can speak of 'need' if you are not prepared to argue that it ought to be met, Drover and Kerans see no reason for being so exclusive about the term. They recognize the 'moral weight' which attaches to need, but argue that this applies only in respect of what they term a 'thin' notion of it, i.e. when we are speaking of needs which are 'abstract, objective and universal' (*supra* p.11). If we are to recognize the ways in which people actually experience and talk about their 'needs', and to give full due to the variety and contestability of claims to welfare, then, they suggest, we need a 'thicker' concept altogether: a concept which may have sacrificed some of its 'moral weight' but has gained instead the capacity to speak to the cultural relativity and particularity of 'needs'.

As they put it:

> ... a thick understanding of need is rooted in an attempt to understand the cultural context in which people name their needs. It relies on interpretive methods to grasp the full particularity of the meaning of social action generally and of need in particular in its everyday context. If welfare is to be understood in the context of people's quest for the development of their human capacities, then the notion of need as that upon which claims for welfare are based, requires such an interpretative reading, at least as a complement to a thin reading. (*supra* p.12)

In a thick perspective, then, if I have understood this correctly, 'need' is not being employed in a way that implies an obligation. Or rather, while claimants themselves may use the concept in a thin sense to bespeak what they regard as entitlements to fulfilment, the social welfare 'hermeneuticist' cannot endorse this interpretation except on pain of recognizing the equal obligation to satisfaction of both racist and anti-racist 'needs', of both nuclear planners and environmentalists and so on.

But how, it might be asked at this point, can we defend the use of the term 'need' while so severing it from the 'conventional' logic of need? Why, in short, are we not here talking about 'interests' or 'preferences', and what, if anything, is to be gained from a welfare point of view by remaining so committed to the vocabulary of needs? The question is an important one, and perhaps most fairly approached by considering some of the reasons in favour of a thick approach.

These reasons relate to difficulties attaching to the theorization of human needs, and in particular to the attempt to distinguish between needs which are common, universal and objective, and all those other requirements variously referred to as 'non-basic needs', 'historically developed needs', 'culturally specific needs', or, indeed as thick. Can we, in short, finally separate the thin from the thick, the a-historic from the historic? Can we ever be sure that in arguments put forward for the universality of human needs we have escaped the thickening lens of our own cultural embeddedness?

These questions obviously have a very direct bearing on the assessment of Doyal and Gough's project in *A Theory of Human Need*, which is surely the most complete and sophisticated attempt to date to defend the universality of needs. I shall therefore postpone discussion of them to the second part of this paper, which is primarily devoted to their work. Suffice it to say here, that if the complaint against a thick notion of needs is that it spuriously legitimates a runaway plurality of wants, and thus risks bringing the whole idea of welfare into disrepute, then the onus is on the complainer to offer us a plausible account of exactly where we should call a halt on the use of the concept of need: to offer us a clear demarcation between what can be said to be needed and what is merely preferred. If this cannot be done, then we may still experience an unease about allowing thick needs talk, but are left with only rhetorical arguments against it.

We might recast this argument in terms which bring out the ambivalence at the heart of the concept of human need, which speaks to us of the 'good' as much as it speaks to us of the bare exigencies of survival. Included, that is, within the idea of human need is the idea of an 'excess' over biological or purely 'animal' need (Soper 1981 ch.1). For whether or not it is correct to speak of animal needs in this reductive way, the philosophical tradition has always insisted from Aristotle onward[1] that in the case of humanity at least, it has fundamental needs for something more than mere survival. It also needs the conditions of the good — and to that extent the idea of human flourishing is built into the idea of human needing. But given the very divergent conceptions of the 'good' that have been found within the human community, how can we be sure that we are not foisting our idea of the 'good' on others in any attempt to speak for their needs in any but a sense so thin and reduced that it no longer serves the purpose of theorizing a distinctively *human* set of needs? In short, might it not be wiser — and more democratic — simply to recognize that there will be many contesting claims about the 'good' and begin at that end of the spectrum in any theory of welfare, as the thick theorists advocate?

This brings us to a further consideration in favour of a thick approach, namely that it has a built-in guarantee against the paternalism, or as some might insist, the inherent totalitarianism, of any attempt to name the needs of others. To insist on the objectivity of needs, it might be said, is to allow that we can have needs of which we are subjectively unaware, and hence to allow that 'experts' can be in a better position to pronounce on these than we ourselves. To focus, by contrast, on 'needs' as these are experienced and interpreted by subjects themselves is to protect claimants from this sort of presumption, and from the inadequate, inappropriate, or downright damaging forms of welfare provision made on its basis. The issues involved here are by no means clearcut since the very idea that 'experts' might be mistaken in their assessments of claimants' needs would seem itself to rely on an objective standard of need-satisfaction; and if 'experts' can get it wrong, then why not claimants too? (Doyal and Gough 1991 pp. 309–10). But the 'populist' sensibilities of the thick theory approach and the critique of positivism which underlies them are an important counter to welfare 'knowingness'.[2] In practice, moreover, we can view the thick emphasis on subjective experience and interpretation as responding to all those ways in which social movement politics have of late been contesting the conventional wisdoms of institutional welfare on gender, sexuality and citizenship.

Thirdly, one might grant the appropriateness of a thick position on needs in the context of welfare theory in virtue of the non-global or nation-specific character of institutionalized welfare provision. The focus of welfare policy is not on the deprivations of the global community taken as a whole, it might be argued, but on the relative deprivations of individuals or groups within a particular nation state. It is about allowing all those within a given community to participate and function adequately *as members of that community*, and to that extent it cannot but be concerned with the particular goods and services which will allow them to do so, even if such goods and services would not be essential to performance in other, less affluent, nations. In other words, if welfare, as many would argue,[3] is about developing capacities — about enabling people to survive and prosper — and people always come placed in societies whose specific structural features determine the conditions of survival and well-being, how can welfare theory abstract from those thick conditions and still function as a guide to practical policy decisions? In the final section of this paper, I shall argue that welfare theory cannot, in fact, be so parochially confined, and must consider as central to its concerns, the more global consequences of any thick needs meeting within particular nation states. But it is nonetheless true, I think, that if there can be a 'general' theory of welfare which is distinguished from a 'general' theory of human needs, then it is a theory which focuses on provisionings and inequities of distribution within discrete communities and not on more global disparities. Its primary concern, as Drover and Kerans imply, is with the consequences for human capacity and enjoyment of the social embeddedness of individuals rather than on the global and long-term consequences of respecting the specifics.

All the same, we can still ask, as Drover and Kerans themselves do, what it is which saves a theory which takes claimmaking as its starting point from being 'simply an account of a struggle over interests'. Their response here is Habermasian. It can only be, they say, because 'a group can articulate needs which are universalizable, hence "true" in the sense that in an ideal speech situation, there can be common consensus' (*supra* p.8). But does this really solve the problem? For unless the 'group' in question is hypothetically extended to include the human community at large, it is not clear how consensus within it solves the problems of irreconcilable claims. If, on the other hand, we do construe the 'group' as all-embracing, then it would seem that any consensus could only be won at the cost of that respect for cultural plurality which the thick approach is designed to secure. Secondly, it can be argued that the 'ideal speech situation' presupposes precisely that capacity for individuals to dissociate from their cultural situation and its formative influence on what they come to perceive as their 'needs' which a thick approach is, in effect, claiming to be unwarranted. And, thirdly, would not this emphasis on universalizability mean that only those claims which would win agreement in an ideal speech situation, could properly be spoken of as claims about need — which is again an implication which risks subverting the priority given by the thick perspective to subjective experience and authentification. Indeed, is not the overall difficulty here that Drover and Kerans want to have it both ways: both to distinguish between interests and needs in terms of the universalizable character of the latter, and to allow that an indefinite plurality of claims can appropriately be viewed as speaking to needs?

They themselves might argue in response that this is but an aspect of the 'duality' of welfare of which they speak: a necessary tension at the heart of its dialectic. Yet I think they may be a little too ready to tolerate tensions at the methodological level which cannot be so easily accommodated at the practical level. One relevant example here would be their endorsement of the ethics of justice even as they advocate the never-ending, individualist dynamic of 'well-seeking' (*supra*; Kerans 1991 p.2). For it is by no means clear how justice in distribution could in practice be secured for the global community, either now or in the future, except by destraining upon the self-developmental capacities of all those individuals currently best placed to enhance their 'needs'. At any rate, there is surely something too abstract about the formulations used by Kerans and Drover in recommendation of a dynamic conception of needs. 'Well-seeking', 'persons rich in need', 'ever newly discovered needs': these phrases sound fine, and no doubt capture something of the way in which individuals actually conceive of their potentials. But unless and until we specify more precisely what kinds of needs and consumption we are here talking about, it is impossible to assess the desirability or practicality of the goals they express. I take it that the aspiration here is not to persons 'rich in needs' for second homes, private planes and motor-cruisers (Castoriadis 1984 ch.9). But if not, what criterion of need is being employed here, and will not any such criterion presume 'objective' rights of discrimination between competing claims?

A UNIVERSAL THEORY OF NEEDS

Granted, however, the dilemmas of a thick perspective, does an anti-relativist approach fare any better as a basis for welfare theory? For the difficulty here would seem to be that acceptance to the idea of objective and universal human needs can be won only at the cost of such a high degree of abstraction from the specific and differential modes of their satisfaction, that the theory of need no longer serves as any practical guide to welfare provision.[4]

Now it is a great strength of Doyal and Gough's argument (to turn now more directly to this) that it represents an attempt to confront this dilemma head-on by offering to defend quite a thick set of needs as universal. What their work shows, they would argue, is that you can chart basic need satisfaction for 'objective' welfare without either embracing relativism or operating at such a level of generality that the pertinence of the theory for specific problems concerning social policy is sacrificed (Doyal and Gough 1991 p.156). Hence they not only tell us what basic needs are (those of health and autonomy), but also offer empirical criteria for the meeting of these goals. They specify, that is, the 'universal satisfier characteristics' (or 'intermediate needs', as they term them) essential to their realization, listing these as: nutritional food and clean water; protective housing; a non-hazardous work environment; appropriate health care; security in childhood; significant primary relationships; physical security; economic security; appropriate education; safe birth control and child-rearing.

Thus, while they readily concede that the specific *form* taken by the satisfiers of 'intermediate needs' will be culturally divergent, the 'intermediate needs' are common to all cultures at all times, and provide a standard of reference by which levels of deprivation within particular groups can be charted and specific welfare strategies defended as objectively grounded rather than ethnocentrically motivated. Abstractly, this standard is defined at two levels: (1) that of the 'participation optimum' (the health and autonomy needed such that individuals can 'choose the activities in which they will take part within their culture, possess the cognitive, emotional and social capacities to do so and have access to the means by which these capacities are acquired'(Doyal and Gough 1991 p.160); and (2) that of the 'critical optimum' (the health and autonomy needed such that individuals can 'formulate the aims and beliefs necessary to question their form of life, to participate in a political process directed toward this end and/or join another culture altogether.') (Doyal and Gough 1991 p.160). Concrete indices of this standard are provided by reference to a wide range of statistical data on the objective welfare of groups or nations in the First, Second and Third Worlds. This allows Sweden to be singled out as the average best performer, and its level of welfare provision established as 'the only logical and moral criterion that can be applied to judge need-satisfaction in the long-term' (Doyal and Gough 1991 p.161).

In a world which might crudely be said to be divided between those who starve and those who diet, I think the political importance of any theoretical project which highlights contrasts in basic need satisfaction must be indisputable. For however well-intentioned the admonitions against 'cultural imperialism' may be, it is a relativist stress on 'difference' rather than Doyal and Gough's defence of universal needs, that is most likely to give comfort to all those seeking to clothe a naked disregard for Third World deprivation with the mantle of theoretical legitimacy.

Yet the political significance of the project makes it all the more important to examine its more problematic aspects; and here I would single out two areas of tension, one concerning the arguments assembled around the concept of 'critical autonomy', the other concerning the objective status of 'intermediate needs'.

As far as 'critical autonomy' is concerned, there are two types of difficulty. The first has to do with a thick–thin conflict between the importance they attribute to the possession of 'critical autonomy' in the assessment of the objectivity of needs, and their readiness to assume a privileged knowledge of needs on the part of oppressed groups (they particularly single out women here).[5] They therefore in some sense also want it both ways: both to allow for a spontaneous, directly experienced apprehension of needs among the oppressed, and to analyse the condition of oppression as one which deprives individuals of the 'critical autonomy' essential to arriving at an understanding of their objective needs.

The other, though related, difficulty concerns the 'objectivity' of the criteria by which they judge the achievement of 'critical autonomy'. For in their discussion of this, they draw on what are arguably very culturally specific ideals of human taste and discrimination (albeit ones which many of us might share).

Thus, in elaboration of their claim that critical autonomy requires the capacity to make 'significant' choices, they argue that 'the choice of a brand of soap powder which is really no different from all the others has more to do with a diminution of autonomy than its expansion'(Doyal and Gough 1991 p.66). But they do not argue through the grounds on which they are making these adjudications. If a Swedish citizen, who on their own argument would be benefiting from optimal levels of basic needs satisfaction, *were* to experience the choice of soap powders as 'significant' on what basis is this sense of significance to be dismissed, and how would Doyal and Gough want to account for the loss of autonomy they claim it would reflect? Likewise, when they cite 'mindless television watching' as evidence of the way in which successful participation in a 'form of life' can be consistent with loss of critical autonomy (Doyal and Gough 1991 p.189), are they not appealing to cultural standards of evaluation whose 'objectivity' is notoriously in question? Some may believe, with Arnold, that 'mankind must be compelled to relish the sublime'. But can they justify this as a need? In other words, if Doyal and Gough are to convince us of the objectivity of their claims about 'critical autonomy', then I think they also have to convince us that what they deem to be 'mindless' consumption and 'insignificant' choice entails serious harm. But can they do this in any non-circular way?

I would argue, therefore, that while Doyal and Gough make out a very strong case for a cross-cultural need for 'autonomy' conceived as a capacity to participate in any 'form of life', they are less persuasive when it comes to defending the need for any more enhanced degree of autonomy (such as would constitute their 'critical optimum') from the charge of being relativistically conceived.

As far as 'intermediate needs' are concerned, the problem has to do with what might be called the 'differential normative status' of the items on Doyal and Gough's list, by which I mean the variable degree to which they can be operationalized (or formulated in terms which would respect differences in individual need while still providing an absolute standard of consumption). Thus, for example, a need for nutritional food can be specified in terms of the requirement of any individual expending a certain amount of energy to consume a certain number of calories, quantum of protein, etc. But it is much less clear how, in the absence of cross-cultural indices for translating the norms of the 'appropriate', the 'significant' and the 'secure' into common 'contents' of consumption, the same could be done in respect of educational, emotional and economic provision.

Indeed, some might argue that phrases such as 'economic security', 'significant primary relations' and the like, are so redolent of contemporary, western perceptions of the 'good' that they very clearly reveal the ethnocentric bias that has been at work in their determination as 'universal'. Doyal and Gough, I imagine, might grant this, but still argue that in the absence of what in western industrial societies is regarded as constituting an 'appropriate' education or 'significant' primary relationship individuals of earlier cultures or elsewhere in the globe, have suffered, or do suffer, serious impairment of health and autonomy. But they can respond in this way only by inviting the objection that they are then defining basic needs too purely analytically in terms of whatever is enhanced by an 'appropriate' level of education or a 'significant' primary relationship.

In other words, I am not convinced that Doyal and Gough do here manage to steer their desired path between the Scylla of relativism, on the one hand, and the Charybdis of politically ineffective generality, on the other. For it would seem that at least in the case of some of their cited intermediate needs, either we claim these to be common to all cultures, but only by remaining wholly non-specific as to their content, or we give them sufficient content to guide welfare policy, but only at the cost of acknowledging the culturally conditioned interpretations we are bringing to these.

BASIC NEEDS AND SPECIFIC SATISFIERS

In this, and my final section, I want to address some complex and inter-connected issues concerning the concept of 'basic' need, the implementation of a 'basic' need programme, and the implications of such a project for our understanding of human gratification. My remarks here will be very general, and have import, I believe, for all theories of need and welfare, universalist and relativist, thin and thick.

I suggested earlier, that the onus was on anyone objecting to a thick perspective, to offer a clear demarcation between 'needs' and 'interest'; and this, of course, is precisely what Doyal and Gough have attempted to provide. 'Interests' ('preferences', 'wants', etc.) refer us to culturally specific desiderata, 'need' to what is common, universal, in effect, 'basic' to human welfare. Yet it is a paradox of this emphasis on the 'basics' — the commonly shared needs for food, shelter, security, education, etc. — that it might be invoked to justify almost any and every form of specific consumption as 'needed'. For an argument can always be made out for considering even the most profligate and luxurious consumption as no more than a 'specific form' in which a primary need (for food, shelter, and the like) is being met. Rather apposite here is King Lear's remark on his daughter's clothing:

> Thou art a lady;
> If only to go warm were gorgeous.
> Why, nature needs not what thou gorgeous wear'st,
> Which scarcely keeps thee warm.
> (*King Lear*, Act II, Scene 4, 264–7)

Quite apart from the interesting questions Lear raises about the status of the urge to be 'gorgeous' (is it mere want or need, and if so how basic?), he clearly targets here the problem of the 'cut-off' point between a needed and less than needed 'satisfier'. Given that a 'basic' need for warmth requires the donning of some apparel, on what criteria exactly would we decide that any item of clothing had ceased to be 'appropriate' to the gratification of this need and had begun to function as the satisfier of a non-basic need or mere want?

I raise these points in order to illuminate what I think is a problematic point of convergence in the two approaches to needs with which I have here been concerned: their readiness simply to accept the very divergent forms taken by the satisfiers of intermediate needs. For while in one sense it would be absurd to deny a relativism of needs at this level, to take it too much for granted is to overlook the critical role of the form taken by specific satisfiers of basic needs in the affluent and 'best performing' nations in creating basic need deprivation elsewhere in the globe. In other words, what has be targeted by a politics of need, so it seems to me, is not only what we share in the way of basic needs or our differences in meeting them, but the causal relationship between the forms in which some are meeting needs and the forms in which others are being deprived. Thus, to cite but one indicator of the very considerable problems raised in this area, which although acknowledged by Doyal and Gough, perhaps deserve more attention: Sweden, as we have seem, emerges statistically as the 'average best performer' in meeting needs and is looked to as providing a moral yardstick for need satisfaction in the long term. But Sweden's per capita energy consumption is one of the highest in the world (Doyal and Gough 1991 Table 13.1 p.289), and certainly not one it seems automatically moral and logical to attempt to universalize — particularly when considered from the point of view of future generations.

ECOLOGY, NEEDS AND WELFARE

This brings me lastly to some considerations about the generalizability of the basic needs model provided by Doyal and Gough. This is a vast and ramified topic, and I shall here address only the ecological dimension of it by posing the following question: if (and it is an all too purely academic 'if'!) all directly economic and political obstacles to the universalization of basic need satisfaction were to be removed, what common standard of living would be ecologically viable (consistent with future generations enjoying the same level of environmental consumption in perpetuo?)

Clearly (as Doyal and Gough imply in their discussion of ecological sustainability) this question is almost imponderable, given the number of over-determining variables of which any projected assessment would need to take account (Doyal and Gough 1991 pp.242–6). All the same, I think we may at least entertain the possibility that even with the best will in the world, and the most equitable and efficient use of resources, we might not manage to attain indefinitely to anything more than an optimal (Swedish level) satisfaction of basic needs. But allowing this hypothesis, what then becomes of their designation as 'basic'? If all that we might be able to achieve consistently with ecological sustainability is to universalize in practice, now and for future generations, what Doyal and Gough theorize as universal, then what are we to make of the idea that these needs are 'basic' because they are the primary requirements which must be met as a condition of any further human gratification and expansion of self-fulfilment?

Doyal and Gough might well consider this to be itself a somewhat luxurious speculation, as in a sense it is. For it certainly seems quite sufficiently utopian for our times to offer the prospect that all now, and in the future, might have access to even half of what Sweden is able to provide for its citizens! But I want to conclude by offering this 'indulgent' speculation up for consideration because of the bearing it has for the conceptualization of certain needs as 'basic', and hence on the whole issue of human welfare. For if it is true, as I am surmising it might be, that Doyal and Gough's 'basic' needs are the most we can hope to realize globally over time, then have we not in a sense surreptitiously subverted the idea of their being 'basic'? Has not their current theoretical designation exposed a certain culturally specific apperception of human potentialities at its heart which should give us pause for thought? Relatedly, should we not submit ourselves to the rather sobering thought that it is an awareness, however subliminal it may be, that a more egalitarian global culture will cut off the prospects of any human 'flourishing' beyond that provided through basic need satisfaction, that underlies the nonchalance of affluent governments, and many of their citizens, in regard to matters of social justice and ecological sustainability? Better, says the voice of affluence, that some should flourish, even at the cost of survival of others, than that all of us should manage little more than to live 'by bread alone'.

Now, it might be said in response to these speculations that they have force, only if we assume that not living 'by bread alone' always means, shall we say, 'eating cake', that is to say, would always involve a refinement and sophistication — a luxurification — of our material needs. Thus, it will be said, it is only if we unthinkingly adopt a 'materialist–consumerist' conception of what it means to 'flourish' or expand on 'basic' need satisfaction, that we shall concern ourselves with these standard, liberal-economic, anxieties about the 'stagnating' effects of an essentially stable and reproductive provision of basic needs for all. If we cut loose from the idea of an 'improved living standard' engendered by a materialist culture, then we need no longer think of 'wants' or 'non-basic' needs always as extensions of, or evermore baroque — and resource-hungry — constructions upon primary physical needs, but as an altogether less materially encumbered, and encumbering self-development and exploration.

By and large, I am in agreement with the spirit of this line of response, with its suggestion that a 'decent and humane' standard of material living for all is quite compatible with the extension in gratification of 'wants' provided these cease to be so fixated on tangible goods, and more directed to so-called 'spiritual' pleasures. Indeed, I would even claim that in restraining our material consumption we shall expand other dimensions of human enjoyment insofar as these are reliant on the less tangible goods of free time, space, safety, a non-polluted atmosphere, and so forth. If, however, these rather general arguments are in any sense valid, what they indicate, I think, is the importance of complementing any theory of 'basic' need with an altered 'imaginary' of human wants: with what I have elsewhere referred to as a new 'erotics of consumption' (Soper 1985, 1990). For if it is true that the more affluent peoples of the world need to reduce their material *wants* if there is to be anything approaching a universal extension of their level of basic *need* satisfaction, then it is surely equally true that a condition of the emergence of a will to sobriety in their material consumption will be the fostering of an altered conception of their pleasures. In this sense, being realistic about needs may require us to be utopian about wants, and the political force of any theory of basic needs may prove dependent on the imagining of a new hedonist vision.

Let me only add finally, that if the primary reference of these rather general remarks on ecological sustainability and human gratification has been to Doyal and Gough's argument, it is not because I regard this as specially open to the criticism that it neglects or abstracts from these issues. On the contrary, I would argue that it is a relativist emphasis on the importance of under-standing and meeting culturally generated and situated needs which may be more properly charged with being nonchalant about the future human and ecological consequences of promoting its particular conception of human flourishing. At any rate, it seems to me important that anyone invoking the goal of persons 'rich in need' and the idea of a never-ending discovery of new needs, should address the issue of the inherently limited (and currently very unevenly distributed) resources available for the realization of such a pluralist utopia of need satisfaction — and also the issue of its compatibility with the 'well-seeking' of future generations. The populist and democratic impulses of a thick theory approach are of critical importance to the avoidance of pater-nalistic and bureaucratic approaches to welfare provision. But it would be inconsistent to concern ourselves only with respecting the subjectively authenticated needs of specific groups within particular cultural settings, without considering the democratic implications of meeting these welfare demands on the need-fulfilment of others elsewhere and in the future. In this respect, Doyal and Gough's emphasis on 'basic' needs, and their commitment to a theory which observes the logical distinction between the 'needed' and 'wanted' or 'subjectively preferred', has for me the very considerable value of allowing us to see how and why a theory of welfare will need to be placed within this broader framework of social and ecological considerations.

NOTES

1 I refer here to Aristotle's claim in his *Metaphysics* that 'when life or existence are impossible (or when the good cannot be attained) without certain conditions, these conditions are "necessary", and this cause is itself a kind of "necessity"'. Ross (ed.) (1956), p.10.
2 So, too, is its injection of a Foucaultian reminder of the intimate connections between knowledge and power.
3 Amartya Sen's work (1984, 1985a) has been of critical importance in the development of a 'capacities' approach to welfare.
4 For what relativists object to is not claims to the effect that we all need the 'good' rather than the 'bad', or even to the effect that everyone has a need to avoid serious physical and mental harm, but to the idea that we can say more exactly in what such harms consist or prescribe the 'universal satisfiers' essential to their avoidance. I am not, however, clear how far Doyal and Gough would accept this general point. In their Introduction and Chapter One, they present 'relativists' of all complexions as united in their rejection of common human needs without much discussion of the degree of consent there would be among them to claims about universal needs of the most formal and minimalist kind. At a somewhat later stage, however, they do suggest that 'even the most staunch relativist would presumably not question the universality of the need for life-preserving

quantities of water, oxygen and calorific intake' (p.69) But given how close this comes to allowing relativists to agree to the existence of basic needs, it is difficult not to feel that Doyal and Gough may earlier have set up a straw-man relativism, when what was really needed was an engagement with relativist objections to the attempt to make any but fairly general claims about common needs. Many of the relativists cited by Doyal and Gough, I suspect, might want to insist that their objections to universalist theory were only intended to come into play at a fairly low level of abstraction.

5   They are understandably loath, in their discussion of women's needs, to offend against a feminist sense that these are not the province of 'experts', but it is not clear that this wariness is entirely consistent with their analysis of autonomy or their claim that groups' interests must not be allowed 'to trump the best available codified knowledge concerning need satisfaction' (p.309). There is the further problem that Doyal and Gough tend to assume a collective agreement among women as to their needs which is not justified by the very different interpretations which feminists bring to the idea of female emancipation. Nor am I entirely happy with the treatment of the need for safe contraception and child-bearing as if this were specific to women. Relevant here are the arguments of Nancy Fraser (1989 pp.161–87), on whose thick–thin distinction Kerans and Drover draw.

For commentary on this chapter see page 270.

CLAIMS AND INSTITUTIONS

5. Economic Institutions and Human Well-Being

Ian Gough

The purpose of this paper is to summarize a longer assessment elsewhere (Gough 1992) of the contribution of different economic systems to human well-being. The criterion of well-being used is the ability to satisfy human needs, based on the concept of human need developed in Doyal and Gough (1991). To assess the potential of economic systems to satisfy human needs, thus defined, I use a family of theoretical approaches from different disciplines broadly labelled *new institutionalist* or *new political economy*. The economic systems to be investigated are first distinguished according to their dominant organizing principle. Following many others I identify three: the market, the state and the community. Recognizing that 'pure' models of each are histori- cally and logically impossible, I evaluate combinations of institutions which are as close as possible to the pure model: minimally regulated capitalism, state socialism and variants of communitarianism. At the next stage I consider three variants of *mixed economy* capitalism. The paper concludes by deriving hypotheses of the effects of differing socio-economic institutions on levels of need satisfaction which I subsequently intend to test against cross-national empirical evidence.

Since this is an extremely ambitious project, it has necessary limits which should be emphasized. First, the sole criterion according to which economic systems are compared is the optimum satisfaction of universal human needs, as defined in the next section. Second, the analysis is conducted at a high level of abstraction, which cannot, without further empirical specification, be applied to specific social formations in the real world. Third, the focus is on need satisfaction within, not between, 'national' economies. It excludes global linkages between national economies. Effectively, this limits my focus to the developed world, though I believe that some of the predictions can be tested for developing nations too. Fourth, it is concerned only with the ability of economic systems to satisfy present levels of need satisfaction: issues of economic sustainability and intra-generational redistribution are left to one side. These are serious limitations, but they are made necessary by the scope of the investigation which remains. The paper is necessarily broad brush and the research relies on secondary sources to buttress many of its claims.

NEED SATISFACTION AS A MEASURE OF WELFARE OUTCOMES

This paper attempts to evaluate socio-economic systems and institutions according to the anticipated welfare outcomes enjoyed by their citizens. Welfare outcomes are conceived of in terms of the level of satisfaction of basic human needs. This approach thus differs from much contemporary research in both comparative social policy and economics. The former has sought to explain variations in 'welfare states' by analysing specific welfare inputs, such as levels of state expenditure on social security, or more recently, welfare outputs, such as the specific social policies or the 'welfare state regimes' which characterize syndromes of social policies. Much economics research on the other hand has concerned itself with the final outcomes of policies, but has traditionally defined these rather narrowly, such as for example rates of economic growth, monetary stability, rates of unemployment, employment and productivity growth (Strümpel and Scholz 1987; but see Putterman 1990).

Both these approaches tend to ignore the final impact of all these factors on the levels and distribution of well-being of the populations concerned, though this gap has been recognized by some (Alber et al. 1987). The major reason for the lack of progress here is an inability to agree on concepts and measures of well-being which have cross-cultural validity. The postwar period has witnessed a growth in research utilizing concepts such as the *level of living, social indicators, basic needs* and *human development*. This in turn has informed comparative research on welfare outcomes in the Third World. However, this work has had little impact due not only to the changed political and economic climate of the 1980s. Crucially, it has been criticized as lacking a unifying conceptual framework (Sen 1987a), and more particularly for incorporating western cultural and political biases in the very notions of universal need and social progress (Rist 1980; Doyal and Gough 1991 ch.8). Though some of these issues have been addressed in some of the philosophical literature on need, there has existed a barrier between this and the more applied development literature. It is this barrier which our book has attempted to overcome.

The absence of a theoretically grounded and operational concept of objective human need has inhibited the development of a common calculus for evaluating human well-being. On the contrary, there is a widespread scepticism that human needs exist, or that, if needs exist, they are in any sense universal. Typical of the first view are neo-liberals, such as Hayek and Flew, together with the dominant strand in neo-classical economics. The second view, that needs exist but are relative, takes a variety of forms. For many Marxists, human needs are historically relative to capitalism; for various critics of cultural imperialism, needs are specific to, and can only be known by, members of groups defined by gender, race and so on; for phenomenologists and certain social researchers, needs are socially constructed; for post-modernist critics and 'radical democrats', needs are discursive and do not exist independently of the consciousness of human agents (Doyal and Gough 1991 ch.1). Clearly, if any of these perspectives are correct, then any common yardstick of welfare is unattainable, and it cannot be used to compare and evaluate different economic institutions and systems.

Our theory attempts to overcome these limitations. The theory is both substantive and procedural: *substantive* in defending, conceptualizing and operationalizing the idea of universal human needs; *procedural* in recognizing the inevitable social determination of products, policies and procedures which satisfy needs, and thus in the necessity for procedures for resolving disputes in as rational and democratic a way as possible. I shall merely list the conclusions of our substantive theory here.

We argue that all persons have an objective interest in avoiding serious *harm* which in turn prevents them from pursuing their vision of the good, whatever that is (Doyal and Gough 1991 ch.4). This pursuit of the good entails, as others have argued, an ability to *participate* in the form of life in which they find themselves. Thus objective basic needs consist, at the least, in those universalizable preconditions which optimize sustained participation in one's form of life. At the most, they consist of those universalizable preconditions for critical participation in one's form of life — the capacity to situate it, criticize it and, if necessary, to act to change it. Basic human needs, then, are the universal prerequisites for successful and, if necessary, critical participation in one's social form of life. We identify these universal prerequisites as *physical health* and *autonomy*. Autonomy of agency — the capacity to make informed choices about what should be done and how to go about doing it — is impaired, we contend, when there is a deficit of three attributes: mental health, cognitive skills and opportunities to engage in social participation.

Recognizing that these common human needs can be met in a multitude of different ways by an almost infinite variety of specific satisfiers, we next go on to identify those characteristics of need satisfiers which everywhere contribute to improved physical health and autonomy (Doyal and Gough 1991 ch.8). These we label *universal satisfier characteristics*, or *intermediate needs* for short. We group these into eleven categories: adequate nutritional food and water, adequate protective housing, a non-hazardous work environment, a non-hazardous physical environment, appropriate health care, security in childhood, significant primary relationships, physical security, economic security, safe birth control and child–bearing, and appropriate basic and cross-cultural education. Nine of these apply to all people, one refers to the specific needs of children, and another to the specific needs of women for safe birth control and child–bearing. All eleven are essential to protect the health and autonomy of people, and thus to enable them to participate to the maximum extent in their social form of life, whatever that is.

As developed this far, our theory of needs is substantive or 'intrinsic' (Hewitt 1992 ch.10). It identifies universal basic and intermediate needs and legitimizes the use of cross-cultural social indicators with which to chart need satisfactions. It thus provides a means of empirically comparing the welfare performance of different societies (Doyal and Gough 1991 chs 12 and 13). However, my purpose here is to investigate *theoretically* the contribution of different socio-economic institutions to the satisfaction of these needs. This leads me on to the procedural dimension of our theory. Here, we identify universal *procedural* and *material* preconditions for optimizing need satisfaction (Doyal and Gough 1991 chs 7, 11). These are attributes of social systems, and it is these with which I am principally concerned in this paper.

Procedural preconditions relate to the ability of a group to identify needs and appropriate need satisfiers in a rational way and to prioritize need satisfiers and the need satisfactions of different groups in conditions of scarcity. In the face of radical disagreements over the perceived interests and needs of different groups, how can this best be achieved? To answer this we draw on the work of Habermas and Rawls. In what follows I shall summarize our resulting procedural preconditions under the following three headings:

P1. *Rational identification of needs.* Needs are defined, and distinguished from wants, by appealing to an externally-verifiable stock of codified knowledge, for example, about nutrition, child-rearing or environmental control. The ability to tap and rationally utilize this stock of codified knowledge — to engage in collectively identifying common human needs — is a first precondition for improving their satisfaction.

P2. *Use of practical knowledge.* At the next level, appropriate need satisfiers have to be selected. Here we argue that the above codified knowledge needs to be complemented by the experientially-grounded understanding of people in their everyday lives. This knowledge can be tapped in one of two basic ways. First there is participation in market relations, where these are unconstrained by contingencies of power or ignorance. Second, there are various forms of political participation and 'claimsmaking' (Drover and Kerans *supra*) — the process whereby people identify their dissatisfactions, name their felt needs and make claims against a variety of institutions.

P3. *Democratic resolution.* If a rational policy to identify and prioritize need satisfiers must draw on both codified and experientially grounded knowledge, then the inevitable disagreements which result must be confronted and resolved in a forum as open, as democratic and as free of vested interests as possible. This is the third procedural precondition by which different socio-economic institutions will be evaluated.

Next, *material preconditions* refer to the capacity of economic systems to produce and deliver the necessary and appropriate need satisfiers, and to transform these into final need satisfactions. We argue that there is a strong moral case for codifying the intermediate needs identified earlier in the form of state-guaranteed rights. However, the *de jure* codification of social or welfare rights is no guarantee of their *de facto* delivery. To assess the latter we develop a cross-cultural model of material production (Doyal and Gough 1991 ch. 11), which yields four material preconditions for improved need satisfaction. These are:

M1. *Production.*   Potential need satisfaction is greater, the greater the total quantity and quality of need satisfiers produced. The efficiency by which need satisfiers are produced is thus the first of our material preconditions.

M2. *Distribution.*   Need satisfaction is maximized if these satisfiers are distributed in line with the needs of individuals. This normally entails in-dividuals-in-households, though for certain collective satisfiers the unit of consumption is different and larger.

M3. *Need transformation.*   These satisfiers are then transformed into individual need satisfactions, a process which predominantly takes place within (various sorts of) households. This, we argue, will reflect the distribu-tion of satisfiers within the household, in particular the degree of equality between men, women and children. Alongside consumption, final levels of need satisfaction will also be affected by the direct effect of production processes and the quality of the natural environment on human welfare.

M4. *Material reproduction.*   The above processes take place through time, which requires that the stock of capital goods, natural resources and human resources should be at least maintained in order to ensure further rounds of production and need satisfaction in the future. Though difficult issues of sustainability are raised here, a theory of human need must encompass material reproduction and must extend beyond short-term horizons.

However, I have already indicated that, to simplify the analysis, this fourth material precondition is unfortunately omitted here. Thus I am left with three procedural and three material criteria with which to evaluate different economic systems.

A THEORETICAL FRAMEWORK FOR MACRO-SOCIAL ANALYSIS

Different economic arrangements are to be evaluated according to these criteria. To do this requires a set of theories and associated knowledges with two major characteristics. First, they should be broadly applicable to a variety of socio-economic systems, yet be sensitive to the institutional variations between them. Second, they should bridge the central fault-line in social science between the disciplines of economics and socio-political science. The body of works which I shall use for this purpose can be grouped under the labels of 'comparative political economy' and 'the new institutionalism'. This has arisen at the confluence of economics and socio-political science as a critique of the dominant paradigms in each: rational choice theory in economics and functionalism/behaviourism in sociology (Cammack 1989). This body of work represents a return to the central concerns of classical political economy of Smith and his followers, and the critique of that political economy by Marx. Both were concerned with the relation between the economy and the state, and the effect of such relations on human welfare (Esping-Andersen 1990 ch.1; cf. Gough 1979 ch.1). Let me briefly consider both strands separately.

On the one side, institutional *economics* has emerged as a result of dissatis-faction with neo-classical economics and a desire to reformulate the discipline in at least three directions (Hodgson 1988; Etzioni 1988). First, technology and preferences are no longer conceived of as exogenous. The economic environment is recognized as affecting access to information and the way that information is processed. This undermines the view that individual agents are continuously maximizing or optimizing in any meaningful sense since their preferences are continually adapting in the light of their experience. Therefore second, the neo-classical assumption of equilibrium is replaced with the idea of agents learning and acting through real historical time. Economic life is characterized by structural, not just 'parametric' uncertainty, which imposes on actors a reliance on routines and habits. These durable patterns of behaviour define social institutions. The third characteristic of institutional economics is thus a recognition of the role of institutions in economic life and a rejection of essentialist arguments about 'the market'. Self-seeking action and institutional structures combine to generate a process through time usually characterized by long periods of continuity punctuated by rapid breaks or institutional shifts.This paradigm also directs our attention to the institutional contrasts between different economic systems.

Within *social and political science*, developments from a very different starting point have resulted in a rather similar set of propositions. In explaining state activity within capitalist societies, the dominant paradigm here was various forms of structuralism, whether the requirements of industrial society, and its economic, demographic and bureaucratic correlates, or the requirements of capitalist society for the performance of accumulation and legitimation functions. In both cases the economy was conceptualized as isolated from social and political institutions, and the latter were accorded no sources of autonomous development.

One attempt to overcome some of these problems can be traced to central European scholars such as Polanyi (1957 [1944]) and Schumpeter (1976), for whom the interdependence of the market economy with the state and the community was a *sine qua non*. Another source has been those scholars recognizing the impact of democracy on state development, stemming from the work of Mill and de Tocqueville. More recently, there has been the project of 'bringing the state back in' with its emphasis on the state as an autonomous or independent actor, with certain specific interests, which can act creatively to define problems and develop policy (Rueschemeyer and Evans 1985; Skocpol 1985). All these approaches attach little weight to the role of particular classes or social agents in explaining state activity (Esping-Andersen 1990 ch.1). A common idea is that of institutional persistence and its corollaries. Institutions are enduring, which means that at any time any particular institution, including state structures, can be 'sub-optimal' or, to use a more explicit and loaded term, 'dysfunctional' for the system as a whole (Cammack 1989).

Another strand in the reaction to structuralist perspectives in social and political theory has identified social classes as a key political agent. Developing from social democratic theorists of the Austrian school, this has emerged as the class mobilization thesis associated with various Scandinavian writers (Korpi 1983; Esping-Andersen 1985). Another source has been a 'contradictory' Marxist analysis which stresses the role of class conflict in shaping social and state development (Gough 1979). Alongside, and partly critical of these, has developed in recent years a broader, more diffuse institutionalism which recognizes the role of other institutions, including firms, other economic organizations and bodies representing class interests. This sociological institutionalism varies according to whether or not it countenances an explicit role for structural or environmental forces alongside institutional behaviour in explaining policy developments (see, for example, Katzenstein 1985; Hall 1986; and Weir et al. 1988; and for a general analysis, March and Olsen 1984).

One prominent characteristic of all these socio-political or 'historical-structural' schools of new institutionalism is a view of institutional change as discontinuous, contested and problematic. Another is the situation of societal and state-centred variables within a more systemic framework. For example, according to Hall (1986) the major components in explaining public policy change are the organization of capital, labour, the state and the political system, and the position of the nation within the international political economy. Within this field however institutions resist change and develop in a path-dependent manner.

Taken all together, these 'new institutionalist' theories mark a convergence between economic and socio-political analysis which provides a fertile framework for a macro-social analysis of economic institutions. In particular, they enable comparison to be made of different socio-economic systems, and ones at different stages of development. It is this framework of institutionalist thinking which I shall use to derive hypotheses concerning the impact of different economic systems on levels of need satisfaction.

A TAXONOMY OF ECONOMIC INSTITUTIONS

Economic debate and policy prescription today is dominated by the respective merits of markets and public planning, so much so that it is tempting to focus on free-market capitalism, centrally planned economies and various sorts of market-planning mix. However, this would be to neglect a third set of economic relationships presently being rediscovered in the economics literature, which can be gathered under the label 'community'. The list of writers thus distinguishing *three* fundamental forms of economic organization is long. It includes economic historians (Polanyi 1957 [1944] ch.4; Boswell 1990), political scientists (Streeck and Schmitter 1985) (though see below), sociologists (Bradach and Eccles 1989), organizational theorists (Powell 1990) and institutional economists (Thompson et al. (eds) 1991). Table 5.1 illustrates the key concepts identified in some of these taxonomies.

Table 5.1 Taxonomies of Economic Systems

AUTHOR	PRINCIPLE	MARKET	STATE	COMMUNITY
Polanyi	Forms of integration	Market exchange	Redistribution	Reciprocity
Streeck/ Schmitter	Principles of coordination and allocation	Dispersed competition	Hierarchical control	Reciprocity
Bradach/ Eccles	Economic control mechanisms	Price	Authority	Trust
Powell	Forms of economic coordination	Markets	Hierarchy	Networks

Drawing on Polanyi (1957 [1944]) and Putterman (1990 ch.1) we can put forward a substantive definition of the economy as the sphere of social activity in which people produce, distribute and consume the material requirements to meet their wants and needs. This generates recurring interactions among elements and agents in the system. According to all the major representatives of classical political economy, including Smith and Marx, a major feature of such interaction is a division of labour, both within 'enterprises' and between them. This division of labour raises productivity, but in turn requires some mechanism or mechanisms for coordinating the actions of the numerous interacting agents. It is to this fundamental question that the three solutions identified above have emerged over the course of human history.

First, markets. Here private agents voluntarily exchange entitlements to goods and services with each other. Where a large number of such commodity exchanges regularly take place we can identify the social institutions of a market. This form of coordination entails private rights in the use, consumption, disposition and fruits of economic resources and goods, and rights to transfer these rights, except the ownership of labour (Putterman 1990 pp.59–60). The prices or terms at which these exchanges take place is determined solely by the free negotiation of the parties concerned. Thus economic coordination is decentralized, *ex post* and unconscious.

The second form of coordination is by authoritative regulations issued in hierarchical organizations. Where these organizations are themselves coordinated by authoritative regulation backed by coercion, we may speak of a state system of coordination. Such a system normally entails state ownership of the means of production, apart from labour. Coordination here is thus centralized, *ex ante* and conscious.

The third ideal-type form of economic coordination is more difficult to specify. Nowhere in the modern world can such a model be found even approximately, though this is not to doubt the existence of such mechanisms in conjunction with markets and state authority mechanisms. Partly as a result of this, 'community' usually appears as a normative model of a desirable economic arrangement, and in different guises. Excluding those who explicitly identify community with pre-modern, hierarchically organized, status-bound societies,[1] we are still left with a great variety. First, there is the idea of communism in radical socialist thinking, such as that of Marx, Morris and Kropotkin (Miller 1989). This has been revived in the last three decades, in response partly to the belief that developments within capitalism are laying the foundations for communitarian economic relationships (in, for example, the work of Gorz (1982) and Van der Veen and van Parijs (1987)). Second, at the opposite pole, there is the libertarian view of community espoused by Nozick (1974). Here, membership of a community is voluntary and self-chosen. Third, there are new attempts to conceptualize a 'democratic communitarianism', drawing upon the currents of decentralized socialism, personalist Christian democracy, ideas of corporatism and civic humanism (Boswell 1990). This strand tends to equate community in the modern world with national citizenship (cf. Miller 1989). The last two conceptions have been explicitly concerned to augment those of market and state, not to replace them, and are considered at greater length when I move on to mixed economic systems. However underlying these differences are some common themes distinct from the other two modes. Economic coordination within communities is by democratic negotiation. Solidaristic sentiments of loyalty and reciprocity within social groups facilitate such consensus-building. The opposition between separatist individualism and state collectivism is overcome by a new focus on the quality of human relations. Coordination may thus be conceived as decentralized, *ex ante* and conscious.

In the next section I shall summarize my analysis of the potential contribution of these three forms of economic coordination to the satisfaction of human needs.

ECONOMIC INSTITUTIONS AND HUMAN WELL-BEING

To begin with I try to abstract from real-world complexities by considering these three economic systems as 'ideal types'. However this is not strictly possible. According to the 'impurity principle', any actual socio-economic system must contain, alongside its dominant principle, at least one other economic structure based on different principles, in order for the whole to function (Hodgson 1984 pp.85–9, 104–9). Thus, market economies must incorporate a system of authority and establish certain normative codes and social relationships. A 'pure' market society is a logical contradiction. Similarly, a centrally planned economy encounters contradictions which can only be resolved via decentralized markets and civil relationships. In these two cases, then, I consider models which incorporate the minimum degree of 'impurity' or contamination by other principles, drawing on empirical and historical evidence where appropriate. The third form of economic coordination, via community networks, poses different problems since it has not existed as an even modestly self-sustaining form in the modern age. Here I consider conceptions of community as an overarching principle of economic coordination, before again pointing out the dependence of such a principle on the other two modes of economic coordination.

The conclusions of this first stage of the evaluation, which is developed in detail elsewhere (Gough 1992), are summarized in Table 5.2.

Table 5.2 Evaluation of Three 'Pure' Economic Systems

CRITERIA	MARKET: UNREGULATED CAPITALISM	STATE: STATE SOCIALISM	COMMUNITY: COMMUNISM
P1. Rational identification of needs	Absent. Unregulated markets weaken 'social capsule'/collective ethic	Prioritization of, but dictatorship over, needs	Rational use of codified knowledge but incorporation of individuals
P2. Use of practical knowledge	Markets tap but distort dispersed knowledge	Absent and discouraged	Rational use of dispersed knowledge within, not between, communities
P3. Democratic resolution	Representative democracy weakened by market exit and inequality	Certain social rights but absence of civil and political rights	Widespread dialogic democracy. Absence of codified rights
M1. Production of need satisfiers	Efficiency in commodity production but market failures and absence of non-commodity forms	Prioritization of need satisfiers, but information and motivation failures	Prioritization of need satisfiers, but problems of coordination between communities
M2. Distribution according to need	No entitlements to need satisfiers	Entitlements distorted by abuse and labour market links	Entitlements to need satisfiers within, not between, communities
M3. Effective need transformation	Potential for autonomous learning harmed by inequality in work and unpaid household labour	Autonomous learning restricted at work, in consumption and via unpaid household labour	Greater free time plus autonomous domain, but gendered/household inequalities

A minimally regulated free-market capitalist society, I argue, suffers from many drawbacks as an institutional setting within which human needs can be optimally satisfied. On both procedural and material grounds it is found wanting. As Polanyi has argued, a strict market economy (even with the concessions to the existence of other institutions made here) is undesirable. The implication of much institutional economic analysis, as well as of political science and sociology, is that to realize their procedural and material potential market relations need complementing with regulation by public authorities and by networks of more solidaristic relations in civil society — what Etzioni calls the 'social capsule' (Etzioni 1988; cf. Wolfe 1991).

Similarly, the weight of analysis suggests that a relatively pure command economy is neither desirable nor feasible, according to our need-related yardstick. This is perhaps more surprising since both the intent and ideology of state socialism have proclaimed the meeting of human needs as an explicit and high-priority goal. Yet the conclusion is clear: a role for markets and networks in civil society is necessary to overcome the deficiencies of a pure central–planning model. And indeed this is what is (or rather was) found in actually existing socialist economies, albeit in distorted forms. All state socialist economies have exhibited, alongside the official economy, what Markus (1981) calls 'second' and 'third' economies: self-employed and private productive units together with 'moonlighting' and other unlawful enterprises, and networks of informal relations between and within the bureaucracy and state enterprises.

Lastly, I contend that 'communities', even democratic and need-prioritizing ones, cannot by themselves mobilize the resources necessary to optimize the need satisfaction of their members. All-embracing communities threaten the autonomy (and hence basic needs) of their members and confront intractable problems of coordination between communities, necessary to realize the benefits of a social division of labour. Voluntary communities on the other hand threaten to exclude vulnerable groups from any community, and thus deny them the procedural and material framework for satisfying their needs. The quite widespread belief that 'community', 'reciprocity', 'networking' or 'negotiation' can by themselves provide a third alternative to economic organization and a surer way to meet human needs is rejected.

We may summarize the deficiencies of the three 'pure' or paradigmatic institutions of economic coordination in another way, by returning to the ideas of need which they each embody. Free-market capitalism essentially equates needs with wants, an equation which is logically flawed and morally untenable (Doyal and Gough 1991 chs 2, 6). State socialism by contrast operates with an idea of universal and objective need, but equates this with the views of the party and state functionaries. Need is identified with one particular form of codified knowledge, which reflects constellations of power incompatible with the pursuit of truth. Communitarian models interpret need as those interests defined by particular cultural groups or communities. They thus relativize the idea of universal human need, and denude it of an evaluative or moral role. None of the three systems embody a notion of human need which is universal and objective, yet open-ended and cumulative.

This leads me on to a second stage of analysis: an investigation of how far this ideal can be realized within various forms of mixed or 'impure' economic systems. I focus here *solely* on mixed *capitalist* systems, that is where markets have a dominant role in economic coordination, and where private ownership of the means of production is the dominant form of property ownership. According to the tripartite model developed above this generates two fundamental forms of capitalist mixed economy.

The first is *statist* capitalism where market coordination is accompanied by a substantial degree of state steering of the economy. According to Putterman (1990 ch.2 p.5) capitalism can be modified by means of four types of state intervention. First, and least contradictory to the essence of capitalism, is to correct for marketing failures, such as monopoly, externalities and the inability to provide public goods. Second is to modify the distributive results of market mechanisms combined with private ownership, via an assortment of redistributive policies. Third, there are a set of reactive macro-economic interventions intended to correct for systemic market failures in the factor markets for capital and labour, of which Keynesianism is the best-known example. Fourth, there are proactive interventions to steer the economy in a desired direction such as indicative planning and specific or 'parametric' industrial policies. I shall define statist capitalism, as an ideal type, as a system where all four levels of state intervention are practised.

The second is *corporatist* capitalism where the market is accompanied by coordination via networks of negotiation between key economic actors. Democratic corporatism has two basic features: first, the centralized organization and representation of major interest groups in society, and their mutual bargaining; and second, their regular incorporation into the policy-making process via bargaining with the state and political parties (sometimes called 'concertion'). Katzenstein (1985 p.32) adds a third: an ideology of social partnership which integrates differing conceptions of group interest with vaguely but firmly held notions of the public interst. He further distinguishes *liberal* and *social* corporatism (Katzenstein 1985 ch.3) according to the absence or presence of strong, politically influential labour movements.

Lastly where both statism and corporatism are absent or weakly developed or deliberately undermined we may identify a third variant: *neo-liberal* capitalism.

Though we are here moving from 'as pure as possible' economic systems to 'impure' or mixed systems, we continue to abstract from the complexities of the real world. The objects of analysis are models of idealized mixed systems. A real-world economy, such as Germany's, will in practice exhibit features drawn from all these in a bewildering array. Again, all that can be offered here is a summary of my conclusions in Table 5.3.

Neo-liberal capitalism, I predict, would be no more conducive to human flourishing than minimally regulated capitalism. Indeed, its defining feature according to Gamble (1988) — a combination of 'free market and strong state' — promises a poorer performance. It is bereft of both the countervailing power

Table 5.3 Evaluation of Three Mixed Economic Systems

CRITERIA	STATIST CAPITALISM	CORPORATIST CAPITALISM	NEO-LIBERAL CAPITALISM
P1. Rational identification of needs	Identification of certain collective interests, but elite domination	Social capsule and collective ethic favour identification of needs	Absent. Both market and state weaken social capsule/ collective ethic
P2. Use of practical knowledge	Indeterminate potential to improve market effectiveness	Potential to combine market and network knowledge, but exclusion of unorganized	Market-based knowledge fostered; claimsmaking discouraged.
P3. Democratic resolution	Wider domain of public sphere, but bureaucratism and/ or clientelism	Nurtures dialogic democracy but exclusion of unorganized	Market and state used to restrict democratic public sphere
M1. Efficient production of need satisfiers	Potential to overcome market failures but bureaucratic failures	Potential to overcome market and bureaucratic failures	Efficiency in commodity production but market failures and absence of non-commodity forms
M2. Distribution according to need	Indeterminate potential to redistribute according to need	Social entitlements to basic need satisfiers likely	No social entitlements to need satisfiers
M3. Effective need transformation	Indeterminate potential to improve labour and gender inequality	Social corporatism; potential to improve labour/gender inequality	Market and gender related inequalities in labour and household

of public authority and networks of public cooperation. This form of capitalism has a poor chance of establishing the procedural and material framework for improving human need satisfaction identified earlier.

The potential impact of statist capitalism on human well-being is, I conclude, indeterminate. Whilst it has a potential to correct for the tunnel vision and market failures of minimally regulated capitalism, it also contains a potential for authoritarian, clientelist and bureaucratic features which distort both procedural and material effectiveness. At best, a proactive state is no more than a means for the achievement of a needs-oriented policy: it may be a necessary condition, but it cannot be sufficient. Statist capitalism may be more conducive to meeting human needs than unregulated capitalism, but the answer is indeterminate in the absence of further information on the direction and nature of state policy.

In principle, corporatist capitalism permits the dominant market mechanism to be regulated by both public action and social constraints collectively negotiated by key economic actors. Thus it has the potential to overcome market and state failures in the material realm, and to foster some form of dialogic democracy in the procedural realm. Against this must be set the danger that unorganized groups will remain excluded from the corporatist decision-making bodies, and thus that their needs will be overlooked or over-ridden. Though this danger is greater under liberal corporatism, it is still present under social corporatism, particularly for groups identified according to extra-economic criteria, such as women and racialized groups.

CONCLUSION

To arrive at some definitive ranking of these different sets of economic institutions is not possible in the absence of explicit trade-offs between our six preconditions. Whilst we argue that Rawls (1971) and the work of some of his followers such as Pogge (1989) provide some important signposts to help in answering this question, we do not pretend to advance a comprehensive solution (Doyal and Gough 1991 chs 7, 11). My own view is that the weight of argument emanating from institutional or political economy theory favours corporatist capitalism on both procedural and material grounds, and within this category favours social over liberal corporatism. Neo-liberal capitalism appears to offer a poorer framework for optimally satisfying universal human needs, whilst statist capitalism is indeterminate.

Let me conclude by noting the two ways in which this analysis could be advanced. One is normative and entails enquiring whether feasible alternative socio-economic arrangements could perform better than social corporatist capitalism in meeting human needs. It is important to repeat that only mixed *capitalist* systems are considered here. The rather more inviting claims of market socialism, for example, are not investigated. The second route is empirical. It entails constructing operational indicators of these idealized economic systems which can be applied to real world national economies. These can then be correlated with the historical record of substantive need satisfaction of different nation states. In this way the conclusions reached in this paper can hopefully be tested against real world evidence.

Acknowledgements: Many thanks to Diane Elson, Andrew Gamble, Geoff Hodgson, Mick Moran and Paul Wilding for helpful comments on an earlier draft, and for the comments of Peter Penz and other participants at the Ottawa seminar. The paper has originated out of, and is indebted to, years of discussion and collaborative work with Len Doyal.

NOTES

1   As do Streeck and Schmitter (1985). It is as a result of this identification that they posit a fourth 'associative' model of social order distinct from that of 'community'. However, I shall argue below, following Boswell (1990), that their associational order can be conceived of as a subset of a broadly communitarian mode of economic coordination.

For commentary on this chapter see page 274.

6. Exchange-Speak, Social Welfare Claims and Economic Policy Discourse

Derek Hum

Conventional wisdom today insists that modern economies cannot afford further expansion of the welfare state. Nations must instead 'restructure' to achieve the necessary flexibility to produce with maximum efficiency, to remain competitive against other nations, and to innovate and create new technologies. These are the modern imperatives.[1] Some obvious reasons behind this sentiment include: a lacklustre economy, government deficits, an accumulating debt load, and disappointment over the persistence of poverty after numerous programmes to help the poor.

What is the future of the welfare state? Is there a trade-off between social transfers and efficiency? This paper considers certain recent economic arguments from the perspective of literary criticism. I shall refer to economic literature which claims that further redistribution is socially costly solely to characterize its rhetorical style. I will neither survey its technical content nor pronounce on its acceptability to the economic profession as a whole. My focus is the policy process from the standpoint of semiotics. Casting this debate as a struggle over a 'text' and establishing 'rules of discourse' for the public at large, I shall argue that important questions such as the amount of redistribution society might wish to have has been usurped from the general citizenry by a technocratic elite. By rephrasing questions and controlling the discourse format, consultation involving the wider public over social questions is curtailed, and controversy narrowed to specific econometric topics. Those without the new 'code' are not allowed to talk at all, and their claims to a share of society's resources can be dismissed. I also suggest that access to information constitutes a significant barrier for those attempting the new policy discourse norms. Given enough time, one can always learn the basic modes of econometric expression so as to present counterclaims to government. However, it is difficult to surmount the many obstacles of time, money, knowledge and competence so as to engage in this discourse. Furthermore, even if one were to overcome all these barriers, there remains one of access to data not generally permitted to those outside government. Consequently, grammar without vocabulary becomes meaningless.

Portraying economic statements as a literary text allows us to see policy development differently. It raises questions aside from content, ones typically not asked when we focus on the 'truth' or 'validity' of economic research. Instead, we are led to ask: have we unconsciously channelled economic discussion so as to disenfranchise many having a serious concern for social welfare? Is there really anything to the 'new' understanding of the costs of redistribution, and the need to restructure the economy and the welfare state?

The next section reviews how economists construct reality through their models, and explains why it is so difficult for economic theory to assign a significant role to the welfare state. The redistributive function of the welfare state is singled out in the following section, with particular attention to the problems of poverty and the efficiency–equity trade-off. I confine my attention, if you like, to one particular 'conversation' among the many taking place in welfare economics. I then consider the nature of economic policy utterances and mention some implications for the policy reform process in the last two sections.

ECONOMIC INSTITUTIONS AND THE WELFARE STATE

The role of the state is problematical for mainstream economists who work within the neo-classical paradigm. Simply put, its role is minimal.[2] The market is the supreme institution, being called upon to satisfy individual wants, guide the allocation of scarce resources, and provide the correct signals and incentives to ensure maximum welfare for all. This modern creed stands in sharp contrast with the thinking of the classical economists. While the classical economists were concerned with the generation, extraction and accumulation of surplus output, neo-classical economists trace their pedigree to a more narrow theory of exchange in which sovereign consumer demand, together with given resource endowments, determine a set of prices capable of sustaining an efficient equilibrium allocation. The classical theory was essentially dynamic, and concerned with economic growth. It was production-oriented, and addressed foremost the notion of viability; that is, whether there exists a surplus above subsistence needs to replace the material basis of production.[3] The composition and distribution of surplus output was fundamental for the classical economists. Wages tended towards socially determined subsistence levels, and profits accrued to property-owning producers. Classical economics, therefore, entailed an analysis of surplus accumulation in an economy clearly marked by class structures and institutions. In the parlance of modern economic jargon, income distribution was a central theme, and a politically charged one.

In contrast, neo-classical theory is static and timeless, according primacy to a-historical individual consumer choices, and dealing principally with exchange relations among individual owners of resources. Production, so central to the classical economists, is relegated to the role of mere intermediation between resource owners and final consumers within the overall requirement of a price-signalling general equilibrium in which there is no unsatisfied demand for either inputs or outputs. The concept of exchange feasibility is paramount in neo-classical models. The classical concepts of viability and surplus output have no meaning or counterpart. Indeed, the notion of surplus is anathema to neo-classical models, since all factors yield services and all types of resources — whether labour or capital — are undifferentiated. Neo-classical theory, therefore, recognizes little need for class distinctions. Each and every category of income is construed as a payment to a factor of production corresponding to its scarcity value. Accordingly, there is no role for social class, nor is there a theory of income distribution apart from pricing resources and goods.[4]

The concern for establishing market equilibrium hides the essential agnosticism of neo-classical economics with respect to welfare propositions. This is evident in the basic theorems of welfare economics as well as the uncompromising standard by which a particular distribution is judged superior to another one. An economy in which there is no excess demand or supply is termed a Walrasian equilibrium. Simply put, all markets are cleared. The First Theorem of Welfare Economics states that a Walrasian equilibrium is Pareto efficient. The Second Theorem of Welfare Economics establishes that a Pareto-efficient allocation is a Walrasian equilibrium for a given initial endowment (and may be achieved by competition) (see Varian 1984). These two theorems together effectively establish a unique correspondence between the clearing of economic markets on the one hand, and a predefined notion of welfare maximum on the other. Little wonder that mainstream economics accord such reverence to unfettered market institutions, with the implied corollary that deviations from market rules must, *a fortiori*, lead to a less than ideal situation for society overall.[5] However, what is often missed is the restrictive nature of the Pareto criterion, and the total silence on the distribution of endowments.

The Pareto criterion is extremely strict. An allocation is Pareto optimal if no reallocation can make at least one person better off without making anyone else worse off. Phrased in this fashion, the approach might be characterized as mildly conservative. But viewed in conjunction with the underlying model of consumer tastes which regards any increment of goods and services as increasing individual welfare, making one individual better off with more commodities without diminishing the satisfaction levels of others is equivalent to dividing the increment of goods among all individuals in society and making all individuals in society better off. Thus is revealed the extreme ultra-conservative nature of the Pareto criterion. Faced with the Pareto guideline as the basic leitmotif for redistributive claims, it is not hard to see how steep and uphill the road to social reform might be, if progress must rely on persuasive dialogue alone.[6]

The Second Theorem of Welfare Economics is also adamant on reporting that its result is contingent upon a particular initial endowment. This bears witness to the observation that neo-classical economics is all (or only) about exchange. Consequently, those with nothing to exchange bring nothing to the institution of the economic market. They have no right to participate in the 'exchange-speak' of the market, an institution in which communication is rudimentary at best, given in bid-and-ask quotes, and in its refined format as practised by professional traders, capable of expression by a limited set of hand gestures and stances, without words, and simplified rules and contexts. Those without endowment are reduced to the sidelines of the market; their only recourse is to shout their 'claim' to goods and services above the din and cacophony of the impersonal market transactions.[7] The state role is therefore minimal, not much more than ensuring that certain fair trading rules are followed, and keeping those without endowments from causing too much of a disturbance to the serious traders.[8]

The debate today concerning the welfare state is as urgent as ever. Writers like Olson (1982) proclaim that western democracies suffer from institutional sclerosis, meaning that their capacity to restructure themselves is limited at best, including their will to rework the welfare state. Others, such as Murray (1984), express doubts about the welfare state to improve individual well being. However, the 'new' new welfare economics (Stiglitz 1985 p.992) emphasizes the information limitations of the government and how this leads to market distortions resulting in a necessary trade off between equity and efficiency. At the same time, Inman (1985 p.849) points out that 'what is "new" in the new political economy [of markets or government as the preferred institution for allocating societal resources...] is the sophistication of analytic techniques which we now bring to answer this important question.' It is precisely this very 'sophistication', along with the uneven access to information, which determines the nature of debate about the welfare state. This matter is considered next.

REDISTRIBUTION AND EFFICIENCY VS. EQUITY

The objectives of the welfare state are many, but most would agree that income redistribution is central. Some suggest that its fundamental role is to provide collective insurance for all citizens regardless of income status (Blomqvist 1985), or to protect its citizens by enshrining entitlements to reduce fear and uncertainty (Courchene 1980). I shall focus on income redistribution, casting, for convenience, my argument in terms of helping the poor.[9]

The research now being published as to whether or not we can afford more redistribution springs from an age-old problem: how should society help the poor? In today's economy, labour services are paid in wages, and even the most basic consumer items cost money. This being so, economists formulate the problem as one of how to transform inadequate incomes among the poor into adequate incomes. With this confined view of the problem, the favoured solution for the alchemical transformation of the inadequate into the adequate in the late sixties and seventies was the Guaranteed Annual Income (GAI). There were two main concerns associated with the GAI: (a) the GAI must not be too costly to taxpayers, and (b) the GAI must not create disincentives among the target population. Since the cost of a GAI would depend to some degree on the extent of work disincentive, several large-scale multi-million dollar and multi year experimental programmes were conducted to test what, if any, disincentive to work would be produced by cash transfers to the poor.

The GAI experiments produced two positive results: they established new econometric techniques of social experimentation inside economics, and these techniques produced more reliable data as opposed to the primitive guesswork of earlier times. However, one negative result of these experiments occurred on a level entirely different from the discussion about incomes and took place at the level of pragmatics. Pragmatics refer to the relationship between the writer or speaker and the reader or listener. The discourse gap separating most of the population from economists was now widened, and the alienated population expanded with the arrival of experimentation econometrics and the form that economic discourse now took. For while the term *Guaranteed Annual Income* would present no difficulties to any competent speaker of English, its reshaping through a semantic or conceptual slippage into *estimated labour supply elasticities* most assuredly did. And that reshaping is not half as bad as *marginal excess burden of redistribution*, the process now taking place in the debate about the trade-off between equality and efficiency. (This is discussed in the next section.)

The central concern about how much, and how best, to transfer income to the poor gets buried in the mystifying discourse of the high priests of economics and public policy. These speakers enter into an exotic dialogue among themselves, but exclude others by silencing the general citizen. To be sure, individual citizens have long suffered from lack of information and voice, but now they can be labelled as 'naïve' and 'uninformed' and their pronouncements called 'mere opinion' because they do not know the econometric discourse codes. In essence, public policy reduces its boundaries yet further to include fewer participants than before while excluding still larger numbers from economic discourse. This sets a technocratic elite off from the body of the polity.

There are essentially two views with respect to the question of redistribution at the present time: (a) one is that we must continue to redistribute income to resolve the problem of poverty; (b) the other is that redistribution of income has not resolved the poverty problem, despite much effort, and therefore we must concentrate on reorganizing the economy and increasing production so as to generate more work and wealth to spread around. The conflict between these two opposing views is referred to as the 'trade-off' between equality and efficiency; it is taking place in journals and books on a textual level, where embattled opposing concepts typically meet. But while these two positions fight it out on the textual level in articles and books, as similar oppositions have done in the past, they do have one characteristic in common: behind their different concepts at the level of their specialized words, these clashing ideologies both share a common discourse form, that of the plain prose discourse which we inherited from the seventeenth century.

The new arguments turn on the costs of reducing inequality, and therefore, appear grounded on a trade-off between efficiency and equity.[10] There has always been concern that transfers to the socially disadvantaged might have undesirable effects on the economy. The so-called *less eligibility* principle is a prime example. Fear that generous cash transfers to the able-bodied poor would destroy their desire to work led to the practice of limiting grant amounts below that which a worker might earn at the lowest going wage. Concern with the work disincentives of transfers remains one of the most compelling worries today. It is a major stumbling block for attempts to bring about any guaranteed income plan, however designed. In short, incentives held to be incompatible with those necessary to the full productivity of the market economy have always been at the heart of the issue. The new element in today's reformulation is its breadth and scope.

Critics of anti-poverty programmes have traditionally held that adverse effects on work effort, personal savings, family structure, and the like call into question the desirability of 'generous' transfers. In the early debates, the focus was on the work disincentive effects of these transfers on the beneficiaries. The arguments largely ignored the taxpayers who would ultimately bear higher burdens, as well as the configuration of the entire economy which would, after a time, adjust to the new regime. Early worries were cast entirely in terms of the dollars given to recipients; that is, the financial cost of the programmes. By focusing on the recipients' responses, the mode of analysis was what economists term *partial equilibrium*.

The early misgivings about work incentives have subsided to a degree as a result of several income maintenance experiments. These massive experiments are apt testimony to the rigour with which the issue of work disincentives was pursued. Research attention has now shifted focus. Recent theoretical and empirical work examine the *marginal excess burden* of transfers. By taking account of the possible distortionary effect of the higher taxes that are necessary to finance further transfers, and by calculating both the revenue and output losses attendant upon the higher taxes, some researchers suggest that the extra costs of reducing inequality are, in fact, very high. The clear implication is that further pursuit of income equality will result in too great a loss in efficiency and output.[11]

The trade-off between a larger pie, and its more equal division among society's members, is given further credence by economic models that demonstrate that any attempt to guarantee absolute equality using only progressive taxes and transfers must, in theory, contain disincentive effects so strong as to cause output to fall to zero (Baumol 1986). For non-Marxists working within the mainstream, the suggestion is that the scales have now been definitely tipped in favour of more efficiency. This gives rise to the stance that we can no longer afford to pursue more equality; furthermore, we were previously unaware of the staggering costs of doing so. The rightward advance of ideological generals is supported, it seems, by an empirical and linguistic infantry.

The economic research on the 'trade-off' has its pedigree in the public finance literature on the *excess burden of taxation*. The modern twist is that the revenues raised from taxation are no longer assumed to be for unambiguously necessary (national defence?) or widely supported public goods (libraries and parks?) but rather for income transfers to the poor. The focus is therefore less on the benefits to the poor than the costs and distortions for other members of society. This loss is termed the *marginal efficiency cost of redistribution* (MECR) and has now become the standard by which we are asked to judge programmes designed to combat poverty and reduce inequality. The early work in this genre initially employed *partial equilibrium* models and often produced widely varying, but sometimes high, estimates (Browning and Johnson 1984; Stuart 1984). For example, the marginal excess burden associated with redistributive programmes could be three times as high as that associated with non-redistributive uses of tax revenues (Stuart 1984). Understandably, the sheer size of estimates such as these drew attention. The most recent work on the 'trade-off' used very sophisticated *computable general equilibrium* (CGE) models (Ballard 1988). Although later work has emphasized the sensitivity of results to the assumptions made, and the particular model adopted, the message has already been transmitted that the social cost of redistribution involves more than the dollars handed over to the poor. A new way of 'seeing the problem' or 'constructing reality' has taken over.

SOCIAL REALITY, TEXT AND ECONOMIC DISCOURSE

Writers and artists make us view the world in a certain way by constructing rules of seeing. For example, the introduction of perspective in painting allowed Euclidean geometry to impose its rules on nature. The use of numbers along with a grid pattern for detailing metre in the Shakespearean sonnet was no accident (Hughes 1986 p.77). Mathematics, another discourse, allowed Newton to dictate how one sees the universe. It is widely accepted that 'the questions scientists choose to ask and pursue are no less products of a cultural context than those with which artists choose to deal...' (Greenberg 1989). Economists are no exception.

Economics has long prided itself as queen of the social sciences. As such, it regards its methods as close to those of the natural and physical sciences; so much so that the various multi-million dollar income maintenance experiments are viewed as endeavours on the level of anything that the natural sciences might do. In essence, economic methodology attempts to imitate those of the sciences, and for that same reason, the awareness by economists 'of their philosophical habits is restricted ... to debates in the philosophy of sciences, or ... to questions of appropriate method.'(Amariglio 1988 p.583). When, in the past, economists strayed from methodological issues borrowed from philosophy of science, their second choice was ethics. Indeed, the economists' distinction between what they term 'positive' and 'normative' propositions reflect just this division. Recently, however, McCloskey (1986) and others have pointed out the need for economists to learn about the nature of their discursive practices. Inspired by modern literary theory, the stress is on the textual nature of our knowledge. Drawing from semiotics, linguistics and semantic analyses, these critics are concerned with neither the 'falsifiability' of economic statements, nor the 'value' position hidden in an economic recommendation, but rather in the diverse literary and rhetorical devices that economists employ in constructing their arguments. They attempt to highlight the 'text' and its role in determining economic and social scientific meaning. By extension, this can be interpreted to include policy development as well. In focusing so clearly on this 'new conversation' in the philosophy of economics, we are forced to confront, in addition to Kuhn, Popper and Lakatos (on method), or Rawls, Nozick and Varian (on ethics), such thinkers as Foucault, whose writings on the nature of discourse, knowledge and power, are more the domain of literature and the arts.

All writers, then, adopt certain types of discourse to create their text, whether it be a poem, prose paragraph, pithy slogan or large-scale mathematical model. The econometric model consisting of hundreds of equations is, according to this view, simply a special text. Writers (including economists) produce their work either in accordance with, or in revolt against, the culturally constructed conventions of their discourse (Hughes 1986). However, it is critical acts which create the categories of classification and thereby constitute 'economic literature'. A second phase in the constitution of this economic literature involves distinguishing economic works as 'rigorous', 'general equilibrium', 'empirically grounded', or 'state of the art', as it likes to think, from those which are 'soft', 'partial equilibrium', or 'purely qualitative and subjective'.

This suggests that we might profit by examining economic writing from the viewpoint of literary criticism. Since economic writing on the 'trade-off' topic is a mixture of prose description, diagrams, tables and mathematical equations, the typical concerns of literary construction (such as rhyme, metre and the like) are not directly relevant. Nonetheless, more general characterizations of the economic discourse can be illuminating. Without attempting to be exhaustive, I shall simply comment on a few aspects.

Virtually all of the writings published in the professional economic journals use the so-called 'plain prose style', albeit liberally sprinkled with specialized terms commonly understood by the profession (e.g., marginal excess burden of redistribution). Immediately, there is a form of tension. People hate economic jargon. Why can't economists use simple English? These readers, however, erroneously assume plain prose discourse to be natural. In fact, 'the plain prose style is not some natural, transparent, ideological neutral conveyer of the truth, [rather it] is currently the most ideological form of any conceivable discourse, for it claims neutrality and naturalness when in fact it is as cultural a construction as any other form of discourse.' (Hughes 1986 p.5). Ironically, it is the presence of the economic jargon itself that dislocates the plain prose style and alerts the reader to the constructed nature of the text.

Economic writing, then, appears to find appealing coexistence in a single text with two conflicting messages. The plain prose style is meant to convey 'truth', and the deliberate jargon is intended to signal its constructed nature and to urge caution. One message is hidden; the other is open and obvious. Why does this go on?

More telling, perhaps, is the underdetermined discourse style of economic writing. Overdetermined discourse refers to the discourse of literature, of fiction. Underdetermined discourse, in contrast, is the plain prose style legitimized by the Royal Society of London in 1662 as the language of science. Hughes (1986 p.11) describes it as follows:

> This plain prose style emphasizes the linear (syntagmatic) syntax (syntax = the order of signs in sequence) : the conceptually horizontal subject–verb–object sentence. It sought to ban metaphor, and aspired to the condition of logic, searching for mathematical precision.... Underdetermined discourse seeks to ... make the signified concepts stand for, or represent things. In this way, the textual world created by underdetermined discourse appears to become the exact naive realist equivalent of the empirical world about

which it purports to speak. In short, underdetermined discourse claims to be the language of Truth. Moreover, it does so in a context which would deny truth to other forms of discourse.

Several observations would appear to follow from the above. Economists, it seems, adopt the underdetermined discourse as a strategy to convey 'truth'. At the same time, they must believe, or hope, that their particular jargon will quietly slip into the mainstream of everyday language, thereby blunting the hint of their constructed narratives. Are not terms such as 'inflation', 'unemployment', 'budgetary deficit', 'transfer payments' or even acronyms like 'GNP' part of our everyday speech, in the media, or items of cocktail party small talk?

As technical words become commonplace, economic discourse strives to invent new terms (e.g., MECR) or new signified concepts (e.g., computable general equilibrium econometric models). Further, the development proceeds so far removed from the general public that the economic profession (including policy advisors) often slides into the view that the system of equations which supposedly models the economy is taken as the economy itself. This act of reification is dangerous since economists now control not only the style of discourse but also what is permitted by way of questions. If the model does not contain an equation for, say, the effect of inflation on poverty, that problem simply does not exist.

As a final observation, consider the role of the economic policy analyst as author and narrator. We cannot suppose in all cases that the author of a text is identical to the narrator. Indeed, they might totally disagree. Typically, however, the authors of economic texts adopt what is called a monological stance. In this mode, the author is behind the narrator and maintains a controlling voice or vision. The author's set of values are affirmed and there is closure, meaning that the discussion is 'closed off' to make the reader feel the object is coherent and complete. There has been 'progress' in terms of movement through a beginning, a middle, and an end.

IMPLICATIONS FOR SOCIAL POLICY REFORM

Whether or not we can afford more redistribution springs from the perennial concern to help the poor. Economists often think it is a matter of more cash transfers but such transfers must not create disincentive to work. Accordingly, a proposal to alleviate poverty through a guaranteed income is restated as a critical empirical need to estimate *income* and *wage elasticity* parameters. As noted, the econometric imperative was sufficiently potent to bring about several large-scale experimental tests in the United States (Basilevsky and Hum 1984) and Canada (Hum and Simpson 1991).

The income experiments not only propelled econometric technique into the methodological world of the hard sciences; they also achieved another purpose. Understanding of the critical elasticities previously permitted was now devalued and replaced by a new meaning in which the experiments' context is central. We don't merely guess at the probable degree of work disincentive anymore; we know from deliberate trials how large the effects are.

Over time, public consciousness of the root question being addressed re-emerged, partly due to popular translation of the economic research, and partly due to public recognition that the question whether or not income transfers engender work disincentives still needs answering.[12] But there now appeared a new restatement in terms of the trade-off between productivity and equality, a more elegant but, of course, less pointed formulation from the viewpoint of the social reform advocate. Just as the matter of a guaranteed income to help the poor was recast as an empirical question about 'estimating labour supply elasticities' through social experiments, the policy touchstone now becomes the 'marginal excess burden of redistribution' as calculated by computable general equilibrium models. The central question about how to help the poor is again buried in language. Given what is needed to establish the appropriate credentials to speak (access to data and publication outlets, competence to investigate economic models, facility with computers, and so on), the vast majority of the concerned citizenry is effectively silenced. In sum, the policy development process is anything but open; the 'right of expression' has been effectively removed from all but a few. The form of discourse favoured by economic writing is one in increasing ascendance among the policy development community. Even if there are those who are willing to learn what Hahn (1973 p.106) calls the 'grammar of arguments about policy', they are still stopped at many turns because they lack meaningful access to the very 'word-data' so crucial to the policy discourse.

This last point is especially significant, for it goes beyond the message that economic models — even when cast in mathematical equations and econometric camouflage — are simply a style of speaking, practised in such manner as to pare down the number of participants. Acceptance of this implies merely that we acknowledge the rhetorical practices of economists. But when government controls access to the very data-vocabulary, criticism of state policies cannot appear credible or coherent.[13] While inherent capacity to criticize is undiminished, the ability to mount an intellectually acceptable counterclaim is absent. No one asks authors to write without certain vowels, nor musicians to compose without using particular notes; yet social policy is often made to take place with one side holding all the 'facts'.

Acknowledgements: I am indebted to Dave Arnason, Glenn Drover, Evelyn Forget, Ken Hughes, and Anthony Waterman for encouragement, discussion and comment.

NOTES

1   Clear statement of this position for Canada can be found in the Macdonald Commission Report (Canada 1985). In the US, Robert Reich (1991 p.52) writes: 'A message for Republicans and Democrats alike: Stop fighting over how much money government is taking from the wealthy and redistributing to everyone else. Start worrying about the capacity of Americans to add value to the emerging global economy.'
2   The political philosopher Nozick (1974 p.ix) also endorses '... a minimal state, limited to the narrow functions of protection against force, theft, fraud, enforcement of contract, and so on.'
3   Society's attack on scarcity might also be a fight against evil. Nelson (1991 p.11) discusses the theological meaning of economic thinking and argues that rational self-interest combined with a belief in the efficacy of economic progress are essential ingredients in the moral struggle against the evil of scarcity. This modern economic theology promising a possible 'heaven on earth' is fundamental to the late-twentieth-century welfare state, and represents a 'continuation in secular form of the Judeo-Christian heritage'.
4   Hollander (1987 pp.4–7, 93–7) sees little change in paradigm or Kuhnian revolution between the classics and neoclassics, arguing that there is a fundamental general equilibrium core in Ricardo (p.7), that the cost price analysis of Ricardo and Smith is pre-eminently an analysis of the allocation of scarce resources in terms of a general equilibrium (p.93), and that, for Ricardo, there is no solution to distribution prior to pricing (p.97).
5   Economic theorists are well aware of the restrictions on the welfare theorems. Atkinson and Stiglitz (1980) list the following reasons for state intervention: distribution objectives, market failure, absence of future and insurance markets, failure to attain full equilibrium, externalities, public goods and merit goods.
6   A change which makes everyone better off simultaneously would require unanimity if everyone votes approval for a given social state (say, a particular distribution of income) purely on the basis of individual self-interest. However, an elegant paper by Sen (1970) demonstrates formally that the Pareto principle is logically incompatible with the principle of individual liberty.
7   Much like the market-institution whereby sports cards are traded, those without any cards to offer receive no cards in return. They can only watch on the sidelines as various deals are made.
8   Economic theory makes reference to the concept of a 'fair' allocation, defined as one which is both equitable and efficient. However, an equitable allocation is one in which there is absence of 'envy' in the sense that no one prefers another's bundle to their own. With the bundles defined ever more widely to include consumption-effort combinations, the problem reduces once again to that of achieving a market equilibrium among voluntary traders. See Varian (1975).
9   For a recent discussion of the efficiency case for the welfare state which derives from imperfect information see Barr (1992). Barr argues that the welfare state is not a subject apart from mainstream economics (p.742) since much of its justification derives from solving a series of principal-agent problems; however, the objective of inequality reduction is almost entirely an equity issue (p.746).
10   Economists often organize their discussion of social institutions along three dimensions — efficiency, equity and liberty. I am concerned here with efficiency and equity.
11   This argument must not be confused with the position that a large government deficit and/or debt precludes further social spending.
12   Greenberg and Mandell (1991) examine two series of experiments — the income maintenance experiments and the work/welfare demonstrations — from the viewpoint of the knowledge utilization literature. They suggest that social experiments are rarely motivated by an essentially rational paradigm, and that the greater the internal consistency among the ideology, interests, and information from non-experimental sources, the less experimental research results will be utilized.
13   Even when access to public data is permitted, the form in which it is available to the general public is daunting. Sometimes the data must be purchased through secondary distributors in the private sector, or it is formatted in such manner as to require the modern-day equivalent of a magic decoder ring to read. Rep. Charles Rose (D-NC) has introduced a Bill (HR 2772) to have the Government Printing Office (GPO) establish a one-stop-shopping window for federal data bases, available at cost, to all citizens.

For commentary on this chapter see page 277.

7. Citizenship — A Feminist Analysis

Gillian Pascall

> Citizenship is a status bestowed on those who are full members of a community. All who possess the status are equal with respect to the rights and duties with which the status is endowed. There is no universal principle that determines what those rights and duties shall be, but societies in which citizenship is a developing institution create an image of an ideal citizenship against which achievement can be measured and towards which aspiration can be directed. The urge forward along the path thus plotted is an urge towards a fuller measure of equality, an enrichment of the stuff of which the status is made and an increase in the number of those on whom the status is bestowed. (Marshall 1963 [1949] p.87)

Marshall's classic analysis of citizenship in the 1940s is a starting point for a new wave of publications forty years on (e.g. Andrews (ed.) 1991, Barbalet 1988, Turner (ed.) 1991). This chapter too begins with Marshall, arising first from my unease that his discussion of the relationship between citizenship and social class was not matched by questioning about citizenship and dependency in the family (Pascall 1986). My concern here is with analysing ways in which women's citizenship in practice is restricted by family dependency, and ways in which these restrictions are reflected in today's citizenship debates.

Some feminists have responded to the citizenship debate by asking for more rights for women (Coote 1992). Others have been more sceptical of the nature of the rights and duties involved, the relationship between them and the citizenship to which they are supposed to add up. Pateman, for example, argues that 'women' have been opposed to the 'worker' and the 'citizen' and that women are confronted with the choice between two paths to citizenship, both doomed to failure:

> The patriarchal understanding of citizenship ... allows two alternatives only: either women become (like) men, and so full citizens; or they continue at women's work, which is of no value for citizenship. Moreover, within a patriarchal welfare state neither demand can be met. To demand that citizenship, as it now exists, should be fully extended to women accepts the patriarchal meaning of 'citizen', which is constructed from men's attributes, capacities and activities. Women cannot be full citizens in the present meaning of the term; at best, citizenship can be extended to women only as lesser men. (Pateman 1989 p.197)

Marshall's fundamental and important question (1963) — which he did not resolve — was whether citizenship was compatible with a class society. Citizenship was both the 'architect of legitimate social inequality' (Marshall 1963 p.73), and a possible engine for 'converting a skyscraper into a bungalow' (Marshall 1963 p.101). Marshall did address some aspects of women's citizenship — for example in his account of the Factory Acts and the way protection undermined citizenship (Marshall 1963 p.84) and his account of women's enfranchisement (Marshall 1963 p.81). But he did not ask whether the contemporary form of family relationships precluded citizenship for women.

Feminists today have made this question harder to ignore. Plant's recent essay ends with an acknowledgement of some of the problems:

> In the case of feminist critics of citizenship, the differences are in terms of the differential positions of men and women in society. This is vitally important in the citizenship debate, because citizenship is about a public identity and a public status that derives from that. However, feminist critics point out that this can be very deceptive in circumstances in which so much of woman's life is privatized in the home. (Plant 1991b pp.255–6)

Feminist debates have made the question of the relationship between the family and citizenship as fundamental and problematic as that between class and citizenship. Unpaid work roles in the family limit women's citizenship through paid work and political activity. Women's dependency within the family reflects unpaid work roles, lower pay and less secure employment than male partners: it also leads to great insecurity on marriage breakdown. Dependency has also been built into welfare policies which often conceive women firstly as family members, thus containing women's special status within the fabric of citizenship. From this flow practical as well as ideological consequences: insecurity within social security and secondary status within citizenship.

So it is at the interface between public and private life that I will focus my argument. Is citizenship irrevocably tied to the separation of public and private worlds that currently exists in western democracies? Do family roles and relationships exclude women from citizenship? Can we conceptualize citizenship in a way that includes women? In locating my argument here I start from the assumption that the division between public and private is problematic, as is women's customary location within the family.

The argument and illustrative material are drawn around notions of universality, rights and duties. The first two were building blocks of Marshall's argument, and all three have played prominent parts in the modern wave of citizenship analysis.

UNIVERSALITY AND DIVERSITY

Notions of citizenship in the modern world have usually been — in principle at least — notions of equality and universality. Marshall wrote of the 'universal status of citizenship' (Marshall 1963 p.121); Hall and Held refer to 'the logic of citizenship, which has tended to absorb "differences" into one common universal status — the citizen.' (1989 p.176).

Drawing on the same tradition, but more conscious of questions of difference and exclusion, Bill Jordan writes that 'There is a tradition which has identified membership of society — citizenship — as the basis of the common good, and hence as indispensable to any form of social morality or good society. The challenge is ... to see whether this active and egalitarian concept of community can be extended to include all the adult members of a large-scale society.' (1989 p.67).

A problem with 'universal' principles is that they may provide a cloak for entrenched differences, making the interests of the powerful appear the interests of everyone. So Anne Phillips argues that the 'ideals of democracy call on us to take seriously the many ways in which sexual difference has thwarted the promises of democratic equality, instead of sweeping this under the carpet with a rhetoric of free and equal citizenship' (Phillips 1991 p.8).

This kind of critique leads Iris Young to an alternative conception of citizenship (1989, 1990a) in terms of group difference: 'a politics that asserts the positivity of group difference is liberating and empowering' (1990a p.166). She concludes,

> the ideal of the just society as eliminating group differences is both unrealistic and undesirable. Instead justice in a group-differentiated society demands social equality of groups, and mutual recognition and affirmation of group differences. Attending to group-specific needs and providing for group representation both promotes that social equality and provides the recognition that undermines cultural imperialism. (Young 1990a p.191)

The problem with a politics of difference is that it provides us with no yardstick to measure past and present injustice or to decide whose claims are acceptable in future. The underlying logic of a critique of injustice against women is that people share some common human need and capacity.

Doyal and Gough have provided us with a powerful analysis of common human need, which provides a moral framework for judging what social arrangements ought to provide and a yardstick for measuring the extent of their satisfaction in practice. The equality embedded in the moral framework contrasts with the inequalities described when the yardstick is employed: in all societies women's basic needs are met to a lesser extent than men's (Doyal and Gough 1991 pp.265–9). The equal recognition of needs — for shelter and food, personal space and time, for social acceptance — and the construction of rights and obligations within such a framework of needs — would be an advance for women. Any analysis of rights and duties in practice will have to show (as the next section does in relation to Britain) that women's 'citizenship' is constructed differently from men's.

Starting from a commonality of needs leads us into a danger that the extent of difference in the provisions required to meet women's needs is underestimated in practice. It is a challenge to citizenship theorists to develop a concept of citizenship which retains its common purpose but is attentive to group difference. History suggests that — in Britain at least — citizenship has had a masculine form; an examination of rights and duties in Britain will show that neither legislation nor literature have taken adequate account of gender difference.

RIGHTS

The limitations of an equal rights perspective in a society of difference have been well aired. Elizabeth Kingdom, in *What's Wrong With Rights?* summarizes the arguments:

> Both in the United States and in the United Kingdom, feminists have been concerned at the inability of the concept of equal rights to address the realities of women's unequal treatment. In general, their concern has not been to attack the achievements of equal rights campaigners. Rather, what is involved is a well-documented awareness that the ideology of equal rights has severe limitations for feminist politics, limitations stemming from its failure to recognize the implications of significant differences and divisions between females and males. (Kingdom 1991 p.114)

The following sections look at some ways in which women's citizenship rights have been limited by relationships, roles and obligations within families.

Civil Rights

It is usually assumed that civil rights are more firmly entrenched than social rights. There have been substantial gains in women's legal rights to person and property, but crucial areas of feminist writing concern the denial of such rights in practice: domestic violence and marital rape, relationships of dependency within marriage, and the 'compulsory altruism' of 'community care' may all be seen as aspects of the denial of women's civil rights.

One of the key achievements of the women's movement has been to uncover the extent of violence within marriage and marriage-like relationships and the lack of public resources that go into their policing. As Plant points out (1988 p.11), civil rights need public resources in their defence just as do social ones.

Within this framework, then, women's civil rights are invaded by the men they live with, and by decisions about policing that define this as beyond the public realm.[1]

Marital rape is only now in 1992 acknowledged within the British legal system. Change in the law, however much to be welcomed, will protect only a few. The extent of violence in intimate relationships, and the relative lack of police protection, suggest that many women will find themselves unable to seek redress.

To what extent do relationships of dependency within marriage and cohabitation allow women the freedom not to do unpaid work? In the context of workfare this is seen as a question of civil rights. Do pressures to do unpaid work not offer a similar offence? Writing about the cohabitation rule within the British social security system (a rule which denied certain benefits to women if they were considered to be cohabiting with a man) Elizabeth Wilson described marriage as a kind of workfare:

> In fact, the cohabitation ruling only embodies in slightly more glaring form the innermost assumption of marriage which is still that a man should pay for the sexual and housekeeping services of his wife. We are so accustomed to this that it seems natural within marriage; the cohabitation rule and its enforcement simply draw back the veil from the general reality of sexual relations within our society, which are, and must remain, distorted and contaminated so long as marriage — like prostitution — remains an *economic* option for women, a job. (Wilson 1977 p.81)

Since this was written, women's increased access to employment has slackened the economic bonds of marriage and cohabitation for many women, loosening the knot between economic security and wifely duty. But women's relatively lower incomes and security from paid work still make women dependent on the men with whom they live; and British social surveys indicate that wifely duties have a reducing hold on peoples' ideals, but are alive and well in practice.

Economic dependence is increased by the physical and emotional dependence of others — of children and elderly relatives. While housewifery as a primary economic role has gone into decline for younger women with access to jobs, policies for 'community care' put pressure on a mainly older and mainly female population to do unpaid caring work.

The question of the freedom to choose such caring relationships has been raised by Land and Rose (1985) writing of 'compulsory altruism'. People who undertake care speak of a sense of obligation, among other motives, such as a strong affection (Finch 1989 p.30). There may also be a lack of alternatives: nowhere decent to go for the person you care for; minimal alternative services at home; no-one else prepared to step in. In the light of their labour market position women may feel most vulnerable to these pressures.

Another aspect of civil rights is raised by the extreme needs of some dependent relatives and the isolation and consequent loss of autonomy of those who care for them. Civil liberty may be at stake in the more severe situations, and again there is an issue of state neglect in providing appropriate alternatives. Janet Finch's review of this literature about caring may be enough to raise this issue:

> A consistent feature of unpaid caring, demonstrated by all the available detailed studies, is that once a particular relative has taken on the responsibility for the care of an elderly or handicapped person they get rather limited support, if any, from other relatives or friends. So the care of a highly dependent person by 'the family' in most cases means care by one relative, usually a female relative ... This can demand a very high level of commitment, in which caring for a relative completely dominates the carer's own life. In their study of 41 women who had cared for their own mother before she died, Lewis and Meredith comment that to an outside observer 'the majority of respondents led remarkably restricted lives' (Lewis and Meredith, 1988: 87). ... One woman compared it to her experience of being in service in the past: 'It's like being in service. I got one evening off ... and one afternoon a month.' (Finch 1989 p.27)

All these examples call into question the extent of women's civil rights and citizenship within the family. Power and privacy in marriage relationships, economic dependency and its link with unpaid work roles, and the 'compulsory altruism' of community care are aspects of family relationships which limit women's civil rights.

Political Rights

> The case of women is the most prevalent and obvious problem of political participation and representation in the policy-making structures of liberal democracies. ... Statistically speaking, women are the most under-represented social group in the elected assemblies of western democracies. (Brodie 1985 p.1)

So begins a Canadian study of the way political recruitment processes affect women. Women's participation as voters and other aspects of citizen politics has not been followed by their participation as representatives in local, provincial or national assemblies. In 1983, 6 per cent of provincial legislators were women, 5 per cent of provincial cabinets, and in 1984, 10 per cent of federal officers and 5 women in the federal Cabinet (Brodie 1985 pp.2–3). In the same era, with Margaret Thatcher as Prime Minister, Britain had 3 per cent women among members of the House of Commons.

Brodie's study of female municipal and legislative candidates concludes that the social valuation of women's achievements, the division of labour within the home and discrimination at party level, with women being given unwinnable seats, were the main reasons (Brodie 1985 pp.122–3).

Anne Phillips, reviewing international evidence, describes the transformation of Scandinavian politics:

> Up till the 1960s there was not much to choose between any of the countries in Western or Northern Europe: a somewhat more damning obstructionism in first-past-the-post systems; a more conservative tendency where the church held its sway; generally just the deafening dominance of men. By 1984, however, women had taken 15 per cent of the parliamentary seats in Iceland, 26 per cent in Norway and Denmark, 28 per cent in Sweden and 31 per cent in Finland. In 1985, Norway took the world record. Women made up 34.4 per cent of the Storting (the national assembly), held eight out of eighteen cabinet posts, contributed 40.5 per cent of the membership of county councils and contributed 31.1 per cent of the membership of municipal councils. (Phillips 1991 p.83)

Phillips argues that proportional representation, the strength of the women's organizations within the parties and the shift in the public/private divide in Scandinavia have all been significant factors. (Phillips 1991 pp.88–9)

Formal rights of representation are only part of the problem. Ideals of participatory democracy have been an important part of some citizenship debates. Oldfield draws on the tradition of civic-republicanism 'to remind people that citizenship has as much to do with the practice of civic virtue in a political community, as it does with the rights of man' (Oldfield 1990 p.ix). He moves straight from the distinction between 'the public life of the citizen, in which individuals live fuller and more satisfying lives, and the private life of the individual, which is restricted to the immediate concerns of family and friends' to a claim that 'the practice (of citizenship) is not gender-specific' (Oldfield 1990 p.159). Nelson argues otherwise, moving from evidence about the limited participation of poor women who 'participated in almost every type of electoral activity except voting less frequently than did poor men' (Nelson 1984 p.216) to a conclusion about 'the inherent tension in liberalism between women's commitment to (and responsibility for) families and their full exercise of citizenship' (Nelson 1984 p.227).

That emancipation of women has not led, in several decades, to the full representation and participation of women, is one of many reasons for wariness about a rights-based politics; though Scandinavian achievement of a greater measure of political rights for women is not an irrelevance.

Social Rights

There is no shortage of evidence about women's unequal position in relation to rights derived from the market and rights derived from social welfare policies (Lister 1990a, b). This section will focus on a topic which has special significance for the public/private boundary — social security rights connected with paid and unpaid work.

The attachment of social rights to paid employment is a significant basis for the recognition of citizens in practice. Beveridge ensured that paid employment was a key basis for citizenship in Britain with his scheme for social insurance: it was elaborated from the notion that the needs to be met were those arising from breaks in men's employment, and that the mechanism should be compulsory contributions while in employment. His clarity about women's work and position in marriage did not lead him to recommend benefits accruing directly in relation to unpaid work: but rather to a very uncitizen-like dependence on their husbands.

The Beveridge solution to the 'problem' of married women was cogently attacked in a Women's Freedom League publication called *The Woman Citizen and Social Security* (Abbott and Bompas 1943). While appreciating the report's 'dawning recognition of our membership one of another', Abbott and Bompas incisively attack the treatment of women as dependents of their husbands:

> The error — an error which lies in the moral rather than the economic sphere — lies in denying to the married woman, rich or poor, housewife or paid worker, an independent personal status. From this error springs a crop of injustices, complications and difficulties, personal, marital and administrative.

They go on to criticize the exemption of married women from contributions and to argue that despite Beveridge's acknowledgement of women's work, 'There is no practical recognition of the needs of this central figure in our social economy. No independent status is given to her as citizen and worke. ... Those who make the very life of the community, are to be treated as merely the means to an end.' (Abbott and Bompas 1943 p.10)

Many changes in the British social security system have adjusted women's relationship to national insurance. Married women now have the privilege of making contributions! But in fundamental ways the Abbott and Bompas critique still has a bearing. By attaching social security to paid employment, national insurance still penalizes women for carrying out their 'vital work'.

There are some policies in which women's unpaid work is acknowledged as entitling them to social rights: credits for family responsibility (counting towards national insurance), and child benefit (paid to women on behalf of their children) are two British ones. But such benefits are lower in practice than the rights accruing as a result of paid work — rights to flat-rate pensions rather than graduated ones, to benefit for one's children but not for oneself.

The Invalid Care Allowance is an interesting British example of a social benefit relating to unpaid work — entitlement depends on giving up paid work to care for others. In some respects it belongs to notions of citizenship. Entitlement is based on the existence of caring needs, not on a contract to carry them out; there is no contract of duties, no procedure to control their enforcement. But ICA is also a critical case for measuring the extent of citizenship rights deriving from unpaid work. At first it was not available to married women on the twin assumptions of natural duty and dependence on husbands: 'they would have been at home anyway.' Now — thanks to the Drake case going to the European court — married women may claim, and do. ICA is becoming a significant social security benefit for women, who constitute 86 per cent of beneficiaries. But its level was originally set at 60 per cent of the level of contributory benefits. The deliberate intention was to privilege contributory benefits over non-contributory ones; this is 'to ensure that the contributory principle, which is the foundation of almost all other non-means tested benefits, is maintained.' (Ungerson 1992 p.16). Citizenship derived from paid employment is thus better than citizenship derived through unpaid work. The result of such policies in Britain, according to a study of ICA recipients, is that 'the data suggests that some degree of financial dependency is commonplace among ICA recipients.' (McLaughlin 1992). The social benefit thus supports a dependency which is already commonplace for women as mothers and as carers of elderly or disabled relatives. While acknowledging the multiple dependencies of all of us on each other, this particular financial dependency of carers erodes their citizenship by any definition.

Patterns of insurance and care-based security have historical roots. Linda Gordon (forthcoming) has described the gendered nature of policy making around systems of insurance. Male reformers with their preference for insurance based on paid work predominated over female reformers with their preference for systems based on relationships. This was parallelled in Britain by Beveridge's social insurance system. The evidence that confronted Beveridge was of a social structure which led to women's dependence on the poor law more than men's. But the core problem for Beveridge was the question of male employment and how to replace the security of men's wages in unemployment, sickness and retirement. The mechanisms established in that period remain with us, however modified. Insurance is still the privileged form of social benefit, irretrievably tied to paid employment (despite family responsibility credits). Benefits arising out of parenthood or unpaid care have their lesser entitlement registered through their lesser value.

DUTIES

The assumption of paid work as the central citizenship obligation underpins many debates — about workfare, training, the conditionality of benefits (Plant 1988 pp.14–15). Certain social rights have followed market rights in being tied to paid work, sometimes becoming a means of enforcement.

But women's access to well-paid work is much less than men's; concomitantly their obligations to do unpaid work are greater. The impact of childcare on women's ability to do paid work and to contribute towards benefits has long been acknowledged. Beveridge, for example, who had a particular significance for the development of the British social security system, made a clear statement of the relative significance of women's duties:

> The attitude of the housewife to gainful employment outside the home is not and should not be the same as the single woman — she has other duties. ... In the next thirty years housewives as mothers have vital work to do in ensuring the adequate continuance of the British race and of British ideals in the world. (Beveridge 1942 p.51)

The significance of responsibility for the care of elderly and disabled adults has more recently been acknowledged, as the work itself has grown. British evidence shows that men as well as women are engaged in caring work, but that women are more likely to bear the heaviest responsibility (Green 1985). Obligations for unpaid care affect women's capacity to engage in paid work and to contribute to social security systems.

But who enforces the duty to unpaid work (Taylor-Gooby 1991)? The literature on the gender distribution of domestic work and on caring shows that there are plenty of free-riders here. In the case of paid work great attention is paid to questions of incentives, so that social benefits do not bring the same rewards as market benefits.

Obligations to unpaid work are not socially policed or materially rewarded. Cultural and economic pressures may suffice to ensure that women do their duty. Men may extract women's work through violence. Women do not use/have this option. Taylor-Gooby and Jordan have speculated about whether we can rescue the concept of citizenship by finding ways to spread the obligation for unpaid work (Jordan 1991; Taylor-Gooby 1991). While I like the objective, I remain sceptical about the means to this end. Neither commodification of the domestic world — with market incentives applied to caring work — nor 'compulsory altruism' (Land and Rose 1985) applied this time to men are particularly attractive alternatives.

RECIPROCITY

It is widely assumed that a claim to the existence of rights must imply the existence of a duty that these rights should be fulfilled. In a very general sense this must be accepted as a logical corollary. Equally, as Doyal and Gough have argued, the existence of duties must imply the existence of rights to the means to fulfil these duties. They also argue that reciprocity depends on a 'network of moral beliefs which clearly specify the conditions of entailment.' (1991 p.93).

But the exact nature of the relationship between rights and duties is another question. Some formulations of citizenship argue that the moral basis of citizenship rests on a direct reciprocity — those who expect rights must also expect to fulfil duties, and in specifying attachments between particular rights and particular duties, as in workfare and Mead's *The Social Obligations of Citizenship* (1985).

Bill Jordan offers us a critique of this notion in his argument about basic income and conditionality:

> This simpleminded idea of correspondence flies in the face of any coherent and credible political theory of citizenship, and neglects centuries of political thought. It is a fundamental principle of any tenable theory of citizenship that its basic rights are only to be suspended for the most serious offences, and then only after very careful judicial consideration. But these acts of suspending basic rights — loss of liberty, of civil or political rights, or of rights to social protection — are seldom directly linked with the obligations that correspond with them ... citizens who refuse to do military service may be imprisoned, but not sent to the front. And citizens who evade income tax may be fined or even imprisoned, but not put on special punitive higher tax codes. (Jordan 1991 p.3)

In practice the relationship between rights and duties is worked out in widely varying ways. Below I consider examples of contrasting models.

Social insurance is a classic case of reciprocity in the public sphere, duties to contribute being closely linked to rights to benefit. It is mechanistic, risk pooling, strictly regulated; contributions have to do with personal responsibility as much as with social duty. There are problems of coverage (or there would be no need for a safety net) and the benefits are uneven; as argued above, insurance tied to paid employment narrows citizenship rights for women. But sharing risks and measured entitlement offer some security to those entitled to benefit.

In several ways these features of insurance as a system of reciprocity contrast with the domestic version of rights and duties. Here are strong notions of reciprocal obligations instead of personal responsibility, hierarchies of duty instead of pooling of risks and entitlements.

In practice reciprocity breaks down in the face of very different levels of need between able-bodied and disabled or frail relatives, causing great distress to those unable to return services: the desire not to be become 'too dependent' becomes a paramount concern. Inter-generational exchanges are one kind of response to this problem: daughters are seen as having obligations to parents (Finch 1989) and may expect to receive service from their own daughters. But there is great imbalance of rights and obligations, and great uncertainty for carers about whether they will be able to call in their investment of duty — and be cared for in their own dependency. Indeed, the classic carer was a spinster daughter who would not be expected to have children of her own (Finch 1989 pp.29–30).

Family reciprocity, then, is the basis for unequal rights. Women doing unpaid work have very uncertain entitlement to return in kind, reducing with family size and the security of marriage bonds. There is no equivalent to social insurance's function of risk sharing. Women often carry the risks and burdens alone. The hierarchy of duty may even let some people off the hook and make it difficult for people such as neighbours to share in caring burdens (Ungerson 1987).

Not all social rights are tied to social duties in the way that insurance benefits are tied to contributions. The looser reciprocity of the NHS and education systems provides another model which I think has served women better. The gatekeeping function of professionals is not without its problems here. But the funding of these services through taxation, with service provided according to need bridges public and private worlds more fairly than social insurance or family duty.

CONCLUSION

Citizenship, in all its components, is problematic for women. Women's civil rights are undermined through violence and rape in marriage, and a state which inadequately invests in law and order in the private world; as well as through pressures to undertake unpaid caring work which undermine their autonomy. Women's political rights give representation at around 5 or 10 per cent of national and provincial assemblies in most western democracies. Women's social rights are undermined by systems of social security which treat them as dependants.

Women's obligations in unpaid work have undermined their recognition through paid work, usually seen as a fundamental component of citizenship, and their membership of those social welfare programmes that are attached to paid work.

Reciprocity is equally problematic. Systems which connect rights and duties directly (as in social insurance) have systematically undervalued women's contributions through unpaid work. Systems based on family duty may provide high levels of care but do not offer great security. Perhaps those systems based on need and human fulfilment (health and education in Britain) have the loosest construction of rights and duties, and in this respect have served women best.

For a feminist all this poses a dilemma. Should we try to achieve citizenship for women, in the knowledge of how inadequately it has served women in the past, and how fundamental are the problems? Should we reject it, as a state of grace reserved for men? Should we try to transform the notion of citizenship, so as to acknowledge the way that the public/domestic divide has undermined women's participation in citizenship as usually understood?

The first route, taking citizenship as it is, runs the risk, as Carole Pateman rightly argues — of condemning ourselves to the status of the second class. Within current formulations, I think duties are more problematic for feminists than rights. The way that unpaid work impinges on the attainment of citizenship status through paid employment has much less public acknowledgement than, for example, the rights of girls to education and women to health services. Only the polities of Scandinavia have taken this at all seriously. Notions of reciprocity make me most uneasy. The more closely that rights are locked into duties (workfare, insurance contributions) the more disadvantaged are those who cannot perform the duties. And this leads to wariness about the citizenship concept as a whole, in that a distinctive concern of those who write about citizenship is often with making rights contingent on duties.

The second route, rejecting citizenship, may be to reject evident goods: the right to ownership of our bodies in marriage, the more established rights to health care and education. The right to services as individual citizens rather than as members of families has positive aspects for women: 'The principle of citizenship rights is the most important political principle which counters a "strong" view of family obligations, because its emphasis is upon the individual, not the family, as the unit of support.' (Finch 1989 p.10).

The third route, transforming citizenship, risks draining away meaning. If the key social roles are those of 'parent, householder, worker and citizen' (Braybrooke, 1987 p.48), then citizenship is characteristically about public life in contrast to private life. To go down this path might be to follow John Major into a citizenship which consists of universal membership of the Consumers Association.

Despite these dangers, reconceptualizing citizenship to acknowledge gender-specific social roles — without entrenching them — is the more inviting prospect. We might detect three different uses for a concept of citizenship, all reflected in Marshall's quotation at the beginning. Marshall writes of 'an ideal citizenship against which achievement can be measured'; the yardstick has its uses. A second phrase — 'an ideal citizenship towards which aspiration can be directed' — suggests a utopia. If this is what we want, then I think we might turn to Bill Jordan's 'The Common Good' which makes a real attempt to shift existing boundaries between the public and the private. The third use is more embedded. The implication of Marshall's analysis is that citizenship is a theory of social welfare development; as such a theory, I think citizenship remains inadequate, too little concerned with social difference and social conflict.

Acknowledgements: My thanks go to colleagues at the University of Nottingham, Becky Morley and Robert Dingwall, for reading and commenting on an earlier draft; and to Lesley Jacobs, of the University of British Columbia, who made detailed comments and helpful suggestions.

NOTES

1   The impact of policing domestic life is contentious, described by Walker (1990) in terms of the risk of substituting public patriarchy for private patriarchy. Morley and Mullender sift the evidence and the arguments in this area from a British perspective (Morley and Mullender 1992).

8. De-constructing Dualities: Making Rights Claims in Political Institutions

Jane Jenson

Since T.H. Marshall wrote it has been impossible to think of welfare without thinking of citizenship. For Marshall, the postwar welfare state had wrought a change; definitions of the rights of citizenship incorporated social and economic rights as well as the more familiar civil and political. His historical survey and typology of citizenship claims made it clear that the progressive social forces which had fought for better representation of their needs and claims in state policy had also reworked the concept of citizenship.

This way of thinking of the links between welfare and citizen rights makes it clear that definitions of citizenship establish the boundaries of social inclusion and exclusion, thereby providing access to full membership in a nation state and the grounds for making claims to that state for rights and welfare (Marshall 1965 [1949] p.76).

Initially, the meaning and practices of citizenship were forged out of efforts to create a certain commonsensical understanding of the vast social changes which reshaped the face of Europe as capitalism transformed economies and the drive for political rights remade state institutions, thereby producing the modern state (Jenson, 1992).[1] Much later, twentieth-century discourses and practices redefined who had the right to representation and the content of social and economic rights which have provided the underpinnings of the welfare system. Women's movements as well as labour and other movements for social reform were central actors for setting out the meaning of citizenship in particular national contexts (Jenson 1989b; Jenson and Mahon 1992).

As a result, definitions of citizenship provide a statement of any society's definition of self, that is the way that it represents itself. This representation identifies aspirants to the condition of citizenship, and in doing so, excludes others. We can expect, therefore, that there will be not only accommodation to the identifying practices of citizenship but also resistance. And, indeed, the last centuries have been marked by the efforts of many different actors to re-establish or gain collective rights denied them in the dominant representations as well as in liberal democracy's representation of the rights of sovereign individuals. Minority language groups, labour movements, many feminists, indigenous peoples, nations within multinational states, and ethnic groups within polyethnic states have, in different times and places, challenged representations of citizenship which did not accommodate collective rights and did not recognize their needs.[2]

Recognizing this story implies an approach to thinking about the processes leading to welfare measures. The first characteristic of the approach is that it sees all citizenship and welfare claims addressed to state institutions as profoundly historical, generated by social movements and other actors anchored in specific time and place. By implication, then, such claims vary in accordance with the political struggles of actors mobilized within the constraints of particular institutions, understood as structured patterns of behaviour. While modern states have obviously shared many experiences and constructed some shared definitions of citizen rights, their story can only be really understood as the result of struggles by actors located in each state. Moreover, historical legacies of past struggles, embedded in institutions, are the constraints within which struggle for changes in definitions and practice of welfare are mobilized. And change they will, because claims for rights and welfare alter — along with much else — in moments of profound economic, social and political turbulence. This is the second characteristic of the approach used here.

The rest of this paper explores the shifts in definitions of citizenship and the rights of claimants by examining recent Canadian history and the way in which struggles about the most basic political institution — the constitution — have challenged definitions of rights. In the last few decades Canadian public discourse has been reorganized in part by the actions of collective actors who have rejected post-1945 representations of economic and social, as well as political rights. In doing so, they have also begun to de-construct the dualisms which have long organized Canadian politics.

After the Second World War the predominant definition of Canadian citizenship which took shape was universalistic and individualistic, identifying only linguistic differences as grounds for recognizing minority rights (Jenson 1992). This conception of citizenship was expressed in postwar social programmes, the politics of bilingualism, and the original project for a Charter of Rights and Freedoms. Pan-Canadian citizenship was doubly dualistic. First, and most obviously, it established the boundaries of inclusion and exclusion, drawing a border around the individuals on the 'inside' and those who were 'outside'. The 'us' was then composed of Francophone and Anglophone individuals endowed with individual liberal rights and some claims to social and economic programmes provided by the federal or provincial governments.

Collective rights were only awkwardly accommodated within this vision. The second form of dualism was the identification of two language groups as fundamental.

This vision of citizenship has been contested in two major ways. One involves a challenge to visions of historical dualisms related to the moments of colonialism and Confederation. The Québécois neo-nationalist movement and the resurgent nationalisms of Aboriginal peoples both date from the 1960s, becoming increasingly important in the last decades as expressions of 'nationalisms against states' (Tiryakian 1985 p.3). These nationalist movements compete with each other over the division of governmental powers and the recognition of collective rights, to be sure. Nonetheless, they both reject the dualisms embedded in pan-Canadian citizenship. However, the nationalism of Aboriginal peoples *also* constitutes a challenge to the dualism of Québécois nationalism, which envisages citizenship rights resting on the historical interpretation of 'two nations'.

The pan-Canadian representation of citizenship has also been contested by the women's movement in the last decade, often in coalition with other social movements. These social movements have been struggling to redefine the political rights of citizenship, including democratic politics. They seek to generate a replacement for the representation of pan-Canadian citizenship and its rights so as to better incorporate notions of specificity and equity. In doing so, they challenge the simple dualism of 'us' and 'them', insisting that 'we' are not only individuals but also collectivities requiring 'different' treatment in order to achieve meaningful equality. They too are trying to imagine an equitable citizenship which recognizes diversity, generates equity and empowers the disempowered.

This paper explores the ways in which contestation over citizenship in the last decades constitutes a challenge to dualism, via a politics which abandons binary representations of Canadian society. This challenge follows from the social movements' and Aboriginal peoples' rejection of representations of citizenship rights as universalistic and individualistic.[3] They seek, instead, access and equity for collectivities and, therefore, collective rights as the basis for meeting needs and generating welfare.

A result has been, in turn, a major challenge to existing systems of representation, both those of intergovernmental relations and of party politics. In particular, there has been a reconfiguration of the relationship between space and powers. Aboriginal peoples make claims for governmental powers which may be defined in other than territorial terms and which, therefore, put traditional federal forms into question. Social movements, for their part, also reject the longstanding premise that guaranteeing equity for regions is the central goal of Canadian politics. They have another equity agenda.

MAKING CLAIMS: AN APPROACH TO ANALYSING REPRESENTATION

Citizenship has been defined here as a way of representing those legitimately able to make rights and welfare claims in a national society. As such, identification of rights and claimants is crucial to the practices of citizenship. These practices are profoundly political. They depend on the forms and outcomes of specific historical struggles. Despite this historical variability, however, most nation states have elaborated three basic types of rights: civil, political and social (Marshall 1965 [1949]). It is worth distinguishing these types because, as will become clearer below, nationalist and other social movements make citizenship claims which affect all three types of rights. Particularly important, however, are the different ways in which claims for political and social rights are made. All those seeking new rights do not present exactly the same challenge to existing practices. It is this diversity in representing citizens and citizenship which in part makes discussions of nation, state and constitutional politics so difficult in Canada. Nationalist movements and social movements work with quite different representations of their rights and claims to political power, economic well-being and social recognition.

In order to address this complexity, this paper considers several dimensions of representation. To be sure there is representation of interests to institutions of the state and civil society. At the same time, however, it is crucial to consider the constitution of the identities of the represented, through political mobilization and policy innovation (Jenson 1990 pp.662–4). The formation of identities defining who has the right to make claims occurs as part of the definition of which interests are in play and the elaboration of strategies to achieve them.

The meanings created by actors constitute a critical aspect of representation. It is by translating meanings into practice — often within institutions — that actors create, sustain or change representational arrangements. The generation of meaning, then, is profoundly political, if politics is considered to include actors' struggles to create themselves and their protagonists by generating support for the formulation of their own preferred collective identity, as well as by enunciating their interests.

The terrain on which actors struggle over representation is the universe of political discourse within which identities are socially constructed (Jenson 1986). Because actors with a variety of collective identities co-exist in this universe, their practices and meaning systems jostle each other for attention and legitimacy (Jenson 1991 p.52). Therefore, politics involves a struggle to be self-naming rather than 'outside-named', as well as to realize collective interests and welfare.[4] Such struggle creates winners and losers. Success in occupying space in the universe of political discourse limits the possibilities of others. As such, struggle over naming involves the exercise of power. This contest may result in an increase or a loss of resources and opportunities.

The style in which national communities is imagined, for example, is part of a competition for discursive space. In the same way, social movements compete to represent themselves as legitimate representatives of particular persons.[5] In this competition, actors are not only constructing their present and imagining their future, they are also creating their pasts. Therefore, social movements making national claims, as all other social movements, write and re-write history.[6] They compose and re-arrange that story in ways which justify contemporary definitions of interests and strategies. The imagined past is often as important a terrain of practice as the present.

Yet, everything is not possible. Collective actors are located in social relations organized in structured relations of power. These social relations set out the places within which action takes place and limit the styles with which such places may be lived.[7] Institutions materialize the power relations of structures, reproducing them through time as well as providing a terrain for action.

Finally, the power of collective actors to be self-naming is affected by the moment of history in which they are acting. Moments of economic and political turbulence — or crisis, as understood here — punctuate periods of greater stability, or regulation. The latter may be thought of as times in which a certain consensus exists around a commonsensical language of politics. Proponents of reform as well as supporters of the status quo *share* a language of politics although their diagnoses of the present and their hopes for the future may vary widely. Included in this language, of course, are the names of the actors. Crises, in contrast, are moments of profound change, in which the familiar is dying — but not yet dead — while the new struggles to be born.[8] They are times of political agitation, of competition among world views and of uncertainty about meaning. At issue are not only distributional and power questions, but even definitions of actors and their interests.[9]

In such a context of crisis some actors defend the past while others promote the future, some actors struggle to maintain their place and others press for wider recognition, some actors stress continuities and others emphasize change. The space within the universe of political discourse for naming new names and mobilizing the resources which such names bring is often larger in such moments of turbulence, with the new sometimes displacing or restricting the place of the old.

With this approach, this paper argues that representation has undergone substantial change in recent years of economic restructuring and constitutional crisis, under pressure from the practices of Aboriginal peoples and from the equity-seeking activities of social movements. New identities have emerged and the actors promoting these identities have successfully represented new interests in citizenship rights, the definitions of welfare which follow from them, and the social welfare programmes appropriate to them.

CHANGING DUALISMS: QUEBECOIS AND ABORIGINAL NATIONALISMS

The efforts of French-speaking residents of Canada to preserve their language and culture has been an enduring nationalist project. There have always been, however, competing ways of imagining how to achieve this end.

One style of imagining Canada defines it as a society composed of two languages with equal rights of recognition and cultural expression. Since 1867 minority language (and some religious) rights have been constitutionally protected in crucial institutions like schools. This representation of Canada as home to two languages was central to the initial project of Confederation and the institutions it established. In 1867 many people insisted that while a new nation might be built, any new 'Canadian' identity must be differentiated because of the diversity of religions and 'races' present in the new country (Simeon and Robinson 1990 pp.22ff.). While the goal was clearly to create a new nation, with a common citizenship, the authors of the BNA Act had a particular concept of Canada as 'a community based on political and juridical unity, but also on cultural and religious duality' (Ramsay Cook quoted in Simeon and Robinson 1990 p.23). Canadian citizenship was not intended to extinguish the collectivist and collectively-defined claims of the diverse communities which it housed. Federalism and other constitutional guarantees materialized this representation of the dual language community in political discourse.

A very similar project gained new support in the 1960s, with the move to represent Canada as a 'bilingual' country. This was also a project of nation-building, designed to identify all Canadians. The identities which followed from it appeared at first glance quite inclusive, designating all citizens according to language preference, as either Anglophone or Francophone.[10] It was dualistic, identifying only two 'official languages' and differentiating citizens by preference for one or the other of these languages.

Through the 1980s and into the 1990s the pan-Canadian and individualist Canadian community was considerably discredited, as a result of the efforts of Québécois nationalists and Aboriginal peoples, both of whom considered a simple language-differentiated citizenship an inadequate expression of their national goals, rights and needs.[11] The ideal of a pan-Canadian unity with linguistic duality collapsed, under pressure from the nationalist movements described here as well as other social movements which made citizenship claims in very different ways. In its place there is now a Quebec nation, facing an 'other'. By the 1990s this style of representing of the Québécois nation had become much more popular, both in Quebec and the rest of Canada.[12]

This shift followed the efforts of Québécois neo-nationalists since the 1960s to construct their alternative to the pan-Canadian model. The community of the Québécois nationalist movement is centred in the province of Quebec, adopting that territory as its homeland. Moreover, by the 1960s the Quebec state was identified by the nationalist movement as the instrument for empowering the Québécois. Provincial control over substantially extended social programmes was a central part of this project, because it would provide evidence of the newly empowered state to provide for the welfare of the Québécois.

The right to be a distinct society within Canada is claimed on the basis of political history, particularly a history of distinctiveness (Nemi 1991 pp.169–71). Confederation is often described as a pact between governments, whose purpose was to realize the benefits of operating within a state form which provided what appeared at the time to be maximum protection of linguistic and cultural differences. But Confederation might also be described as a re-grouping of autonomous communities in a new state. Either way of imagining the history of the national community identifies the government of Quebec as the nation's state (Gagnon and Montcalm 1990 p.169).

For all of these reasons, then, the identity of the Québécois has been represented by the nationalist movement as requiring access to new governmental powers, so as to exercise sovereignty, and the right to recognition of societal distinctiveness. Both are essential to the national project, practically expressed in the language of federal–provincial negotiations. The goal is to work institutional change so as to provide what the movement defines as acceptable political representation.

While the Québécois project has contributed a great deal to challenging the dualism of pan-Canadian definitions of citizenship, its own representation is also dualistic. The 'other' created by the Québécois nationalists is 'English Canada'. The movement's project also posits a traditional link between state and nation, claiming that state forms must follow the borders of nations. Therefore, there are demands to alter governmental institutions, so that the nation-building project can be effectively realized. The calls for constitutional recognition of Quebec's 'distinct' status and greater powers for the province of Quebec than for the other nine provinces are part of this dualistic and territorially defined nationalism. This dualistic representation has been challenged by the movements which have gained political importance in the recent years of economic turbulence. As Canada has confronted pressures for economic restructuring, the traditional relations of postwar federalism have come under political pressure and faced demands for change.[13] Calls for constitutional reform are part of the response by Canadian political institutions to the new circumstances of globalization (Breton and Jenson 1991). In this turbulent moment social movements have been promoting different rights claims and definitions of equity. In particular, the Aboriginal peoples and social movements both refuse — and in doing so begin to de-legitimatize — the dualism upon which Québécois nationalism depends. They refuse the mirror which Quebec holds up to them, insisting instead on alternative images which reflect both Quebec and the rest of Canada in much more fragmented ways and identifying other grounds for claiming citizenship rights.

As a result of these alterations in the universe of political discourse, neither the federal government nor Québécois nationalists has been able to bound the discourse of representation sufficiently to maintain a Quebec Round.[14] The boundaries have shifted as public discourse has opened to accommodate another understanding of Canadian history, in which more than two nations participate and in which citizenship claims are no longer confined to the traditional language of either pan-Canadianism or 'two nations in a single country' and routed through intergovernmental institutions.

This shift has happened in large part because of the success Aboriginal peoples have had in rejecting their classification as part of a 'multicultural' Canada. In the original discourse of multiculturalism of the late 1960s and 1970s, Aboriginal peoples were sometimes included as simply another cultural group (Cameron 1974 pp.11–12).[15] Their recently acquired ability to mount nation-based claims has required a long struggle. Some, albeit limited, success has given them additional power in the political discourse of Canada which has been, since the 1960s, open to national claims as a result of the struggles of Québécois nationalists.

In turn, however, the nationalisms of Aboriginal peoples have contributed to undermining the dualistic nationalism of the Québécois. On the one hand, Aboriginal groups made claims as a people in terms of a *rights* discourse. This strategy directly challenged the efforts of the Québécois to enshrine their definition of their unique collective rights — because of being a distinct society — in the Constitution. On the other hand, Aboriginal groups also made claims for access to governmental *power*, which if realized would fundamentally alter institutions of federalism upon which the Québécois claims have also always depended.

As Aboriginal peoples pushed for recognition of their 'nation-ness', they effectively undid the representation of Canada as composed of two linguistic communities and/or two nations which had for so long defined the identity and interests of both the pan-Canadian and Québécois nationalist movements.

They are also making a significant contribution to shifting longstanding representations of actors and politics in territorial terms. Many Aboriginal peoples lack a recognized land base and therefore cannot imagine their citizenship right to self-government in traditional territorial terms.[16] To the extent that it makes claims for a reassignment of governmental powers from the federal and provincial levels where they are all currently located, Aboriginal nationalism undoes the link between territory and nation which traditional nationalism has always maintained. Since the nineteenth century nationality and citizenship have been linked through claims to a form of territorial sovereignty.

These are also claims to a new relationship to the Canadian state. If recognized they would involve a significant redefinition of citizen rights in Canada. Peoples without a relationship to a clear land base would gain access to governmental powers now exclusively assigned to territories. If a third level of government can be imagined and implemented which would provide governmental powers without locating them within clearly defined territorial boundaries this would constitute a major shift in the political rights of citizenship.

With such practices, Aboriginal groups are claiming new citizenship rights of all three types described by Marshall. They are, for example, making claims for basic civil rights when they demand treatment consistent with recognition of their dignity and respect as a collectivity. They demand the political right to self-government. Moreover, in doing so, they make the argument that self-government within the Canadian state is not simply their right as peoples; it is necessary because only self-government can effectively deliver economic and social citizenship and overcome the appalling conditions within which so many of their communities live.

Therefore, the nationalism of Aboriginal peoples presents real, political challenges to both Quebec and the rest of Canada's ways of conceptualizing citizenship, territory, state forms and history. Such challenges form part of the everyday public discourse. But they also represent, even more profoundly, a rejection of dualistic representations and a refusal of binary distinctions. In effect, the challenge is to replace the longstanding dualism of traditional readings of Canadian history by a non-dualist one. Once a third term — Aboriginal nations — is introduced, the stability of the hierarchy and the forms of contestation collapse. The effect of reclaiming and revalorizing threatened Aboriginal cultures is to introduce into everyday discourse resistance to the existing — albeit contested — discourse of two nations.

In the ways they are made such formulations not only expose the racialism — and therefore racism — of what went before. Being an argument which re-identifies Canada, by labelling both Anglophones and Francophones as colonizers, they collapse distinctions based on language and culture. At the same time, by claiming something similar to that which Quebec wants in being recognized as 'distinct', such claims open up the possibility of fluid alliances around a discourse of three. For example, if Québécois suffer the effects of colonization, they can recognize themselves in the experience of Aboriginal peoples. Yet, obviously, the Québécois have also participated in colonization.

The resulting instability of representation, which mirrors the Aboriginal peoples' own experience of identity-instability, provides grounds for the recognition of diversity, fragmentation and uncertainty in identity formation. This instability of identities has several sources. Long subjected to outside-naming (under the Indian Act for example) Aboriginal peoples have struggled to be self-naming, in a situation in which the boundaries of communities are not fixed but established through action. Secondly, the presence of the Métis nation, which represents a situation where its members also have identity choices, is an additional factor which reveals the instability and choice dimension of identity. Finally, the willingness of communities to accept as full members those accepted by the community simply formalizes the idea of identity as choice.[17] Thus, the Aboriginal peoples' political work around naming has exposed the impossibility of relying on any form of racialist essentialism, whether the result of self-identification or court-based definitions (Chartrand 1991 pp.13–15). Their nationalism relies more on fluid forms of entry and exit from the community than it does on racial or even cultural markers.

In this way, Aboriginal nationalists challenge traditional Canadian and Québécois readings of history and their practices of representing themselves in terms of linguistic difference and national dualism. When the definition of 'nation-ness' is clearly exposed as a politics of choice and as a strategy, essentialist definitions can no longer be sustained.[18] Such stances, then, both support and are supported by other movements' — especially feminists' — refusal of essentialist categorizations and celebration of diversity.

CHALLENGING DUALISM: CANADIAN CITIZENSHIP AND EQUITY-SEEKERS

Traditionally, citizenship provides definitions of inclusion and exclusion. It draws boundaries around the group which is 'us' and distinguishes it from the 'others', in much the same way that traditional nationalism makes a clear we/they identification, usually based on cultural markers. Dualism is embedded in such understandings of citizenship. Both liberal democracy and social democracy promote the notion that citizenship rights are 'universal', accessible to any group or person included in the definition of citizen, because that definition establishes the boundary between 'us' and the 'other'.

Several decades of political mobilization by women, visible minorities, disabled peoples and other groups have challenged this dualism by rejecting the premise of 'universality' of citizen rights. Their practices have legitimated affirmative action — i.e. differential treatment to achieve meaningful equality — as a recognized route to access of the economic and social as well as political rights of citizens. They have sought, instead, a definition of equity which can recognize and protect equality in difference.

Such politics have been directed against the pan-Canadian national identity generated in post-1945 Canada (Jenson 1992). After the Second World War political discourse had begun to represent Canada as a single space north of the 49th parallel, having one labour market, universal standards for social programmes, and a central government with responsibility for assuring the well-being of the whole. A centralized system for income security was created, paying benefits to individual citizens (Jenson 1990 pp.681–2; Simeon and Robinson 1990 ch.7).[19]

With these moves toward a welfare state, a recomposition of national identity had begun, centred around a basic discursive and policy consensus. It redefined the identity of 'citizen', addressing individuals who had access to countrywide, or pan-Canadian, institutions and protections. Creating as it did countrywide, individual-based institutions with little capacity for recognizing difference beyond language, it is not surprising that resistance to these institutions arose as social movements claiming both the right to 'difference' and recognition of their particular needs appeared in the period of economic restructuring and political crisis of the last two decades.

Many groups are now making claims in the name of collective rights and solidarities, seeking state-guaranteed mechanisms to achieve equity. They are claiming 'categorial equity' (Jenson 1992). Demands for alteration in the original proposal for the Charter of Rights and Freedom in 1981–82, for example, were mounted by those who sought to embed in that document a recognition of the limits to formal equality and a representation of those categories of citizens who required particular attention. Defined in terms of affirmative action and collective rights, equity claims resonated through the constitutional debate before 1982 and then after.

Armed with their arguments about fairness, these movements have been calling on the state since the 1960s to guarantee effective justice in the face of a situation where formal equality of rights — supposedly guaranteed by a pan-Canadian citizenship blind to gender, race, or history — has failed to generate institutions representative of currently widespread representations of the categories of Canadian society. These claims antedate the Charter of Rights and Freedoms. Indeed, the Charter, as a *compromise* document, reflects the power of groups mobilized around collective identities in opposition to liberal individualism to mount successful claims for collective rights in 1981–82.

It is nonetheless clear that social movement organizations representing those long-disadvantaged by the universalistic standards of pan-Canadian citizenship are not simply claiming the right to better access to the social rights of citizenship. They are also attempting to expand the spaces of politics and generate more democratic politics. The movements' demands for 'categorial equity' involve extending democratic practices and they often take the institutions of intergovernmental relations as the opponent, arguing that the workings of these institutions, as well as electoral politics, suffer from a serious democratic deficit.

The new social movements of the 1970s and 1980s rejected the longstanding notion that the pre-eminent political spaces were Parliament, workplace and nation. As these movements now struggle to elaborate their own identities and to legitimate them in political discourse, the spaces for and of politics proliferate.[20] But behind all of this is a renegotiation of citizenship, and in particular the insistence that more actors 'belong' in the political process than can be recognized by a single countrywide undifferentiated definition of the citizen and that these actors, defined in categorial terms, will exercise their political rights well beyond electoral politics and intergovernmental institutions.

Feminists, for example, have sought not only the right to strive for equality with men but also the recognition that achievement of that goal could involve at times acceptance that women are a collectivity distinct in many ways from men. This was the motive for lobbying to entrench not only liberal equality rights but also affirmative action guarantees in the Charter of Rights and Freedom in 1982 (Simeon and Robinson 1990 pp.298, 323). Other equality-seeking groups (representing the poor, visible minorities, the disabled, for example) have not confined themselves to using the courts as the route to redressing the disadvantages they face as a result of systemic discrimination. They too have joined the call for a statement of social and economic rights in the next Constitution, as testimony to the importance of social solidarity. For these equality-seekers, only fair social programmes can provide real equity.

Women's and minorities' longstanding search for equity has led them to mobilize in constitutional debate, to approach the courts, and to engage in coalitional politics on punctual matters, like the free-trade agreements and constitutional controversy. In doing so, they have effectively shifted the locus of political action away from both party politics and intergovernmental institutions.

Many of these collective actors dispute the definition of constitutional politics as being about federalism and the idea that politics occurs primarily in elections and the institutions of executive federalism. These groups frequently bypass issues of federalism, intergovernmental institutions, and certainly the brokerage party system (Breton and Jenson 1991 pp.210ff.). Critiques of the democratic deficit of the Meech Lake negotiations led many groups to press, individually and together through the Action Canada network, for example, for opening up the process of constitutional negotiations in 1991–92 (Breton and Jenson 1991 pp.201–2). Not only did 'intergovernmental' meetings involve more kinds of actors — the territorial governments which were not yet provinces and Aboriginal peoples who did not yet have self-government. That negotiation process itself lost some of its legitimacy as a result of calls for other decision rules, including referenda and a constituent assembly. Such changes were pre-figured by the constitutional conferences held in the winter of 1992. Those conferences provided categorial representation — via group identity, including that of 'ordinary Canadians' — and promoted the notion that the citizenship of the twenty-first century will continue to recognize difference.

With such calls for recognition of many categories of citizens, the previous dualism of the 'citizen' and the 'other' has been fragmented. Now alternative representations of citizenship exist which define citizens in terms of their different status and needs and which seek effective state as well as private actions for providing 'real equality' via 'different' and equitable treatment.

CONCLUSION

This paper has shown the ways in which struggles for representation by collective actors so as to carve out space for their identities and interests in the universe of political discourse, are now challenging dualistic understandings of citizenship rights and the link between state and nation utilized by both the pan-Canadian and Québécois nationalist movements. Whereas it was the challenge of Québécois nationalism which first helped to undermine the pan-Canadian idea, in more recent years that movement has also lost its ability to bound political discourse to a focus on its claims and to make gains on its agenda. In large part this difficulty is explained by the success of alternative, non-dualistic readings of history and understandings of rights and powers.

In particular, such politics have begun to undo the straightforward tie between 'citizen' and 'nation' which has existed since the French Revolution. The revolutionaries of 1789 constructed a way of thinking about citizenship which linked nationalism, state power, territory, and universal rights. In late-twentieth-century Canada, the nationalism of Aboriginal peoples challenges the idea that nationality and governmental power must always coincide in a territory. In doing so, they compel a rethinking of the politics of territory which has always underpinned the notion that territorially defined government — such as traditional federalism — is the appropriate way to recognize citizens' right to self-determination in a culturally divided space in which several peoples claim political and social rights not as only individuals but as distinct nations.

Processes of globalization contribute a great deal to such de-linking by making the borders of nation states permeable to economic, social and political forces from 'outside' and encouraging communities to think of themselves as part of transnational networks. Both Aboriginal peoples and social movements represent themselves in part in terms of such transnational politics, seeking legitimacy, allies and justification for their rights claims in international covenants and organizations, as well as among transnational social movements.[21]

Social movement politics also challenges one of the legacies of 1789 when it organizes claims for greater political as well as social and economic equity. By making claims for equity, social movements are rejecting a conceptualization of citizens' 'universal' rights, in which little differentiation or specificity is recognized. Instead they claim that formal equality is insufficient to meet the needs of particular groups and that meaningful access to citizenship involves 'special' treatment. In this way, many social movements inject into a 'rights discourse' the language of diversity.

In addition, many social movements as well as Aboriginal nationalists seek to empower the politically weak — whether workers, women, Aboriginal peoples, the disabled or children — and seek to do so not only by claiming new rights but also by expanding the spaces for democratic politics. Therefore, a central element of contemporary politics involves critiques of traditional forms of self-government — the right of citizenship *par excellence* — and mobilization to generate meaningful democratic practices. All of this reconfigures, in profound ways, the longstanding Marshallian definition of citizenship rights from which so much of our post-1945 understanding of 'welfare' derived.

NOTES

1   The concept is a modern one, invented in the eighteenth century as an element of the emerging system of capitalist nation states in western Europe. Citizenship became a principle of political thought and of the system of modern states coming into existence at that time (Breuilly 1982, Introduction). Therefore, while its philosophical roots might be traced to Athenian practices, it is most appropriate to discuss citizenship in terms of post-Enlightenment politics and the invention of the concept of the 'sovereign individual' (Abercombie et al. 1986).
2   The notion of multinational states and polyethnic states is from Kymlicka (1991). These two terms replace the highly problematic term 'multicultural'.
3   On feminism's longstanding rejection of dualism and binary distinctions see Benhabib and Cornell (eds) (1987).
4   The term 'outside-naming' is adopted from Chartrand (1991 p.2) who describes naming by those outside the community — whether state actors or others in civil society — as an indicator of a relatively powerless community. Achieving the ability to insist upon one's own name and achieve recognition — to be self-naming, that is — results from a shift in the balance of power. Of course, resistance to 'outside-naming' may also take the form of assuming and reworking the name assigned by others.

5   For example, one of the most difficult conflicts when the women's movements first appeared in the late 1960s was between feminists who would style all women simply as 'women' and the labour movement which struggled to maintain its power to represent 'working women'.

6   All social movements must write their own history, and thereby rewrite that of others. An obvious example comes from contemporary women's movements, which have explicitly undertaken to 'make women visible' in history, to rewrite the story by placing themselves in history, and, in doing so, to recompose the discipline of History itself. For a discussion see, *inter alia*, Scott (1987).

7   For a discussion of the links between structural processes setting out the 'places' of social relations and the 'styles' for living those social relations, see Jenson (1991 pp.54–6).

8   While the allusion is to Gramsci, the definition of crisis which follows is based as much on the concept as developed within the French regulation approach. See, for example, Lipietz (1989).

9   For a discussion of crises as moments of competition among representations see Jenson (1990, 1991).

10   In its recent post-1960s incarnation support for this definition of Canada has come primarily from political parties and the federal government, promoted first by the Liberal party, adopted by the other parties, and organized by state institutions. Social movements, with the exception of Francophones outside Quebec and some parts of the 'English-Canadian' nationalist movement, were not major advocates of this project.

11   Of course, both sets of nationalists also vehemently rejected any tendency to represent Canada in 'multicultural' terms. Neither Québécois nor Aboriginal nationalists were prepared to acknowledge that ethnic or racial difference was equivalent to their national status. Multiculturalism was a policy to deal with cultural pluralism arising from immigration, which had generated a polyethnic society. Both the Québécois and the Aboriginal peoples were struggling to define Canada as a multi*national* state (Kymlicka 1991 pp.239–41).

12   To say it is hegemonic is not to say that it is uncontested. The question of *who* can identify as Québécois is a thorny problem within the province. Whether commitment to the French language is sufficient or whether one must share in — or at least identify with — the historic experience of those who first settled the colony is hotly debated. At issue is recognition of French-speaking immigrants, whether from France or ex-colonies of France, as well as immigrants who have adopted French after immigration.

13   Jenson (1989a) explores the links between economic and political institutions and the reasons why the economic restructuring of recent years has been accompanied by challenges to federal–provincial relations.

14   The discourse which labels 'constitutional rounds' is a particularly important indicator of conditions in the politics of representation. The Meech Lake Accord is usually considered to have represented a 'Quebec Round'. This involved the recognition of Quebec's insistence that its claims were more important than all others, and had to be settled first. Only then, could attention turn to Aboriginal peoples and other matters, like Senate reform, which were of major concern to the West. This view of how to make change, by recognizing a hierarchy of claims based on supposed historical precedence, was clearly a fundamental blow to Aboriginal peoples as well as to all those whose vision of federalism is of ten equal provinces. The 1991–92 'Canada Round' was deliberately labelled as such by the federal government, in order to address the wide variety of claimants pressing for recognition.

15   Another effort to assimilate Aboriginal peoples' situation to that of the rest of Canadian society was also launched at the end of the 1960s. The Liberal government's White Paper on Indian Policy in 1969 translated a philosophical commitment to embodying liberal rights in individuals into a policy proposal to eliminate their special status in law and to treat Aboriginal peoples as a 'disadvantaged' social group. This threat of assimilation was a catalyst for creating stronger and more nationalist organizations in the mid-1970s (Barsh and Henderson 1982 p.69; Long 1992 pp.120–1).

16   The relationship to a land base is complicated and varied. While Status Indians do have land bases, they are small, not economically viable and not contiguous. Therefore, even they must rethink the relationship between institutions of self-government and territory. For off-reserve Aboriginal persons and the Métis there is no land base. For Aboriginal peoples involved in comprehensive land claims, while settlement may resolve the question of title to land, it does not extinguish the notion that a people's traditional territory extends beyond the borders of the land assigned in the settlement. Therefore, the issue is a pertinent and pressing one, particularly as social change swells the ranks of urban and Métis Aboriginal persons.

17   There are clearly limits on this choice. Racism is an obvious one. In addition, the Canadian state still retains the power to name 'Indians', as those granted status under the 'Indian Act'. In the same way, to the extent that courts maintain the power to define 'Indian-ness', or who is an

Aboriginal person, the power and flexibility of self-naming practices are reduced. On the 'outside-naming' practices embedded in the Indian Act see Chartrand (1991).

18 Such practices of 'self-selection' characterize much of contemporary nationalism (Rogowski 1985 p.377).

19 According to Banting, Ottawa could gain access to the field of income security because of '... the special nature of income security as a direct exchange between citizen and state, which bypasses other social institutions' (1987 p.51).

20 In effect, such movements reflect a shift in the locale of politics, from the almost exclusively national to include both the global and the local. Feminists, anti-racists, ecologists, gays insist on creating new space for new politics in the family, the city, the environment and the community. Geographical space contracts, as such movements develop ties around the globe (Jenson 1991 pp.47–8).

21 On the strategy of Aboriginal peoples in using international and transnational actions see Jhappan (1992). On the general point see Breton and Jenson (1992).

9. Private Pains in Public Places: The Uses of Criminal Justice

Ronald Melchers

Contemporary representations of criminal justice have often tended to focus on its repressive character as state institution and on its functions within the modern state. Academic treatment of criminal justice has thus been focused on three main issues: the normative character of the criminal law, criminalization as the extreme marginalization of groups and individuals, and the use of force and legal constraint in the exercise of state power through criminal justice. This essentially functionalist perspective on criminal law and its administration has also held a privileged place in critical reflection on criminal justice, the nuances of which have often only served to consolidate a fundamental consensus on a central vision of criminal justice as the exercise of state power.

It is the contention to be developed in this paper that such a view fails to consider both the macro processes by which this category of law is produced, and the micro- and macro-processes of human agency by which the criminal justice system is supplied by the elemental social matter with which it is seized in its day-to-day existence. The dual nature of formal institutions as both resource and constraint is very much in evidence in the area of criminal justice. In this paper, we will examine the notion of criminal justice as resource and explore the dynamic of its use by social actors.

WELFARE AND JUSTICE: NEEDS AND RIGHTS

It may appear incongruous to include an examination of criminal justice in a collection of papers exploring the possibilities of the construction of a general theory of welfare. Criminal justice is not traditionally a significant producer of goods or utilities and so does not address 'needs' nor create 'welfare' in any empirical sense. This is changing rapidly in most jurisdictions as utilitarian conceptions of the role of law are gaining sway. We will return to this point.

Criminal justice is centrally driven by a conception of rights, not of needs. As such, in a reverse and yet symmetrical manner, we see operating in criminal justice the same struggles which Drover and Kerans (*supra*) describe in the production of welfare: that for identity in its dual role as both reflection and autonomy; for normativity in the dual capacity of social actors both to reflect norms and to create counterfactual norms; and the struggle for the universalizability of defined needs through the recognition of their 'justness' or justice.

Similarly, in criminal justice there is tension between agency and structure, engaging the processes by which agents affirm and create identity and their relations with structures as both enabling and constraining forces; that between rights, borne by individuals or collectivities yet invoked or consumed publicly, and utilities, the latter consumed privately yet created within social space; and the tension between 'thin' and 'thick' needs, the first referring to abstract, moral and universal needs and the latter to those needs which are concrete, named and particular to specific individuals or groups.

Justice is principally concerned with the validation of identity, the formal recognition of citizenship rights, with determination of the 'justness' or universal character of claims and with the delivery of abstract moral redress. Yet, it is also called upon to play a significant role in the production of welfare and interacts with these processes, as described by Drover and Kerans, as both resource and constraint. For the bearer of needs must first be determined to be a subject of rights, in order that these needs may be considered universalizable and thereby considered to ground legitimate claims against state institutions. Criminal justice, in conferring status to received claimants by assuming the onus of criminal pursuit on their behalf, identifies these claimants as citizens of the state, abstract subjects of law and the subjects of rights. It is this historic and traditional role of criminal law which permits us to engage the notion of criminal justice as resource.

THE ORIGINS OF CRIMINAL LAW

Nowhere is the apparent contradiction between formal representations of criminal justice as state repression and constructivist analyses of the production of criminal justice more evident than in the growing body of recent work in France, Belgium and in progress in Canada on the historical origins and conditions of production of contemporary criminal codes. Lascoumes et al. (1989) reveal the French penal code of 1791 as an arm of the Revolution, the companion piece to the Declaration of the Rights of the Citizen of 1789. The code operationalized and entrenched the principal of the primacy of law articulated in the Declaration. In this articulation, penal law derives, not from the absolute power of a Sovereign, but rather from the social contract which links the people and the state. It is in this way that the code was seen by its contemporaries as the arm of liberty striking a blow against arbitrariness and absolutism. The French penal code of 1791 thus consecrated the people's right to lay claim to the pursuit of justice by the hand of the state.

The rhetoric reflects only a partial reality and the new codes which emerge throughout the nineteenth century owe much to the regimes which preceded them and in many ways constitute a reactionary rather than revolutionary process. Castan (1980) portrays the French penal code as a sort of reverse image of the justice of the *Ancien Régime*; the notion of a single uniform code outlining and limiting positively the authority of the state in penal law replaces in 1791 the plurality of sources of legal authority and private procedural arbitrariness in penal matters under the *Ancien Régime*; the idea of a public and popular procedural justice founded in positive law responds to the essentially private character of the King's justice, seen as the vehicle of absolutism. Public and unified criminal codes thus themselves laid the foundations of the state power which they have come to symbolize.

Nonetheless, the principle is established whereby the initiative in criminal prosecution lies first and foremost with the people, in whose name alone the state may take up cause against a citizen. The increasing predominance of public prosecutions at the expense of private prosecutions, beginning in the second half of the nineteenth and continuing throughout the twentieth centuries, further consolidates the public character of criminal law. This public character of penal law means that a cause, once taken up by the state, ceases to be a private matter. The individual citizen whose claim initiated the action is relegated to a supporting role and deprived, in principle, of the faculty of making private claims for retribution, restitution or reparation — often in practice seen as, in principle, mutually exclusive. The citizen who claims the former forgoes any individual claims or compromises the universalizability of the greater claim, not for redress but for recognition as a citizen. The resolution of a criminal matter is therefore essentially symbolic rather than utilitarian in nature, the true crime under consideration being the abstract, moral and universal violation of the state as embodied by the citizen rather than the actual substantive damage incurred.

The codes of the nineteenth century, although they emerge from rather different contexts than that of Revolutionary France, carry the seeds of this libertarian conception rooted in the notions of individual rights and the social contract with its public character was one of the major influences in the early development of American criminal law and procedure. In this manner these codes function, at least in part, by conferring to the citizen an individual entitlement to personal safety, to well-being and to the legitimate enjoyment of property which is materialized by the creation of an individual right to lay claims for state action in a limited number of areas. In these areas, the violation of the rights of the citizen invokes a duty on the part of the state symmetrical, in the formulation of Weber, to the state's monopoly over the legitimate use of force.

CRIMINAL JUSTICE AND RIGHTS

Unlike the essentially regulatory character of other forms of state intervention, in criminal law, as in other forms of legal recourse founded in rights, it is incumbent upon citizens to materialize their right through the making of claims. Legal norms intervene in the judgement as to the receivability of a claim and in its subsequent re-ordering by institutions, but are not determinant other than by reflection in the processes by which a claim is initially made. In the main, criminal justice functions more along the lines of the liberal justice model than the utilitarian welfare model (Rawls 1971) and it is thus that any consideration of the function of criminal law must primarily focus on its character as a resource. Nonetheless, from Pound to Kelsen to Althusser, it is a fundamentally utilitarian, or instrumental, conception of the production and interaction of formal legal norms, and its underlying balance of notions of *libre arbitre*, on the one hand, and welfare and constraint, on the other, which dominates thinking on the social foundations of the criminal law.

It is my purpose here to demonstrate that it is this historic and yet still operational understanding of modern criminal law and procedure, founded in classic liberal thought, which justifies their reconsideration in terms of the making of claims against the state in the same sense as the claims for welfare and social justice in the broader sense to which Drover and Kerans refer (*supra*).

Some current developments in criminal justice are following a course opposite yet symmetrical to that which Drover and Kerans lay out for social welfare.[1] Critical theory, by addressing the normative character of social welfare, challenges its traditional utilitarian conception. It has, in criminal justice theory, often served only to confirm the traditional focus on the production of legal norms. Critical legal theory rejects the Kelsenian approach to the production of legal norms according to which all law is derived by deduction from a few 'original' principles in nature, in favour of a theory which considers the production of law as derived from relations of domination, principally those of class, race and gender. Thus much critical examination of criminal justice has focused on the role of law in the production of inequalities, in the marginalization of individuals and groups and in the repression of specific social practices of marginalized groups, all 'useful' productions for the maintenance of existing relations of domination, and has led observers of criminal justice to embrace ever more tightly the notion of criminal justice as a producer of utilities.

While such consideration of the utility of criminal law to dominant groups provides a useful and essential perspective on criminal justice, it leaves aside its more fundamental normative character. I refer here not to the normative character of law as traditionally defined in the legal positivist tradition, but rather to that which Drover and Kerans address (*supra*). As any normative system, criminal justice thus possesses a dual nature, both ascribing and reflecting identity to its actors, acting simultaneously as constraint and resource, and functions as a conceptual framework within which individuals and groups engage in the process of defining their needs and identities.

The work of John Lea and Jock Young (1984, 1986)[2] in the past decade in developing an alternative to mainstream critical theory in British criminology, under the name of new or left realism, is an interesting parenthesis. Lea and Young effectively point out the limits of a theory which ascribes to criminal justice intervention an essentially repressive character in the exclusive service of the dominant classes of society, illustrating their argument by the massive preponderance of the marginalized, the poor and the excluded among those at whose call and in whose name the state intervenes. They offer a stinging rebuke of the underlying vision of crime as proto-revolution which such a theory requires.

The left realists thus open the way for a consideration of criminal justice as an arena for the interplay of claims from various users located differentially within relations of domination. Yet, in refusing to abstract from the concrete experiences of the communities they survey, they fail to construct an effective alternative to what amounts to an essentially positivist notion of crime in their effort to describe the interactions between the social actors of criminal justice. To paraphrase Drover and Kerans, the left realists are caught attempting to reconcile the 'thick' needs of communities under duress with the 'thin' institutional responses of the criminal justice system. A more dynamic vision of criminal justice as the site of structured relationships and intersecting claims for identity and inclusion is necessary for left realist criminology to begin to understand the highly mediated and transformative links between claims and institutional responses.

THE SOCIAL PRODUCTION OF CRIME

A first obstacle to the consideration of the normative character of criminal justice arises from a historic misunderstanding of what comprises the subject matter of criminal justice. This can be illustrated by examining the debates between functionalists and interactionists over what precisely is measured by criminal justice statistics, in particular, the production of that part of criminal justice most in contact with the public, the police, and its public representation of its own subject matter.

It is the case with most public institutions that the issue of the representation and measurement of the matter they are established to address precedes their existence. So it was that the fascination for a sort of *moral epidemiology*, proposed initially by the Italian positivists and realized in the '*statistique morale*' of the Belgian demographer Quetelet among others, preceded the emergence of the first modern police organizations in the mid-nineteenth century. Upon becoming available, the operational records of the new institution were transformed by some philosopher's stone into that socially relevant measurement of essentially abstract social phenomena so long searched for.

Records of insured medical acts have similarly been expected to reveal the health of a population; claims for unemployment relief, the state of the economy; and so the volume and pattern of police-recorded incident reports are seen to reflect the moral state of a people. The ontological implications of this process are worthy of more attention than can be given here. The essential point to be made is that the social use of such information is generally little related to the actual conditions of its production, obeying an intent and purpose which often precedes and usually remains unrelated to the existence, much less the practices and structures of the institution which produces them. Yet it is often this use which subsequently determines the dominant representations of the institution and its subject matter.

Cicourel and Kitsuse (1963) in their now classic criticism of Merton's use of police statistics point out that the statistical records of institutions cannot by virtue of the very conditions of their production directly inform of socially relevant behaviour nor of individual acts. To so argue would be to ignore that there is an essential distinction between a phenomenon and the ways in which it may be known, between an event and its seizure within professional and institutional practices. The latter involve operations of selection, reduction and reconstruction which are specific to the institutional rationality of the recording organization. However, these specific record-keeping practices, to the extent that they are represented in their final product, can be extremely relevant sources of information on how the institution interacts with the individuals and groups which constitute its public. Thus, police statistics provide a glimpse into how criminal justice interacts with individuals and groups, as well as into community attitudes and the professional practices of institutional agents.

Police are massively reactive in their intervention and exercise little direct control over the volume and nature of the material submitted to them. Diverse estimates have situated the volume of matters which arise from the proactive intervention of police at between 14 per cent (Bottomley and Coleman 1981) and 20 per cent (Lévy 1985) of the total number of recorded incidents, excluding traffic offences. These involve, in the main, public order offences, enforcement of non-code statutes or regulations and secondary offences such as refusal to appear or to comply with an order. These estimates of the volume of such incidents in police statistics overestimate the actual importance of this source of incidents in the day-to-day provision of police work, due to the certainty of their inscription even where police action is neither required nor even possible. Many such incidents are discovered and closed simultaneously as a consequence of factors influencing the laying and prosecution of charges and thus involve little or no intervention nor interaction with the public.

Perhaps another 25 per cent of recorded incidents are the result of calls from other services, organizations or institutions (Bottomley and Coleman 1981). These incidents are principally composed of small thefts, frauds, vandalism and public order offences, often reported by private security personnel. The interaction of criminal justice with institutional actors is a phenomenon of considerable and growing significance (Shearing and Stenning 1987; Brodeur 1988).

Not all illegal acts, even those resulting in injury or loss of life, are equally likely to result in recording by criminal justice institutions. Acosta (1981) has advanced that certain potentially criminalizable acts committed in certain contexts comprise zones of 'privileged illegalisms'. Many such acts become the subject matter of other non-penal institutions such as labour inspection, industrial health and safety boards, grievance procedures and labour arbitration, public complaints bodies, commercial or administrative tribunals, regulatory bodies such as securities commissions, environmental protection agencies, professional disciplinary bodies, or may become the subject of civil actions. These may ultimately either precede or follow criminal pursuits in some cases, but this is the exception, and in such cases the logic by which these incidents come to be recorded by criminal justice agencies is entirely different from that which governs individual complaints. This is relevant, however, to the study of how non-institutional groups interact with the criminal justice system and we will return to this point.

For an increasing majority of incidents reported by police, however, intervention was initiated by a call for service from a private citizen, usually a complainant or victim. In fact, the place of such incidents in the supply of subject matter to the police is far greater than their share of recorded incidents would indicate in that, unlike matters arising from police or other institutional initiative, not all private calls for service lead to the recording of a founded incident.

Local police services maintain extensive reporting systems for recording calls for service. Only a selection of these, however, wind up being reported to central statistical agencies, generally those which can be mapped onto the classification system of these agencies. Systems, like Canada's Uniform

Crime Reports, despite recent efforts to the contrary on the part of agencies which design them, remain bound to the legal categories of the Criminal Code, the acts, statutes and regulations of Parliament and of provincial legislatures and municipal by-laws. Much of what police do is not related to legal categories or is not seen by them to be so and thus much of this matter may not be recorded in official central registers. Therefore, a great deal of information on claims for intervention is lost. This particularly affects emergent claims where rules of reporting or entrenched attitudes and practice discourage formal reporting and intervene especially where groups of individuals are not socially recognized as full rights-bearing citizens. In operational terms, such systemic lack of recognition occurs, for example, as negative judgements about the credibility of testimony, the receivability of evidence, the formulation of intent or, conversely, of consent, or the real possibility of legal sanction such as payment of fines or compliance with orders. In Canada, claims for criminal justice intervention by natives (in contrast to those made against natives) and, in the not so long distant past, by women may not have always been recorded.

In a classic study of calls for police intervention and police response in three American cities, Black (1970) identifies five factors which influence the decision to report. The first refers in operational terms to the officer's on-the-spot estimation of the likelihood that the incident will be retained and pursued at subsequent steps in its treatment by the criminal justice system: within the police hierarchy, by the prosecuting authority, by the magistrature, by those charged with executing an eventual sentence and, increasingly, by influential groups or institutions outside the criminal justice system — social movements or the media. This assessment is based on accumulated experience, either direct or vicarious, of the individual officer at the moment that the decision is made to retain as founded or to reject an incident.

The other factors identified by Black refer to the relational context of an incident: the insistence of the complainant that the officer pursue the complaint; the complainant's deference to the authority of the officer; the officer's perception of the social status of the complainant; the existence and nature of a relationship between the complainant and the suspect. These factors interact with each other to influence both the likelihood of reporting and the selection and representation of the specific elements of the incident which will define the substance of the report. In a general way, each of these factors addresses the same issue, the capacity of the actors to mobilize various social resources in the pursuit of a claim for intervention.

Thus complainants who are informed and insistent of their right to demand intervention, investigation and eventual prosecution, yet who at the same time show deference and respect to the responding officer, who are perceived by the officer to have sufficient status and resources to successfully support their complaint and who appear unlikely to favour non-penal means of obtaining satisfaction or of redressing their situation are more likely to have their causes taken up by the criminal justice system. Many of these characteristics of 'successful victims' are those of individuals and groups with a vested interest in the status quo, those who have been successful in ensuring the universalization of their concrete needs.

Complainants are less likely to see their cause assumed by the state: if they seem ambiguous as to whether their injuries or loss are subject to criminal action; if they appear mistrustful of the criminal justice system and its agents; if, in the perception of the responding officer, they may be unable or unwilling to participate effectively in an eventual criminal prosecution; or if they seem to show preference for more material forms of resolution. By way of illustration, a poor, black woman with young children, faced with charges of assault being laid against her male companion, may not be afforded full consideration by the attendant officer as a citizen of the state if she appears to weigh the consequences to her family and her community. In this example, concrete interpersonal solidarity and abstract citizen rights appear at odds.

Therefore the initial processes of the production of crime accounts are highly localized and reflect the actions, the experience and the representations of the immediate actors at the site and moment of their production. As a consequence, comparisons of records over time and across local jurisdictions may reflect the interplay of factors in their production: changes in the knowledge and in the self-identity of individuals or groups which affect their use of institutions; the interplay of identity, of status and of mobilizable resources; the availability and attractiveness of other means of recourse.

Once a call has been initially judged receivable and worthy of recording, it must consequently be mapped onto the reference system of official record-keeping operations. These categories are derived from law and legislation and refer each to a limited number of articles of the Criminal Code or other legislation and by-laws. It is curious to note the extent to which each party in a reporting relationship finds it entirely normal to categorize and classify events in this manner. In part this is the consequence of the success of initial selection processes. However, a number of studies have noted the stability of event classification (Pepinsky 1976; Bottomley and Coleman 1981; Robert 1985) from the initial call to police and its recording by a telephone operator through to the possible laying of charges and prosecution. Cicourel (1963) noted the persistence with which classification agents map all events onto a criminal justice classification system, even when no possibility of legal pursuit exists:

> The police must locate events and objects they investigate in some legal context, or characterize the situation in such a way that their presence or interference can be warranted

now or later on if further justification is required. The police must map the event and social objects into socially and legally relevant categories as a condition for inference and action. (Cicourel 1963 p.113)

Even in victimization surveys, in which there is no such obligation or encouragement to report incidents of harm or loss using criminal justice classi-fications, the tendency among respondents to do so is massive without regard as to whether or not an incident was actually reported (Robert 1985; Zauberman 1985; 1991). This has led a number of observers to describe this process as a sort of automatism.

This observation is important in understanding the nature of the interface between the criminal justice institution and its users. One cannot pose the anteriority of the potentially criminalizable event in the process of the produc-tion of a criminal incident. As Acosta (1987) has pointed out in his study of public breach of trust investigation, it is not possible to consider events as pre-constructed matter, thereby respectively positioning civil society as the *place of origin* of a criminal incident and the criminal justice institution as the *place of control*. A now considerable volume of work examining the role of 'social representations' in the relationships between individuals and groups and the institutions with which they interact, '*les mecanismes de renvoi*', demonstrates the impact of institutions in forming the mental schema, under-standings and behaviours which condition their use (Faugeron 1978; Faugeron and Robert 1976; Robert and Faugeron 1978; Moscovici 1976; Herzlich 1972; Belisle and Schiele 1984a, 1984b; Jodelet (ed.) 1989). The process of report-ing and reception of incidents and the entire social matter of institutions, the social production of crime, is one of complex co-determination, not always intentional in nature.

SOCIAL ACTORS AND CRIMINAL JUSTICE

A productive way to examine this process occurring at the interface of institutions and their social matter has been suggested by the Belgian clinical psychologist Christian Debuyst at the University of Louvain, initially intro-duced in 1985. In his subsequent work, Debuyst has moved beyond the study of the intimate ethological processes which underlie the bringing of private pains to public places, the condemnation of the acts of others and the process of the production of the criminal law, incorporating into his work the insights of Alain Touraine (1984) concerning social agency.

This original and somewhat unusual evolution has opened a number of new perspectives for the study of criminal law and justice from many disciplinary perspectives. In September 1989 an international scientific gathering in honour of Debuyst, involving several hundred researchers and research institutions covering many disciplines, attempted to bring together these new perspectives. Thirty from among the papers presented have been published in a collection in honour of Debuyst (Mardaga 1990).

The notion of social actor enables legal theorists to transcend the traditional paradigm of free will and constraint and the methodological individualism of positivism. It places the cognitive and interpretative dimension at the centre of the study of the production and the institution of criminal law and further recognizes that this dimension is comprised of 'fictions'. These 'fictions' are dynamic in that they express not passive modes of knowledge but incorporate a capacity for transformational vision. Debuyst uses the term 'utopia', in the sense of its use by Mannheim (1956) and by Bloch (1959), to express that the 'fiction' of crime is, by its very essence, indissociable from an elemental discord or conflict between experience and identity (injustice) and from an individual and collective desire to realize identity (justice). In this way, criminal justice and social movements are nourished from the same substance and social matter and are equally dependent upon a capacity for abstraction from this matter.

Finally, the notion of social actor, as put forward by Debuyst, places the subject of law firmly within the framework of social relations and human agency:

> C'est dans le cadre sociétal ou dans celui des inter-relations que l'homme est appelé à être acteur, c'est-à-dire 'agissant' ou intervenant, 'qu'il s'y trouve confronté à des règles c'est-à-dire à un langage selon lequel il importe de s'exprimer, confronté également au fait de se trouver constamment pris dans des jeux de pouvoir' et de vivre dans ses relations avec les autres à l'intérieur ou au-delà de ces jeux, des processus de reconnaissance ou de non-reconnaissance qui paraissent essentiels dans l'élaboration de sa propre identité. (Debuyst 1985 p.26)

The diversity of contributions to the 1989 gathering in Brussels reflects the fecundity of the notion of social actor. Discussions ranged from the physiology of the human brain and the study of intimate cognitive processes to collective action at the level of peer groups, professions, institutions and social movements, from the processes by which actors are socially constructed to those by which actors become social actors. But the most significant contribution of the introduction of the notion of social actor to the study of criminal justice is to the study of the roles of individuals and groups in the creation and the institution of criminal law itself and to the social processes which underlie the processes of incrimination and criminalization.

SOCIAL MOVEMENTS AND THE CRIMINAL LAW

Philippe Robert suggests that two stages intervene in the production of penal norms. The first of these is that of incrimination, or of the production of the possibility of penal sanction. The second is that of criminalization, or the actual recourse to penal sanction by diverse actors. The first process has been relatively more examined than the latter. Recent work on violence (Walker 1990), the reform of sexual assault laws (Pitch 1985; Pires and Roberts 1992), on the production of traffic laws and the creation of the infraction of drinking-driving (Gusfield 1981; Leboeuf 1990) have all explored the role of various interest groups as social actors — bureaucrats, professions, social movements — in the production of law.[3]

However, the latter process, that by which the law is utilized as a resource by individuals and groups in social interaction and, both conversely and simultaneously, that by which the law orients and defines the identities, intentions and actions of individuals and groups, has been relatively ignored. Nonetheless, the formal possibility of criminalization does not render its realization inevitable nor determine its use. Some sources of potential criminalization or penal sanction are seldom if ever used and thus seem to fulfil their purpose by their existence alone. The creation of a legal sanction is the least costly manner for a government to take action. Some sanctions serve only to define or generate norms. Others are effectively neutralized in the play of competing forces in their application. Among the social actors in force in this process, claimants to intervention or 'victims' be they direct or indirect, individual or collective, play a central though not a dominant role.

Such a focus on the place of the victim as claimant runs counter to a recent but influential utilitarian tradition in criminal justice literature which also examines the role of the victim but in a radically different manner. This 'victimology' literature simultaneously positions the victim in the liberal positivist tradition as the individual bearer of a right to claim that the state substitute itself for the victim in a state action, and in a utilitarian welfare model as a privileged consumer of state resources to indemnify harm or loss. In some ways, this current reflects symmetrically the traditional welfare rights debate, and carries with it the same problems inherent in the fundamentally contradictory framing of rights as utilities.

We have referred already to this growing utilitarian trend in criminal justice to understand intervention as a producer of concrete, material benefits to those who invoke it. It is the consequence of the relatively recent large-scale incursion of social movements into criminal justice and of their efforts to transform criminal justice intervention into a 'weapon of the weak'. By arguing for more systematic charging and prosecution of those who harm their constituents, social movements increase the status of their members by portraying them as bearers of rights to be included in the state. From this stance of inclusion it is then more easily argued that the concrete needs of the constituency are legitimate and merit priority over the competing needs of others in the allocation of resources.

This is only true, however, of those needs which arise from the criminalized action and not of other substantive or identity needs of claimants. For instance, it is not the need for housing of women-led families without adequate income from employment which is met by the women's shelter movement, but rather the need for immediate and temporary redress of the harm incurred by the victim of a criminalizable assault. The costs of assuming the victim role are therefore high, both for the individual and the social movement, and its consequences ambiguous. As Walker (1990) points out, positioning claims in this manner can facilitate their absorption by the state.[4] The growing use by the state of criminal justice to impose specific definitional frameworks on situations and to control access to or to distribute resources palliates its incapacity to ration resources in a time of fiscal crisis. Yet, for highly marginalized groups these 'weapons of the weak' may be the only initial recourse.

In the strict sense, the satisfaction of needs, even those of victims of criminal acts, is not the business of the criminal justice system. Opposition to the proliferation of services to victims within the criminal justice system comes from those quarters who hold to a formally legalist definition of the role and scope of criminal justice. In this view, criminal law is distinct from other areas of law in that it neither remediates nor indemnifies but merely determines culpability and punishment. Criminal law must be used sparingly and without design. The use of criminal justice as a means to gain access to, or to distribute resources is anathema to such a formal legalist view, in that it can only be at the expense of its more fundamental role to include or to exclude individuals as regards the rights and freedoms of citizens, and can only lead to a massive inflation of the matter criminal justice is called upon to consider.

The opposing utilitarian view is that the rights of citizens, as materialized through the criminal justice system, comprise more than the formal rights of inclusion or exclusion as regards citizenship, but also extend to the normative claims of citizens to security and safety. Thus, criminal justice must do more than merely determine culpability and punishment, but must also protect and indemnify citizens from harm. In this way, criminal justice operates increasingly as a welfare service system. Community policing, victim's rights, indeterminate sentencing, offender classification and treatment of offenders are all features of utilitarianism in criminal justice.

The study of how criminal law and the use of penal sanction is brought into play in particular situations of conflict or of blockage by both individuals and groups must examine their role not merely as abstract bearers of rights, nor as consumers of utilities, but as social actors. Competing interests seek to impose specific definitional frameworks upon situations and behaviours which may emerge as public problems. Some interest groups in any particular situation attempt to influence perceptions so as to increase the importance given to the particular aspect of a 'problem' to which they direct their intervention. Conversely, other interest groups may seek to diminish the perceived importance of aspects for which they may be deemed responsible.

Interest groups may demand the criminalization of situations and an increased police role. The criminalization of a problem can often enhance its symbolic status. Victims of criminal acts are perceived by definition as rights-bearing citizens with legitimate claims against the state. For interest groups representing segments of the population which have not traditionally had access to full rights of citizenship, the call for increased police attention to the sources of their victimization can be a means of achieving higher status and greater access to resources. Other groups will struggle to avoid criminalization or even order-maintenance interventions by police organizations. The capacity to avoid criminalization of forms of deviance common to a group is traditionally a good indicator of a group's status. Professionals, employers, commercial interests and other elite groups have succeeded quite well at maintaining internal control over disciplinary functions and keeping their deviance out of the criminal justice system.[5]

Collective use of claims for criminal or legal sanction may figure into the strategies of social actors to serve ends other than criminalization. Even where the possibility of criminalization may not exist, the use of criminal metaphors to describe the experience of a group can serve to legitimize its other claims for resources. Such has been the strategy of some women's groups around some issues of abuse and neglect. Child welfare advocates have similarly made use of criminal justice metaphors. Conversely, criminalization, real or rhetorical, may also serve to withhold resources, as in the case of substance abuse and prostitution, for example. Certain uses of criminalization are founded on understandings of its consequences which are dubious at best: a faith in the deterrence value of penal sanction or in the real potential for incapacitation of the perpetrator. Many groups active in the process of criminalization have contributed to the diffusion of a large number of myths pertaining to the substantive effectiveness of criminalization, either strategically or unwittingly. The dangers inherent in the use of criminal justice by marginalized groups are often not well understood.

Finally, a programme of investigation is needed to examine how the use of criminal recourse interacts with other forms of redress and the establishment of identity. The constant and considerable inflation of the matter of criminal justice in the postwar period reveals that recourse to criminalization has long ceased to constitute an ultimate recourse but has become a response to conflict.

Yet, this phenomenon has been little studied. The increasing criminalization of all forms of violence, including symbolic forms of violence, reveals a loss of capacity on the part of individuals and groups to achieve recognition and resources through other means. Yet, the micro-processes at work are not fully understood.

NOTES

1   Such divisions are extensively explored by Delmas-Marty (1992). Baratta (1991) proposes a nomenclature defining two schools of thought on the functions of criminal law: the classical school, which we associate here with the primacy of inclusionary rights, and the social school, which we refer to as a utilitarian model of criminal law.
2   See also Mathews and Young (eds) (1986).
3   For an excellent review of French research in this area over the past decade see Faugeron (1991).
4   Using the methods of institutional ethnology, Walker (1990, 1993) has examined the processes of institutional absorption of the issue of wife battering. She has thus addressed the complexities of individuals' and groups' roles and relations to the institutional forms by which power is exercised and domination maintained. Thus she focuses on the actual organization of the state and its institutional mandates. She shows that the constraints which women experience are traceable to jurisdictional and bureaucratic practices.
5   On this point, the work of Pierre Lascoumes (1985, 1986) on such diverse objects as public breach of trust, fraud, environmental 'crimes', and the use of penal sanction in administrative law has been fascinating.

CLAIMSMAKING AND COLLECTIVE ACTION

10. Social Movements and Social Welfare: The Political Problem of Needs

Henri Lustiger-Thaler and Eric Shragge

It is long overdue that critical thinking about social movements be evaluated in light of a general theory of welfare. It comes as no surprise, therefore, that contemporary social movements, in their many voices, identities and forms of claimsmaking, are capturing the attention of a wide range of disciplines. With mounting attacks on the welfare state, mixed with the massive impact of global restructuring, the contemporary role of social movements is high on the analytical rosters of a good many theorists.

Our interest is to explain processes of mobilization around collectively defined and provisional needs. The argument we put forward states that the manner in which social movements frame and interpret needs is critical to the elaboration of any future democratic design of the welfare state, and the well-being one nominally attaches to it. We will be arguing, with the help of some concept building and selected case studies, that the trajectory of social movement analysis, to date, can be fruitfully advanced through a consideration of how welfare needs are collectively articulated, and of the environing universe of interpretations which surround them. We make no attempt here to engage the 'deeper' nature of human needs as outlined by Doyal and Gough (1991) or Drover and Kerans (*supra*) though our mezo-theoretical approach for a theory of social action has obvious implications for collective forms of mobilization around issues of need satisfaction as a measure of welfare outcomes.

We will be making frequent reference to the importance of 'social rights' and 'rights of inclusion' inherent in the structures of formal democracy. We will also be alluding to 'counter-rights' (gleaned from the Critical Legal Studies School) as a way of speaking about the political practices of movements within formal democratic processes. We mean the following when referring to these differentiated rights: social rights refer to the outcomes of conflicting need interpretations that rule work, income, health, education, etc.

These are the rights T.H. Marshall brought attention to in his seminal discussion of social citizenship (Marshall 1965 [1949]). Our own understanding of these rights, however, is based on a critical appreciation of the inherent limits of pluralism, by dint of the fact that these rights are constituted by the exclusion and subordination of rights in other categories of human activity. The notion of *rights of inclusion* refers to the struggles of movements to secure a place in the political sphere, underscoring goal-oriented movement behaviour as a conscious *politics of recognition*, pursued within formal political channels. As concerns our case studies this refers to community organizations seeking inclusion within a welfare and social policy decision-making framework. Rights of inclusion are indicative of a liberal-inspired moment of participation, based on universality. They are operative in the traditional *political relationship* that formal democracy leaves relatively open. Social rights are operative in the traditional *welfare relationship*. Both are premised on a property-based liberal version of rights underwriting universality, and the need for integrating new forms of political representation in the management of social equity.

In contradistinction, *counter-rights* refer to actions by movements to create different forms of political and organizational praxis. These practices initially start outside the state, but move into a closer relationship with the state as groups receive funding and credentials. We make no sharp distinction between counter-rights and the terrain of liberal rights. This is in keeping with what we understand to be the deep nature of their contradictory and dialogical relationship in liberal discourse. Counter-rights are counterfactual moments and can be invoked on the level of the goods that liberal discourse most cherishes, for example, economic independence, ability to enter into social relations on an equal footing, etc.[1] Counter-rights take seriously the dynamism of bourgeois society and the rapid changes in its relations of social contact. They are invoked within communities as mobilized expressions of needs dissatisfaction. These rights function within and outside the state, with the telos of transcending the contradictions and paradoxes of liberal discourse, while being deeply enshrined in them.

In brief, these instances within the contradictions of liberal discourse underscore the political imaginary of movements, exercising, as Jean Luc Nancy so aptly put it, their ability to think 'on the limit' of the political (Nancy 1991). This characteristic also distinguishes the type of movements we are examining from regressive and reactionary backward-looking expressions of collective behaviour. The singular premise that these social movements do not seek to undermine the ethical basis of liberalism, but rather extend its contradictions towards mediated forms of communicative rationality, attests to their forward-looking agenda.[2]

This renders the relationship of social movements to the state a functional paradox, rather than a contained series of self-limiting practices.[3] The paradox is socio-political in that formal democracy is incapable of revealing its own inequalities, thereby consistently nurturing negativity (social movements), which in turn brings out the central liberal contradiction that the type of society it hopes to constitute 'can be conceived only as a consistent realization of the high principles of formal democracy' (Heller 1988 p.141). By drawing attention to this basically conflicting matrix of social rights, rights of inclusion and counter-rights, we hope to bring to the foreground the importance of social movements in the radicalization and interpretation of claimsmaking within a context of welfare, creating, as it were, new discursive surfaces for political and social action. We shall be supporting our contentions with case studies on alternative service organizations (ASO) and community economic development (CED) in Montreal. These case studies are focused on the practices of groups interfacing with the state on a continuous basis, involved in the political organization of needs, rights of inclusion, counter-rights, but perhaps most importantly, the establishment of alternative forms of welfare provision.

Thinking about a general theory of welfare also has several implications for contemporary social movement analysis. The following are some tentative suggestions:

a) The matrix of material and post-material values integral to a theory of welfare makes it clearly inadequate to view movements simply as socio-cultural phenomena, as in the New Social Movements literature. Neither can one only view movements as rationally fixed on inclusion processes (as is the case in Resource Mobilization Theory). The traffic on the bridge linking institutionalized and non-institutionalized practices and forms of action necessarily flows both ways. Nowhere is this clearer than when examining the socio-political context of movements and their relationship to different orders of government and the state.

b) An adequate theory of social movements should demonstrate how movements enter the political field and produce knowledge about that entry.

c) Social movement analysis must be redirected towards a consideration of what is really at 'stake' in new forms of political representation, above the clash of 'identity wars'; for example the differential distribution of what we refer to here as rights of inclusion, the conflicting production of counter-rights, and their impacts on institutional transformation and institution-building.

TOWARDS A DEFINITION OF PARALLEL AGENCY FOR SOCIAL MOVEMENTS

Bringing together the problem of movements and of welfare requires a model of social action that can accommodate the interdependency of both the normative and the analytical, whilst maintaining the usefulness of their separate standpoints. Our use of the term parallel agency (PA) hopes to bridge these two important criteria. PA explains the capacity of social movements to inscribe dual sets of meaning within state and society. We will be building this concept in a very tentative manner. It will be employed as a conceptual construct through which to view the process of inclusion of movements within the state (rights of inclusion) and how the meaning and knowledge produced by that socio-political process bears consequences for other areas of movement activity. PA is a way therefore to decipher and examine the logic of various simultaneous collective actions, or how movements gesture in several directions at once.

It is useful to draw out two distinct yet interrelated moments in the parallel agency of movements (PA1 and PA2). In PA1, inclusion within the formal political process, or regulatory environments created by the state, are *prima facie* to the activity and mobilization base of social movements. The politics that emerge from this are issue oriented and contain an ethic of participation. This occurs both as a need in civil society, for representation, and as a response to the regulatory state for innovation in areas of welfare. The type of political agency that emerges out of this deals with rights already built into the statist checks and balances of a given political system and its level of democratic accountability.

Inclusion of movements in the state is concretized through the formalism of funding, which appears hand-in-hand with the ever-present threat posed by the withdrawal of financial aid to projects. As movements interface with the state, forms of political agency emerge, based on status attribution and limited forms of social partnership. These practices partially reconstitute the normative claims of movements by marking off boundaries and spheres of reciprocity and power. These also partially define and structure public and private space around work, the family, etc., as movements are encouraged to clientalize and personalize their local constituency.

PA1, therefore, represents an institutional moment which gives voice to movements through the language of rights of inclusion, within the state. There is a politics of risk involved here in that this allows movements to articulate needs (on however small and limited a scale) that merge contradictory divisions in the liberal foundations of the capitalist state. This creates a double-edged sword for both movements and the state. Local economic development is an excellent case in point. CED initiatives create linkages between the economic and political, integrating welfare and market concerns within given spatial areas. This builds a haven for the development of alternative responses to local markets, which remain structurally hostile to these types of initiatives.

The liberal democratic state, while transferring statutory functions and responsibilities towards voluntary groups, in a sense creating a 'welfare community' (through its need for innovation in urban partnerships) offers the strategic possibility for movements to claim political expertise in problematic social areas. This appears to be one of the new logics of flexible welfare provision. Through a general upgrading of local politics in the overall political system, the urban movements we are looking at have become adept at channelling the contradictions of the state off the terrain of national and regional social policy and into recesses of local society.

As the process led by CED organizations takes shape around the integration of market and welfare, the state in its efforts to tap endogenous sources emerges as a key partner in community initiatives. In this, a definition of rights of both an individual and collective nature is functionally cast. The state chooses winners and losers, reinventing movements as subjects with responsibilities, conflating their subjectivity with a proprietorship over rights of participation and inclusion. This actually deepens the political crisis within the state by bringing the normative dimension (radical need interpretations) of social movements onto the terrain of the state, thereby ensuring mobilization beyond its frontiers.

Because of the inherent contradictions of the state, this process accords movements a property right in new if ambivalent political spaces. One manifest contradiction is that in so doing, the liberal capitalist state demonstrates its inability to distinguish the type of social and political relations that it itself contributes to through its necessary interaction with movements. The urban-based movements we are examining suggest that this tension and interplay of normative contraries is not lost on local actors. The meaning movements bring to the state cannot therefore simply be seen as part of a process of co-optation or appropriation of statist or 'movement' values. Rather, as social movements interface with the state there is an overlapping of critical moments which produce political rights of inclusion, a reanimated local discourse around existing social rights, and knowledge about both forms of rights. It is in this morass of social rights and rights of inclusion that social movements become agents through the state, extending the politics and contradictions of their newly acquired political form into the public orbit of civil society.

The second moment in parallel agency (PA2) is concerned with forms of praxis and intersubjectivity which occur outside the state as such. It is here that the putative framing of needs by the liberal state (a state which sees all rights as equally endowed) meets a counterfactual interpretation of power. This moment is concerned with the socio-political context of social movements, as actors with extraneous sources of legitimation in everyday life. Rights of inclusion as a form of action and meaning become an issue *beyond* the state, as they are brought to civil society through mediation networks that have emerged out of the process of status attribution discussed above. It must be clearly stated however that the precondition of the relationship between PA1 and PA2 is the existence of the democratic-legal state. It is on this political and cognitive basis that social movements (immersed in the social conditions for the enactment of rights of inclusion and social rights) have a powerful basis for formulating 'counter-rights' (radical needs interpretation) in opposition to the property-based and commodified model.

Unger (1987) is useful in elaborating a more precise definition of counter-rights for social movements that has resonance for the building of alternative welfare institutions. Unger speaks of the essential contradiction of liberal rights, building his critique on the basis that goods (rights of inclusion, social rights) within the liberal state represent an important political territory for radical thought. He argues that liberal rights, around economic independence and the right to enter into a social relationship on an equal footing, should be challenged by rights which protect the very goods valued by a liberal sense of justice. *Immunity rights* would protect bodily and spatial security against organizations. *Destabilization rights* would protect actions aimed at disrupting social hierarchies that insulate themselves from contestation and threaten self-government. These rights would guarantee participation. *Market rights* would entitle individuals to a share of social capital, reducing the economic power of elites to withhold the means of livelihood and provide a basis for workplace democracy. *Solidarity rights* would express and generalize communal ties and expectations of mutual reliance. However the counterfactuality of these claims are indicative of the challenge that movements bring to politics as increasingly legitimate actors, creating a normative basis for new knowledge about the boundaries of freedom and equality.

PA1 and PA2 are therefore by their very nature, normatively based phenomena as well as analytical constructs, and must inevitably be thinly sliced.[4] It is here that one can reasonably talk about contemporary movements as representing a new praxis of social citizenship, by giving voice and perception to those political conditions and anomalies underlying the general social environment of structured inequality.

THE POLITICAL INTERPRETATION OF NEEDS AS A FORM OF SOCIAL MOVEMENT PRAXIS

To recapitulate our argument to this point: social movements contain two types of discourses regarding the political interpretation of needs — a discourse of rights of inclusion within a political system of action, and an overlapping discourse of counter-rights directed towards institutional transformation and institution-building. These rights and practices are not mutually exclusive, but dialectically intermeshed through the parallel agency of movements themselves which tightly meld together these forms of action with the state. For example, the liberal state has a property-based and commodified notion of needs that is imposed upon local movements. Operating through the state, movements are immersed in a liberal process that emits contradictory signals. This process, though appealing to universal principles, is undermined by a market rationality that intrinsically places some needs over others, reproducing the power relations of a class, gender and racially structured society. This creates a hierarchy of needs and *need dissatisfaction* at the very core of the welfare state and increasingly the *welfare community*. In this sense, the building of counter-rights by social movements underscores their desire to restrict the liberal *levelling process*, by bringing up issues of structural inequality amongst all needs.

In this analytical process, to overly separate state and civil society obscures the importance of how social movements in society engage the political sphere. Clearly, the relationship between movements and the state has moved faster than the still Manichaean view of many movement theorists, particularly on the question of institutionalization. Perhaps one of the most critical elements this underscores is that social movements, as actors through and beyond the state, are agents of knowledge, by their very inclusion within a process of institutional transformation that cuts across the boundaries of state and society. Their contradictory *Realpolitik* is such that they express needs through formal institutions and political parties that are not always structured around radical demands or counter-rights, as we described them above. Social movements, as political actors, are embroiled in the contradictory process of formal democracy, inasmuch as the liberal democratic-legal state becomes the basis for their action.

Equally important, however, are the forms of representation which social movements build within society. The creation of alternative institutions around counter-rights is a key function of contemporary movements in the field of welfare. This distinguishes them from loosely-based interest groups. Counter-rights as practices create a critique of reigning understandings of needs. This critique must secure a representational political space outside the capitalist state, though always using its liberal democratic base as a point of dialogue and contestation. The state as a political sphere for the enactment of counter-rights is inappropriate for two reasons: firstly, decision-making within the liberal-capitalist state is reached through ideological priority given to equally legitimate needs. Agnes Heller's (1985) work is instructive here. She argues that the pluralistic state can never be the source of elaboration of new systems of needs, due to its legalistic structure. Only public life can be a channel for the critique of needs. Social movements as harbingers of a grounded grassroots understanding of social citizenship are indicative of the premise that needs can never find their origin in the state. At most, the state can establish a framework for the social decisions of a more decentralized structure of power. Secondly, social movements, through their alternative projects, create knowledge within and beyond the state. On this critical basis they represent one of the few authentic socio-political voices that can speak of a different kind of state.

ALTERNATIVE SERVICE ORGANIZATIONS AND COMMUNITY ECONOMIC DEVELOPMENT

We have chosen to look at Alternative Service Organizations (ASOs) and Community Economic Development (CED) groups drawn from practices in the Montreal area. Both are organizations that address needs which reorder spaces between the state and society. These social movement/community organizations combine the radicalization of everyday life with a service orientation that addresses needs of specific populations.

The link between service and politics is both the source of tension and a means of promoting social change. Furthermore, in the development of forms of social provision, and the process of making new claims on the state for the support of these initiatives, these organizations have played an increasingly important role. They have not only promoted innovations but also have presented prototypes which the welfare state has either copied (without their more radical content) and/or integrated within a logic of political cultural practices underscoring the new flexible welfare design.

ASOs have been described as organizations founded by local initiative to offer an alternative to established human services. This service is an alternative because it offers a different product (e.g. shelters for battered women), employs a different method of intervention (e.g. hotlines), or targets a different population (e.g. services for people suffering from AIDS). ASOs fill gaps in the existing social services by providing innovative social service delivery as well as promoting social change. The demystification of professional knowledge is a related feature. These organizations tend to resist bureaucratic structures and process (Powell 1986). ASOs have developed democratic forms of organization that encourage the participation of staff, volunteers and community representatives. In general, ASOs combine both service delivery and an agenda for social change linked to the empowerment of the population served, within a democratic structure. As mentioned earlier, mechanisms of change and the vitality of social practices depend on the ability to adapt to new conditions and embrace often contradictory components.

The relationship between an ASO and the state is central, particularly on questions of funding. An ASO lives a delicate balance between its autonomy to build an alternative practice, and becoming an extension of a state-defined service provision. In the present context in Quebec, the provincial government, the principal funder of the health and social services, has linked funding of community organizations to a partnership in service delivery, underscoring the new flexible welfare model. ASOs have fought for many years for the right of inclusion and legitimacy as agents of service delivery. The consequence of these new policies is to shift the terrain of struggle. This shift from an *ad hoc* relation to the state towards a formal right of inclusion and politics of recognition by the state will increase tensions for ASOs in maintaining their autonomy and locally defined practices.

CED has taken a variety of forms and orientations. It has been promoted as a new approach to community organization that broadens the self-management movement to include the creation of community-based economic initiatives. It is a strategy used by low-income communities to stimulate economic development, particularly through job creation and employability strategies. Furthermore, CED embodies a vision of an alternative form of economic development that links the need for job creation with locally controlled and self-managed enterprises that address social needs and encourage local empowerment (Shragge 1990). The same tensions between social and political change and service provision faced by ASOs are similar for CED. From a social movement perspective, the conflicts are between traditional forms of economic development and employability measures for local residents, and approaches that argue for a social economy, democratically planned and controlled, with cooperative principles as the means of organization.

ASOs: from Mobilization to Service Delivery

The ASOs that developed in Montreal during the 1960s and 1970s emerged out of the student, feminist and community organization/new left movements. Clinics were put in place by alliances of 'radical' professionals and students, community organizers, local residents, the women's movement, and by the youth culture of the period. Examples include the Pointe St. Charles Community Clinic, a health clinic in a working-class neighbourhood that was established in the early 1970s and continues to provide a combination of traditional medical services with preventative programmes and forms of political action and advocacy.

The most successful of the ASOs were those organized by the women's movement to address issues of rape and violence. These have been organized in many communities with a variety of models including collective decision-making processes and political mobilization. In addition, these groups have organized *regroupements*, or coalitions, for legitimacy in the wider community and with government, both to protect and increase their funding, as well as to educate the public on these questions.

There are two areas of practice important to ASOs: first are the links created by these organizations between the delivery of services and the promotion of social change, either as advocates for the population that they serve or through its mobilization. Second is the chosen form of mobilization and organization which defines internal principles of non-hierarchical modes of organization and/or greater community participation.

Within the general sphere of services, provision and demands for social and political change are usually separated. Direct service provision is often viewed as a professional and technical relation between service providers and clients. 'Personal troubles' are not acted upon as though they were 'public issues'. The private and the public are clearly defined. In contrast, many ASOs have engaged in a wide range of struggles which implode this distinction. For example, much of the recent struggle against a retrograde welfare reform in Quebec came from community clinics either through the 'lending' of staff to coalitions directly engaged in that struggle or through the mobilization of welfare recipients in their own communities. Shelters for battered women and rape crisis centres have been in the forefront in both public education and lobbying for changes in government policies. Many of the ASOs in Quebec have formed *regroupements* of their own in order to pressure and lobby government for funding (demanding inclusion within the provision of welfare) and in the process have politicized that funding.

The current debate has been one of the legitimacy of autonomous community organizations to provide a service and to decide locally the nature, content, and form of organization of that service. The resulting tension has not only been the amount of support that they will receive from government, but also the conditions of funding, including the relationship to other state institutions such as the social services or state community clinics (CLSCs). The form of parallel agency (PA1) that ASOs engage in, and the rights of inclusion they are negotiating, are central to new and emerging regimes of flexible welfare that seek not only to incorporate these services, but also to do so in a way that implies only limited obligation for adequate and long-term funding.

The internal forms of organization of many ASOs have reflected their commitment to a radical democratic orientation. This is indicative of the process of parallel agency (PA2) in which radical needs and practices are linked to an extension of democratic rights, particularly the right to control social institutions, even though these are increasingly negotiated through the state. The democratic practices of ASOs are expressed in three ways. First, the structure of boards (required by law in order to receive funding) can be selected in a democratic way. The clinic mentioned above has an annual general meeting in the community which elects the majority membership of the board, with staff representatives making up the rest. Similarly, other ASOs draw their board from an open membership process. These structures keep the organization both grounded and accountable to the needs and priorities of the local community. Second, internally, a characteristic of the ASOs is their attempts to avoid or reduce hierarchical structures. Collectives with shared decision-making, and equal salaries, continue in women's shelters, rape crisis centres and some clinics. This process of inclusive decision-making fosters alternative perspectives. The third aspect of democratization is anti-professionalism through the use of volunteers. ASOs clearly represent a concrete link between movement ideals and institution-building around needs satisfactions.

Community Economic Development: from Movement to Institution?

The CED projects were a response to the failure of the local economy in Montreal to provide jobs with adequate wages to working-class neighbourhoods. The 'deindustrialization' of these areas and the inadequate opportunities for immigrants and refugees arriving in Montreal has created a situation of chronically high levels of unemployment and related elevated levels of poverty. CED was a recognition by community organizations that new initiatives and interventions were required if these problems were to be addressed. With a revival of an entrepreneurial culture in the province at large, communities have been given status by the provincial and local state as necessary players in economic development and welfare distribution. Indeed, the state through its support of community economic development encourages the mixing of market and welfare for growing clients of a devolving welfare state. Yet there is a risk here, particularly for the local state. The question is what kind of player, and what kind of vision and orientation will the new CED develop. A contradiction has already emerged in the actual practices of CED in Montreal between the competing traditions of a community movement and a market and private business orientation.

This alliance is inherently contradictory since the local state allied with local business interests pushes for market-driven models of development while the community component demands both jobs, which address poverty and unemployment, and an economic development plan, which contributes to the social development of the community. The stakes here certainly are higher than at any other time in the relations between urban social movements and local government in Montreal. The process of devolution of the welfare state and the upgrading of local politics have created a local welfare corporatism in which movements (through their community organizations) are now credentialed and recognized players.

A further point of conflict emerges between the social movement/community's tradition of a radical participatory democracy that stands in contrast to the private sector belief that ownership implies control of all economic decision-making. A variety of approaches to CED have been attempted ranging from new partnerships to achieve capitalist forms of development to initiatives to create democratic economic experiments.

The policy of the City of Montreal is to give priority to two areas of CED practice. These tend to push the CED organizations in a more conservative direction that emphasizes traditional forms of economic development. As a means of addressing the high levels of unemployment and poverty, employability programmes are put forward as a major area of activity for the CED organizations. The consequence of this priority is to push the CED organizations in the direction of individualized service delivery, thus diminishing the more collective forms of action that are associated with community organizations, and changing these groups into service programmes that are the extension of the usual functions of the state. The second priority is *concertation* between unions, business and community in order to promote solutions to the problems of local economic development. This configuration of interests expressed through the boards of these agencies along with the pressures of funders for saving local business and promoting small and medium-size enterprises have further pushed the CED organizations into the economic mainstream. This orientation sets out the parameters in which CED is practised; however, the CED organizations, largely from the pressures exerted by community groups and agencies, have developed both a political voice and forms of alternative economic development.

With this voice, CED has challenged the traditional rights of those who make unilateral economic decisions, without concern for the social costs or alternative social benefits that might be derived from the project. For example, RESO, a CED, resisted the zoning conversion of one area from light industry to middle-class condominiums in order to protect at least some industrial jobs. It challenged McGill University's buying of an old industrial building and converting it into dormitories. As part of the compromise, McGill was forced to guarantee the renovation and maintenance jobs to local people, and invest $500,000 in social housing. The other CED organizations have not moved as clearly in this direction, but the community voice on several of their boards is pushing for an orientation that emphasizes the social dimension rather than only the economic. With the exception of RESO, these organizations are only at most a few years old and are struggling for a social perspective to put forward.

The second component is the creation of new forms of economic practice that can be described as linking the social with the economic and finding new ways to build democratic alternatives that can reach marginalized groups. There are many examples which attempt to reach these objectives. The most innovative practice has been developed by Centre d'Innovation Développement Economique Locale (CIDEL), which has recently become a unit of one of the CED organizations. It has used an empowerment approach in which projects created are controlled by the participants. These include: the establishment of a community loan fund to support micro-enterprises and social housing; loan circles composed of women working in small independent production and offering mutual aid, technical support and small loans; women's production cooperatives; and collective kitchens and a 'popular' restaurant as a means of addressing hunger. None of these are on a large scale, and make little impact on the level of unemployment, but they do represent an economic practice that emphasizes democratic control.

The economic problems faced by the city of Montreal have forced it to search for new partners. Neighbourhoods have gained access to this process and consequently this right of inclusion has led to new resources being available to community-based organizations. This has opened up possibilities for nurturing a legitimate oppositional voice on social priorities for the urban economy. Counter-rights to redefine what is considered economically legitimate appear to be the terrain of the new social and political citizenship sculpted by social movements.

THEMES AND ISSUES

ASOs and CED organizations were built as community-based initiatives and as a means of addressing social problems and issues in such a way that members and those served could have a greater control of their economic and social lives. These organizations began in contested struggles, often with an historical adversarial relationship to the state and the private economy. On the one hand they demand a right of inclusion in order to receive support and recognition; on the other, they are part of a struggle for counter-rights. ASOs and CED display a parallel agency that places them at the juncture of the state and society. Living this process is obviously tricky and the stakes for these community organizations and the state are high.

We have described organizations that have been financed by the state, but at the same time, they have been able to protect their autonomy in order to preserve and extend more radical programmes, participate in community struggles, govern themselves democratically, and find ways to empower their members. One of the questions that follows from this is why the state, through different levels and departments, has allowed or needed this to occur. In the current period, there are several important factors that contribute to the state's support for these activities.

ASOs in Quebec are in the midst of negotiating a new status with the provincial government. In this reform ASOs will receive both formal representation in regional decision-making structures, as well as more clearly defined and predictable funding. Given their lack of funding alternatives, there is no other choice but to enter into this partnership. However, the structuring of flexible welfare and its dispersal of services gives some play to this relationship. In the 1960s and 1970s, the welfare state was established through large-scale institution-building. With attempts by the state to cut back on government spending and find more flexible ways to provide services, community organizations have become a low-cost option, if they can be integrated easily into state structures and processes.

Similarly, the CED organizations have entered into partnership with the local state. The city is facing the deterioration of the local economy propelled forward by globalization, free trade and cutbacks in financing from higher levels of government. It clearly has limited means at its disposal to promote economic growth. The city would like to see the CED organizations as promoters of private accumulation and growth, and play a role in labour market integration; but because of the traditions and interests of the CED groups, another vision has become present — one that puts social needs, innovation and a democratic economy as a priority.

An immediate question arises. What are the factors that allow for a level of autonomy for ASOs and CED organizations? The historical origins of ASOs as social movements point these groups in radical directions. Yet, the power of the state, particularly through funding arrangements, acts to constrain and to reshape these initiatives. Community groups have used the following practices to reduce pressures from the state. They have maintained strong linkages with the local community. This includes the ability to mobilize both local organizations and individuals in order to defend the programme or practice of the ASOs or CED organization. Both the Pointe St. Charles Clinic and CIDEL-GP have to some extent defended themselves against changes proposed by the state that would have restricted their practices. Linkages with similar organizations have also been helpful. ASOs in Quebec, particularly those providing services to women through shelters and rape crisis centres, have used their *regroupements* as a means of pressuring government.

These services have gained a degree of legitimacy on particular issues, although they remain underfunded. In both CED and ASOs, there is a high turnover of both staff and board members. Community groups have nurtured practices that both maintain and revitalize their political and social vision in order to have a chance at resisting external pressures. The existence of non-hierarchical internal structures, and community forms of participation have contributed to the vitality of the organization and its ability to develop autonomous practices. The practices of CED and ASOs are prefigurative of the type of *market rights* and *solidarity rights* that Unger (1986) speaks of, in which individuals demand a share of social capital as part of their interpretation of needs. This has led to a redefinition of the means of livelihood, as well as expressing and generalizing communal ties and expectations of mutual reliance.

The argument implicit in our paper is that ASOs and CED, through a complex series of intermediations, rights and parallel agencies, emerge as a democratic alternative to the more centralized and bureaucratic welfare state. This begs the question of universality. What happens to communities unable to organize themselves, to build those olinion or points of service? Does centralization, as a means of administering and planning a universal welfare state, automatically imply the loss of empowerment by communities? Alternatively, what is the future of the *welfare community*? The relationship of local to central authority is a critical question, as universal standards for health care and social services will necessarily require greater defence in the future.

In other words, can there be local radical democratic control with higher levels of government playing a redistributive role? The ability of local communities to play an important part in creating institutions to meet various needs through democratic structures is clear. Critical issues to be addressed include the access of these organizations to resources, the consequences of localism for wider access to these services, and the autonomy of the local initiative. This is particularly the case since the new flexible welfare envisages a decentralization of services, though largely maintaining centralized decision-making powers or subcontracting them out to the local state. Welfare provision is clearly in a state of flux. It is very likely that social movements are stationed at the precipice of a relatively new political situation in which the logical boundaries of formal democracy and needs provision are in a deep state of crisis and transformation.

Acknowledgements: the authors would like to thank the Social Science and Humanities Research Council and Fonds FCAR for their support.

NOTES

1 We take our notion of counter-rights from the work of Unger (1987).
2 We thank Claus Offe for his helpful commentary on our paper regarding this particular point of conceptual clarification.
3 One of the main proponents of the view of movements as 'self-limiting' agents is Cohen (1982); see also Cohen and Arato (1984).
4 We are indebted to our respondent Alan Scott for bringing attention to this critical aspect of parallel agency.

For comment on this chapter see page 281

11. New Patterns of Collective Action in a 'Post-Welfare' Society: The Italian Case

Ota de Leonardis

After the crisis of the welfare state and the exhaustion of neo-conservative onslaughts in late industrial societies, a new phase has opened, which I define as *post-welfare*: the growing ineffectiveness of social policy to face basic problems, which I will discuss in the first part of the chapter, makes us question the possibility of maintaining at a conceptual and practical level, the same objectives and criteria which characterized the last fifty years of welfare development. This ineffectiveness demands a reconceptualization. We can work towards this goal by deriving some suggestions concerning method and content from new forms of collective action, which I will examine in the second part of the chapter with reference to the Italian experience.

THE INEFFECTIVENESS OF SOCIAL POLICY

Problems of inadequacy, of regulatory unreasonableness and of injustice plague social policy in such manifest and deep-rooted ways as to lead to the hypothesis that the continuity of social policies with the gains made, is already impractical. Two crucial factors influence this ineffectiveness: the uncertainty of citizenship and the scarcity of resources.

Uncertain Citizenship

The first problem consists in an uncertainty about citizenship, and in the consequent necessity to rethink the fundamentals. Citizenship has become uncertain because its boundaries — the lines separating those who belong from those who don't, 'us' from 'them' — have become confused, and because the content of citizenship, the web of rights and obligations it creates, is no longer clearly defined. Two complementary tendencies which characterize this post-welfare scenario mark this uncertainty: the first is relative to the spread of the discourse of rights, the second, by contrast, pertains to the growth of 'no-man's lands' within the fabric of our civilized societies.

Rights Discourses

The long curve in the development of the welfare state has been accompanied in different forms and levels in the various industrial countries by two complementary processes: the general acceptance of civil rights and the introduction of social rights. These two developments have modified the standards of relationship between citizens and institutions, and have given rise to new rights discourses, a social understanding of needs, of resources and of services. In these discourses civil liberties lose, on the one hand, the negative status typical of the liberal tradition (freedom *from* external interferences) and acquire a positive meaning (freedom *to* gain access, for example); and on the other hand, some basic social needs acquire the status of rights. These two processes enrich citizenship with new guarantees, powers, and the resources to implement them. The holders of this citizenship are no longer passive recipients of institutional interventions, but active, competent and also conflictual partners in the decisions that affect them. The presence of this active citizenship, of this 'new civil society' or 'new civil community' as defined respectively by Touraine and Dahrendorf, is a characteristic of the welfare civilization substantially untouched by either the crisis or neo-conservative reactions.

But now this active citizenship demands to be legitimated as an important resource in the new post-welfare phase, otherwise it will degenerate in opportunistic directions and create free-riders.

No-Man's Lands

The second tendency goes in the opposite direction: it is the structural and massive growth of new forms of poverty, disaffiliation and marginalization. This phenomenon, with diverse origins and manifestations, constitutes a structural component of our advanced societies, rooted in the connective fabric of civil society.

The phenomenon of homelessness is the most dramatic highlight of this marginalization, but is only the most visible of general processes which render vulnerable sectors which were hitherto protected (Castel 1992). Its most manifest symptoms are riots, but no less serious are daily wars between the poor, and discourses of inequality, of oppression and of exclusion. This new marginalization is fed either by internal dynamics: above all, by long-term unemployment and more generally the crisis within the 'work-society' (Gorz

1988; Negt 1988); or by international dynamics: the growing discrepancies between North and South, the dissolution of the eastern-bloc countries, the growing number of areas affected by more or less open warfare, which feed massive migrations which, in turn, as documented by UN agencies, will in the near future change the face of our societies in important ways. In the very heart of our opulent cities roams a heterogeneous population of demi-citizens (Balbo 1991) who do not put down roots and do not possess any definite social identity, however deviant, an alien population, which cannot be confined in a ghetto.[1] I have elsewhere called this population the *new vagrants* because it is reminiscent of the type of vagrancy which marked the dawn of industrial civilization (1992).

Differences and Inequalities

Both these tendencies make visible the uncertain status of citizenship rights: the use of *both* systems of rights and criteria of belonging. The crucial knot around which the question of citizenship turns is 'the dilemma of difference', to use the expression of Martha Minow (1990). Changes in norms and institutions have introduced guarantees of the recognition and respect for difference and at the same time have produced fissures and fragmentation in the legal framework. The first horn of this dilemma consists in the duality between assimilation and differentiation (examples are the problems of minorities, the education of disabled children or the work of women). It is difficult, as Minow suggests, to limit inequalities without denying and violating differences; and vice versa, it is difficult to acknowledge differences without creating inequalities. The second horn of the dilemma consists in the fact that these developments have fragmented or 'deconstructed' the subject of law — the abstract, autonomous, sovereign individual. But this undermines the basis for the guarantees of the neutrality, coherence and impartiality of justice. Today the citizen has acquired concrete and multiple configurations which place him/her in a network of social relationships. This makes it impossible to reduce individual differences to deviations from the norm. It is difficult to design a system of rights which is neutral but not neutering, impartial but articulated to deal with differences.

These are, in summary, the uncertainties that the dilemma of difference creates for a system of citizenship rights and the challenges that this dilemma poses for social policy in the post-welfare state. This would involve not only expanding charters of rights, but redefining the subjects, powers and social processes around which such charters are built. As Minow notes, in elaborating her perspective on 'rights in relation', we must from the beginning adopt a viewpoint which is not 'from nowhere', but avowedly from a social location and which gives rise to a perspective. From such a viewpoint, differences are no longer deviations *from* the norm, but are differences *among* subjects, and are therefore relationships and interdependencies. People are, therefore, the bearers of rights inasmuch as they are located in these relations of interdependence, and bound by limited autonomy and responsibility.[2]

The Question of Scarce Resources

The second reason for the ineffectiveness of post-welfare social policy consists in the scarcity of resources to be distributed. I would like to examine three aspects of this problem.

First of all, the quantitative sum of human, financial, technical and structural resources which welfare agencies have at their disposal (be they public, private or voluntary) is inadequate, whether in view of the enormous quantitative growth of social problems, the more visible aspect of which is the new marginalization I previously referred to, or whether in view of the qualitative growth of active citizens' (legitimate) expectations. Privatization and cost-cutting have worsened these problems.

Secondly, the question of scarce resources has critical civil, political and ethical effects. Scarce resources cause problems in the allocative criteria and make useless the principles (the right to health, to study, etc.) that welfare agencies are called upon to honour. In this regard, Elster raises the problem of 'local justice' (1990, 1992): that is, justice, as concretely administered by institutions, is by definition essentially plural and local. That is, the rules are differentiated according to the problems with which these institutions deal and according to the criteria and procedures which guide the allocation of goods and selection of clients. 'Every institution is more or less free to choose its own allocative criteria'; or rather, as Mary Douglas (to whom Elster refers) puts it, there are concrete institutions which are decentralized, which differ in their procedures and the benefits they allocate, and which nevertheless 'make life and death choices' (Douglas 1986 ch.9; Elster 1990 p.140). One cannot escape the 'tragic' nature of such choices: constraints on resources and the selections that their allocation entail are no longer opaque natural events, accepted unquestioningly by a justice discourse. They are 'cultural tragedies' (Calabresi and Bobbit 1968; see also Donolo and Fichera 1988 ch.5) which become apparent at different levels: for example, on a microscopic scale in the allocation of vital resources such as transplant organs; or on a broader scale, in global dilemmas that affect the life chances of entire continents, or in choices which have a decisive effect on future generations. Here too the limits of the local dimension of justice persist.[3]

Last and perhaps most important, scarcity of resources is thus not an objective fact but a paradigmatic assumption: the paradigm of marginal economics, developed for the marketplace and industrial production, has permeated methods to identify problems and solutions even in the welfare field, and in general in social reproduction. As Hirschman remarks, the scarcity of resources is a problem of the 'parsimony of economic theory.'[4] (1985). Above all, studies on women with respect to welfare (i.e., regarding 'time to care' and the social wealth produced by the unpaid labour of women in social reproduction) help to redefine various problems: what are the resources in the field of welfare beyond the quantitative criteria of the market; what other agencies and actors besides the state produce their resources; and how can they be utilized other than through the mechanisms of distribution and commodification. Thus, one can maintain the idea that scarcity of resources is much more a problem of conceptualization (but with operational consequences), rather than an objective fact. This opens the possibility of overcoming the constraints which scarcity poses for social policy.

NEW FORMS OF COLLECTIVE ACTION: THE ITALIAN CASE

If these are the problems and the challenges that the ineffectiveness of social policy present, it would seem that the politics of defending and reforming welfare as we have known it, (ie, claims for rights and resources) is a thing of the past and doomed to failure. However, new forms of collective action are emerging, with contents and strategies that seem appropriate to the radical nature of these challenges. In this second part I will focus attention on these new forms, and in particular on some significant examples from the Italian scene. I will try to bring out emerging changes in the goals and criteria of social policy.

Social Actions Across Institutional Boundaries

The development of the Italian welfare state has been characterized by two elements. First, this development has been accelerated and, more importantly, politicized in the sense that the management of this development has constituted an important contested terrain between the political forces of the left and the right. During the decade between the late 1960s and the 1970s, the welfare state was an important political battleground between the workers' movement, which saw opportunities for political hegemony (such as gaining control of the local administrative apparatus of the National Health Service) and the forces of conservatism (particularly the Christian Democrats) who consolidated their own particularistic and clientelist orientation (many votes, for example, were 'bought' by granting disability pensions). The growth of democratic discourses and universal guarantees in various welfare fields produced by this process has been enormous. However, the most manifest and problematic turn in the recent past has been a kind of 'take over' of welfare institutions by political parties, sometimes on behalf of recipients but sometimes for electoral or even business purposes. This hypertrophy of politics and of the party system feeds the present crisis in two main ways: the legitimacy crisis of political parties and of the political system, and the fiscal crisis of welfare state whereby rising costs go hand-in-hand with the declining efficacy of policies.

The second element consists in the fact that the discourses and strategies of social movements which have accompanied the development of welfare in Italy have been directed much more to producing innovations and transformations from within institutional structures than to making oppositional claims and protests from outside.

Significant movements of professionals, e.g. in the field of public health, often allied with consumers and local administrators, have produced important changes in the ways the institutions function. A good example is the process of de-institutionalization which the movement of mental health professionals has guided for more than 25 years. This movement has caused profound changes in professional practices on illness and care, and has achieved a progressive law. The movement has also shaped the implementation of this law, mobilizing new actors (such as associations of patients' next of kin, and social cooperatives), experiencing new models of administering resources, animating forms of self-organization and consumer partnership. To avoid any misunderstanding, let me say that in Italy, in contrast to English-speaking countries, the notion of de-institutionalization means neither abolitionist criticism with regard to institutions (typically anti-psychiatry), nor an administrative measure of de-hospitalization. De-institutionalization has been in Italy a long, slow and daily process of dismantling and transforming (from the inside) psychiatric institutions to change the complex of relationships between citizens and services (consumers–users, families, local contexts) such that these partners became active as well as conflictual subjects, and no longer objects, passive recipients of interventions.

One could construe de-institutionalization to be a strategy by which institutions are socialized.[5] The case of de-institutionalization is important in this context because it forms, directly or indirectly, the background of discourses and practical experiences characterizing the forms of collective action, which I will now go on to illustrate. Above all, the case of de-institutionalization shapes a leading idea of their strategies. This is the idea that innovations in institutions may be produced on the terrain of their daily concrete inner life, and that the changes occurring on this terrain affect, at the same time, both the institutional structures and the cultural orientations of the actors.[6]

Active Citizenship

Active citizenship is the first kind of collective action which I would like to examine: associations, groups, citizens' networks which emerge to deal with policies which directly affect them. The most significant cases are found in the fields of mental health, of drug dependency and domestic violence against women and children. In the area of mental health, for instance, a national network of associations of ex-mental patients and their families have developed self-governing structures, run jointly with the public services, and have promoted local initiatives to guide the implementation of the mental health legislation. Associations of family members of drug addicts work in a similar way. Here the case that stands out is the *madri coraggio* group in Naples, a group of women from the underclass who live in neighbourhoods where drugs are the basis of the economy and a normal way of life. In this environment they care for their children and, in the absence of services, undertake the dangerous job of prevention and control in the face of the pushers, and — though often illiterate — combat their isolation with action to expose and publicize the problem, learning the language of the mass media, of the law, of rights and resources (Turnaturi 1990). Other analogous forms of association emerge in the care of the chronically sick and disabled (for example, those eligible for organ transplants, or terminally ill patients) as well as around the issue of battered women.

The organizational forms differ widely, from models of self-help to models of advocacy. There is nothing new here in comparison with forms found in other industrial countries. What is different in Italy is that these organizational forms are often mixed together and that in their implementation, protest, self-help and the promotion of local community resources, are mixed together. Many are families of users of services, many are women.

Notwithstanding the enormous differences between them, on this and on other levels, these types of collective action have two key elements in common. The first is their relation to the political. These citizens have no political training and use neither its ways nor its political jargon. They begin, simply, from a personal pain or problem (usually confined to their private sphere) and transform them into public issues, translating them into a civil and ethical, though not directly political language. Their action evolves along the boundary between the social and political. While it deals with the questions of rights, of the workings of institutions, of responsibilities, of resources and powers, it produces collective processes of moral learning (Turnaturi 1990).

Self-respect seems to be the motive, the guiding principle for facing and interpreting these questions. Self-respect derives from the possibilities of becoming active political partners; competent in defining and resolving problems. This is the second characteristic which unites these forms of collective action, with regard to their relation to the institutional structure of welfare. The most interesting fact is that these associations, even when aiming toward self-help solutions, do not act independently from, or as alternatives to services. Rather, they act in unison, both cooperatively and conflictually, in a close relationship with the personnel and the structures of welfare agencies. These associations receive tasks, financing and even personnel from local government. They provide services and create and manage important positions. They participate in the everyday work, resolving problems and at the same time effecting changes in both the cultural orientations and structures of these services. Thus they become enmeshed and often develop a synergy with the welfare agencies, complementing the activism developed in the agencies. I will pursue this point in the final section of the paper.

Social Enterprises

The second form of collective action had its origins in the administrative and operational structures of the welfare state itself, through the initiatives of both administrators and social workers. This collective action consists of a strategy of auto-transformation, whether of particular services or of entire service systems at the local level. The central challenge of this strategy is to be able to overcome the constraint and the logic behind the scarcity of resources. The unmet needs which result from these constraints have given rise not to accusations, protests and demands for answers and resources from the state, but rather to working experiments with qualitatively different responses. These experiments mobilize new actors and invent new resources and new ways of using those available, changing accordingly the institutional tasks, responsibilities and organizational patterns. They mobilize and bring together a mix of public resources, local economic and community resources. Above all, they acknowledge and mobilize the resources of the consumers themselves, that is, their capabilities, interests and skills. Collective action is a part of daily work; militancy does not express itself separately from the context of work and life in the social services. What creates the collective identity is participation in specific local issues and working projects, and shared criteria of quality applied to the products of work and the processes of production. This cannot be called a movement; at most it represents a network of initiatives that provide an opportunity to exchange ideals, problems and projects. Still, this network does produce a culture of innovation and quite well-defined set of goals for change in the logic and powers which govern social policy.

The most complete expression of this strategy is the transformation of services into *social enterprises* (de Leonardis 1990, ch.6; Gallio (ed.) 1991). This notion is evidently an oxymoron in which elements usually kept separate are united. On the one hand it speaks of enterprises, since the daily work of the participants (personnel, consumers, administrators and common citizens) consists in investing either public welfare funds (local, national or international, such as EC social funds) or private funds derived from the creation and management of productive enterprises in the local community. Usually they are cooperative because these types of economic democracy and of participatory management are, as we shall see, important for the focus of these enterprises. These enterprises operate in the most diverse sectors of the marketplace and in accordance with its norms. The social enterprise of Trieste, for example, is a consortium of five cooperatives with productive activities in services (restaurants, bars, hotels, transportation, etc.) in cultural services (radio station, publishing house, information agency, record library etc.) in design industries (interior-decorating, fashion jewellery etc.) with a total membership of 300 and a budget of $5 million in 1991.

On the other hand, these enterprises are social, meaning that the main objective and the criterion for evaluating results is the ability to produce well-being — health, aid, rehabilitation, integration etc. — of participants and members. Even more, the goal is well-being for those most in need — the mentally ill, the disabled, drug-dependants, impoverished senior citizens, drop-outs, ex-convicts, etc. I summarize here the main points of this strategy.

(a) In order to reverse the process of marginalization which welfare services bring about through their screening (through their mechanisms to select, to screen out, to render passive), it becomes necessary to redefine the rules of intervention. The interventions are organized no longer negatively around users' shortcomings — deviance, handicaps, inabilities — or to cure or remedy, but rather positively around their abilities — their resources, energies, competencies, talents, interests — in order to promote and to exercise those abilities for the validation and development of the users.

(b) Consequently, the traditional, separate and specialized structure of service collapses. Instead, intersectoral programmes are set up, which on the one hand jointly confront all forms and degrees of marginality found at a local level, and on the other hand, create coalitions centred on common objectives rather than on the diverse abilities, responsibilities and various interests of the different actors.

(c) This strategy makes the dimension of production (professional training, work, market) the key factor — not in the traditional sense of discipline, normalization, or a reward system for those who do well. On the contrary, the idea is that on this terrain real social exchanges take place, that interests are enriched, that room for autonomy is expanded, that conditions to take risks, even to make mistakes and to learn are encouraged. In this way, workers are allowed each in their own way (some better, some worse) to exercise their initiative. These are preconditions and not rewards for subjective and intersubjective growth, which are given and guaranteed for all.

(d) Finally, investment is centred on quality: on the quality of production which depends on the intelligence and the manual ability of the cooperators; on the quality of the contexts and social processes of production; on the quality of the local social community.[7]

In summary, the oxymoron *social enterprise* points to a strategy of transforming the workings of welfare in a productive sense beyond the limits of distribution, beyond the constraints posed by the scarcity of resources, beyond the mechanisms of dependency and passivity of the recipients. The above characteristics have marked the welfare state in all its forms, from its origin to its crisis.

SOME DIRECTIONS FOR RESEARCH

New forms of collective action point to a key set of reasons for the crisis and ineffectiveness of social policy, both from the point of view of right and of resources, as I have shown. The set of reasons come to this: the provision of welfare is so structured that it is paternalistic and creates dependency. This is the basis for many of the neo-conservative criticisms. However, these arguments are overturned and redirected by the new forms of action. Even when social interventions are distributed on the principle of recipients' rights, these are passive rights, that is, rights to be protected from social injuries and to receive goods or services; they are not rights of agency — to act, to do, or to have the ability to act. Thus, when scarcity of resources demands that interventions be reorganized, recipients will continue to be seen as problem and expenses, not as resources; their resources (competence, intelligence, ability) will be wasted and ignored. If one takes the path suggested by these forms of action, one perceives the possibility of new ways to confront the problems of social policy. I will take this path for a few steps by reworking the notions of rights and resources. To do this, I will use conceptual tools derived from Amartya Sen's notion of basic capability.

Basic Capabilities

The main thought behind the notion of basic capability is that the crucial parameter for a standard of living is not a certain basket of goods, but the possibility to exercise basic capabilities (Sen 1987a). Therefore, a crucial parameter for social justice is not primary goods to be redistributed and guaranteed, but the basic abilities of each person. 'The value of the living standard lies in the living and not in the possessing of commodities, which has derivate and varying relevance' (Sen 1987a p.25) and,

> Living consists in a series of functionings, such as being nourished, being sheltered, being clothed, being able to move about freely, being able to meet friends and to be entertained, being able to appear in public without shame, being able to communicate and participate, being able to achieve fulfilment of one's creative instincts and so forth. (Sen 1988 p.7)

The heart of Sen's proposal consists in directing our attention 'from commodities to capabilities' (1985a), from goods to what they allow human beings to obtain (Sen 1987b); and finally, from objects administered and distributed by social justice to subjects who are both recipients and interlocutors.

Rights and Capabilities

Let us examine the elements of this proposal, and the change of perspective which it introduces, above all with respect to rights. The rights to exercise basic capabilities (Sen 1982b, 1985b) are different in three ways from the traditional rights of citizenship.

(a) *The principle of liberty*: the perspective of guaranteeing the exercise of basic capabilities strengthens the shift from the classic negative meaning of freedom as 'shield' to a positive meaning, as a granting of conditions for exercising freedom (Sen 1985b).

(b) *The principle of equality*: equality, as equal access to an equal basket of primary goods (which has guided and supported the development of welfare state) still does not resolve, as we have seen, the problem of differences, of the 'basic differences among human beings', as Sen himself says. Equality of basic capabilities (1987b) is a 'complex equality' because it takes as a point of departure the differences and varieties of human reality. The basic capabilities of individuals are composed of elements (both subjective and objective) which are particular and differentiated. These capabilities have therefore a constitutionally social and intersubjective character, in which the plurality of forms — the differences — are no longer criteria of discrimination in the negative sense, but intrinsic requirements for the life of individuals. Thus, we can see that the basic capabilities approach moves in the same direction as 'rights in relation' (Minow 1990). Being able to appear in public without shame, an example which Sen gives, can be an absolute parameter for the principle of equality. All that varies are personal and social resources necessary to exercise this capability.

(c) *The principle of subjectivity or entitlement to rights*: the notion of capabilities contains a reflexive principle, because one of their fundamental elements is the act of exercising them, of making them objects of choice, of discourse and of action. Therefore they imply freedom of choice and action; the sovereignty of the subject implies the ability to exercise its own basic capabilities (that is, *second-order* capability). This reflexive component redefines the status of the subject of rights. To be the subject of rights is no longer simply to be a recipient of goods and services, but a bearer of the right to exercise capabilities. This subjectivity, in terms of social justice, consists in the ability to self-evaluate (Sen 1987a p.32) and to act according to basic capabilities. As such, s/he is a participant in and not a recipient of institutional choices concerning rights which affect him/her, a participant competent to define both problems and solutions.

   To conclude this section, it seems to me that the basic capabilities approach provides us (on these three points) with the basis for redefining the status of rights in social justice, and conversely the criteria for the institutional responsibility to administer it. Above all, it seems to me that on these grounds there is the possibility of facing the paternalistic implications of social justice bestowed by welfare institutions without resorting to the minimalist solution of the liberal model. The basic capabilities approach, as I have argued, shifts the problem of justice from the objects to the subjects of justice — that is, to the actions and interactions which comprise justice. Therefore, on the one hand, it safeguards the principle of redistribution on the basis of individual or group needs but does not profess to give an external and objective definition of needs which would legitimize institutional interventions for the good of these individuals or groups. On the other hand it guarantees the freedom of individuals (or groups) to define their own needs, but places these freedoms not outside — where they have the right to refuse, claim, protest — but inside the social processes which produce justice. These freedoms are powers to decide and to act; those who exercise these freedoms are producers (not recipients) of justice and the social policies based on it.

Resources and Capabilities

Let us finally examine what the capabilities approach implies regarding resources. Because this approach changes the criteria and objectives of justice from the distribution of goods to the exercise of capabilities, the ways to identify and utilize resources change as well. Resources able to produce capabilities have, says Sen, a constitutive plurality (1987a p.2). If one begins with goods — as is usual — they are simply data, and the problem becomes the method of distribution within a 'competitive' logic, according to which distribution to some means denying others. Thus, the constraint of scarcity gives prejudicial results and blocks allocations.

   Conversely, if we begin with capabilities many other resources become relevant and visible beyond those goods which are institutionally defined and constitutionally scarce. The development of a person's basic capabilities draws on a variety of resources, public and private, familial and local, material, symbolic and relational, as well as inner resources. Furthermore, capabilities are acquired through their exercise, their use; they are produced by exercising them. Therefore, capabilities themselves are also resources. Indeed, to go back to a point already made, subjects, far from being simply recipients of interventions in the name of social justice, are recognized as producers of resources — of energies, talents, intelligence, interests, experiences, beyond material resources. This enormous wealth, usually wasted in those marginal environments where exclusion and insoluble problems accumulate, can be invested in social justice — concretely in social policies. A justice that takes account of basic capabilities is not just an allocative justice but a productive justice whose purpose is to activate and increase wealth. This justice redistributes power and not just goods (Walzer 1992). It considers not only what is given to each person to guarantee their capabilities, but also to what is given 'from each according to his ability.'

NOTES

1   Into it fall the leftovers from the process of redistribution of social rights, which skims off and rejects everything which in any way resists assimilation into standardized patterns of normality and deviance; conversely, in this zone the generalized rights of freedom assume a merely negative form and appear as rootlessness, abandonment and a lack of institutional responsibility.

2   See also Pitch 1989. The debate on the theory of justice offers other insights in this direction. I cannot deal with it because it is very intricate and controversial. I will touch upon this problem again in the third part of this work, which deals with Amartya Sen's 'basic capabilities' approach.

3   Nevertheless this conclusion does not lead us to condemn the arbitrary character of justice, nor does it force us to relativism. As I have tried to demonstrate elsewhere (1992), justice as seen in its local dimension focuses on institutions as a crucial point of a theory and of a politics of justice. This displacement reformulates the central problem of justice to be no longer the abstract principles upon which it is based, but rather those functioning standards of institutions, and those relations between citizens and institutions on which it is built and defined. From this emerges the view of justice as a social process, where many forces, which influence individuals' lives, are beyond their control, but where by the same token abstract instances and principles beyond judgement and conflict are not possible. Thus we find that the field of justice is full of injustices and insoluble dilemmas. And yet these dilemmas come back in allocative decisions and in subjects with a limited responsibility and rationality, which accomplish them. We cannot take away from the tragic character of these decisions, but they now begin to comprise the moral tenor of social relations and partake in the moral identity of each of us.

4   On this subject one can point to various crucial currents: the tradition of social economy, beginning with Polanyi (Bruyn (ed.) 1987); the critique of the bureaucratic paradigm (Crozier 1987); some Keynesian thinking (Meade 1989); critical elaborations of utilitarian theories (especially Sen 1977 to which I will return).

5   See more details in de Leonardis, Mauri and Rotelli (1986).

6   One can perceive here the possibility of outlining a prospectus for change beyond the usual dualities — *movement–institution, social–political, ideology–structure* — which have so deeply marked the entire history of the Left.

7   To place welfare state structures into the framework of material and cultural growth in the quality of local life, and more generally, the strategy of transforming these structures into social enterprises has many commonalities with other experiments and projects in diverse contexts: e.g. OECD projects of *urban regeneration*; WHO projects of *health promotion*; experiments of community economic development and of social investment. (On this last point, see the work of Lustiger-Thaler and Shragge (*supra*).

12. Welfare Work: Discursive Conflicts and Narrative Possibilities

Michael Bach

The case of *Clark v. Clark* begins:

The respondent, J.C. [Justin Clark], was born on September 21, 1962. He was cyanosed at birth necessitating resuscitation. Development was abnormal and cerebral palsy, hydrocephalus and mental retardation were diagnosed at the Hospital for Sick Children in Toronto. At the age of two, the respondent was admitted to the Rideau Regional Centre where he still resided at trial. On admission to the centre, he was diagnosed as severely retarded and suffering from cerebral palsy. Physically, the respondent was still extremely disabled at the date of trial. He was confined to bed and a wheelchair. He could not speak. However, he had learned to communicate through a system known as Blissymbols....

In 1981, arrangements were made for the respondent to visit several placement homes in Ontario and Quebec as a first step to a possible move out of the Rideau Regional Centre.... Because he feared that his son could not cope outside the centre, the father applied for a declaration that the respondent was a mentally incompetent person. The judge, not being satisfied beyond a reasonable doubt that the affidavit evidence provided that the respondent was a mentally incompetent person, directed a trial of the issue.

Judge Matheson closes his written judgment of this case with:

the spirit of that liberty which Learned Hand tells us seeks to understand the minds of other men, and remembers that not even a sparrow falls to earth unheeded, I find and I declare Matthew Justin Clark to be mentally competent.[1]

Shortly after the case concluded, Justin Clark left Rideau Regional Centre to live outside of the walls of that institution, which once housed over 2,000 people. He had challenged his father's claim that he was incompetent and, with his Blissymbol board and his supporters, argued instead that he had a right to make his own decisions and a right to leave the institution. The outcome of this case suggests that in the course of the various activities that led up to the court proceedings and that constituted these proceedings, Justin Clark sought and obtained his 'welfare', in the sense that Drover and Kerans (1993) define that term: 'human flourishing' (Kerans 1993) and 'autonomous self-actualization... through social action, ...in the context of and with regard to others.' One might argue that court proceedings over competency determinations are not very welfare-producing at the best of times. However, it is certainly the case that through these proceedings Justin obtained welfare to a much greater extent than if the ruling had gone against his claim of his own competency and for enjoyment of the right to make his own decisions.

How are we to account for the welfare that Justin did obtain? How are we to theorize this man's possibility in a theory of welfare? As readers of the court's judgment, how do we know him? How do the others in his life know him — his father, friends, psychiatrists, expert witnesses, Judge Matheson? How do they, who have so much power in his life, come to see his welfare? These are critical questions to address, because Justin did not obtain his welfare through the mechanisms we have come to associate with the welfare state, mechanisms for determination of needs and public provision of income, goods and services. Assessments of his needs, organized through the discourses of medicine and psychometric testing, were being mobilized in the court proceedings to strip him of his rights and to keep him confined to Rideau Regional Centre. And, it was a mode of welfare state provision of supports to people with disabilities — institutional care — that Justin was struggling against in making his claim for autonomy.

It is not news that the welfare state, as well as the institutions of the market and the family, do not secure welfare. For many, they systematically undermine the possibility. Given these limitations, and their argument that contractarianism and utilitarianism do not provide adequate theoretical accounts of the production of welfare, Drover and Kerans (*supra*) seek to re-theorize welfare. They provide an account that makes the activity of needs interpretation, claims-formation, and claimsmaking foundational to welfare. In the discussion that follows, I will critically draw upon their account of welfare, for light it can shed on how welfare came to be produced in Justin's life. In particular, I will explore Justin Clark's case against the account they provide of the welfare-seeking self, which they suggest resides in a 'genuine' narrative of self, a 'genuine autobiography'. The welfare seeker and obtainer becomes the 'definitive judge with respect to the meaning and coherence of [his or her] life,' albeit within a social and linguistic context where one must write with and against language, and the interpretations of one's self that are constructed by others.

With the framework Drover and Kerans provide, can we move beyond a declaration of the failure of the welfare state to produce welfare when it came to Justin Clark? Can we begin to see the possibilities for his welfare in the interstices of narrative production, claimsmaking, and discursive conflicts played out in *Clark v. Clark*? I want to argue that we can, not as an apologia for the welfare state, but as a path to reconstructing the work of producing welfare, in the sense that Drover and Kerans refer to that term. In the case of Justin Clark, the state presides authoritatively, it speaks a patrician voice, it reproduces a binary opposition between competency and incompetency. Yet, the case displays an irony: for Justin, among the most marginalized of marginalized, the state is emancipatory and liberating. To recover from this case the possibilities for obtaining welfare, and reconstructing welfare work, I will work through four steps. The first step is to justify a narrative construction of self. Secondly, we must make visible the multiplicity of narratives which come into play in *Clark v. Clark*, and the conflicts set in motion by their performance(s). Third, we need to distinguish the different kinds of knowledge-making practices which organize the acts of recognition of self and other, acts which are constitutive of the narratives and their performance. Self and other appear in different ways depending on the forms of recognition constructed into the narratives. Certain forms of recognition, I will argue, make possible a genuine autobiography, the *autonomous*, yet not *liberal*, self, to which Drover and Kerans appeal. Other forms of recognition result in relations of domination between subjects. Finally, we need an ethical stance with which to judge acts of recognition and the knowledge-making practices which underlay them. I will argue that in a claims-sorting process these acts and practices *can* be judged so that it is, indeed, welfare-producing claims, and genuine autobiographies, which are validated.

THE NARRATIVE STRUCTURE OF THE SELF

The notion that the self is narratively structured, that it comes into being only within the context of a story woven of past, present and future, is gaining increasing credence in moral philosophy (MacIntyre 1983; Taylor 1991, 1989; Benhabib 1986a), psychoanalytic theory (Benjamin 1988); and medical ethics (Brody 1987; Elliot 1991; Miles 1990; Cassell 1991).

Like these writers, Drover and Kerans reject the 'methodological individualism' of the liberal conception of the self — an isolated, autonomous self, born and contained entirely by an instrumental rationality. A narrative of self is not freely chosen; its construction must take place by drawing boundaries. Taylor (1991) has defined the boundaries with which we construct our narratives of self as 'horizons of significance' that appear in different regional, cultural, and historical contexts. Kymlicka has argued that in our current era where there is an increasing pluralism of cultural groups seeking recognition of language and cultural rights, we must recognize cultural structure and cultural membership as defining the boundaries of the 'life-plans' or narratives of self that we write. This is because 'the processes by which options and choices become significant for use are linguistic and historical processes. Whether or not a course of action has any significance for us depends on whether, or how, our language renders vivid to us the point of that activity... in its capacity of providing meaningful options for us [cultural structure aids] our ability to judge for ourselves the value of our life-plans.' (1989b pp.165 6).

The narratively-produced self is not fixed, but multiple, continually written and re-written through time. It is a 'self-in-process' (Lorraine 1990), actively re-interpreting in the face of contingencies, and always confronted with new possibilities for making meaning. Joan Didion (1979) has written of how she felt as though she had mislaid her 'script' when she experienced the onset of multiple sclerosis: 'I was supposed to hear cues, and no longer did. I was meant to know the plot, but all I knew was what I saw: flash pictures in variable sequence, images with no "meaning" beyond their temporary arrangement, not a movie but a cutting room experience.... We tell ourselves stories in order to live... [with the onset of multiple sclerosis I] began to doubt the premises of all the stories I had ever told myself.' The narrative structure of the self means that we can reflect critically on the 'scripts' by which we have lived, and write ourselves anew, write ourselves new scripts of possibility (Heilbrun 1988), albeit with and against the boundaries, and by virtue of the discursive resources, that Taylor and Kymlicka point to.

Self does not precede the writing, the writing precedes the self. As Kristeva writes, 'Writing is upheld not by the subject of understanding, but by a divided subject, even a pluralized subject, that occupies, not a place of enunciation, but permutable, multiple, and mobile places...' (1980 p.111). In Mead's terms, it is the standpoints of other individuals and of the 'generalized other', from which the self comes to be perceived and recognized, that precede the grasping and the writing of the self. 'The individual experiences himself as such [as a self], not directly, but only indirectly, from the particular standpoints of other individual members of the same social group or from the generalized standpoint of the social group as a whole to which he belongs.' (1964 [1949] p.202) For Benhabib, it is with standpoints provided by the 'generalized other', the socially organized standpoints in law, institutions, and 'universal' principles to guide action, *and* the standpoints of the 'concrete' others, the flesh and blood beings with whom we come face-to-face, that we construct an identity: 'At any point in time, we are one whose identity is constituted by a tale. This tale is never complete: the past is always reformulated and renarrated in the light of the present and in anticipation of a future. Yet this tale is not one of which we alone are the authors.' (1986a p.349).

The fact that autobiographies are bounded by historical, social, cultural and linguistic contexts; constructed from the standpoints of many 'others' that organize our lives; and bring into being a self, *ex post facto* as it were, seems to occlude the possibility of making visible the 'genuine' narrative so central to the account of welfare Drover and Kerans provide. And yet without being able to select the genuine narrative, from among the multiple interpretations of self, we won't be able to see or know the welfare-seeking self, and hence any adjudication of claims on this basis seems a mirage. In the Justin Clark case a particular set of narratives were ultimately valorized as 'genuine'. Ronald Clark's story about himself and about Justin was rejected, in favour of Justin's own narrative of self, and the complementary narratives produced by others.

MULTIPLE NARRATIVES

The event of the court proceedings in *Clark v. Clark* shows us that many constructions of the self parade under the banner of a name, in this case the name of Justin. These narrative productions are not *exclusively* differing narratives of Justin, from among which the most 'genuine' was selected as the basis for adjudicating and resolving the conflicting claims. Justin also appears as a character in the claim statements of others, in the narratives others write about themselves, others who are struggling to put together and to write 'welfare-seeking selves'.

In writing Justin the way he does, one could argue that Ronald Clark is putting together his own autobiography, and seeking his own welfare, just as much as he is his son's. He is probably not a malevolent being whose entire aim in life is to lock Justin away. If he is at all like hundreds of thousands of other parents in Canada who have sons and daughters with disabilities, he is deeply concerned about his own welfare, *and* that of his son's. He was likely told when his son was an infant that the institution was the only option, and given the nature of supports to parents who had young children with disabilities, it probably was. Justin's father may have heard the horror stories about all forms of abuse and violence that have happened to people with disabilities who leave institutions to live in the 'community', perhaps choosing not to hear about similar incidents visited upon those who remain. Ronald Clark is also aging. Like many other parents in his situation, he probably doubts that financial and service supports promised to his son to enable him to live in the community will be long term; he fears that he will be hit with huge financial expenses to support his son in the final years of his life; and wonders whether his son will be taken care of when he passes on. These are well-founded fears and concerns. Social provision of income, goods and services to meet disability-related needs are not granted by entitlement in this country. They are often inadequate, provided in ways and for periods of time that do not provide security of provision, much less enable self-determination (Rioux and Crawford 1990; Torjman 1988). The Rideau Regional is an imposing, grand structure. Even if it is the architecture of confinement, it bestows permanence. To Ronald Clark, it could appear like a safe haven for his son.

Similar to Ronald Clark, the expert witnesses, the psychiatrists, who are called to give evidence about Justin's 'competence', are participating as much in the work of establishing the validity of Justin's claim, as they are in producing their own narratives. The assessments of Justin over his many years of life in the Rideau Regional were carried out by professionals whose education trained them to recognize and encode Justin in certain ways. Their livelihoods, narrative identities, indeed the organization of welfare state provision, depend on the work they perform of drawing boundaries, like competency/incompetency, across certain human acts and flesh. In Smith's terms, these expert witnesses wrote across Justin's 'primary' narrative, how he lived and what he did and what he wanted, with an 'ideological' one (1990), whose terms found their power to define and encode in the professionalizing and dominating discourse of psychiatry. When people are viewed through such a discourse, they lose their particularity, their life histories, and their hopes for the future. This is the stuff of a narrative of a past and future self. The process of labelling, through diagnoses and a history of treatments, is a process of fitting the person into a general framework of categories through which medical and service systems can then frame an 'appropriate' response. In such a scheme, the standard for appropriate treatment decisions is related to whether the treatment corresponds to the person, not as an individual with a particular narrative history and future, but as one instance within a generalized category of diagnosis (Elliot 1991). As the case bears out, however, the discourse of psychiatry is not a monolithic one, applied in uniform ways. It is contested. How Justin is to be encoded by it, how he appears through the terms of this discourse, is not ruled entirely by the logic of the discourse. Matheson ultimately draws upon the narratives of those who knew Justin personally, who could write, in Benhabib's terms, from the standpoint of the concrete other.

While contestation over a 'genuine' narrative of Justin is organized in part along the boundary of the concrete v. the generalized other, there is more than one generalized other that is writing the accounts of Justin. As Judge Matheson points out in his ruling in *Clark v. Clark*, the psychiatrist and psychologist speaking on Justin's behalf, also have philosophical and ideological commitments to 'normalization' — the theory and set of principles that people labelled as mentally handicapped should be supported to live as 'normal' lives as possible, in normalizing environments, etc. (Wolfensberger 1972). Whatever one may think of a theory and guiding principle that may disregard difference in favour of a norm, the point here is that these general commitments offer a standpoint to carry out a discursive contest with the ruling discourse. The standpoint of the generalized other is not, by definition, a hegemonic standpoint. It can be a site within the dominant discourse that is drawn upon and re-invested with meaning to mobilize a counter-hegemonic claim.

Contest over the genuineness of Justin's narrative is also cast within the binary opposition of the generalizing categories of competency and incompetency, a boundary established and legitimated through the Ontario *Mental Incompetency Act*. Matheson's work is to safeguard the 'integrity' of the Act, by ensuring that the boundary is appropriately drawn when it comes to Justin Clark. A dominant icon of our political culture undergirds the distinction on which the legislation rests, and is the guiding standpoint for this case: the freely contracting agent, market man, the rational, independently autonomous self. Protection of the ruling force of this icon gives reason to legislation, and to the conduct of the case. Narrative productions about Justin are written within the terms the legislation makes available: Is Justin 'competent' or 'incompetent'? Justin's counter-claim to his father, that he is indeed competent, finds its force not only from his capacity to produce a coherent narrative of him/self but because he positions his counter-claim within the discourse of the generalized other of universal human rights; in particular, his right to self-determination. Matheson writes: 'This case, in Justin's mind, revolves around his right to make a decision, about the friends he chooses to have, where he wishes to live and how he chooses to lead his life.' The discourse of rights is mobilized to re-draw the boundary of competency/ incompetency in a way that can include rather than exclude Justin. In doing so, the 'independence' features of the icon, which have been paradigmatic of the self-determining, rights-bearing man, are let go. Justin is granted a right to self-determination, if only because he passes the competency test, but in spite of the fact that he has many dependencies. He will exercise his right only via technological supports, many friends around him, and public provision of various personal supports and services.

Justin does not produce the rights discourse that gives his claim force, he draws upon a discourse that is actively being written across a number of sites. Nor is his counter-claim spoken from an organizational site within a social movement. Nonetheless, he takes advantage of the human rights discourse the disability movement began to attach itself to and mould in the late 1970s, a discourse which now drives the claims of the various disability organizations, and likely those who supported Justin as well. By mobilizing this discourse, the disability movement makes available icons, and subject positions, and identities counter to those configuring people with disabilities as 'incompetent'. These identities are made available discursively. To obtain the identity discursively does not necessarily require active participation in an organization, though it does imply some form of 'consciousness-raising' or critical education. Consequently, we need not see welfare-informed needs interpretations and claimsmaking as co-terminus only with the organizational space of new social movements. Rather, we need to understand the discursive and regulatory 'co-ordering' of social movement organizations and the institutional framework of state, family, and market (Smith 1987; Walker 1990).

At the same time, we cannot simply assume that 'counter-hegemonic claims' are embedded in 'counter discourses'. Indeed, while there is much evidence of the former in the Justin Clark case, the latter seems without a referent. For example, organizations of and on behalf of people with disabilities are increasingly claiming for them the right to be 'consumers' in service markets rather than 'clients' of state-run or state-funded institutions and service agencies which often end up regulating and controlling them, denying them their autonomy. Consumers with cash have contractual power and can determine terms and conditions for those who will touch them, bathe them, toilet them, etc. Needless to say, governments pursuing a strategy of privatization and devolution of state-funded and -regulated services are beginning to look seriously at proposals to shift the dollars into the hands of the consumers and away from the institutions and the agencies which have controlled the expenditure of these public funds.

So a challenge to the discourse of 'incompetency' and 'dependency' that has ruled the lives of people with disabilities is being mounted in the terms of the discourse of consumer sovereignty, markets and privatization, and all in the name of the principles of autonomy and self-determination. What will save the link between the subject position of consumer and a 'welfare-informed' self-determination in the case of people with disabilities, one that will resist the slide into 'possessive individualism', is precisely the link to the disability movement. This is a movement struggling against rules of exclusion and seeking to invest 'consumer' with a meaning that will counter the histories of marginalization, and abuse, and control that have been written for people with disabilities.

In order to understand these contradictions, and the kinds of discursive and narrative conflicts played out in *Clark v. Clark*, we need a theory of the relationship between social movements and the institutional framework of society which makes visible their 'co-ordering'; we should not assume a simple opposition. We need a theory, also, that situates the role of social movements in making available discursive positions which can be drawn upon across a wide range of sites, including the individual contractual transactions that take place in markets, and competency determinations that take place in court.

Justin appears as a node in a network of narrative production, a man of many faces. He gains his 'agency' and his 'welfare', not simply through the assertion of a singular narrative, but in the context of a discursive struggle in which he is situated in multiple narrative accounts and discourses which come into conflict. The case illuminates the poststructural insight that, as Valverde writes, 'subjects are not the authors of social meaning... recognition of the multiplicity and ambiguity of social discourse [means that] social subjects can start to exercise some agency if only by using one discourse against another.' (1991 p.183).

ACTS OF RECOGNITION

The discursive conflicts and multiple narratives brought into play by Matheson and the various claimants and witnesses, do not in themselves secure a distribution of welfare that would meet our principles of justice (whatever we decide they might be). Nor does a genuine narrative, pristine in its clarity, necessarily arise from the landscape in which the conflicts are played out, and thus provide a basis for adjudicating claims. The valorization of the claims organized through one narrative and set of discursive strategies may meet the 'needs' of one of the claimants in the discursive battle; and, at the same time, disenfranchise 'others' that appear in the narrative. Simply put, if it was his father's welfare claim that was met, Justin Clark would still be in the Rideau Regional today. His rights to self-determination would have been legally removed from him, even while one might argue that his father had obtained welfare.

How do we sort our way through an apparent minefield of narrative production, organized by terms of discourse that carry institutional force, in order to give moral weight to some claims over others? In other words, how can we deliver on Fraser's assumption that 'we *can* distinguish better from worse interpretations of people's needs' and, as she adds, make such distinctions at the same time that we allow for interpretations to be continually thrown open to question (1989 p.181)? We have seen that criteria of 'genuineness' of narratives are not simply constructed, nor could they be simply applied to make better/worse distinctions. Claims are made in a discursive space of multiple and conflicting acts of recognition of the self and others. Thus the subject/self may appear in many places at once, in each cast in a different light. At one moment, in one narrative, Justin is 'incompetent'; in the next, his 'Blissymbolic' performance of self is read by Matheson as impressive evidence of his competence.

Justin Clark's case makes clear that the possibility for a narrative-writing self lies in its intersubjectivity. The standpoints which organize his *auto*biography, and his biographies, are socially organized. They are provided by the personal and institutional 'others' he encounters. That the self is intersubjectively born, through acts of recognition from the standpoint of others, is Mead's basic insight. Benjamin (1988) argues for an intersubjective theory of the self based on psychoanalytic theory and practice and on a psychoanalytic reading of *The Story of O*. She examines in her reading of the film, how certain acts of recognition, or mis-recognition, of the other result in domination: the instantiation of an object, where a subject should be.

If we are produced by acts of recognition deployed by self and others; if this is the stuff of our intersubjectively-born narratives of self; and if it is such narratives that give our claims meaning and voice and passion, then to what is it that we are applying judgement when we seek to sort claims and give moral weight to some over others? Claims we voice and narratives we write are founded in certain acts of recognition. Because of this, it is the acts of recognition of the self and other, and the knowledge-making practices mobilizing such acts, that must be brought into question in the sorting of claims; in making distinctions between better and worse interpretations of needs. An intersubjective theory of the self can thus shift the analytic focus in determining the 'moral weight' of claims from judging the 'genuineness' of a narrative of self, to include analysing the various acts of recognition and interpretation of others which position the narrative-writing self in certain relations of domination and subordination.

It is, in fact, the acts of recognition about Justin, and the knowledge-making practices that underlay them, that Matheson brings into question in *Clark v. Clark*. In the face of conflicting narratives, he must sort and adjudicate among the claims:

> Where there are marked differences of view the court is compelled to prefer one expert opinion to another. It is necessary to examine and weigh the facts upon which each such expert opinion claims to be founded.

Matheson 'weighs' the claims or 'opinions' about Justin's competence, by judging the knowledge-making practices that 'founded' certain acts of recognition over others. For example, 'exhibit #4' is a hospital record about Justin entered by a paediatrician who speaks in support of Ronald Clark's claim. The paediatrician states in the hospital record that, in his 'professional opinion', Justin continued 'to be incompetent to manage his own affairs.' The certification of incompetency was made when Justin was five years old. The paediatrician entered his confirmation of incompetency when Justin was eight, and shortly thereafter ceased being responsible for his medical care. The fact that the physician had not known Justin for many years, and had supported a declaration of incompetency to manage affairs when a child was a mere five years old, led Matheson to state that his testimony 'sheds very little light' on the issue at hand.

Matheson also calls into question instruments that have been used to assess Justin's competency. Evidence of Justin's 'incompetency' provided by Dr

McCreary, a consulting psychiatrist, is questioned because the assessment instrument he used took no account of the actual context in which Justin had lived for many years. Matheson writes:

> Now I was not tremendously impressed with the testimony of Dr. McCreary who would appear to have based his opinions largely on the Peabody picture vocabulary test. Considering that a young man had only commenced to communicate at 13 years of age and had lived in the not too stimulating society of seriously retarded patients at Rideau on the multi-phasic unit all his life is it reasonable that he should be exposed to vocabulary tests which distinguish serpent from snake, cascade from waterfall or faucet from tap? It would seem to me as reasonable to test Tarzan's intelligence by tests that were appropriate to the environment of his friend Jane.

There are other knowledge-making practices at play which make Justin visible not as an instance of a generalized category of diagnosis, or as an instance on a continuum of intelligence scores, but as a particular 'person'. It is these other knowledge-making practices that decide the day in court. Matheson writes in his ruling:

> On behalf of the respondent Justin Clark a number of close friends and hospital staff were called, perhaps more partisan and certainly more zealous than the witnesses called by Ronald Clark. They had the incalculable advantage of personal knowledge of Justin and proved eminently to the Court that they knew him as a person and I therefore prefer their testimony to those witnesses for the applicant. The testimony of the experts [who spoke on Justin's behalf]... were noteworthy for insight, approach and common sense. Philosophically these three were ideologically committed to what is called the 'Normalization Principle' developed in Scandinavia by Nirje and elaborated in America by Wolfensberger.

'Personal knowledge' and 'philosophical and ideological commitments' are legitimated in this case as alternative standpoints for writing the narratives in which Justin appears. They reflect different practices for knowledge making than that of the dominant psychiatric discourse. In Benhabib's terms, the standpoint of the concrete other comes to hold sway in contradistinction to the generalized other of the categories of psychiatric discourse and psychometric testing. From Judge Matheson's perspective, knowing someone 'personally' matters. It provides insight into the person that cannot be obtained by applying the generalized categories of assessment. By taking up this standpoint the psychiatrist and psychologist, who give evidence on behalf of Justin, are able to resist the totalizing effects of the discourse that has legitimated them as expert witnesses in the first place.

NEED FOR AN ETHICAL STANCE

Matheson's judgment does not give us insight into the ethical stance he drew upon to judge more valid those acts of recognition formed out of personal knowledge of Justin. He simply states that because they 'knew him as a person', he preferred the testimony of the expert witnesses for Justin, over the testimony of expert witnesses for his father, 'the applicant'. While his position undoubtedly holds appeal, it begs further justification and clarification. What does it mean to suggest that acts of recognition of an other, based on personal knowledge, provide for 'better' interpretations of claims and need statements, than acts of recognition based on knowledge-making practices which seek to objectify the person into certain categories of diagnosis, etc.?

Forms of knowledge making about the other, have been distinguished by the extent to which the acts of recognition they make possible, bring the other into view as a subject. Smith has suggested that the impetus for a 'feminist sociology' is to challenge the 'universalizing' practices which have rendered women invisible as subjects in their own right. To universalize subjects out of existence is to perform, in Haraway's terms, the 'god-trick'. It is a 'conquering gaze from nowhere', in which the particularities and actualities and activities and agencies of those across whom the gaze falls, are simply not seen (1991). They are read, if at all, not as subjects, but as instances of the limited 'masculinist' categories which focus the gaze. Theweleit (1987) has examined personal letters of officers in the *Friekorps*, writing home in the 1930s from the front of the rising Third Reich, as narratives which activate the authors' recognitions of women. He shows how women came to figure both as objects of desire and as objects of fear, and how such positioning organized the *Friekorps* relations of violence and sexuality with regard to women. His analysis adds to the universalizing knowledge-making practices, those which objectify the other, and those which figure the other as object of fear or disgust and thereby set the other up for annihilation.

Benjamin argues that when recognition is granted to others only in ways that universalize or objectify them, and deny their subjectivity and personhood, then the seeds of domination are born. For Benjamin, women come to be dominated by men, where men do not recognize women as subjects in their own right, and where women do not claim their own subjectivity. Mis-recognition, she argues, finds its source in the gendered structuring of nurturing where mothers often do not appear as subjects; and in masculinist cultural practices and forms of rationality which associate subjectivity with an independent self and a denial of the subjectivity of others. In her analysis of literary narratives written by men, de Beauvoir argues that the mark of gender difference is not in itself the foundation of the dominion of men over women. Rather, women have been made 'other' to men in ways that deny them subjectivity and personhood in the eyes of men, in ways that deny them a 'reciprocity' with men. Men have represented the world from their own vantage point, 'which they confuse with the absolute truth' (the god-trick), and in these representations women have been made less than, evil, objects of desire, etc., but always without the dignity of subjecthood which men maintain exclusively for themselves. For de Beauvoir, this particular relation of domination between self and other is not intrinsic to the relations between selves: 'It is possible to rise above this conflict if each individual freely recognizes the other, each regarding himself and the other simultaneously as object and as subject in a reciprocal manner.' (1974 [1949] pp.157–64). With de Beauvoir, Benjamin argues for what we might call an 'ethic of mutual recognition' as a way out of the logic of masculinity in which the other is defined by his standard and his desire:

> To halt this cycle of domination, I have argued, the other must make a difference. This means that women must claim their subjectivity and so be able to survive destruction.... The conception of equal subjects has begun to seem intellectually plausible only because women's demand for equality has achieved real social force. This material change makes the intersubjective vision appear as more than a utopian abstraction; it makes it seem a legitimate opponent of the traditional logic of subject and object.... This means not to undo our ties to others but rather to disentangle them; to make of them not shackles but circuits of recognition. (1988 pp.220–1)

To posit that a 'person', a 'subject', actually exists in our field of vision, a person with whom we come face-to-face through personal knowledge, is not necessarily a strategy for re-centering the subject in a way that sets him or her up as a subject of tyranny or an object of domination. Rather, as Kearney argues, even if the postmodern deconstruction of the fixed subject has no epistemological limits, 'it must recognize ethical limits.' At some point in time and space, we do indeed face 'others', who themselves persist through space and time. We come to a point where 'here and now I face an other who demands of me an ethical response.' (1988 p.364). The self exists, even if its boundaries are made fluid by shifting acts of recognition. The ethical requirement, for Kearney, is to recognize the persisting yet fluid other as a subject.

Implicitly, Matheson is judging the various acts of recognition at play in *Clark v. Clark* against an ethic of mutual recognition between subjects. Those acts that render Justin a subject, are those that are legitimated as the basis for claims that should receive moral weight in the claims-sorting process. In doing so, Matheson is judging, not singular narratives of self or other, or singular acts of recognition, but the spaces of intersubjectivity that are carved out by many acts of recognition of self and other. It is in these spaces of intersubjectivity that light is cast on Justin in certain ways. The intersubjective space carved out by the expert witness accounts supporting Ronald Clark's claim objectify

Justin beyond the possibility of subjecthood. Justin's Blissymbolic performance of self, and the testaments of his friends and expert witnesses speaking
on his behalf, desire a space in which he appears as a subject. These narrative
accounts, constructed out of deep personal and 'situated knowledge' of Justin
(Haraway 1991), which reflect 'philosophical and ideological commitment' to
his personhood and self-determination, trumped those acts of recognition
organized through a viewing lens embedded in the discourse of psychiatry.

Nonetheless, theirs was not an intersubjectivity free of acts of recognition
that reproduce domination. Justin did have to pass the test of putting together
a narrative of 'competence'. The state-enforced boundary of competence/
incompetence was re-drawn to include him in the former term, but the
dichotomy persists. In Matheson's written judgment, Justin appears against
the backdrop of the 'not too stimulating society of seriously retarded patients
at Rideau on the multi-phasic unit....' His construction of competence requires, in this case, a motif of madness. The subjectivity of those in the back
wards of Rideau Regional must be consigned to silence, or to an incomprehen-
sible babble, in order to hear Justin's personhood.

In conclusion, an ethic of mutual recognition can deliver upon Fraser's
hope: it can keep open the interpretive moment about the subjects and others
which appear intersubjectively in any discursive space, while at the same time
judging better from worse acts of interpretation and recognition. In other
words, we need not condemn the emancipatory account of Justin that appears
intersubjectively, because of the motif upon which it is constructed. Given the
accounts of Justin that were available, the better ones *were* valorized, if the
ethic of mutual recognition is to be our guide. We can applaud the narrative
productions of his subjectivity, and affirm them, while at the same time
recognizing the partiality of perspective and the limiting discursive boundaries which gave Justin his emancipation. As Harding (1986 p.194) suggests,
in relation to a feminist epistemology which maintains the possibility of
'objectivity': 'By giving up the goal of telling "one true story," we can
embrace instead the permanent partiality of feminist inquiry.' 'Emancipatory
epistemologies', Code argues, require that we begin with subjectivity as the
ground of knowing and judging, and that means giving up on the possibility of
absolutist truths (1993). With an ethic of mutual recognition, Matheson does
'objectively' choose one set of accounts over another. He incites an emancipatory epistemology by searching for Justin's subjectivity as the ground for
sorting the conflicting claims in the case. However, at the same moment that
he redraws the boundary of subjectivity and competency to include Justin he
unwittingly casts light on those who remain trapped by the 'god-trick' he does
so much in this case to undermine: the 'seriously retarded... on the multi-
phasic unit...' at Rideau Regional. Narratives which make possible *their*
reconstruction as subjects, a necessary condition of their welfare, are yet to be

performed, or heard, in the places where it counts. For them, we cannot have the ethical response Kearney imagines until, and unless, our knowledge-making practice enables us to come face-to-face. Or as Justin Clark put it, in a presentation he made at the 1991 National Conference of the Canadian Association for Community Living: 'If people think of you as a person that has many possibilities... they will create the space for you to grow.'

NOTES

1   *Clark v. Clark* (1982), 40 O.R. (2d) 383 at 392 (Co. Ct.) *per* Matheson J.

13. Framing Claims and the Weapons of the Weak

Bill Jordan

I should start this paper by acknowledging that my own claims to be a theorist of welfare are shaped by my early experiences as an activist in a poor people's movement (the claimants' unions), by twenty years' service as a social worker, and by our empirical research project (of six years' duration) on decision-making in low- and higher-income households. What I have to say will therefore be strongly practice-orientated (in the broad philosophical sense of the term).

The second half of my title refers to the work of James C. Scott, whose study of everyday peasant resistance in Malaysia is firmly rooted in an analysis of class and power, but gives close attention to the practices of subordinates (Scott 1985). His more recent book, *Domination and the Arts of Resistance: Hidden Transcripts* (Scott 1990), broadens out his critique of the dominant ideology thesis. It draws on historical and literary sources for an analysis of how and why subordinate groups use the repertoires of the powerful to frame their claims, and employ individual absenteeism or banditry (defection, pilfering, small-scale sabotage, go-slows, shoddy work, slander) against their oppressors.

Scott's work has helped me make sense of some aspects of my experience and research which seem relevant to the issues of framing claims. First, although poor people seldom spontaneously organize to frame welfare claims against the rest of society, my experience of involvement in such a movement (Jordan 1973) was not of struggling to overcome false consciousness, but of building on well-established practices of resistance and discourses of dissatisfaction while formalizing and strengthening social networks. Second, although clients of social work agencies seldom reject professional analyses of their 'problems' openly, they are nevertheless skilled in subverting agency goals, and in pursuing their own purposes and interests within the roles and rights accorded them: social workers only crudely capture their artful practices with such words as 'manipulative' and 'dependent', since clients transform the nature of transactions, rather than simply seeking more of what professionals aim to provide (Jordan 1972). Third, in our research on household decision-making we found that subordinates (poor people, women in better-off households) adopted the normative frameworks of powerholders (the ethics of hard work and family responsibility), but adapted their rhetorics to justify practices which diverged from the conventional interpretations of these norms.

None of this — which will be developed in the first part of my paper — is intended to discredit analyses of welfare claims in terms of institutional structures and power relations. Clearly claimants, clients and women were all systematically subordinated by officials in social service agencies and men in households. However, they were able to gain room for manoeuvre by some fancy discursive footwork in two ways. First, although they could scarcely be said to develop a moral analysis of social relations, universalizing their claims through the deployment of abstract principles of justice (Habermas 1987), they were able to pick out parts of the dominant ideology, in terms of which others justified their authority over them, and employ these against those powerholders. Second, although they did not develop their own alternative understandings of their social worlds, or elaborate these in terms of a new blueprint for social relations, they did interpret the apparently consensual standards of their transactions with powerholders in radically divergent ways. Claimants cobbled together their version of a good life out of bits of animal, fish and bird breeding, poaching, clothing club agencies and casual and undeclared work, using repertoires borrowed from the social security regulations and the enterprise culture. Clients interpreted their wilder practices — drunken nights out, flights from hearth and home, occasional flings with those who took their fancy, spending sprees or shoplifting expeditions — within a solemn psychological vocabulary of panic attacks, depressive episodes, stress, crisis or discovering their true selves. Middle-class women interpreted their accountability for making something of themselves in the labour market in terms of a self-developmental rather than a resource-incremental version.

This, at least, was their story as told to me, variously a political activist, mildly subversive social worker, and member of a qualitative research project team. It was not necessarily the same story they told at the pub or the launderette, nor was it more or less true (Mulkay and Potter 1985). While it is important for theorists to postulate authentic autobiographical narratives (Fay 1987) and ideal speech situations (Habermas 1987) for the analysis of how justice relates to welfare, self to community, and autonomy to structure, the everyday order of such people's lives depends on giving more or less convincing accounts (Silverman 1989) of themselves and their actions in a whole series of different interactive contexts (Silverman 1985; Cuff 1980). The accountability frameworks and discursive repertoires of the claimants' union meeting, the social work visit and the research interview are all adapted to the public, 'on stage' nature of the performance (Scott 1990; cf Goffman 1959, 1969): they are not the same as what Scott calls the 'hidden transcripts' (as opposed to official texts) of the pub or club. The latter are far more likely to refer (though often through humour, myth, symbol or folklore) to an alternative order, with radically redistributed roles, rights and resources (Scott 1990).

Such claims are seldom made public because they are too costly, not just in terms of the rejection, marginalization or stigma that they might entail, but also because of what subordinates have invested (Popkin 1979) in the prevailing order. Open, concerted, coordinated claims against powerholders are rare, because they are unlikely to be conceded, and because there are always chances to subvert the system, making opportunistic gains, threatening or embarrassing those in authority by using their own rhetoric against them, opting out of unwanted or exploitative obligations, getting satisfaction from symbolic or substantive revenge, and so on.

This revisionist view clearly overstates its case, since claimsmaking social movements do develop among subordinates (though seldom among the most powerless members of the claimant group — see the Black and women's movements). However, successful organized resistance usually develops out of this informal everyday variety, rather than through the separate development of counterhegemonic ideologies and practices. Subordinates who have made some opportunistic gains consolidate these through coordination: subordinates in a tight spot support each other in defence of traditional practices. Radical rhetoric is only a useful adjunct to the hidden transcript of indigenous resistance if it brings with it useful allies, if it disconcerts powerholders, or if it can legitimate longstanding unorthodox practices.

In the next section I shall analyse (from my experience in those three fields) everyday resistance to power and try to show how the everyday practices of subordinates relate to the exercise of authority over them. In the final one I shall argue that welfare claims are usually framed in terms of a reciprocal relationship between powerholders and subordinates and in line with established practices, rather than in terms of abstract justice. Hence — and this is my conclusion — successful social movements for disadvantaged groups contain some backward-looking elements that appeal to tradition and strengthen existing practices, as well as postulating future ethically-superior social relations. I shall weave into my argument an account of why this is necessarily so: that the everyday order of social relations is made up of interactants' artful practices (Garfinkel 1967), rather than reproducing social structures (Giddens 1984), and hence that we must understand practices in their own right (Anne Rawls 1987, 1989) rather than as reflections of an institutional order of power relations. I trust the examples will be read as critically self-reflexive autobiography and not as self-indulgence.

THE PRACTICE OF RESISTANCE

My interest in this topic goes back to the very first day of my working life when (as a 21-year-old Oxford graduate with an overdeveloped social conscience) I took up a position as a 'discipline officer' in Her Majesty's Prison Service. It did not take long to discover that neither the official authority to control the lives of prisoners, nor the official duty to attend to their rehabilitation, were easy to implement. Inmates did not organize themselves into unions or protest movements, nor did they generate an ideology to counter Home Office policy: they carried out a kind of guerrilla warfare in which they maximized their scope for autonomous action in pursuit of their versions of the good life in a very restrictive environment. In the daily bickering and skirmishing that made up prison life, they cleverly drew on whatever the official line of the moment might have been (welfare and rehabilitation or clear-cut rules and punishment) to construct rhetorical justifications of, or arguments for, their chosen practices (Mathieson 1965). The art of being a prison officer, I quickly learnt, lay not in the authoritative deployment of the disciplinary code (unless you were very physically intimidating), nor in cultivating a compassionate concern for inmates' well-being, but in mustering an equally ingenious rhetorical defence of the regulations. My masterpiece was, when a group of prisoners argued that queuing for a mass X-ray screening constituted non-working time, and hence a smoking break, to insist that this was out of order, on the grounds that the X-ray picture would be obscured by the smoky inhalation.

This was my first clue in the development of a line of thought which I would now put as follows: the interactive order of face-to-face relations is constituted by artful practices through which individuals produce selves, create meanings and actively pursue purposes (Garfinkel 1967; Goffman 1969). The institutional order (formal roles, rules and structures) provides the boundaries and limits to this local order, and interactants are accountable to each other in terms of that institutional order (Rawls 1989). Hence, interactional competence is the primary requirement of the face-to-face situations in which claims are negotiated (Redley 1991), including highly regulated ones like prisons and social security offices (where I spent many of my prime years), though even there competence lies in the artful deployment of arguments derived from formal rules and standing orders. Any satisfactory theory of welfare claims must take account of this fact (the *sui generis* nature of the interactional order, as Anne Warfield Rawls (1987) puts it), since ethical claims must always eventually not only be codified within the institutional order, but also implemented within the interactional order. They must be operationalizable by the skilful practitioners of the everyday encounter, whether in the lockup, the social services office or the kitchen.

If I fondly imagined that a professional qualification and a battery of therapeutic skills would overcome the difficulties I faced as a fresh-faced and slightly-built screw, I was quickly disabused of this fantasy by my experiences as a probation officer and a social worker (1965–85). To read the professional texts and training manuals of the day was to enter an ideal world of psychodynamic omnipotence (Ferard and Hunnybun 1962; Goldberg 1963), in which the all-wise practitioner was always one jump ahead of the client's (necessarily infantile and irrational) resistances, transforming them into positive energy by penetrating interpretations. My first book (Jordan 1970) was an attempt to make sense of the hectic and blundering quest for survival that made up the bulk of my work with my most deprived clients. Written within the psychodynamic idiom of the day (and hence couching its claims to originality with the modesty required from a novice who was, at the time of writing, still a mere practitioner with no university post) I argued that the accepted orthodoxy on the social work relationship underestimated the active and purposeful aspects of client behaviour.

> I believe that such under-educated, economically hard-pressed, impulsive, anxious people can provide many clues about what is wrong with the doctor–patient way of thinking about the social work relationship. By refusing to play the game according to the rules of casework theory, they indicate the weaknesses of these rules. The biggest weakness is that the game is formulated in such a way that it often seems as if only the social worker has aims and plans and things he is trying to do to the client. It fails to take account of the things that the client is trying to do to him. It is like describing the game of cricket purely from the bowler's point of view, acknowledging that the batsman may do things that make it difficult to get him out (the client may have resistances against treatment) but failing to recognize that the batsman is aiming to make runs off the bowler. (pp.45–6)

Writing as someone who had had several very quick centuries scored off his bowling, I analysed the patterns of transactions between a well-meaning representative of agency powers and resources, and young couples living on the far edge of their social capabilities. Their facility for making me do their emotional and material legwork, by presenting problems in the form of almost daily dramatic crises, was impressive: my self-imposed earnest reliability required me to do all the fielding of their powerful shots, while my colleagues watched with quiet amusement. As in classic relationships of patronage, the combination of fear and gratitude, coercion and partnership, inequality and community, dominion and exchange (Unger 1987 pp.135–40) that characterized such repeated transactions gave my clients an interest in preserving their bond with me: we depended on each other for our strange and primitive identities.

Increasingly aware of the weaknesses of these approaches to social deprivation, I took the fleeting opportunity in 1972 to catch the final wave of the

Protest Movement as it gently lapped the Devon coastline. The recession of that winter had thrown out of work many of the radical elements (International Socialist persuasion) of Newton Abbot's industrial workforce: claimants' unions had been developing in other towns, and out of a series of unpromising local meetings there developed one of the most prominent in the country. Our success stemmed from several factors. First, the organizational experience of the politically conscious was grafted onto a close-knit network of indigenous claimants — irregular workers, people with disabilities and chronic illnesses, single parents — with well-established grievances and everyday resistance skills. The latter (many of whom were known to me in my social work role, but who magnanimously overlooked my other identity) formed the bulk of the membership, and provided the most effective and ingenious advocates over individual welfare claims: the political element dealt in strategy and organization. Second, due to a flair for publicity, we accumulated quite extensive resources (vehicles, gardens, offices, cash) from which we provided tangible benefits for members (parties, outings, weekly supplies of vegetables, meeting places). Third, we were able to create a very successful advocacy service, winning handsome sums from the supplementary benefits system. Fourth, we won a political battle over an administrative reorganization of the emergency payments system, as a result of which we were able to gain cash payments for people facing standard systems failures (delays, lost papers, etc.).

Although from today's perspective claimants of that period had a good situation, there was a culture of discontent and criticism of the benefits system on which the political element could build. Supplementary benefits were a national means-tested scheme that represented a semi-decommodified (Esping-Andersen 1990) income provision: they were supposed to be an entitlement, but long-term claimants had to satisfy irksome conditions to receive them (work tests, incapacity tests, cohabitation rules, surveillance). The indigenous element were well-versed in the ways round and through these obstacles, and there was a shared wisdom on the most effective rhetorical devices for outmanoeuvring the authorities, which the union merely codified and systematized. Indigenous members sat politely through the political items on the agenda of meetings, and many were apparently genuine in their support for the policies (such as an unconditional guaranteed income, now called Basic Income) and strategy (pressure on local managers over oppressive rules) of the union. However, the day-to-day lifeblood of the association, and what secured loyalty and solidarity on other issues, was its work on individual claims, and its own mutual benefits. These were the products of a strengthened network of indigenous resistance and cooperation, rather than of new consciousness or social identity. Active members certainly gained sufficient confidence to render a public performance of their artful practices hitherto reserved for pleading their own case, or for recounting their experiences in private, but this was putting 'on stage' the hitherto hidden transcript of individual resistance.

Almost twenty years later, doing qualitative research on how members of low-income households made decisions about whether to take casual work or claim benefits, I recognized much the same arts of resistance in interviewees' accounts. Here is Mr Bow, father of 3 children, explaining why he is unable to take low-paid employment or accept a place on a government training scheme, and why instead he does undeclared cash work 'on the side'.

> *Mr Bow*: ... I goes down the Job Centre quite often, but there's not many kind of jobs what I wanna do, see. I want to ... wages about 150, something like that [...] No. It's like ... they asked me whether I'd wanna do these government schemes, you know, it's ... it's not the same, you know, it's ... it's, well I've tried 'em before and there I was working three days, three days a week I think it was and 50 odd pound, something like that. And it was just so silly. I thinks it's disgrading a man, you know, to work for that wage — would you? [...] You know, it ... actually we don't have anything, any luxuries or anything like that [...] I been married 7 years now, I don't think my wife's ever had steak. 7 years. That's been working, mind you, and on unemployment [... account of various short-term employments] And then I just pick up jobs, I, you know ... I worked for, what do they call it, they call 'em travellers, they come down and they do roads and all that lot, and I do roofing for 'em. They come down and they offer me, what, 2 or 3 weeks' work. And I go and do roads for 'em, tarmac the roads and that lot [...] 'Cause the money's there, see, the money's actually there [...] 'Cause with these jobs here they only last about, maybe 2 weeks, see, and it's, I can't actually sign off the dole ... 'Cause if I sign off the dole I'm gonna be out of work again in another 2 weeks' time see. I gotta go all through the rigmarole of signing on and all this lot and [...] when you resign on ... you're like 2 weeks in arrears [...] and I'd be worse off and ... then back in debt again [...] No, it wouldn't be worthwhile, so ... I just takes a chance of finding a bit of work [...] 'Cause the moneywise here — the money on social security, it's not great, you can't, you know I, my wife can't live on it, she's always arguing all the time 'cause she haven't got the money, she ha'n, can't go to the shop and get this and get that. [...] But that's the only way: it's either that or go out, go out pinching. Now if I go out pinching I'm in prison. (Jordan, James, Kay and Redley 1992 pp.239–42)

Here Mr Bow constructs a classic case for claimants' informal interpretations of the work ethic, bending the rules on earnings and expanding his weekly entitlement. Like any self-respecting worker he is unprepared to take employment at wages that give him no dignity; like any responsible spouse and parent, he is unwilling to keep his family short. Shunning idleness, yet frustrated in his best endeavours by the shoddy administration of the public assistance service (delays, red tape), he does the right entrepreneurial thing, calculating only in terms of his family's needs, and making his contribution to the economic infrastructure. Rather than see his wife deprived of the ordinary decencies of life in a consumer society, he takes a warrantable risk, as the only alternative to dishonesty. It is a masterly weaving together of elements of the New Right orthodoxy (enterprise plus family responsibility) with its critique of the state system, yet implicit acceptance of the constraining rules under which it is operated.

However, later in the interview Mr Bow surpasses even this artful justification. Asked about his several animals, he replies:

> *Mr Bow*: I got 4 ... well 4 dogs, they're all curled up see. I go out hunting with 'em. That's the only, that's me, you know, that's the enjoyment I get [indistinct] that's the only enjoyment I get really ... going out with 'em. [...] Night times [...] I been going out once every ... about week now — I used to go out now about 3 or 4 times [...] a week, see.

> *Q*: Can you sell ... I mean is it rabbits you catch?

> *Mr Bow*: Yeah. Yeah, rabbits. Rabbits, hares, foxes, deer or you know that's ... well it's ... ain't s'posed to some of the thing's but ... most of it I, I get it all [...].

> *Q*: Right. Is there a danger of the taxman catching up with you?

> *Mr Bow*: ... Well I spose they could really because I sells most of the stuff, like the rabbits I s..., I sell, I sells 'em. You know, on an average night there'll be 15, 20 rabbits, that's maybe, that's what, 20 pound i'n'it ... and maybe ah ... someink else ... talking about maybe a hundred pound hmmm ... S'pose it is in a way. It's like ... social security, if they found out I was [indistinct] rabbits, selling 'em [indistinct]

> *Q*: [indistinct] the risk.

> *Mr Bow*: Yeah, but I, I don't I don't look at it myself 'cause it's, 'cause what it is, I'm looking at it as ... if I go out rabbiting or ... go out, I go out, it's me dogs do the work, see ... And that money don't go into me wife's ... or me, it goes back into food for the animals ... It don't actually, I don't actually go and spend it on meself or me wife or children; it goes back in what they need. If they need a sack of dogfood I get a sackfull. And if they need tablets, they need milk, all kinds of tablets and stuff ... which that goes back into they. Do'n'actually go to me, so ... (Jordan et al. 1992 pp.315–16)

In a creative move (a variation on one used by the claimants' union in my day) Mr Bow here shows that his dogs, which are not claiming benefit, are both the workers and the beneficiaries of his hunting activities, and hence he is within the rules of entitlement. This is the very stuff of everyday resistance among poor people, conjuring up a vivid image of a kind of poaching which is specially constructed within the social security regulations, taking place at night (hence leaving him available for employment during normal working hours), and involving neither labour nor reward for the hunter, who merely observes his dogs earning their keep, and enjoys himself.

This discursive bending of the rules, to seek a degree of autonomy and space for the practices of a good life, was characteristic of the accounts by irregular workers, men and women, who formed two-thirds of our sample of 36 couples. Rather than challenging the fairness of the rules, or proposing alternatives, they interpreted them in such a way as to give themselves room for manoeuvre in managing their resources (Jordan et al. 1992 pp.316–21). In this way they were less 'trapped in poverty' than theoretical analyses (Parker 1989) or econometric modelling (Beenstock et al. 1987) of their situation suggested, and they described their decision-making as constrained more by the administration of the system than its regulations (Jordan et al. 1992 pp.161–8). In practice, they had invented for themselves a kind of Basic Income system, by expanding the disregarded portion of their occasional earnings (from about £5 per week in the official rules to around £30–50 in their informal ones), and by granting themselves more extensive tax allowances when they did come off benefits and take paid work (not declaring all their earnings to the tax authorities). But only one couple argued for a change in the system to legalize these practices, along the lines of the Basic Income proposal.

If the Newton Abbot claimants' union of the early 1970s had offered no more than a counter-ideology and a vision of a world in which all benefits were as automatic and unconditional as child benefit, it is doubtful whether it would have won any support from indigenous long-term claimants: other unions were made up almost entirely of middle-class members, such as college drop-outs, or members of fringe political groups. Our union had a mass membership (400 subscription-payers at its height) because of the respect we paid to indigenous everyday forms of the resistance, and the fact that we were careful to frame our welfare claims in terms which built on, rather than cut across, their identities and practices. The particular version of post-industrial, post-socialist human flourishing to which we appealed owed as much to Mr Bow's account of the good life (a self-respecting tarmac-layer and responsible husband and father by day and a law-abiding poacher by night) as to Marx's famous image of the polyvalent citizen of a communist utopia.

A more puzzling issue over the relationship of resistance practices to welfare claims arose in our research on decision-making on higher-income (i.e. above average earnings) households: why did only one of the 36 women interviewees use a feminist discourse in their accounts of how they chose what employment to take and what hours to work, and how they reconciled their choices with those of their partner? Instead, they saw themselves accountable as Durkheimian individualists (Durkheim 1933 [1893]), telling us what they had made of themselves in the world of work, but assuming (apparently unquestioningly) their primary responsibility for childcare and domestic work. Given the wide accessibility of feminist analyses of the domestic division of labour (in the popular media as well as books), the costs of adopting some of its rhetoric to justify practices, or criticize those of partners, seemed far lower than were the costs of radically redistributive welfare claims for the poor. Although these women as a group had exactly the same educational qualifications as their partners, and most had started down the road towards professional or managerial careers, they now earned on average one-third of their husbands' salaries, and were concentrated in junior, part-time, clerical or manual posts. Only Mrs Palm, a senior teacher, used a feminist repertoire to legitimate her career (she was the highest earner among the women respondents) and to justify a role swap with her husband when the children were young (he had since qualified as a barrister, but still earned less than her salary). The rest took for granted a change to less demanding employment or hours of work on the birth of their first child, and seemed to have invested more in protecting their partners' careers than in developing their own.

Were they unaware of the subordination and dependence built into their patriarchal domestic relations? (Walby 1990). Had they swallowed the Thatcherite ideology of the family, or was this the 'new realism' of the 1980s? (Finch and Morgan 1991). Did they practise resistance, but say little about it to two male interviewers? (Finch 1984). Some clues to the answers to these questions are given by Mrs Beech in some repartee with her husband and the interviewer during their joint interview (which followed each one's individual version of their decisions). Mr Beech had mentioned in his individual interview that he would not mind a role swap with his wife — something that was feasible, given that they were both practising solicitors, though at the time she was doing part-time work.

> *Q*: Wouldn't you give him the chance?

> *Mrs Beech*: What, to sit at home while I went out to work? Well, because I'm probably on to a winner, you know. Basically because society accepts the fact that women stay at home, the man goes out to work, and as long as that traditional role is established I would like to sit around …

Mrs Beech is overstating her case, of course. Like the other women in the sample, she has demonstrated her willingness to contribute to the household's income, as well as protect her husband's career — she actually rescued his ailing practice, taking it over at a point when he was forced to seek other employment. However, in a joking way she seems to be putting into words the practices of many of the women who, having got off the professional career bandwagon, see opportunities for autonomy and self-development within the role of mother and part-time worker. Several other women spoke of their preference for part-time work allowing more autonomy and self-development than their original occupation and one went as far as to pay demure tribute to her husband's career success for making this possible!

The artful practices of resistance by these middle-class women can call on a far richer diversity of vocabularies and resources (including those of feminism, where these prove useful) than are available to their low-income counterparts. But the common feature is that, for purposes of everyday interaction, and in public accounts of their lives, they choose not to challenge the dominant order, but to seek a measure of autonomy and opportunistic gain within it.

POWER, RECIPROCITY AND JUSTICE

In this brief concluding section, I shall consider Scott's contention that powerless and dependent groups, in generating their own discourses of dissent from official transcripts of power, emphasize dignity and autonomy rather than justice (Scott 1990 pp.xi–xii, 112–15), and that they have an interest in reinforcing hegemonic appearances (for instance, by stressing the duties of the powerholders within existing relations) rather than challenging the social order (pp.85–107).

This rings true to my experience in the three fields discussed in this paper: it seems to be the indignities associated with the exercise of power that most move subordinates to anger and resistance, yet this usually takes the public form of appeals to the obligations that accompany power, rather than attempts to discredit that authority itself. And this seems in turn to be related to the importance of the interactional order as a source of meaning, self and purpose. Whatever its structural form, power must be exercised in a public performance, and where this is experienced as denying subordinates the scope for displaying a creditable 'face' (Goffman 1955), then it can be turned against those who use power, to discredit them also. Power is fragile, insofar as it can perhaps best be sustained by allowing its subjects some dignity and autonomy, yet these are likely to be used to develop resistance practices. Accommodating some such practices, yet setting effective limits around them, is presumably one of the arts of effective rule. All this prompts the disturbing thought that welfare claims have little to do with justice, and much to do with the interactive theatre in which people play out their unequal roles.

Scott's analysis of autonomy and dignity as foci for resistance is rather underdeveloped in his work. However, the examples he gives concern appeals by subordinates against being treated as 'animals' or 'insects' by the powerful. 'The practices of domination and exploitation typically generate the insults and slights to human dignity that in turn foster a hidden transcript of indignation' (Scott 1990 p.7). He also writes of the sense of self-respect and personhood of those who, after long enduring indignities and humiliations in silence, finally speak out against them (p.210). Casual workers among the low-income interviewees in our research frequently spoke resentfully of such treatment (Jordan et al. 1992 pp.94–9; cf Sennett and Cobb 1972), leading them to leave their jobs.

Scott's analysis of why subordinates reinforce the appearances of legitimate power relations emphasizes the risks of open defiance, and the advantages of covertly pursuing divergent interpretations of hegemonic norms. However, he develops his arguments from examples of slave, serf and peasant societies, and hence from highly coercive forms of power, where the risks of challenging authority are extreme and brutal. The interesting point about applying his theories to forms of subordination in advanced capitalist societies is that many of the same phenomena are identifiable, even when the threat of coercion is much reduced. This suggests that the discourses of dissent generated by indignities, and the appeal to reciprocity within existing social relations (such as boss–worker) relate more to an interactional order, in which self and meaning depend on not giving offence to the 'face' of the other. In the process, reciprocity is not so much about the duties that legitimate power, as about the rituals, courtesies, skills and competences by which interactants understand each other, and communicate mutual recognition. Hence the complaint of the oppressed is in one sense more fundamental than a welfare claim. It is that the exercise of power does not give them the opportunity to be a human self, or that it mortifies the self of the subordinate (Travers 1992), by destroying the trust on which sustainable selves and communication depend.

If this is so, then it implies that the notion of welfare in academic social policy analysis is abstract and generalized in the same sense as the concept of justice in political theory. Practices of resistance and discourses of dissent relate primarily to people's experiences of power, in particular social relations — and hence their attempts to gain autonomy and dignity within a given social order. The ability to frame welfare claims is dependent on the achievement of a viable social identity: but this requires the experience of a meaningful interactional order, for the production of self. We all learn interactional skills — the ability to carry off the public performance of self — in subordinate roles, as children. We are socialized into the reciprocities of trust and mutual commitment in relations of dependence. Perhaps the weapons of the weak and the discourses of discontent hark back to the universal experiences of humiliation in childhood, rather than expressing universalizable ethical welfare claims. Indeed it may be that ethical analyses of justice and welfare are based on reflective consideration of experiences of domination and being dominated. Such reflection is perhaps most likely to arise when groups have had an experience of social mobility (either upwards or downwards), and of the dissonance between exercising power and being under authority.

Scott's analysis of power relations, and his critique of the dominant ideology thesis, emphasize the use-value of hegemony for subordinates, and their strategic adoption of a camouflage of dominant discourse to cloak the practice of resistance. His thesis is that they are able imaginatively to reverse or negate ideological legitimations of power, but are constrained at the level of political action and struggle to mask their subversive intentions. 'The conflict will therefore take a dialogic form in which the language of the dialogue will invariably borrow heavily from the terms of the dominant ideology prevailing in the public transcript.' (Scott 1990 p.102). Hegemonic discourse is therefore 'an invitation to a structured argument' (p.102), in which 'the basic terms ... are shared but in which the interpretations follow wildly divergent paths in accordance with vital interests' (p.100).

My argument in this paper is that Scott overstates the strategic element in resistance practices, and underplays the interactive element in keeping up the appearances of power. Reciprocity is not just a contingent feature of the particular power relations of landlord and peasant or patron and client: it is a necessary condition of the communication on which the interactive order is based. In any dialogue, the best way to keep up one's own appearances (to pull off a public performance of oneself) is to keep up the appearances of the other (to sustain the other's 'face', by avoiding giving offence). Formal power relations require the rituals of 'giving face' in interactions to be asymmetrical (in terms of authority and deference), but the principles of mutual commitment still apply. Dominator and dominated depend on each other to achieve interactionally what their formal roles prescribe: they have an interest in saving each other's face.

In our research study on decision-making by higher-income couples, we noticed that — with very few exceptions — women deferred to men in the joint interview situation, modifying any discrepancies between their individual account and that of their partner, and avoiding challenges or disagreements. The exceptions were all couples where the man's 'career' was foundering, or the woman disputed her 'non-careerist' partner's account of her work as 'career'. We also noticed that we, as interviewers, were embarrassed by these few open disagreements that did occur, and tried to preserve the interactional order of the interview by comments or questions which, by restoring 'normal appearances', saved not only the man's face, but also our own.

Mr Birch, a research scientist who moved first into management and then (under threat of redundancy) into starting his own small business, gave an upbeat account of his entrepreneurial venture: his wife, in her individual interview, said it was losing money and that she had been slightly reluctantly driven into pursuing her career as a teacher because this was now the main source of family income. In the joint interview, she was asked if she would give up her job to help with his business.

Mrs Birch: No, not until it actually makes money. I have to keep the job to bring in the money to keep the household going. We simply can't do without my salary at the moment, but there again I don't know if I'd want to. [...] We're not managers or business people at all.

Mr Birch: That's not true, I'm a manager.

Mrs Birch: Nigel's getting there more quickly than I am.

Mr Birch: I've been a manager for six years, so I have the production and technical experience. What I lacked was probably the financial and sales side. The financial side of a small business is not all that daunting. The sales is an area which does require learning about. I've employed as I told you earlier, a part-time salesman and also been on courses and club meetings with Enterprise Agency workers, very helpful.

[pause]

Q: My turn to speak now, isn't it?

Here Mr Birch stops speaking, and domestic power relations dictate that Mrs Birch should say something (if only a murmured endorsement) to validate his account of the business's good prospects, but she pointedly does not. After an awkward pause, the interviewer tries, half-jokingly, to restore normal appearances and interactive momentum by referring to the formal roles and rights of the interview situation. This moment (and another later, when Mrs Birch responds to her husband's comment that some couples have separate bank accounts by a throwaway 'Good idea, why haven't we discussed this earlier?' followed by a laugh) breaches the deferential norms of patriarchy, and at the same time ruptures the interactional order of the interview. In failing to give her husband face, Mrs Birch brings about a moment in which all the participants temporarily lose themselves (Travers, forthcoming).

The final section of this paper has necessarily been rather speculative in its attempt to link resistance practices and appeals to reciprocity with the interactive processes that make up the everyday world of power relations. The turn taken by ethnomethodology since its promising beginnings, and some arid disputes between quantitative and qualitative sociologists, have led to missed opportunities in the development of theoretical analyses of the interactional order. There are signs that this damage is being repaired, and that microsociology can make an important contribution to epistemology and social theory (Anne Rawls 1987, 1989). In reviewing my experience of practice and my more theoretical writing (Jordan 1989, 1990), I am increasingly drawn towards a closer attention to the way in which members artfully sustain meaningful exchanges under unpromising conditions. Just as puzzling as understanding how some groups with which I was associated framed welfare claims is the question of how prison inmates, clients, claimants, interviewees and students enabled me to get by in the various power-laden roles I have occupied as a practitioner. In most such situations, it seems as if the interactive fairness of giving and saving the other's face overrides the requirements of justice in welfare shares.

This should not be taken as a defection from my twenty-year commitment to a restructuring of the welfare state in line with a new, more universalizing, individuated principle of justice in distributional shares (Basic Income). That principle (which I believe is the way to operationalize many of the arguments deployed in the early chapters of this book) also seems to me to be a necessary condition for the development of diversified autonomy among new groups (often emerging in partnership with staff in social services) and the transformation of local politics, discussed in the later chapters (Jordan 1992). If post-modernity is really to be 'modernity come to its senses' (Bauman 1992) rather than a chaotic cacophony of new voices and claims, basic social rights should become more abstract and unconditional. The practices of regulation and resistance and the improvisations of the interaction order are inescapable features of social relations: they are not justifications for domination, whether in the form of workfare or patriarchy.

For comment on this chapter see page 284.

14. The Theory and Politics of Helping in Feminist Social Service Collectives

Janice L. Ristock

> Hierarchical divisions — whether between men and women, the caregiver and the cared-for, the administrator and the direct service worker, the professional and the volunteer, the principal and the teacher, the doctor and the nurse, the theoretician and the practitioner — all reflect differences in power, esteem, and autonomy. Dichotomies of this nature ensure rigid role definitions and organizational structures that fail to uncover the complexities and solutions involved in arriving at a collective responsibility for caring. (Baines 1991 p.68)

In a field characterized and dominated by traditional government-style power structures, feminists have a different approach to the provision of services and social change work. A collective structure has most often been the preferred *modus operandi* for feminist organizations such as rape crisis centres, sexual assault centres, shelters for battered women and women's resource centres. These non-hierarchical, participatory democracies are seen as being consistent with feminist philosophy in that they embody a praxis that fosters social action and empowerment. Zofel's (1985) definition of feminist work neatly defines a collective structure: 'There are no hierarchies, knowledge and information are shared (and not used as oppressive instruments of power), responsibilities are rotated and everybody learns and is capable of doing any of the jobs. There should be as little specialization as possible or rather: everywoman is a specialist in all tasks' (p.25). The collective structure can be viewed as an attempt to adhere to certain feminist principles such as equal power, equal pay and equal work. The collective structure is also in keeping with the feminist belief that our surest route to personal autonomy and political change lies in the strength we have when we work together. Women who work collectively, then, are working within an alternative culture with specific norms, values and practices (Ristock 1989).

The ideal of feminist social service collectives is to work towards eradicating sexist, racist, classist and homophobic oppression within our society, as well as to provide empowering alternative services to women by placing their welfare and experiences at the centre of service provision. My own research and work with feminist collective organizations has shown that they are a viable force in their efforts to retain consistency between their ideology and structure. Yet, collectives struggle with their contradictory location within a mainstream social service system that gives rise to power-over relations. Collectives, therefore, have been easy targets for allegations of inefficiency, tyranny, conflicts and personality problems (see for example, Freeman 1973, 1977; Mansbridge 1973; Riger 1984; Vickers 1991). The criticisms have come not only from right-wing forces who are opposed to the underlying feminist values operating within a service delivery system but also from within feminist circles, from women who have had negative experiences of collective work. Despite the many real difficulties of such work, feminist collectives can offer us a vision of an alternative approach to providing services and fostering human welfare. Understanding this vision, however, requires an insistence on and acceptance of multiplicity. We cannot simply view collectives from a binary perspective as, for example, either social service organizations or social movement organizations; structureless, inefficient models or the uniquely feminist model. To do so diminishes a thorough comprehension of their praxis. Viewing feminist collectives from a perspective of multiplicity means acknowledging the seemingly contradictory aspects of their work or areas of tension within their praxis that occur in the context of the norms and values of the dominant social order. In other words, understanding feminist social service collectives requires an understanding and emphasis of both/and (multiplicity) rather than either/or (dichotomy). In this chapter I summarize some of the information that I have gained from studying feminist collectives and propose a model for understanding their social context. Examining counter-hegemonic discourses operating within and through collectives will assist us in our efforts to develop a general theory of welfare.

Historically and at present, hierarchical bureaucratic institutions with their centralization of power and rigid rules, have served, inevitably, to continue the oppression of women and other powerless groups. Collectives offer an alternative structure with practices such as sharing power and skills, everyone participating in decision-making, and acknowledging the individual worker's needs. This is all in accordance with the fundamental feminist principle that 'the personal is political'. Working collectively allows for women's life experiences to have a place in the work environment by providing a structure that may foster a sense of belonging. This in turn often places a political analysis around those experiences and encourages work for social change. These reciprocal foci of service delivery and social activism have been central to feminist collectives.

Despite the normally intense political and philosophical commitment to feminism behind efforts to retain this structure, many difficulties have been associated with working collectively. Feminist groups tend to become exclusive and remain small in size, due to the requirement of participation by all in every decision (Freeman 1973). They are also known for slowness in decision-making procedures, again because everyone participates and must come to an agreement. There may also be emotional intensity in collective interactions from differing approaches to common cause, and inequitable influences amongst collective members arising from the varying degrees of skills and friendships that may exist within the collective. Further, there may be difficulty in holding members accountable due to the high degree of commitment required (Riger 1984; O'Sullivan 1976). In addition, other difficulties, which are unique to the feminist collective structure, may arise from the lack of a formal authority structure and decision-making structure (Freeman 1977) as well as from the political and service nature of their work.

Above all, writings on feminist movement organizations emphasize the difficulty of providing services at the expense of social activism (e.g., Ridington 1982). Riger (1984) sees this contradiction (between service delivery/social control work and social activism/work for social change) as resolving itself by groups focusing either on the provision of services or on social change. Yet this dualistic construction of social service and social change misses the essence of the values, work and incentives that operate within feminist social service collectives that I have re-searched. Freeman (1973), although critical of collectives, states a social movement organization's basic purpose in terms that any collective social service would wholeheartedly endorse: 'to put itself out of business by changing the situation that gave rise to it and thus eliminating the need for it to exist' (p.43). Feminist collectives view the collective structure as important to maintaining consistency between feminist values and feminist work, specifically in that its non-hierarchical, participatory structure provides for an intimate connection between the best care for women who are in need of service *and* working for social change. Ideally they will work until there is no longer a need for such services. In the long meantime, the organization finds itself in the rather contradictory position of being part of the growing institutionalization of such services while resisting a socially controlling function and retaining a transformative vision. But rather than looking for this contradictory location to devolve into a single focus in the way Riger (1984) and others predict, we might better see the contextual predicament of feminist social service collectives as the unsolvable reality in which they work. In this light, the predicament becomes a framework that is itself necessary to understand if we are to promote and foster the development of alternative settings in the social services. Kathy Ferguson in *The Feminist Case Against Bureaucracy* (1984) comments, 'entry into the public realm, now increasingly a bureaucratic realm, is necessary for any voice of opposition that wants to be heard...it comes down to the tension between living/surviving in the world as it is and making the world into what it should be.' (p.180). This tension merits further explora-tion.

In sum, the alleged dichotomy between social service and social change is not experienced as problematic within feminist collectives. But there are tensions. The difficulty of achieving consistent feminist praxis has been usefully summarized as a struggle between two poles of attraction: disengagement and mainstreaming (Adamson et al.1988; Briskin 1991). This model theorizes feminist strategic practice and emphasizes the context surrounding feminist practices rather than presenting a standpoint of theory alone or theorizing from experience alone, which often individualizes or personalizes experience. Disengagement is a form of practice that operates from the position of critiquing the system while standing outside of the system. When operating from this standpoint, there is a desire to create alternative structures and ideologies and promote a vision of social transformation. According to Briskin (1991), the motivation for a standpoint of disengagement rests on an understanding and analysis of the patriarchal nature of institutions and on the evidence that women have been excluded from power in the public realm. Mainstreaming is the form of practice that works within the existing system. Implicit in this standpoint is the commitment to transform the everyday lives of women by focusing on particular issues and offering popular and practical solutions. The desire is to reach out to the general population and interact with major institutions such as the family, workplace and the state, to challenge the public/private dichotomy that exists and affects women's lives. As Briskin (1991) explains, 'both mainstreaming and disengagement are necessary to the feminist vision. The goal of feminist practice is to maintain an effective balance between the two; the dilemma is the tendency for feminist practice to be pulled toward one pole or the other.' (p.10). The risk of operating solely from a disengaged position is marginalization while the risk of operating solely from a mainstreaming position is institutionalization. A single feminist collective can and should operate from both positions of mainstreaming and disengagement while providing social services to women and working for social change. For example, a sexual assault centre operates from a mainstreaming position by ensuring that it has working relations with police, medical and legal systems so that the collective can facilitate the process for women who choose to press charges against their assailant. Collectives may also accept funding from government departments that are decidedly mainstream but they would probably not accept funding from the Secretary of State in Canada, which does not support advocacy of gay and lesbian rights or freedom of choice on abortion. They operate from a disengaged position by offering women counselling services that presents an analysis of sexual assault as part of a continuum of violence against women, the roots of which are in patriarchal society. They are also critical of police, medical and legal systems' response to sexual assault where women must endure a second rape that begins in the form of a medical exam for obtaining evidence.

THE THEORY OF HELPING IN FEMINIST COLLECTIVES

A feminist approach to the delivery of services is multi-layered in its goals and actions, and different from the traditional approach to service delivery. Firstly feminist collectives that provide social services are involved in care-giving and relatedness by both their collective structure and their social service function (Ferguson 1984; Gilligan 1982). Workers offer support to one another at the same time that they provide empowering services for women. The feminist adage 'the personal is political' that operates in collectives legitimates individual experiences (including feelings) as sources of knowledge that are to be valued (Morgen 1983). Secondly, feminist collectives are involved in external activities for major social/political change such as pressure group strategies, letter writing campaigns, lobbying, testimony, demonstrations and coalition groups. Finally, the workers feel that the provision of service to clients is itself social action.

I am proposing that a feminist approach to social change through their provision of services can be summarized by four concepts. It is the essence of these concepts that underlies a feminist approach and that is best represented in the collective structure. These concepts in turn can be contrasted to the approach of traditional mainstream (or 'malestream') organizations. And it is the co-existence of both feminist and traditional ideological ideals that comprise the larger social context that collectives work within and are shaped by. My conceptual framework is presented below in the form of a chart followed by a discussion of the concepts in greater detail:

FEMINIST APPROACH	TRADITIONAL APPROACH
1. Empowerment	*1. Power*
–collectives as role models	–workers as leaders
–sharing knowledge between women	–distributing facts and information
–value experience	–value specialization
–'the personal is political'	–value expertise
–comes from within	–comes from above
2. Choice	*2. Direction*
–non-judgemental	–decisiveness
–present options	–choose one route
3. Ethic of Care	*3. Ethic of Justice*
–relatedness	–rights
–identity of connection	–identity of separation
–responsibility	–individualism
4. Survival	*4. Access*
–based on women's history of oppression	–based on the power of patriarchy

It is my contention that a feminist collective's approach to social change and social service delivery is underlined by an adherence to the concepts of empowerment, choice, and an ethic of care and survival. The feminist approach and the traditional approach, as outlined, represent the perception of feminists of the opposing ideological ideals existing within the context of social service delivery. But rather than seeing these as binary oppositions, they can also be viewed as attracting poles within the social service context that parallel the theoretical conception presented by Adamson et al. (1988) and Briskin (1991). A feminist approach to the delivery of social services and social change would ideally be disengaged from the mainstream social service system: it is an alternative approach with different values and goals operating. Yet it is often involved in that system in the normal course of working for service recipients' immediate best interests. In this sense, collectives would be operating from a mainstreaming orientation: the desire is to reach out directly and interact with the existing social institutions. These poles present a tension for feminist social service organizations and reflect the struggles of collectives not to be marginalized, on the one hand, or co-opted and institutionalized, on the other.

Feminist collectives struggle with the tension between disengagement and mainstreaming and with the opposing value systems that operate in the social service work context between traditional systems and feminist systems. I will elaborate on the four components of each system as illustrated on the chart. I will be emphasizing the experiences of feminist collectives and their perceptions of how they are different from traditional agencies. Empowerment operates as a central value within a collective structure where power is diffused and experience is valued. In my survey of Canadian feminist collectives, empowerment is strongly identified as a component of what it means to work collectively (88 per cent [*n*=30] of the collectives who responded to a survey about their work indicated that empowerment was a value central to their work environment). Empowerment conveys a meaning of mutuality and sharing. Active involvement in and control of your work environment, input into decision-making at all levels within the organization, having a sense of interdependence and validation of opinions, ideas and experiences are all ways in which empowerment is enacted within collectives. Empowerment is also a goal of the service that they provide to service recipients. Collective workers feel that they act as supportive role models who work in a way that does not involve oppressive, power-over relations (Ristock 1989). Service recipients — reconceived as participants — are also validated and encouraged to expand their self-awareness through a social service organization that fosters connections through women helping women. The empowerment within these organizations is both psychological and organizational. Recent literature within the field of community psychology has differentiated between these forms of empowerment. At the individual level, psychological empowerment includes participatory behaviour and feelings of efficacy and control. Organizational empowerment includes shared leadership, opportunities to develop skills and effective community influence (Zimmerman 1990). Empowerment, then, can be contrasted with the traditional notion of power. This form of power is found in hierarchies where it is centralized and often oppressive because it remains with a select few. The world of power-over relations has been identified by feminists as conceptualizing women as 'other' and creating separateness and powerlessness.

The concept of choice is then contrasted with the notion of direction. Feminists value the freedom of choice that comes from an approach that is non-judgemental, shares knowledge and presents options for both workers and service users. Thus a service recipient who has been sexually assaulted will be presented with a variety of options when she seeks support: she can receive supportive counselling for her traumatic experiences; she can find an advocate who will assist her should she decide to press charges; she can get referrals for appropriate medical attention. The focus is on placing the service recipient at the centre of the services and letting her make the decisions as the person best informed about her life. She may, for instance, decide not to press charges and she would be supported in her decision. Traditional organizations, on the other hand, value direction and decisiveness. This is readily apparent in many of the protocols and policies that have been established for the social services (e.g., the sexual abuse protocol — once sexual abuse is reported or suspected victims must go through a series of steps including a medical examination and police involvement).

This analysis of the difference between feminist and traditional organizations can further be extended to the moral and ethical values that underlie our service and change approaches. A feminist approach for change is informed by an ethic of care (Gilligan 1982; Ferguson 1984) as found in the collective structure and in the act of caregiving. Caregiving and relating to others is part of a process for change. An ethic of care assumes interdependence and connection to others rather than independence and individualism. In psychological terms then it recognizes self-in-relation-to-others and the environment. Feminist psychologists have been arguing that existing theories of psychological development emphasize some form of autonomy or separation as the main component of the human developmental path. Yet women's primary motivational thrust concerns growth within relationships. Connection with others is a key component of growth (Kaplan 1991). This is in contrast to the ethic of justice that operates as the normative moral orientation in our society based on an emphasis of justice, rights and equality (Gilligan 1982). This ethic, I believe, is supported by hierarchical, traditional organizations where service provision is rooted in individualism and change involves adapting the individual. A justice perspective draws attention to problems of inequality and oppression and holds up an ideal of equality and reciprocity. A care perspective focuses on problems of detachment or abandonment and has an ideal of attention and response to need (Gilligan and Attanucci 1988). Recently Carol Gilligan and Jane Attanucci (1988) have been exploring the meaning of these two different moral orientations and their association to gender. They suggest that these two dimensions — care and justice — are universal experiences in that no one survives in the absence of attachment and we all live in a system of inequality. Yet their research on how men and women analyse moral dilemmas found that while men and women use both moral orientations when thinking about real-life situations, they tend to focus on one set of concerns — men on justice and women on care — and minimally represent the other. Their work does not lead to essentialist theories of moral difference between men and women but, instead, suggests that our society emphasizes a normatively male ethic of justice with a focus on autonomy and separation. Thus collectives are offering an alternative to this normative stance.

Finally, the feminist approach to social change and social service also involves the notion of survival. Feminist collectives reflect women's position in society as an oppressed group. Funding is always an issue, while the demand for the services continue to grow. The vast majority of sexual assault workers are unpaid, and therefore, survival of the organization is always an issue that impacts and informs service and change strategies. Traditional groups, in contrast, have access to the larger power structures because of their normative, status quo orientation. Their funding tends not to be precarious. This then impacts on the types of actions and services they can provide. They also have an interest in maintaining their access and therefore the status quo.

A MODEL FOR UNDERSTANDING ALTERNATIVE SETTINGS

Existing within this social context that includes a tension between feminist and traditional ideals of welfare means that collectives (or any alternative model that opposes the norms, values, forms of the dominant society) cannot exist in their pure or ideal form. Even if a group views itself as being separate from the norms of society (a disengaged position), it is still controlled to some degree by society's rules. Individuals within these settings have still been socialized with the values of mainstream society and bring that history with them to alternative settings despite their intentions about re-socialization. As well, the larger group itself is often forced into relations with society that again affect the attainment of this ideal form. Yet theories on organizational development and social psychological theories of group behaviour have been inadequate in offering explanations of behaviours within alternative settings, such as collectives. For instance, according to Kathy Ferguson (1984) arguments for the inevitability of bureaucracy are either psychological or technological at bottom. They do not account for the social forces that demand bureaucracy. According to Newman, in her study of collectives in the 1960s, collectives that became bureaucratic hierarchical organizations did so because of encroachment from outside bureaucratic forms, not from an internal desire for hierarchy. As well, theories such as social identity (Tajfel 1981) reflect a lack of understanding of the external context. For instance, social identity theory suggests that the need for positive social identity leads to intergroup discrimination. Thus an in-group struggles for a homogeneous, positive social identity in order to obtain higher status. Minorities within the in-group who do not fit with this social identity will experience discrimination from group members. This theory explains what happens within groups and in this case within collectives, but it does not attribute these social psychological phenomena as arising from a larger context. Thus there is a need to understand the effect of external pressures and to suggest ways of preventing in and out groups from forming, rather than seeing them as inevitable outcomes of group development.

A consideration of the framework provided enhances our understanding of the work of collectives and the understanding of any alternative structure attempting to exist within society in that it suggests that we cannot dichotomize our understanding of social service and social change; the collective and the individual; traditional and feminist approaches; us and them. These poles co-exist. We will be better able to change this context and promote welfare by first acknowledging our multiple and contradictory locations within it. The challenge for feminists is to create our own theories that explain and account for the maintenance of balance within a contradictory context such as this and to resist hegemonic constructions of our own. As Sheila Neysmith suggests, 'There are no fixed, universal meanings of caring as it relates to community and family ....Until now the discourse on the nature of the welfare state has excluded the voices of women.' (1991 p.296). A feminist discourse on the provision of services that I have outlined brings forward women's experiences and demands an understanding and analysis of the larger, contradictory social context.

Understanding the larger social context of collectives points to the social construction of collectivity and does not provide easy answers for developing feminist praxis. Yet it does describe more accurately the complex and contradictory reality within which we work. Poststructuralists — in particular de-constructionists — stress an understanding of the positioning and fabrication of subjects within the social relations of power and desire. They see relations as ever-changing rather than as static symbolic order. De-constructing and understanding the produced social positioning and practices can lead to their transformation (Weedon 1987). In my view the task for collectives is to understand their social positionings within a constantly changing context rather than within a context of dichotomous oppositional poles which assumes unity in each pole. Understanding collectives within this framework requires our ideal, our conceptual vision to shift from that of creating a homogeneous community (a unified ideal of collectivity) to what Iris Marion Young (1990b) has called the model of 'an unoppressive city'. In other words we need a vision of service delivery and social action that provides an alternative to traditional systems yet resists hegemonic constructions of our own. The vision of an unoppressive city is an interesting analogy to consider for developing general welfare theory. Within this vision there is an understanding of social relations in which people live together in relations of mediation among strangers with whom they are not in community. In other words this ideal assumes openness to unassimilated otherness. The goal is not for social wholeness. Young (1990b) mentions two factors which are necessary in the model to encourage respect and prevent domination and power-over relations from emerging. The ideal insists on a politics of difference which recognizes and affirms differences. It does this in two basic ways: it gives representativeness to group interests and it celebrates the distinctive cultures and characteristics of different groups. The image of a city is more complex than that of a community. The city is meant to describe a kind of relationship of people to one another. City embodies difference — strangers live and work together, there are communities and also public meeting places, areas where you can meet strangers and encounter difference. This ideal assumes that group differentiation is a given of social life for us. Of course many questions are raised by this vision such as, 'how to do this?' 'how do we make the conceptual shift?' 'what defines a group that deserves recognition and celebration?'

The issue of working with diversity has been taken up by some feminist collectives. For example the Toronto Rape Crisis Centre uses a model of 'group and caucus' as a way to address dominance and difference within their organization. Women with varying positions of privilege — white skin, middle-class, heterosexual — meet in groups to gain awareness of how they may use their positions of privilege in oppressive ways, while women who experience additional levels of oppression — women of colour, lesbians, working-class women — can caucus to support one another and challenge any oppressive practices within the collective (Toronto Rape Crisis Centre 1988). Thus women are using their identities as a political base to build cohesive and visible communities within organizations where those identities have been marginalized, made invisible or silenced. Yet one of the potential dangers of addressing diversity through the 'politics of identity' is the division of women into oppositional categories — white women versus women of colour, lesbians versus heterosexual women, etc. (Fuss 1989). Further, the focus on identity denies the multiplicity of our subjectivities and the various competing and contradictory aspects of our identities as, for example, is evident for a Black Jewish lesbian mother of sons. Although the struggles of these collectives are noteworthy, it remains a challenging task to make the conceptual shift that is required to resist hegemonic and binary constructions. My research on collectives has indicated that there is a need to go into the grey area between the poles and grapple with the contradictions of practice. This analysis is unable to occur within a model or vision that values the homogeneity of feminism, ideal feminist structures and dichotomous opposition.

FEMINIST COLLECTIVES IN CANADA

The existence of collectives in Canada since the second wave of the women's movement has challenged certain academic theorizing. Despite organizational theory which predicts that ideology cannot have a sustained influence on structure (Katz and Kahn 1978) and despite the critiques that urge the formalization of leadership and authority as a way of preventing oligarchical arrangements from forming (Michels 1962 [1915]; Freeman 1977; Epstein et al. 1988; Vickers 1991), feminist social service collectives have maintained and are continuing to maintain a relationship between their feminist ideology, and their collective, horizontal structure. My research has documented this consistency by examining their internal practices (Ristock 1987, 1989, 1990, 1991). Most use consensus decision-making, sharing and rotating job functions and retaining control over hiring and firing practices, despite, for example, having a traditional board of directors. As well, this consistency between ideology and structure has been evident through examining the feminist values contained in their public documents. They believe in empowering women, valuing experiences and working for social change and they see this as being offered in a structure that is consistent with democratic principles.

In keeping with their internal operations and philosophy, feminist social service collectives engage in social activist work beyond their social service work, often involving themselves in pressure tactics that have been identified as strategies for social change (O'Sullivan 1976). As with theories of participatory democracies which state that working in environments where there is control over the workplace encourages political involvement (Greenberg 1986), there is a reciprocal relationship between service provision and social activism.

In summary, the existence of feminist social service collectives can best be understood by viewing these settings (1) as alternative empowering services with their own culture and sense of community (Repucci 1973); (2) as feminist movement organizations which are part of the larger women's movement (Riger 1984; Staggenborg 1989); and (3) as small groups with specific group norms, properties of membership and cohesiveness, and a specific group structure (Brown 1988; Baron and Byrne 1987). Collectives challenge many of the assumptions of what it means to work within a group, organization and community. The challenge of collectives to these assumptions has also meant that they live with contradictions. For example, they are both empowering services and services with power and control over women. As well, they view workers as equal but do not adequately address the diversity and differences amongst women that reflect social inequality (Ristock 1990). They also have a positive in-group identity but experience difficulties because of the hegemonic construction that can occur of what it means to be a 'collective' (Ristock 1991). Thus collectives hold multiple and contradictory locations. The framework that I proposed encourages us not to lose sight of the social context that gives rise to tensions and difficulties when struggling for a new vision. Difficulties stem from this context as well as possibilities for developing and forwarding alternative services and theories of welfare.

The study of feminist social service collectives in many respects is the study of a cooperative society on a micro-level. The struggles to develop and exist within a cooperative, caring context in a world that values individualism, competition and violence, are great. Yet the fact that these collectives exist and continue to exist, working out an integral relationship between theory and practice, is a hopeful one. Their survival is a testimony to the possibilities for transformation.

For comment on this chapter see page 288.

CONCLUDING COMMENTS

15. Interdependence, Difference and Limited State Capacity

Claus Offe

What I have to offer as a conclusion is a number of unsorted thoughts that I have organized around three topics that have come up again and again at this conference. The first has to do with interdependence, the second with difference and the third with state capacity.

One question that has recurred concerns the problem of how we define legitimate needs and tell them from illegitimate ones — legitimate needs being those needs that can be the foundation of rights to welfare or well-being. On what grounds can any reasonably specific list of such rights be defended? This is a question that has both a philosophical dimension concerning both normative theories of social justice, and very importantly, an empirical dimension. The latter can be summed up in the question: what kind of arguments and defences are empirically employed and turn out to be successful in motivating individual actors and social groups to grant such rights and agree to share the burdens that are involved in granting such rights? It is only what passes through the filter of given attitudes and intuitions about justice prevailing in society, as well as through the routines, values, and traditions embodied in the institutions of policy making, that rights will eventually be established, implemented and enforced as social or positive rights. Rights, in other words, are contingent upon the actors' preparedness to validate, acknowledge and redeem such rights.

This preparedness can be hypothesized as being more precarious the *more costly the granting of rights becomes* to those who are not immediate beneficiaries relative to those rights, and the *greater the social distance* that lies between those who grant the rights and pay the costs, on the one hand, and the beneficiaries, on the other.

What we might call the 'welfare transaction' is thus regulated by moral and political intuitions about rights and duties, and arguments that activate or invalidate these intuitions. These intuitions are not established once and forever, but unfold and shift within changing political and economic power relations, perceptions, and situational contexts. We can thus address the question: what type of argument 'makes sense' to what kind of agents within which context, and how robust is the power of such arguments concerning rights and duties likely to be? To what kind of moral resources and commitments can claimants appeal in order to motivate those who must fulfil the duties that correspond to rights to actually do so? Or, putting the same question negatively, who denies such rights, what mechanisms and what power positions make these rights inoperative?

This transaction can be framed within a simple supply and demand model. In trying to understand the shifting balance and the moral and political discourses in which it is embedded, we can either focus on the demand side, the claimants' side, or look at the supply side, the provider of rights, i.e. the side of those who tolerate, support, and pay for the claiming of others' rights. From the first point of view, we focus upon normative arguments such as equality of status and opportunity, need, and desert. From the second, the emphasis is upon equality in the allocation of burdens as well as the efficiency and effectiveness of programmes designed to improve the well-being of claimants.

Rights always involve obligations, duties, and burdens. That is the case not only with social or 'positive' rights, but even with civil and political rights. If someone claims *civil rights,* such as the freedom of property or of religion, then there must be a willingness on the part of 'everyone else' to tolerate the use of these rights. The same applies to *political rights* — freedom of communication, freedom of association, freedom of participation — all of which presuppose that everyone else accepts his or her obligation to tolerate the use of rights, or to honour the rights without discriminating and punishing the actors using these rights. The duties that these rights impose upon everyone else do not only involve the moral effort that is necessary for tolerance, but also the very tangible costs caused by the maintenance of the court system or the institution of general elections and parliamentary representation.

Sometimes rights and duties coincide in the same person, sometimes they are entirely separated. A market transaction is an instance of the former case. A person's right to the item purchased is entirely contingent upon *this very same* person's willingness and ability to pay the respective price. But even this may not be a 'pure' case, since the tolerance and consent (or lack thereof) on the part of third parties may make a difference, as we see if the supposedly 'private' market transaction in question happens to be a case of drug-dealing or prostitution or, for that matter, rental of a rent-subsidized apartment to which a specific category of persons, but not others, are entitled. At the other extreme, we can have a virtually complete social separation of rights and duties. Newborn babies are probably the purest case in point, but only for a while, until rudimentary forms of reciprocal duties emerge in the parent–child interaction. An intermediary case, located closely to the market transaction, is the notion of the *deserving poor*. In this case, the right to (very limited) transfers is made conditional upon the recipient's compliance with (very strict) behavioural rules and the approval of his behaviour on the part of a paternalistic agency. Close to the other end of the scale, we would locate Basic Income schemes which provide for unconditional rights to income to every citizen, regardless of his or her desert or even need. We thus see that there is a zero-sum relationship, or sum-constancy relationship, in the allocation of obligations. The more obligations apply to the bearer of the rights, the less to the general public, and vice versa. One of the questions that several people have addressed though not resolved at this conference is how great is the burden in terms of moral effort that is required in order to accept rights that are *not* complemented by *individual* obligations of the beneficiary of the rights.

Sometimes this moral burden is alleviated through material or immaterial returns. For instance, we can say we accept obligations pertaining to us because (a) there will be some material benefits, or the avoidance of a *collective evil*, as a consequence. Examples may be taken from health policies where it is often argued that the prevention and treatment of diseases serves 'all of us', not just the patients. An alternative to this type of utilitarian calculus of second-order benefits is that (b) we develop *external* preferences, i.e., preferences involving the well-being of other members of *our* community for whom we feel sympathy. A further alternative is the Kantian solution, (c) of making a principled commitment to general obligations, regardless of the identity of the beneficiaries of these obligations. But in all of these cases, though to a varying (and probably, as we move from (a) to (c), quite steeply increasing) extent, a measure of moral effort will always be required to honour the social and other rights of others, even if, as in (a), it is only the effort to act prudently rather than in short-sighted ways. There must be some compelling supportive intuition that certain rights of others are worth honouring. The question, as suggested by the perspective of a sociology of morals, is this: 'What is the repertoire from which a society can draw in order to alleviate these obligations so as to make them widely acceptable?'

My second point, having to do with *difference*, is that the process of structural differentiation of societies and the perception and active proclamation of differences will make it more difficult to provide reasons to accept obligations, and thus cause this repertoire to shrink. Again, the political problem is to mobilize moral resources that lead to the effective recognition of welfare rights and the preparedness of everyone else to grant such rights. But given the emphasis on difference and differentiation, and looking at political macro-trends in western societies, it is clear that the question of welfare rights or the rights to well-being is not one on which we can take the offensive, make further or more far-reaching claims to rights and corresponding obligations, because that would clearly overtax the preparedness of everyone else to accept the obligations. On the contrary, as we would probably all agree, we are in a defensive position. We need to mobilize reasons to defend, as it were, the status quo.

The three (and only three) types of substantive arguments with which we can possibly try to activate and to mobilize moral resources that lead to the acceptance of obligations, have to do with entitlements, deserts and needs. This tripartite division is not to be confused with the above three types of theories about distributive justice, namely utilitarian, communitarian, and Kantian, although there may be elective affinities that I cannot go into at this point. Let me briefly discuss these three types of substantive arguments.

For the first, entitlement, we can claim welfare rights because they are attached to *codified citizenship rights*. However, this argument is often not good enough, not sufficiently compelling or convincing to motivate the willingness to accept obligations. Note that citizenship rights are by definition 'positive' in the dual sense of (a) obliging the state to some specified kind of active provision and (b) being susceptible to legislative revision. The entitlement argument comes in a utilitarian and in a communitarian version. As to the first of these, the general form of the argument is something like this: for the sake of farsightedness and prudence we must be prepared to accept the obligations attendant upon rights to well-being because they constitute a sort of investment in collective peace and the avoidance of collective evils. We see that this presumed equation (rights generate collective utility), to which much of the welfare state owes its existence, is not as plausible today as it was in the past, perhaps during the inter-war period. For the conflicts and disturbances that result from, or must be anticipated as a consequence of society's failure to grant social citizenship rights are uncertain and controversial as to their incidence and costliness, especially if balanced against the direct as well as indirect costs of granting these rights. Moreover, the utilitarian calculus invites the consideration that there may be other and better, i.e. more efficient and productive, ways to deal with the provision of public goods or avoidance of public evils. As a consequence, the notion of social citizenship rights would have to compete against those alternatives which would amount, for instance, to insulating the vast majority of society against the negative collective effects of, say, unmet health needs rather than approaching the problem through the granting of citizenship rights to therapy. Instead of granting relief we would thus build higher thresholds in order to escape the collective negative consequences of unmet needs.

Therefore, secondly, entitlements deriving from citizenship must be defended, if they are to be defended at all, on some subsidiary communitarian argument. Such argument would recognize and emphasize some communality of culture, history, language, nationality, ethnicity, religion, and then proceed to derive a solidaristic obligation of a quasi-familiar sort from these shared commonalities. That, however, presupposes that such communalities are actually present and considered sufficiently salient to provide a basis for obligation. If we look at the history and the level of development of welfare states in a comparative perspective we will see that this homogeneity argument has helped a great deal to support the development of demanding welfare state arrangements. Within the OECD world, the most homogeneous society in ethnic, religious and linguistic terms is probably Sweden, and the most heterogeneous is probably the United States. And the levels of welfare state provision and spending correspond to that homogeneity. The appeal to homogeneity is a powerful mobilizer of solidaristic willingness to accept obligations, and, inversely, perceived social, cultural and geographic distance or difference undermines the willingness to share. What seems to follow from these observations is that, as societies become more differentiated, more multicultural and stratified according to complex and multiple dimensions of inequality, communitarian arguments fail to make sense. In other words, it becomes more facile to say that a particular category of people do not deserve 'our' solidarity simply because they are not 'our kind of people'.

As entitlement arguments based on citizenship do not seem to fare well in post-industrial social structures in either their utilitarian or communitarian version, much of what these arguments fail to accomplish would have to be substituted for through *desert* arguments. Desert arguments establish an equivalent between the *value* of a person (usually measured in market terms, such as income) and the claims he or she is legally entitled to. As we have seen, the model case is the purchasing interaction. But also all contributory schemes in social security rely on desert arguments. In pension rights, the kinds of arguments employed is this: as a given person has worked for 40 or 45 years, and has earned such and such an amount of income, thereby demonstrating his or her worth in society and to society, this person deserves old-age pension or health provision in reward of this active service. Correspondingly, all current income earners (within pay-as-you-go contributory systems) are obliged to honour the desert-based claims of the retired (or, for that matter, the unemployed) through paying a share of their income into the common fund. The well-known by-product of this logic is that contributory schemes are exclusivist. They impose a pattern of normal life-course that is neither empirically nor normatively defensible as 'normal'.

When the question is posed, what happens to those who do not benefit from the moral foundation of obligations achieved through desert principles, the last alternative, after entitlement and desert, is to base transfers on *need* as a basis for solidarity and obligation. The *dependency* discourse that, as Ray Plant shows (*supra*), is so prominent in the recent writings on the social philosophy of welfare, alerts us to the fact that 'thoughtless' giving to the needy may fall short of actually 'helping' them. We must thus beware of our mindless inclination to compassion. Another popular argument holds that not only the condition of need, but also the institutional conditions of helping the needy are stigmatizing — and hence not really helpful — which also undermines the sense of obligation to the needy. Furthermore, popular social science as well as medical knowledge has given rise to the widespread understanding that much of what appears as 'need' is actually 'deserved' in the negative sense, as it can be causally attributed to objectionable modes of behaviour that must not be rewarded. Such knowledge invites an attitude of victim blaming, or the tendency to respond to the incidence of need by saying 'I told you so' — or 'such and such professionals could have told you so' — your teacher, your doctor, your social worker, your employer. All of these arguments and the spread of knowledge on which they are based are likely to further weaken the operative obligation to practise solidarity with the needy.

My third point concerns *state capacity versus civic agency*. The state has a limited repertoire for dealing with needs, even if there were an abundant supply of willingness to accept obligations and the material consequences of such obligations, namely sharing resources, sharing income etc. This limited repertoire of modes of intervention of the state is restricted to the attribution of rights, of funds and of information and education. As a combined consequence of (a) the decline of the moral and political support underpinning welfare generating state activities (the point I have argued so far) and of (b) the categorical limits of state capacity to provide for well-being (which is my concern here), we see a broad trend in almost all political camps since the seventies to replace or to complement welfare state arrangements with something that in dozens of recent papers, books, and articles, is called *welfare society*. The welfare state must be complemented, or to that effect a very broad consensus seems to have emerged, by welfare society arrangements. I think this has also become very evident in the course of our discussions at the present conference: networks, movements, communities, households, self-help arrangements, self-defence arrangements, self-organizing, self-prevention are supposed to increase the capacity for coping, for fate-control, for self-provision within civil society, in addition to what a shrinking scope of welfare state provision is able to accomplish. To rely on these forms of activity and intervention, most of which start with 'self' and are located within civil society, is not to deny, however, the essential role of state-guaranteed and state-enforced institutions, in spite of the limits of what I have called state capacity. It is not justified, I think, to denounce such state-organized institutional frameworks in the name of a somewhat post-modern 'difference happiness' or the romanticizing celebration of particularistic identities. If in the field of social welfare and social services the formation of 'competent agents' with 'critical autonomy' and the basic capabilities that are needed for implementation of all these transactions of self-help and self-organization etc. is to succeed, this is unlikely to happen, in my view, without their being assisted, encouraged and protected by state action and state provided funds.

In conclusion, let me highlight one area that has appeared in our discussions several times where these capacities for self-organization are particularly significant and called for, namely concerns of physical integrity and physical well-being. Physical integrity of the human body in society concerns not just health, but something that has been called body rights. These are rights that have, among other things, to do with consumption, with all aspects of health, with ecology, with the built environment, with crime, with violence, with drugs, with transportation, with sexual relations, and with nutrition. I think these concerns practically cannot fully, nor even to a significant extent be guaranteed by the state beyond perhaps police protection and regulations concerning health and safety at work. But much of the physical integrity that is threatened, that is rendered problematic or precarious under modern living conditions, needs to be protected and cultivated through forms of individual and collective activity, such as preventive health initiatives, that come out of a civilized and responsible self-organization within civil society rather than any kind of police-enforced state regulation. In my view, it is this 'self-serving' provision of welfare in kind that must be integrated into, as well as partly replace, provisions of the welfare state.

16. What Welfare Theory Hides

Dorothy E. Smith

I have proposed elsewhere that women's standpoint casts the knowing subject in a distinctive relationship to the text-mediated discourses of the social sciences (Smith 1987, 1990). It locates us, I have suggested, in the actualities of our lives so that theory and discussions of theory such as those that generated this book, become visible as the ongoing practical activities of actual people, situated at some determinate time in a particular local site, the site of our bodily being and consciousness.

This means that theory itself is taken as a feature of an ongoing and actual social organization. Discussions, such as those we were engaged in back in September of 1992, now embodied in this book, are themselves seen as located and embedded in a complex of social relations and of social, economic and political processes that is implicit in our theorizing and discussions. And theory is an organizer of social relations, one of the reasons presumably that a theory of welfare is useful and interesting. It also entered into the ways in which discussion could go forward among us. It set up definite conceptual boundaries, bracketing actualities.

My comments look for ways of breaking out of those boundary conventions, returning us to the ineluctable setting of all our work, the lived world in which theorizing goes on but that isn't comprehended in theory. Topics that never became topics can be noticed. For example, that participants in discussion brought to it relevances that coordinated it with relations beyond that present: Nancy Fraser valued contributions that would serve as arguments against right-wing policy proposals being promulgated in the United States; Ian Gough, on the other hand, addressed issues likely to arise in developing welfare policies in the context of the rational conduct of established welfare administration and the actual or potential uses of experts, such as nutritionists, in determining need; and so on. Related to these were issues — which Nancy Fraser began to open up towards the end of our meetings — of national differences in welfare institutions. Theory was stretched and pulled like taffy by discursive relations beyond the setting of our talk.

Our focus on theory displaced the world beyond and embracing theory. We did not talk about the more general 'historical' setting that has, presumably, precipitated the crisis in welfare theory that was our concern. I take it that issues for welfare theory emerge as established welfare institutions are dislocated or discredited as solutions to problems created for people's lives and living by the contemporary dynamic of capital. The crisis is more than theoretical. Rather it arises as established theory — or ideology — loses cogency[1] as contradictions emerge in new forms in the context of an irrevocable transformation of society and economy.

The context most relevant to our theoretical debates on welfare is the uncoupling of society and economy. Society or nation state no longer coincides with the operative boundaries of economic organization. In the past, government could conceive of 'managing' a national economy that operated to a sufficient extent as an autonomous functioning system. Though that autonomy was no doubt always less than represented by the economic ideologies based on Keynes, it had practical cogency as a working assumption. Keynes theorized a system in which the conflicting interests of capital, government, and wage-earners could be seen as working together for a shared societal good.

The uncoupling of state and economy destroys the practical cogency of that assumption. The uncoupling appears at multiple sites and levels of economic organization: governments are not free to manage a deficit wholly in relation to a national economy's internal problems. National economic policies are at the mercy of fluctuations of the bond market or exchange rates; the wages of workers in newly industrialized countries compete against those of the first world; corporations are no longer tied to a particular national basis (it is no longer correct to think of these as forms of empire); the fiscal basis of the government of the nation state is decreasingly based on national capital and more and more on the incomes of individuals. New transnational institutional and administrative forms emerge, transgressing national boundaries; for example, the great chartered accountant firms, such as Price Waterhouse, operate in multiple national sites and internationally, serving their corporate clients with a knowledge of how to move the latter's assets among different national tax jurisdictions to their best advantage as well as in pressing national governments to standardize taxation procedures to facilitate standardization of internal corporate accounting; the infrastructure of a Europe-wide labour market calls for designing procedures to standardize skills and educational qualifications across national boundaries; and so on. The uncoupling of nation states and economy is progressive, multi-layered, and driven by the dynamic of global economic forces.

Under previous conditions, the notion that conflicting economic interests could be reconciled made some practical sense. Divergent interests of individuals and class could be reconciled in a practical recognition of a common societal interest in public education, health, unemployment insurance, and the economic support of those unable to work in paid employment. Even the idealization of a corporate state could be seen as a practicable project. But as state and economy are uncoupled, the theorizing of such reconciliations loses cogency. The interests of wage earners whose tax payments support the fiscal basis of the state are not easily reconciled with the use of public monies to support people who do not earn. The interests of capital in lowering the national deficit conflicts with those who identify the interests of workers with government investment in rebuilding infrastructure, maintaining public services in education, health, and housing, and providing extended unemployment payments. It seems that such divisions can no longer be reconciled in practice and in rhetoric as they once were with reference to the effects of state intervention in a relatively autonomous national economy.

This, I suggest, is the setting of our workshop and our work in welfare theory. Our work was, and is, situated in what I've come to call the relations of ruling. This isn't intended as a theoretical concept. Rather it points to relations that we're active in as members of an intelligentsia, connecting what we do and produce into objectives beyond our intentions. The term is used to designate a distinctive organization of social relations that become visible from a standpoint in the local and particular as extra-local, generalized, generalizing and objectified. The social relations of ruling are an objectification, or socialization, of what were formerly and are otherwise the individual functions of knowledge, judgement and will. They are bureaucracy, professions and professional organization, management, formal organization, text-based and test-mediated discourses in science, culture, technology, and so on. In a sense they are a specialization and differentiation of the social functions of organization, control and management that were formerly embedded in relationships among particular people.[2] They form a complex, coordinated in various ways, but far from monolithic. They are fissured with contradictions and contestation as the dynamic of capital feeds stresses, problems, disorganization, into at least temporarily stabilized alliances, reconciliations, compromises, and solutions. And people go to work within them, as we have been doing, to figure out how to redesign, patch, cobble, reweave, reorganize.

Theory inserts its distinctive modes of social organization into these processes. In addition to the boundary conventions that restrict how topics and relevances can be introduced into a theory-governed discussion, theory also structures the subject–object relations in which we are active in our theoretical discussions. It places us, readers and writers of theory, in a definite relationship to those who become its objects. The categories of welfare clients or recipients, their motivations, their problems, and their potentialities are structured theoretically. Concepts such as 'need' expropriate and displace the desiring, wanting, subject; concepts such as 'self-actualization' impose values and objectives on her/him. Relationships set up theoretically replicate the subject-object relations of the relations of ruling, tracing the contours of the institutional order.

Welfare theories do not provide a place from which others might speak from beyond the objectifying categories. They don't expose us, its practitioners, to encounters such as Karen Leander's (n.d.) who introduced criminological theories to a group of women criminals she was working with in a Swedish prison. She describes how embarrassing it was to speak in the objectifying language of criminology to the people it theorizes. I remember a speaker in a panel of older women at a meeting of the National Women's Studies Association in the United States mocking the objectifying language of gerontology and decrying the relations of dominance it embodies. Theories conceal the actualities of people's lives that they might speak of and from if we knew how to hear them.

In our theorizing, a particular structuring device contributes powerfully to our blindness. Welfare theorizing, again following the contours of welfare practices, isolates the individual (or family unit). This is a feature shared by our various disciplines: economic theories are based on individuals making rational choices; in welfare theory models of the needs of individuals can be constructed; in sociology properties of social relations and organizations are represented as properties of individuals — for example, the notion of dependency is necessarily relational, yet we treat it as an attribute of an individual. The actualities of people's lives and ways of getting their living, however, may not correspond at all to that individuation. In some of the papers given or the discussion of paper, there are glimpses of lives beyond the relations of ruling and how it defines them. There is, for example, Mr Bow in Bill Jordan's paper. Mr Bow is active in the work organization of what we might call a life-support economy.

Mr Bow appears in Jordan's paper in the welfare office, perhaps hoping to wheedle something out of Bill. He's obviously a familiar figure there. But welfare isn't the only basis of his life-support economy: he poaches; people buy the rabbits he catches; he keeps dogs; he shares a household with his wife; he deals with local stores. He is rooted in a work organization that produces his living and is bound up with a local network intersecting with the life-support economies of other households.

The notion of a life-support economy directs attention to economies the relations of which are not mediated by money, though money is surely an important, if not essential, resource. Mr Bow's story gives us a glimpse of an organization of the work that directly produces his and his family's living. Of course, it isn't an individual production. His wife is also at work and so are others. Though the household is central, this work organization isn't reducible to it. Such a life-support economy does not coincide with a definite social unit, but operates across several. The 'wages for housework' movement, at one period, put forward a generalized conception of housework as all that work that people do behind, beyond, around, and sustaining the economy of markets and capital. Driving to paid work, as well as domestic labour, was considered *housework* in this sense. The notion of a life-support economy is analogous. People coordinate the economy of wages, retail outlets, services, home appliances, leisure activities, rental or mortgage payments, and so on, to produce their own living. They don't do this all by themselves. Their work is concerted with others, inclusive of but not restricted to the household.

People are active in keeping their life-support economies in order and the way they want them. Life-support economies constitute *regimes* in the sense of being regulated and controlled through the exercise of informal powers. For example, Mr Bow poaches, so most likely he has a deal with local police who get occasional gifts of rabbits in exchange for turning a blind eye to his activities. The domestic side of life-support economies has privileged men to use violence in subordinating their wives' work. In the stories of battered women, these are some recurrent themes: being beaten because supper was not on the table, and *hot*, when he got back from work at whatever hour; or because he didn't like the food prepared; or because she wasn't ready for sex when he was. As with Mr Bow's poaching, men's power to regulate women's contribution to the household through the use of physical force has been, and probably still is, supported locally by informal police tolerance.

The notion of 'life-support economies' doesn't describe a particular type of work organization or a particular class. We should imagine them as specific to how the local effects of the monetary economy articulates to local conditions for sustaining life. And hence they are necessarily very various and often specific to local conditions. Welfare or unemployment insurance payments may be an integral part of them, as they have been seasonally in the Atlantic provinces of people depending on fishing. 'Welfare' can become one component of a life-support economy. Indeed this is one of the contradictions that welfare theory theorizes, though it tends to do so in terms that ascribe *dependency* to a quasi-psychological state of individuals. We would not know without investigation what the character of a life-support economy might be for different classes or regions.

Our own experience will tell us that people work out more or less stable ways of producing their everyday living under conditions of stability in the monetary economy, but the dynamic of capitalist economy with its perpetual and essential drive of accumulation propels changes into local life-support economies from sources external to them. And currently such changes are rapid and sometimes entirely unanticipated. People's life-support economies may be completely disrupted and repairs or alternatives do not come readily to hand. The effects of financial transactions internationally may result in plant closures or restructuring that transform a local economy and permanently disorganize the local life-support economies. The transition from 'Fordism' to 'post-Fordism' (whatever that will turn out to be) has been a major disorganizer of locally stable life-support economies among the North American working class. The movie, *Roger and Me*, depicting the effects of the closing of the General Motors' plants in Flint, Michigan, gives us some notion of what this means. The widespread encouragement by governments of industrialized nations of the immigration of workers prepared to accept lower wages than the native population transforms local labour markets and disrupts the labour market conditions of local life-support economies. June Nash's historical anthropology of a Pennsylvania city describes the life-support economies of multi-generational family organizations that were organized on the base of the city's fifty-year stable industries, a base that disappeared as the mergers of the 1980s forced 'restructuring' (Nash, 1989). The history of the black ghetto in Los Angeles is the story of black immigration from the South to work in the wartime aircraft industries. By the 1960s the stable employment basis of its life- support economies had already been eroded. They were further disorganized in the 1980s by the erosion of public schooling and other public services resulting from the passing of Proposition 13.

Yet, life-support economies are conceptually invisible. The appearance of people in the welfare context as individuals or as nuclear families detached from their locally embedded life-support economies is an artefact of a welfare theory, welfare categories and welfare administration. The theories and categories of economics deal with relations mediated by money and commodities or social forms that can be translated into their simulacra; the economies that mediate the money economy and how people actually live are not visible to it. Existing forms of political representation do not necessarily give public voice to the disorganization of the life-support economies of those who have no organized representation. But people are not, of course, inert. They work to repair and reinstate; they act, protect, rebel. I suggest we might better grasp the basis of the racist attacks on foreign workers' hostels in Germany, or the invasion by Nova Scotia workers of a fish processing plant threatened with closure, if we examined how the vagaries of capital's dynamic and its state facilitation disrupt regional life-support economies.

Our theorizing in general has not been directed towards people's efforts to repair and reconstitute local life-support economies, or their attempts to defend them against locally experienced threat. We have talked about problems of dependency created by welfare, about the importance of empowerment and self-actualization, but we have talked about these as if they were ours to give, ours to manage, ours to administer. Only Ota de Leonardis has put forward a version of welfare that seeks to support people's efforts to remake the local economies that support their lives. It is a version that recognizes that people have resources, skills, abilities, energies, and initiative — among them, of course, irritating competencies in manipulating welfare administration.

In constructing an objectified world that we, as subjects, stand outside and independent of, theory deceives us into imagining that, at least for the then and there of our discussions, and the whenever it may be of this book, we stand outside what we are talking about. Theory created objects or others for us as theory's expressions. Occasionally in what people wrote or said we could get glimpses of actual lives going on beyond our theorizing and evaded by it, but that was all.

A different theorizing is called for. Or perhaps rather less theorizing and more exploration. The dynamic of capital feeds changes into people's established ways of putting their living together that disrupt and disorganize. There is a problem of theorizing that does not know how to construct a standpoint from which those effects can be made visible. A woman interviewed on television about new child-support measures introduced to reduce overall government expenditure says, 'They don't know how we exist.' A theorizing complicit with 'their' ignorance will not serve policy or practice, let alone people, in these new times.

NOTES

1   The notion of the cogency of ideological organization avoids issues of truth or representational accuracy and, recognizing the significance of ideology as a constituent of organization, draws attention to the effectiveness of a given ideology under actual conditions of governing, administration, or other forms of ruling.
2   Weber's account and analysis of transitions from traditional to rational–legal forms of authority addresses this differentiation though not, of course, in these terms.

Afterword: Sorting Claims

In our early formulation of the central problem of welfare theory, we placed an emphasis on 'thin' and 'thick' notions of need. However, after reviewing the papers which are presented in this volume, we see the distinction as one which, while helpful, gives rise to difficulties which can be solved only by examining the tension between a *universalistic* and a *particularistic* approach to welfare questions. Universalists argue that the particularist stress on cultural difference is irresponsible because, philosophically, it leads to relativism and, empirically, because it is extremely difficult to distinguish between reasonable and unreasonable, serious and frivolous, just and unjust claims. Without a clear, formal criterion, the political process becomes a free-for-all, where groups are encouraged to make unreasonable and non-negotiable claims, which in turn can lead to the balkanization of the social. We want to examine the assumptions which we think lie behind this criticism, and then try to develop some positive arguments to suggest that beginning with social action does not necessarily lead to the relativism and chaos which we, along with those who have criticized us in this text, find threatening and problematic.

1. POLITICAL RESPONSIBILITY

Offe's reminder of the spectre of balkanization enables us to make one important clarification. Our theoretical frame of claimsmaking and response presupposes a stable civil society, protected by a state which is recognizant of diversity and of rights. If this were not the case, it would be important to recognize that claims which are taken by others to be inordinate and non-negotiable could push the tolerance of others past the breaking point. The result would then be — as we see in many places today — an endless cycle of violence. Hence, the stress so many of the papers place on difference and particularity only brings out that contesting groups must have something in common in order to communicate, to negotiate, to contend. The question then becomes how what is held in common relates to what is contentious.

In response, universalists insist that the universal notions which all have in common ought both to supply the criteria for settling the differences and to set limits *a priori* to the extent of those differences. Soper (*supra*) makes this point by concluding that we 'advocate the never-ending, individualist dynamic of "well-seeking",'(*supra* p.73) and 'allow that an indefinite plurality of claims can appropriately be viewed as speaking to needs'(*supra* p.73). She warns us that 'admonitions against "cultural imperialism"' are in effect a 'relativist stress on "difference"'; this is 'most likely to give comfort to all those seeking to clothe a naked disregard for Third World deprivation with the mantle of theoretical legitimacy.' (*supra* p.74).

In defence, we would say that our exploration of difference is nothing more than a recognition of the multiplicity and diversity of claimsmaking. As a matter of fact, there are a variety of groups and movements who insist that their voices should be heard in the political process. And equally important, it is difficult to see by what criterion an outsider — or a theorist — could judge ahead of time that there should be no more distinctive voices added to the political chorus, that enough is enough, that life is already sufficiently complicated.[1] Furthermore, we argued (*supra* p.16) that people who have experienced oppression will have great difficulty in articulating their aspirations and making claims. While claimsmakers who are members of the hegemonic group are quite capable of making self-serving and even frivolous claims effectively, most people, and certainly marginalized people, must ordinarily work in groups to overcome the cramping effects of oppression (*supra* p.26). Thus, serious claims are sorted from frivolous claims even before any public process begins. Claims which emerge from groups of those who have been oppressed and marginalized will already have undergone a screening process. Those who grant recognition to the uniqueness of persons struggling to articulate their aspirations and goals are aware of the struggles which await them once they have come to agree about their goals and make public claims. Implicit in their encouragement to others to explore those aspirations is a commitment to solidarity in the ensuing struggle. By the same token, a demand is being made that the exploration be on serious ground. To the extent, then, that a claimsmaking group lacks power, its claim will not only be scrutinized once made publicly, but also in the process of its articulation.

Lurking behind Soper's concerns, however, are two important questions: one is the function of the notion of need in a theory of welfare; the second is the epistemological status of need. Soper seems to be presupposing that there is a clear and fast demarcation line between 'need' and 'want', determinable according to strict criteria. Thus need, once so established, can be deployed to set up a matrix (much like the schema of intermediate needs so brilliantly worked out by Doyal and Gough) which will provide a series of benchmarks to determine which sorts of claims should be validated and which should be prioritized (Braybrooke 1987 pp.68–74). She seems to be suggesting that if we abandon 'need' as this kind of criterion, we invite chaos. While Offe is arguing at a very different level, dealing as he does with questions of practicability, he seems to share this concern.

Offe (along with Preuss) has also recently turned his considerable analytic skills to the question of democracy, and his reflections there shed light on his concerns here. Democracy, they argue, requires moral effort: it requires more than recording the 'empirical' will of the people, but rather their 'reasonable' will (Offe and Preuss 1991 p.158). Democratic institutions must do more than simply involve people in participatory processes; they are limited unless they 'help to improve the quality of citizens' involvement in the democratic process.' (Offe and Preuss 1991 p.170). Is political involvement an end in itself, they ask, or should it be conceived instrumentally, as a process to transform the economic and social order so as to promote some substantive notion of justice and the common good?

But this last question seems to point to not one tension but two. While there is an irresolvable tension between the demands of reasonableness and the claims which people actually make, there is also an irresolvable tension between the demands of justice and the institutional conditions in which people live their lives. No set of democratic institutions can, in principle, fulfil all the promises of democratic ideals. Any attempt to alleviate the first tension by ruling out claims which are on *a priori* grounds deemed to be unreasonable, will have to show that it is not simply an exercise of power designed to obscure the second tension.

Even scientific findings are not immune from this demand. While we (*supra* p.5) have made much of the shortcomings of needs-as-known-by-experts, Doyal (*infra* p.273) has remarked that 'The issue of expertise posed by Drover and Kerans is a red herring.' Doyal is doubtless correct at a certain level of abstraction. However, as he and Gough have admitted (1991 p.125), there are times when, because of mistakes and/or abuse, expert opinion is correctible by the views formed on the basis of the everyday experience of those whose social conditions have been affected by the policy decisions of experts. In other words, science is much more than a method for attaining a certain kind of truth (no matter what the historical importance of that truth). Because of its very success, science has also become institutionalized, not only with strict rules about the behaviour of scientists as scientists, but also with enormous power to allocate resources and to exercise social control (Harding 1986 pp.16, 222–3). For this reason alone there is room and need for a sociology of scientific expertise, to explore which interests are served (if only coincidentally) by the findings of experts.

Perhaps a quick overview of one important recent debate will make this point clearer. In the early 1970s, in reaction to the worsening terms of trade between North and South, and the resultant immiseration of so many countries in the Third World, and as an attempt to challenge economic definitions of development, people at the Fundacion Bariloche in Argentina worked out what became known as the *Basic Needs Approach* (Mallmann 1980). In their attempt to base their moral objections [2] against current economic practice on universal and objective criteria, they rooted their notion of need in states of illness or disintegration, states which were to be determined by the latest scientific research. What is interesting from our viewpoint is that this definition, so evidently drenched in objectivist assumptions, was quickly supplemented by 'insistent calls for popular participation in the definition, implementation and benefits of basic-needs strategies.' (Sandbrook 1982 p.1). Since most of the scientific capability was in northern countries, the criteria as initially defined were easily controlled by the very people who had caused the problem in the first place (Chichilnisky 1982 p.5). While Doyal and Gough (1991 p.154) construe this turn in the debate as 'the relativist wave...eroding the conceptual foundations of [the basic need] strategies', others have argued that true development must mean that communities in the impoverished countries have to discover their own deficiencies, set their own priorities and develop their own capacities to meet their goals (Smith 1980; Gronemeyer 1988; Sachs (ed.) 1992).

Our point here is not that there is no objective distinction between basic needs and frivolous wants; our only point is that an attempt to determine that distinction scientifically leads to further questions. We do not wish to question the possibility of an objective notion of need. Rather we query the central function of such an objective notion of need in a theory of welfare.

Our approach to welfare theory begins, instead, with social action. Thus, our focus is on the naming of need and on the claimsmaking processes which lead to an authoritative interpretation of need, rather than to the notion of need as sharply distinguished from want.

2. WELFARE

But the persistent question is how can it be determined that 'welfare' is the goal of the socio-political processes which contributors have been exploring throughout this volume. Some of them have bracketed the philosophical question, but eventually a theory of welfare must deal with it.

Our approach implies a notion of welfare with three aspects. First, in line with Plant (*supra*), we begin with an individual aspect which bespeaks flourishing, that is the development and enjoyable exercise of uniquely personal capacities and the autonomy to choose which capacities will be developed. Secondly, lest the centrality of autonomy be misunderstood as individualistic, we have also stressed an interpersonal aspect, or interdependence. Individual flourishing can happen only within the context of a community characterized by relationships of mutuality. If one approaches claims from the viewpoint of social action, claims are seen to be made in light of goals to be attained. For these goals to be conducive to a person's welfare, they must be goals autonomously chosen. Autonomous choices, however, are difficult work, especially for those who have been marginalized and oppressed; hence, as several contributors have shown, autonomy is achieved through the mutuality and respect which people experience in certain kinds of groups. Finally, there is an institutional aspect of welfare. The personal flourishing within a context of mutuality must be understood as embedded within the larger society, where one encounters all the complexity of power imbalances, resource scarcities and competing demands. It is, of course in this wider forum that claims are recognized, given low priority or rejected; without this recognition, claims remain claims and are not transformed into entitlements. Thus, the third aspect of welfare is the characteristic of institutions which is a precondition for individuals successfully to pursue their welfare; and this, as Jacobs (*supra*) rightly highlights, is tied to the controversial issue of equality.

With respect to the first aspect, welfare is an attribute of the good life. It has to do with people's sense of themselves, with their aspirations with their identifying themselves with a certain community, with certain values. Looking at the moral dimension of welfare, however, puts us into the middle of the controversy between those who, since Kant, identify morality with universality and those who, harkening back to the arguments of Hegel and even Aristotle, insist that morality can be understood only within the authoritative horizons of a particular community which has identified itself with certain goods.[3] The Kantian view is that welfare concerns are 'ethical', grounded in universalizable principles. On the other hand, communitarians see this key part of human experience as an aspect of morality which beckons us to a passionate commitment, to identify ourselves with the common values and goods around which a community coheres.[4] However, while Taylor often speaks of a plurality of goods, the cruel question of allocating the resources necessary for each of those pursuits must be faced. Scholars such as John Rawls and Habermas would insist that this makes distributive justice the central public virtue, such that morality requires not passionate commitment but the olympian coolness and detachment of a 'moral geometer' (Benhabib 1990 p.356). In making claims, however, people manifest both commitment and principle, involvement and detachment, action and reflexivity. Hence, the moral and the ethical are held in tension, framed in discourse, challenged on the margin, continuously re-evaluated. And the reason why this occurs is related to the second aspect of welfare, the continuous taking into account of someone else, the necessity, either because of power or through mutual respect, of recognizing counter claims, of contextualizing one's own sense of well-being, of being dependent on others.

The third aspect of welfare therefore, the characteristics of institutions required for welfare claims to actually contribute to the welfare of the claimsmakers, entails a technical precondition and a moral precondition. The technical precondition is that there be institutional reliability — social stability and civil peace, as well as economic stability and some degree of prosperity (SPARC et al. 1993). The moral precondition is that claimsmakers be heard as equals by others. Equality is a criterion which cuts two ways: on the one hand, claimsmakers must accept that all other members of the political community who would be affected by their claim being accepted have a right to partake in the decision concerning their claim; on the other hand, welfare is served only if the claimsmakers are also heard as equals.[5] However, we must specify more clearly what we mean by 'heard as equals'.

We have argued that claims are made on the basis of a thick, contextuated knowledge of need, arrived at in a common struggle by groups which cohere around relationships of mutuality and a common commitment to the goals which give rise to those needs. But putting the matter this way only serves to highlight the problem: on what grounds will other members of the wider community feel constrained to recognize those claims as valid welfare claims (i.e., to meet needs)? There is also a second and related question: on what grounds *should* they feel constrained to recognize those claims as valid? We shall explore the empirical question first, and for that we need to clarify how we understand the social context in which claims are made.

2.1 Empirical Probability of Acceptance of Claims

The first step is to specify what is meant by 'the wider community'. If the question is dealt with in terms of institutions, it is difficult to avoid speaking here of the nation state, since it is the institution in modern times which controls the resources over which claims are made. However, it has been argued that claims are first sorted at the level of the 'social', or in civil society (Cohen 1982; Fraser 1989 p.156). To introduce this distinction points past the organizational aspect of institutions to the discursive resources of what Braybrooke (1987) calls a 'linguistic community'. Hence, claimsmaking groups have to draw on the stock of discursive resources of their linguistic community to make their claims, even though the assumptions and connotations embedded in the discourse are saturated with structured inequality (Fraser and Gordon forthcoming). A variety of institutions maintain control over this hegemonic discourse and its assumptions. While the state maintains overarching control, other institutions, for example, professions such as economics (Hum *supra*) or psychiatry, also exercise effective control. But as the word hegemony implies, there is also more diffuse control exercised. As we have noted earlier, the hegemonic order accords some people privilege over others: property owners over the dispossessed; employed over the unemployed; men over women; whites over coloured people; the able over the handicapped. For the claims of the underprivileged to be accepted, the privileged at every level of society must be willing to imagine a society where the benefits of common bonds and a small gain in equality would be preferable to the enjoyment of privilege.

However it is exercised, the result of discursive control is to render the claimsmaking — at least in any public sense — a 'non-event'.[6] One way to manage the exclusion of a claim from the realm of public discourse is to insist that the issue is private, and inappropriate for public discussion. A more radical method is to deny that the experiences upon which the claim is made ever happened. Claims made by women concerning physical and sexual abuse within the family have been dealt with in both ways. Perhaps the most famous example of the second method was Freud's ascribing to fantasy his patients' recollections of incestuous assaults in their childhood (Masson 1984). A less extreme, but more common method is to accuse claimants of exaggeration, irresponsibility or simply mistakes in their analysis. In general, exclusion of claims from public discourse is possible by so managing the public discourse that the categories emerging in the claims are denied validity. For their claims to be made public, to become part of public discourse, requires changes in the hegemonic discourse (Fraser 1989 pp.6, 130, 164–5; Laclau and Mouffe 1985 p.129–30). Hegemonic control is often successful in resisting the changes.

An even more obvious reason for resistance to new claims is the ostensible scarcity of resources, whence the appeal of utilitarianism. Yet it is difficult to know just how scarce resources are in terms of justifiable claims; the scarcity which is built into the models of economics is, from one point of view, simply definitional: because the models of economics take as data (without any ethical inquiry about justifiability) a potentially inexhaustible effective demand, there is by definition scarcity. Both Hum (*supra*) and Donaldson (*infra*) have explored implications of this definitional scarcity. By setting the allocative question within the context of environmental concerns, Soper (*supra*) has pointed towards a new dimension of real scarcity, while de Leonardis (*supra*) has argued that claimsmakers can themselves be construed as resources, thereby suggesting that the notion of scarcity must be reconsidered. Whatever the exact dimensions of scarcity, it seems clear that both claimsmakers and their political interlocutors must examine the allocative implications of a claim, since real choices have to be made. If claims are not rejected out of hand, it will be necessary to rank the relative importance and immediacy of the claim with respect to other claims, past, present and indeed the foreseeable ones in the future.

There are, then, many reasons to deny that there is any sense of commonality, by which claims can be adjudicated, beyond the mutual recognition inherent in social movements and self-help groups. Is there only imbalance of power, and the amoral exercise of that power, as many have implied since the time of Hobbes? Our insistence on the qualitative differences among groups only seems to exacerbate the larger lack of commonality. Offe (*supra* p.235) and Pinker (1971 pp.171–5) have pushed this point very effectively by noting that the greater the social distance and difference between the claimsmakers and those who will eventually have to bear the cost of validating their claims, the more difficult it will be to make the claim effectively. Offe further argues that abstract pleas based on the universality of the rights of citizenship will not be sufficient. People, he concludes, will have to recognize the claimsmakers as 'our kind of people'.

We would suggest that, while his general argument is clarifying, especially in its implicit warning against straining the tolerance of a community beyond its limits, his contrasting examples of the United States and European countries are misleading. That many European nation states have a deep sense of cultural solidarity and that their welfare-state programmes are rooted in this cultural homogeneity is doubtless true (Esping-Andersen 1990). Indeed, as many contemporary events seem to show, the negative face of their sense of cultural solidarity is xenophobia. But his counter-example of the US is misleading. The US is indeed culturally and racially heterogeneous; it is the paradigmatic nation of immigrants. But it is not the heterogeneity which necessarily accounts for its underdeveloped welfare programmes. Offe and Preuss (1991) have argued that the general sense of democracy in the US is liberal rather than republican; that it seeks no more from its political institutions than a balance of interests. One could press that argument to suggest that there is nonetheless an image, an icon of the one pursuing the interests: a male, white, anglophone property owner. Despite the profound cultural and social heterogeneity to be found in the US, and despite some attempts by the courts to recognize that diversity, there is, we would suggest, little political or social validation of that heterogeneity.[7]

Despite the enormous cultural influence exerted by the US in Canada, the Canadian experiment with heterogeneity is quite different. It has historical roots: when in 1760 the British armies took over Quebec from France, the newly established imperial power recognized the shakiness of its hold over two culturally diverse peoples, especially in the light of the growing restiveness of the colonies to the south, the francophone Quebeckers and the many Native tribes who still constituted a military threat. The upshot was a pair of remarkable decrees, a Royal Proclamation in 1763 and the Quebec Act in 1774, recognizing and granting protection to the cultural diversity of the Natives and Quebeckers respectively. Subsequent imperial administrators looked on the Quebec Act as a temporary measure, and finally in the 1840s Lord Durham would counsel London to stamp out the distinctiveness of Quebec, but by then the institutions were in place to protect it and the Durham Report only served to strengthen the resolve of Quebeckers for *la survivance*. The diversity was once again institutionalized in the Canadian Constitution of 1867, where the provinces were given exclusive jurisdiction over health, education, welfare and, by extension, cultural concerns. While the cultural integrity of the Native peoples was for a century ignored and then actively suppressed, their resilience has outlasted Eurocentric oppression. Jenson (*supra*) brilliantly analyses how the experience of obstacles in the pursuit of social and cultural diversity have undermined the sense of universal and univocal citizenship in Canada. It is, perhaps, a more fruitful counter-example to reflect upon than the one which Offe has used.

What the Canadian counter-example shows is that claimsmakers do not necessarily face a dichotomous choice, as Offe has argued, between an abstract argument from universal rights and a contextuated argument from their own lived experience and choice of a form of life. As Jenson has implied, the aboriginal nations have perhaps been most successful in presenting to the Canadian public a set of claims for self-government which appeal both to the commonality between themselves and their interlocutors and at the same time insist on the particularity of their experience and its cultural context. They have ably made the point that the deprivation they suffer is not of their choosing; commonality is implied by triggering the question: how would you feel if so deprived? They only want to build a life in peace and dignity as does everyone else. At the same time, the substance of their claims highlights that their values and culture are different, that their history gives them the moral and constitutional right to be different. Nor should this approach be surprising. It is neither the case empirically nor is it sustainable philosophically that there is a list of basic needs common to everyone and then on top of that a second list of '*additional and specific satisfiers*' particular to a certain group (Doyal and Gough 1991 p.74). That which makes one group of humans different from another is not some specific characteristic apart from their generic common humanity; quite the reverse, it is precisely their common humanity, their creativity, their ability to weave webs of cultural significance, which give rise to the differences among them.

To the extent that this commonality is recognized, despite people's proclivity to cling to the privileges accorded them by hegemonic order, and to the extent that it is embedded in a language of mutual respect and common rights, no matter how vague and abstract, to that extent one can speak of a 'wider community'. When the communitarians speak of a community with a commitment to common values, they seem to have in mind the nation state.[8] However, even internationally, there has been developed, through the instrumentality of the UN, some common language of rights. Certainly the very existence of multi-nation states (Kymlicka 1990 p.231) has as its point a framework of mutual respect and rights common to each of the national groupings.

What this language of commonality points to is a set of social commitments, usually to ideals the implications of which are only dimly seen.[9] The process of invoking these ideal commitments is not a straightforward deductive process. It seems rather to be a complex hermeneutic process, the crux of which is the appropriateness of a principle to shed light on and to provide the basis for a particular moral judgement with respect to the circumstances out of which a claim arises.

As Bach (*supra*) has shown, claimsmakers draw on cultural resources in the work of constructing their autobiographical narrative. In so doing, they both use the principles and values to interpret their experiences and, reversing the order, they re-interpret or even reformulate the values and principles, in the light of their emerging sense of the integrity of their own lives and aspirations. Ristock (*supra*) speaks of the tension among members of alternative service collectives between mainstreaming and disengagement; this movement back and forth is not simply vacillation, but depends upon a reading of circumstances. This is a way of speaking of a hermeneutic circle. Scott (*infra*) criticizes a categorical reading of the distinction between PA1 and PA2 suggested by Lustiger-Thaler and Shragge. He argues that they should be ideal types which vary over time; this presupposes an interaction between the critical demands of claimsmakers and the resilient responses of institutional actors. The appropriateness of each will be determined by interpretative methods. Jordan (*supra*) has given examples of people and groups who, he argues, having accepted the regulating principles which they inherit, create interpretive space within which to lead their lives. Jenson analyses an example where the principle of fairness itself, as it has been formulated, is being challenged. Citizenship and the rights which adhere to that notion have been assumed to accrue universally and uniformly to individuals. In Jenson's example of the Canadian constitutional debate, that assumption is being challenged, such that the rights of citizenship would be construed to accrue to groups differentially, in accordance with the particular obstacles they face in the pursuit of their aspirations (which would, as we have argued, have to be accepted by the rest of the community as morally valuable). Pascall grapples with the same issue when she considers whether and on what terms citizenship represents the reality of women. The invocation of values and principles is used to shed new light on the particularities of social context, such that those particularities take on a new relevance. That new relevance in turn leads to a reformulation or reinterpretation of guiding principles.

2.2 Beyond Particularism and Universalism

On the face of it, our approach would seem to put us in the communitarian camp. Welfare is, after all, a matter of shared answers to questions concerning the good life. Still, there are reasons why we cannot accept the communitarian view completely. First, within that philosophical tradition, community seems to mean a shared conception of the good; to us it is less that than a locus of mutual recognition and respect. Secondly, communitarians presuppose that people find themselves in community, or, more precisely, that they find their constitutive principles only by treating community values as 'authoritative horizons' which 'set goals for us'(Taylor 1979 pp.157–9). But like so many builders of grand theory, they seem to have in mind those members of the community who have good reason to accept communal values and goals, those whose lives have been rendered 'functional' by this acceptance — that is, the relatively successful, mainstream members. Community in the sense they use the word rarely connotes exclusion.

Our theorizing, by contrast, begins with another kind of person, one who has experienced exclusion, or marginalization: a person whose social circumstances, because of structured inequality, constitute an obstacle to their living 'functionally' or indeed to their sense of well-being. Such people are caught in a dilemma. The larger society in which they find themselves provides them with an identity and concomitant values and role expectations, but acceptance of these entails a repression of autonomous aspirations or of a positive, developmental sense of self. On the other hand, what other linguistic and cultural resources does such a person have to begin the work of self-appropriation, except those provided through the normal socialization processes? Guided by the literature on colonized, oppressed peoples coming to emancipation, including feminist literature, and by our own experiences with groups of the marginalized in Canada, we have suggested a two-stage process. Admitting the need for communal processes of developing their own vision of the good, we have argued that oppressed people initially form groups characterized by mutuality and trust (whether of family, friends, or those who come together around a common issue). But such groups must also find both social validation and resources for their newly achieved identity and enter into a complex discursive interaction with the larger society. Our reading of the communitarian literature has not helped us to grasp this complex process, which includes oppositional elements as well as attempts to find common cause. That is, the communitarian approach seems to shed light on the rich complexity of the quest for welfare by people who find themselves at home within a larger, historical community, but not on the problems of those who experience exclusion.

On the other side, one of the strong points of a universalist position, as developed by Habermas, is that universal moral principles provide the oppressed with grounds for criticism of their circumstances. The early Habermas (1975) equated need with generalizable rather than particular interest, and subsequently (1990) developed a 'communicative ethics', where he shifts the kantian principle of reversibility of standpoint which focuses on a monologic subject or self to a principle of dialogue among all those parties who would be affected by a decision. One of the great strengths of his position is he makes central to morality that each social grouping must be heard as equals by all the others (Fraser 1989 p.135). Gough (*supra* pp.88–9) makes this point central to his analysis as well.

But, as Penz (*infra*) argues, there can be a weakness in this reading of universalizability. Benhabib has been a persistent critic of this weakness in Habermas' universalism:

> By identifying participatory democracy with the notion of an ideal community of reconciled intersubjectivity, Habermas interprets all diversity of interests leading to conflict as illegitimate particularisms…a human society freed from all sources of conflict and diversity of interests cannot be conceived of without eliminating the radical plurality of ways of life, of cultural traditions and individual biographies which differentiate humans from one another. (Benhabib 1982 pp.71–2)[10]

Habermas has revised his position in the face of this sort of criticism. First, he has pointed out that the argument of 1975 is essentially negative; that is, he traced the social structures which emerge from the repression of generalizable interests, and the substitution of particular interests (i.e., of the powerful) for generalizable interests.[11] Furthermore, he has modified his position substantially. He no longer locates *need* at the level of a formal principle of justice, since this latter is radically open, formal, and procedural.[12] Need is categorized as one of several competing material principles of justice along with merit and equality and, as such, must be shown by claimsmakers to be the appropriate norm to be invoked, given the circumstances which have led to a claim (Habermas 1992 p.250). He thus accepts explicitly the argument which Günther (1988, 1989) has developed, to distinguish sharply between foundational discourses, where the stake is the validity of universalizable moral principles, and questions of the appropriate applicability of those principles. Günther argues that there is a procedure for showing the appropriateness of a norm to a given situation which is quite separate from that of demonstrating the validity of the norm. To invoke a norm as the appropriate one to apply to a given situation is challengeable (just as is declaring a norm to be valid) and must be justified. The justification, which demonstrates that the invocation of a particular norm as appropriate has not relied on a selective, biased or distorted account of the situation, consists, according to Günther, of giving an exhaustive account of all relevant features of the context.[13]

As we have already suggested, however, this does not square with the process which claimsmakers actually go through. Indeed, the insistence on the exhaustiveness of the list of relevant features is misleading. The central issue is usually the relevance itself of features rather than the completeness of the list, since the assessment of relevance can be sharply divided.[14] It would seem that Günther's account is shaped as it is in order to show that applicability discourse would also rationally compel universal consent, just as the discourse leading to the justification of principles is said to do.

On our account, an assessment of relevance is achieved in a circular, hermeneutic process whereby people draw on a matrix of concepts and principles to interpret our social reality in light of our needs, but then in light of our reflections on our experience, revise the matrix. We have argued that such circular processes are what groups go through in formulating claims and what the larger political community also must go through to respond to claims.

Benhabib (1988 p.14; 1990 p.350) has suggested that consensus with respect to questions of the good life, among which we would place questions of welfare, is not a desirable goal. She has argued that the universalizability of a standpoint refers not to the universality of consensus with respect to it, but to its reversibility: 'we come to terms with and appreciate the others' point of view.' (Benhabib 1990 p.358). She has often used the term *complementary reciprocity* to designate the moral standpoint, that is, the readiness of one person to affirm not only the humanity of the other, but her individuality, with needs, talents, capacities. The overall framework she has advocated she calls *historically conscious universalism*:

> The principles of universal respect and egalitarian reciprocity are our philosophical clarification of the constituents of the moral point of view from within the normative hermeneutic horizon of modernity. These principles are neither the *only allowable* interpretation of the formal constituents of the competency of postconventional moral actors, nor are they unequivocal transcendental presuppositions which every rational agent, upon deep reflection, must concede to. These principles are arrived at by a process of 'reflective equilibrium' ... What one arrives at ... is a 'thick description' of the moral presuppositions of the cultural horizon of modernity. (Benhabib 1990 p.339)[15]

Wellmer (1991) has also criticized Habermas for the idealistic reading he gives of universal consensus. He suggests instead a 'fallibilistic' interpretation of consensus that focuses on the adequacy of the comprehension of complex situations but also recognizes the historically variable ways in which people see themselves and the world. Moral dialogue — or, in our case, the negotiating which must go on as claims are processed — is designed, he says, to 'eliminate nonsense' (1991 p.196). This is done through questioning the collective matrices of interpreting situations; this questioning (as we have also tried to argue) takes place not so much as argument as 'under the *pressure* of a struggle for recognition and under the *influence* of new experiences'(1991 p.198). The moral vector in these movements is the reduction of inequalities.

As we see it, our theory of claimsmaking is closer to Benhabib and Wellmer than it is either to Taylor or Habermas. We have suggested that among the institutional preconditions for claims to be seriously entertained is that the claimants be heard as equals. The claimants clearly bear the responsibility also to attend to the economic, political, social and environmental implications of their claims. But they ought not be dismissed without a serious hearing, where the process is characterized by complementary reciprocity. Their claim might only entail a new interpretation within the framework of collective matrices already agreed upon or it may entail a radical reworking of those matrices.

What we have not begun to do is explore the actual parameters of the social and political processes which would lead to decisions about new claims. Nor, therefore, have we made any suggestions about who will appropriately make those decisions. But as western industrialized democracies struggle to achieve new political paradigms after the collapse of the earlier Fordist arrangements, we would suggest that theory cannot expect the social and political pressures to come from the classical actors (labour and capital) but should be prepared to develop frameworks which take account of the immense and invigorating variety of welfare claims now emerging.

Acknowledgements: we acknowledge helpful comments on earlier drafts by Michael Bach, Tim Stainton and Alan Scott.

NOTES

1   Jenson made this point very forcefully during the seminar.
2   Penz (1990 p.7) defines basic needs as 'those interests to which distributive justice, by virtue of their basicness, accords moral priority.'
3   See Plant (*supra*). Anglo-American philosophers tend to speak of this controversy as that between liberals and communitarians. Habermas' communicative ethic posits a similar Kantian universalism, but he does not share the liberals' social assumptions.
4   See Taylor (1989 pp.14–15) Taylor speaks of three axes of moral thinking: strong evaluation of questions such as what kind of life is worth living, what kind of life would fulfil the promise implicit in my particular talents; respect for others and the choices they make with respect to the first axis; questions with respect to attitudinal dignity. These square rather broadly with the three aspects of welfare which we are presently exploring.
5   Wellmer (1990 p.317) argues that dissenters must know their basic rights will be recognized. Only when 'individuals know their common interests are recognized in the insitutions of society and thereby at the same time recognize one another reciprocally as free and equal persons.' He concludes that the real utopian horizon is that domination-free discourse is possible within basic social institutions.
6   Offe (1974 pp.38–40) developed the notion of class-specific selectivity, the ability of political institutions by their internal structure to reduce certain social actions to the status of non-events because their recognition as events would serve as a basis of resistance to accumulation. We are

only broadening the use of this notion, to include other institutional actors and other axes of oppression.

7   Perhaps the most obvious way in which pluralism is prejudiciously categorized in the US is through racialist and, therefore, racist categories. See, among others, Omi and Winant (1986) and Goldberg (1990.) In recent months, the American right-wing has very adroitly sought to minimize any changes Clinton might implement, by insisting on the universality of individual rights, and denying any validity to the diversity implicit (as the arguments of so many of the chapters in this volume show) in the claims of groups. See, for instance, Steele (1992).

8   While Walzer speaks of spheres of justice, Taylor speaks often of patriotism.

9   Bach (1992 p.15) has given a detailed account of the sources of this language of commonality.

10   Wellmer (1990 p.304) makes this same point by reformulating Hegel's objection against Kant that his universal moral principle is empty: its emptiness lends it a transcendental illusion, namely its universality, so that it can become the source of arbitrariness and therefore terror. There is, in other words, a massive confusion between the 'validity' of a moral principle and people's willingness to commit themselves to it.

11   See Hum (*supra*) for an analysis of one important example of this substitution.

12   'The element which can convince *everybody* is narrowed down to the *procedure* of rational will-formation itself.' (Habermas 1992 p.248).

13   The rendering of this phrase in Habermas (1992 p.250) is 'the fullest possible description' which mutes the full meaning of the German 'eine vollständige Situationsbeschreibung' (Günther 1989 p.177) especially given Günther's repetition of the phrase '*alle* moralisch relevante Merkmale', his italicizing '*alle*', and his contrasting this with 'a selective reading of the situation'.

14   For example, while Canadian law sets three years as the maximum penalty for a murder committed by someone under the age of eighteen and who is tried in juvenile court, the US Supreme Court has found no reason to stop the execution of a man for a murder committed when he was fourteen.

15   Scales (1986) has proposed a similar construct which she calls concrete universality.

COMMENTS

COMMENT ON DROVER AND KERANS

Tim Stainton

In thinking about new approaches to social welfare theory in late modern society we are confronted with a range of new and often paradoxical challenges with which we must contend. We can no longer simply consider a limited range of 'safety net' or welfare state provisions; an adequate theory must address itself to questions of rights and citizenship, the problem of difference, and the inherent discursivity of those notions.

We are immediately confronted with a series of social and political oppositions or dialectical tensions: liberalism vs. communitarianism; the difference dilemma; modernist vs. postmodernist; socialism vs. capitalism. The challenge seems to be not in the resolution of those tensions but in embracing them, in finding a means to provide a degree of social stability while reserving sufficient social space for the discursive constitution of claims and the recognition of difference.

Much of the current discourse seems to be coalescing around the concept of autonomy, the idea of self-actualization and self-determination. The debate has shed the metaphysical necessity of Kantian notions of autonomy in favour of a more discursive, political conception. There is also to some degree a rejection of classical liberal assumptions of atomistic rational actors competing for scarce resources. In its place is a more social concept of autonomy as something which requires a socio-cultural context-discursive realm where identity is forged not as a radically situated subject, but as a social being.

One of the difficulties in conceptualizing this problematic is that it occurs in related yet distinct realms of discourse. Often what is posed as an opposition is in fact a problem of confusing these discursive realms. This problematic is made more acute by the fact that these realms have traditionally been the domain of distinct academic disciplines, each with its own methodological and discursive forms. In these brief remarks I would like to offer a preliminary typology of these realms and suggest the critical questions which each must address. Considerations will also be given to how they interrelate in terms of the overall problematic of social welfare theory.

The Thin Realm

In this first realm there has emerged a rich discourse around the idea of autonomy as a first principle of social organization. Here, most paradigmatically, we find the debate inspired by John Rawls on justice, right and needs; Sen's work on basic capabilities (1987a,b), Doyal and Gough on needs (1991) and the plethora of work on rights and citizenship. This realm also encompasses the somewhat more structural debate on basic institutions clearly evident in Canada with the current debate on the constitution and in Europe with the debate on emerging nations and the EC, particularly around the idea of social rights.

Here the fundamental problem is the articulation of a 'thin theory of the good'. Put another way, the defining of a non-neutral liberalism, where autonomy acts as a 'meta-good', defining generally necessary conditions for individuals and collectivities to define and pursue particular, or 'thick' notions, of the good. It is non-neutral in that — *contra* classical liberalism — the state is not required to act neutrally with respect to threats to these meta-goods, or generally necessary conditions for autonomous action. Further, the state is required to act positively to secure these conditions. Yet these goods are less than fully normative in that they do not define or prescribe particular ideas of the 'good'.

Decisional Distance

This second realm is in many ways the most difficult to conceptualize. Here we are concerned with the interface between the claims based on 'thick' or particular good and the more universal 'thin' goods. Here the difficulties stem from the increasing uncertainty, grounded in the profound diversity of 'goods', or needs. Further complexities result from the asymptotic nature of claims related to thick needs and the discursive nature and inherent instability of identity. The communitarian notion of 'constitutive attachments' wherein identities are forged too often ignores the complexities wrought by the fact that in late modern society our 'constitutive attachments' are multiple, often contradictory in nature. Hence the possibility of merging the realms of thick and thin through unitary shared notions of the goods is practically eliminated.

The problematic in this second realm then is concerned with what Foucault (Kritzman 1988 p.168) has called the 'decision distance' between the subject(s) and the state. Hence in rejecting the Manichaean argument of state vs. civil society, the scope of this second realm becomes clearer. That is, it is concerned with how claims are filtered, weighed against each other and legitimated against the more universal thin goods. Here we are concerned with institutions and processes of representation, procedural structures and, on a more intimate level, social policy structures which provide fair procedures for both the framing and adjudication of individual and collective claims against the state.

Strategy and Identity

Finally we move to the realm of practical life, the experience of civil society. The chief concern is that of identity formation, the basis of claims, and the articulations of thick needs. Here we find a rich diversity of forms, most notably, the emergence of new social movements. Here there are two central challenges: the primary one of identity formation through rational discourse; and, the strategic challenge of altering the dominant discourse and putting claims forward. This realm is in many respects the most critical for the development of a new theory of social welfare in that it defines the 'social'; it is here that the forces which shape the former realms emerge. This highlights the central paradox which must be embraced by a new theory of social welfare. The state must provide the stability necessary for identity formation through definition of the former realms, yet allow the discursive space for identity formation and allow itself to be shaped by the claims and challenges which emerge from these multiple discourses.

Autonomy, Universality and Particularity

In conclusion I would like to briefly discuss the interaction between the three realms I have outlined and return to the central idea of autonomy. While it may appear that a hard line can be drawn between thin and thick needs, this is something of an illusion. Autonomy is best construed as a continuum, along which the demarcation of what constitutes thin or universal needs and what constitutes thick or particular needs is socially determined. Social, economic and cultural factors will all contribute to this demarcation and as such it is impossible to define a permanent division between the two. Certain thin needs, such as bodily integrity, may indeed be near universal *vis-à-vis* autonomous action, but the specific means of maintaining and satisfying such needs will remain relative to socio-economic factors. Hence what constitutes a feasible level of basic health care, the right to which may be enshrined in a basic document such as a constitution, will vary considerably between states. On a more complex level, a hard division between thick and thin contradicts the essentially discursive nature of autonomy, which will change through the process of identity formation and redefinition. Thus the identification of what constitutes thin needs in a given society will never be a fixed immutable set of universals, rather, they will remain socially and temporally relative. In light of this, the second realm, concerned with decisional distance, becomes critical in that it defines the way in which civil society and the state will interact to define the nature of thin needs.

A new theory of social welfare must address each of the three realms I have described. While most of the papers presented at the seminar address themselves to one of these realms, we cannot take this as an indication that a new theory of social welfare will be found in a single realm. Rather, the challenge lies in the integration of the work in each of these realms into a synthetic theory that articulates how welfare claims are formed, how they are adjudicated, balanced and addressed, and the basis upon which they are legitimated or rejected.

COMMENT ON SOPER

Len Doyal

There has been much recent debate about the degree to which it is possible to found a theory of welfare on universal principles. Drover and Kerans (*supra*), for example, have argued that what is required is a 'thick' theory which leaves space for welfare claimants to determine the substance of their needs. This will help to avoid the abuses of the concept of need which have been perpetuated by experts dictating to clients rather than listening to them. It will also act as a corrective for various forms of cultural imperialism which neglect the plurality of discourses which give meaning and moral significance to the lives of individuals within different cultures. In short, the people know best about both their needs and the most appropriate ways of satisfying them.

In our book, *A Theory of Human Need*, Ian Gough and I develop a theory which in the preceding terms is more 'thin' than 'thick'. It argues that all humans have the same basic needs. Cultural diversity does nothing to negate the moral importance of equating human welfare with the universality of such needs.[1] In her paper, Kate Soper compares our positions, offering criticisms of both. I agree with much of what she says about Drover and Kerans' attempt morally to legitimate claimants' demands. Here, I will respond to her criticisms of our work, returning at the end to the dangers which we both recognize with theories of welfare which gain their 'thickness' from a misconceived populism.

Soper's Criticisms

In her paper, Soper argues that we do not convincingly distinguish between the types of choice which are associated with ordinary autonomy which all basically competent individuals possess and those more liberated choices which represent the exercise of what we call critical autonomy. It is certainly true that we do differentiate between choices which entail an objective expansion of the spectrum of choices open to individuals *within* a form of life and choices which do not. We also distinguish informed from uninformed choices *between* forms of life themselves. Although strictly speaking we concentrate on the latter in our conceptualization of critical autonomy, Soper's argument concerns both.

As regards the expansion of autonomy within a culture, an example of the uncritical exercise of autonomy is choosing between different brands of soap powder which are all basically the same. Researching and selecting the one available ecologically respectable brand illustrates a more critical approach. What is wrong with this? Here we have a choice of ecological respectability on the basis of acquiring an informed moral and prudential understanding. This clearly demands more autonomy in objective terms than the false consciousness of mindless consumption which feels like choice but in reality is not. One could make the same point about participation and choice within any culture.

In her critique of our conception of critical autonomy per se, Soper is also mistaken. She argues than an 'evaluative standard' is smuggled into our analysis of the emotional, intellectual and social preconditions for choice between forms of life and not just within them. We would be guilty of trying to force a specific vision of the good on others if we dictated what their choice between forms of life should be. With one exception, however, we specifically do not.

For example, a woman in a certain Islamic sect may flourish within her form of life, depending on the level to which her non-critical autonomy is developed. To say that she should be able to exercise her critical autonomy as regards choosing to stay or leave her culture on the basis of, among other things, some understanding of alternative life styles, is not to predetermine her choice. As many women have in such circumstances, she may decide to stay. As far as we are concerned, this is both her right and just as much an expression of her critical autonomy as a choice to leave.

Soper does have a point, however, about the evaluative character of our concepts of both autonomy *and* critical autonomy. This concerns the degree to which we argue that individuals have a right to high levels of both — whatever their culture. Yet contrary to her argument, our position is not substantively evaluative in that we nail our colours, so to speak, to one version of the good. Our argument rather is logical and highlights the moral inconsistency of imposing moral duties on others without at the same time supporting their autonomy to do what we expect of them.

Consistency dictates that individuals are not forced to accept moral duties designated by others if these duties are in any sense to be regarded as their own. Hegel, of course, outlines similar illogicality in his analysis of the relationship between master and slave. Thus the evaluative character of our theory of autonomy is hardly 'perfectionist'. Our only plea is again to consistency, not to any set of substantive cultural values. In short, the fact that some western liberal values which take individual rights seriously follow logically from our analysis of the moral implications of human need does not, therefore, convict us of the charge of duplicity which Soper makes.

Soper then argues that so long as we do not normatively dictate what *should* count as an acceptable satisfier for our list of needs — so long as we accept that these satisfiers rather than the intermediate needs themselves will be culturally determined — then we ourselves appear close to embracing the same relativism which we claim to reject.

This is puzzling in light of the way in which we take care to define intermediate needs in our book. They are the 'universal satisfier characteristics' of the basic needs for health and autonomy. Thus, for example, in whatever culture within which it is in the interest of the individual to participate, it will be necessary for her or him to have an 'appropriate' formal and informal education. What the content of this education might be is an open anthropological question which will depend on the normative character of the form of life in question. Yet against the background of our theory of rights which has already been outlined, to state as much does not entail relativism.

For again, it is the degree of intermediate need satisfaction — whatever the cultural content of the satisfiers themselves — which is the real focus of debates about relativism. It is one thing, for example, to accept that an appropriate education for women within certain types of cultures is much more restricted in its content than it is within the same culture for men. The relativist would say so be it if that is what the culture dictates. We argue that even within the confines of such a culture this leads to the sorts of logical/moral contradictions which have already been outlined.

Slavery does not have to be at the point of a gun. Again, the point at issue is not the substantive content of satisfiers of intermediate needs, accepting that our list of intermediate needs is more or less complete. The issue is the acceptable degree to which citizens are allowed access to these satisfiers and to alternatives to them.

Soper's final argument is divided into two components. First, she maintains that we do not adequately distinguish between basic and non-basic needs. We certainly try in our book when we argue that the appropriate level of need satisfaction is that where minimal input yields optimum output. Take nutrition or appropriate education as examples. This would entail minimum food of sufficient quality and variety to yield the optimal level of physical health for the least well off, a level which would have to be justified as socially and economically sustainable. The same line of reasoning applies to appropriate education as regards more min-opt levels, say, or specific vocational training.

Desire for types and quantities of satisfiers over and above these min-opt levels becomes a question of wants and not needs, as does the choice of more than less expensive satisfiers which conform to the min-opt criterion. For example, one can achieve min-opt levels of nutrition without eating in expensive restaurants!

This leaves Soper's final argument which concerns the global and ecological sustainability of need satisfaction in the terms elaborated by our theory. These problems become amplified by the problem of our moral duties to future generations. She suggests that when we really confront the realities of these issues, satisfiers of needs which we deem 'basic' become the only types of goods and services which can be unambiguously generalized over space and time. If so, and these needs become the only ones worth discussing, then why refer to them as 'basic' at all. They become the sum total of human needs — end of story.

In one sense, she is right. Our argument about the conceptualization of basic human needs is both logical and empirical: they are the objective preconditions for successful participation in any form of life. Given this conceptualization, the word 'basic' does suggest that other needs might exist which are not so fundamental and to this extent, it is somewhat misleading. Yet this point has nothing to do with whether or not basic needs in our terms can now or in the future be universally satisfied in the optimal ways for which we argue. This question must be confronted independently of the conceptualization of human need as such, always remembering that what constitutes optimum levels of satisfaction is always variable over both space and time.

Thus her argument about sustainability is really more about levels of both types of need satisfaction — how much counts as basic rather than what does so. And on this we are very clear in our conclusions. As already indicated, appropriate levels of need satisfaction should be pegged at min-opt levels. Further, to the degree that it can be demonstrated that these levels must be reduced in order to meet our moral obligations across space and time, then so be it. It is unclear how Soper would conceptualize her own approach to the universal prioritization of goods and services relevant to need satisfaction if not in precisely these — our — terms.

Finally, if the role of social policy becomes focused on this task — on searching for a balance of optimal production and distribution directed toward meeting the basic needs of the less well off — then how can we take people with us in political struggle to this end? It surely doesn't sound like much fun, this world of deprioritized desire. Through our concentration on the satisfaction of universal and objective basic needs — and the moral imperative of satisfying them in a just and fair way — haven't we neglected the question of why those who already have reasonable levels of need satisfaction should join the political struggle which we implicity advocate in our book? There we concentrate on the irrationality of doing otherwise but this is surely not enough.

Soper's conclusion — one which I completely endorse — is that alongside a coherent theory of need we must begin to formulate a new and morally responsible 'hedonistic vision' which is compatible with it. This will entail a new and more imaginative approach to the conceptualization of wants or desires. In short, we must begin to learn to have fun in morally responsible ways. To do so will still require, however, an adequate understanding and specification of the objective and universal preconditions for doing so. It is this which I still believe is provided by *A Theory of Human Need*.

Conclusion

Drover and Kerans argue that a commitment to universalism creates an over-dependence on experts or codified knowledge. Like Soper, I'm not convinced.

For example, as regards health, we understand perfectly well what is meant by disease and illness in universalistic terms and we have a great deal of universal understanding of the types and causes of both. The fact that individuals or cultures may think or feel otherwise cuts no ice as regards their objective ability to flourish in the terms which Drover and Kerans advocate in the introduction. There is nothing 'thin' about this understanding, as one day in any busy hospital anywhere in the world will testify, institutions which are indeed inhabited by experts. We show in our book that similar arguments and examples can be brought to bear as regards the concept of autonomy.

The issue of expertise posed by Drover and Kerans is a red herring. Of course, domination by dogma of any codified kind is a problem for the conduct of inquiry. However, it does not follow from this that some understanding is not better — more correct — in technical, hermeneutic or critical terms than other understanding. If this is the case then the issue is surely how to harness inputs of whatever kind to rational inquiry which stand the best chance of leading to effective solutions to the problems under investigation.

In short, claimants cannot be protected from getting it wrong, unless it is argued that they always get it right. However, to do this would undermine the admitted universalist strands in Drover and Kerans' own epistemological and ethical position. Conversely, if it makes sense, as they rightly suggest, that claimants sometimes do get it right, it follows, again, that they can also get it wrong. Claimants, after all, might support slavery and completely disagree about basic ethical principles and the nature of human flourishing. In other words, there is a real danger here of throwing out the baby with the bath water.

I feel particularly strongly about the dangers of epistemological and moral populism having grown up in the environment of populist racism in the American South. In what I feel at times reduces to a purely pragmatic argument against the tyranny of experts, Drover and Kerans run the risk of replacing this with other equally abhorrent tyrannies.

Acknowledgements: thanks to Ian Gough for helpful comments.

Note
1   See summary of the book in Gough *(supra)*.

COMMENT ON GOUGH

Peter Penz

The recent work of Ian Gough and his collaborator, Len Doyal, is extremely valuable for several reasons. (1) It can help rejuvenate the traditional egalitarian vision after the rather successful onslaught of the New Right in the 1980s. (2) It bridges political philosophy and political economy. For some time now I have been concerned about the restrictive divide between these two fields. Political philosophy focuses on social justice (among other ideals) and political economy on power, each generally ignoring the other. The book by Doyal and Gough, *A Theory of Human Need* (1991), consists primarily of political philosophy, but it also develops the connection with political economy. In the paper under discussion, Ian Gough lays the groundwork for the political-economy half of the project. (3) Their book is also valuable for the systematic manner in which it develops this bridge between political philosophy and political economy. It is a complex, but clearly recognizable structure of concepts and relationships that moves from the formulation of ethical principles, focusing on the moral centrality and priority of human needs, to normative policy requirements and on to the implications for economic structures and political processes.

Against the background of my general appreciation of this project and in the spirit of wishing to see it progress, I want to offer some critical observations on Ian Gough's paper. I intend to bring these out by referring to a comparative study of the politics of poverty alleviation in the Third World. This needs to be justified, given that Gough meant his analysis to apply primarily to the highly industrialized countries. The reason for my move, apart from the fact that my own concern is now mostly with basic needs in the Third World and it is on my mind as a result of an extended research stay in India recently, is that the issue of social welfare is relevant not merely to highly industrialized countries. Moreover, Gough does say in the paper, 'I believe some of the predictions can be tested for developing nations too' and the longer-term project seems to be designed to cover the less industrialized countries as well (see Doyal and Gough 1991 ch.13).

The Third World study I am referring to is the comparative analysis by Atul Kohli (1987) of reforms to reduce poverty under different political regimes within India's federal system. Using the theoretical orientation of the bringing-the-state-back-in school, Kohli (1987) compared three state governments in India in the late 1970s whose performance was noticeably different with respect to poverty. One regime was a government of the party that traditionally held monopoly control over state power in India, the Congress Party, but one that was headed by a populist leader, in the southern state of Karnataka; a second was a government formed by a party that had just broken the historical monopoly of the Congress Party on state power in India, the Janata Dal, which also came to power in the huge northern state of Uttar Pradesh, the object of Kohli's second case study; and the third was a government formed by one of India's Communist Parties in the eastern state of West Bengal. The comparative analysis revealed that the least effective in tackling poverty was the government of the Janata Dal in Uttar Pradesh which had fragmented leadership and was dominated by the land-owning peasantry, while the most effective was the Communist government in West Bengal, and the populist Congress government in Karnataka was in-between in its impact.

Particularly interesting for us here are the reasons for this differential performance. Kohli (1987 ch.6) concluded that the decisive explanatory variables of effective anti-poverty policies were the nature of the respective regimes, in particular the cohesiveness in leadership, an ideology clearly committed to redistribution, an organization both disciplined and extensive in reaching into the countryside and, finally, relatively high autonomy from the propertied classes. This suggests a conflict perspective, which is in striking contrast to the consensus perspective that seems to predominate in Gough's analysis, despite the thrust of Gough's earlier work (1979). This consensus perspective shows up on two levels: (1) the collective interest is seen as readily coinciding with the priority of human needs; (2) economic governance is seen as most promising when it emerges from cooperation between propertied interests and other powerful economic groups, ideally but not necessarily including labour. Both points are, I believe, dangerous as guides to political action aimed at putting needs first, and they warrant elaboration.

Consider first the relationship between needs and the collective interest. The conception of human needs presented in the book by Doyal and Gough, because it focuses primarily on the question of *what* should count as needs rather than *who* is needy, gives the impression that satisfying needs is in the interest of all of us. While the distributive dimension of needs is acknowledged, it is not really treated as fundamental. Perhaps implicit in this equation of needs with the collective interest is the concern that the deprived will not win a distributive struggle and that only a solidaristic policy will serve them.

Even if it is true that only a solidaristic policy will help the deprived, the institutional aspect of Gough's consensus orientation raises the question of what kind of solidarity is effective. Gough concludes, in a manner similar to Ramesh Mishra (1984), that corporatist capitalism (ideally social corporatism) is the most promising politico-economic structure to give priority to human needs. This conclusion partly rests on the range of options that he selected for analysis. It excludes, for example, market socialism, without a justification being offered. This is, I believe, a major limitation.

Beyond that, however, Gough's analysis of processes advancing solidarity under capitalist corporatism seems to me problematic. Corporatism is in effect a negotiated solidarity of the powerful. It is not apparent why the various centres of power would be concerned about the plight of those too disadvantaged to harm the privileged. Trust and cooperation apply to the mutual interests of the powerful and are different from altruism towards the needy or from a sense of social justice. I find it difficult to see how the need-satisfaction *potential* of corporatism emphasized by Gough can be seen as a need-satisfaction *propensity* of such a structure. It is true that social corporatism is a promising option, but only in those countries (unlike, for example, Canada, as well as practically all less-industrialized countries) where the labour movement is powerful and is willing and capable of insisting on participation in socio-economic governance and where it does not merely represent a labour aristocracy. The nature of the solidarity that is required for an effective needs-first regime may well have to be of a quite different kind from that of corporatism.

My distinction between potential and propensity suggests, furthermore, that the structure of the politics *within* economic systems may be at least as important as the politico-economic systems analysed by Gough. Whether basic needs are attended to or not may in the first instance depend on political mobilization. Part of what the Communist Parties in India have accomplished in two states is the mobilization of the lower classes and castes. Such mobilization can lead both to the coming to power of needs-first regimes and to the legitimation of the construction of institutional structures that then protect basic-needs programmes, such as in India's state of Kerala, which has one of the Third World's outstanding records in meeting basic needs. I suspect that this point also applies to highly industrialized countries.

Applying the model of need satisfiers (summarized in the early part of Gough's paper) to the evaluation of economic-political structures seems to me to be a very illuminating way to proceed. The thrust of my critical commentary has been that there are two important restrictions that limit the usefulness of Gough's analysis in terms of informing political strategy for the minimization of deprivation. One is in the range of options considered. The other is the exclusive focus on structural shells, the most promising of which leave great indeterminacy concerning their impact on human needs. In fact, it is only by viewing the possibilities of such structures in terms of a consensus perspective that they become promising, as distinct from simply open-ended. This suggests that another level of political structure, that of the nature of regimes and their bases of support, may in the end be at least as decisive as the structures for mediating between the state and the economy, which is the focus of Gough's analysis.

COMMENT ON HUM

David Donaldson

In his analysis of the discourse surrounding economic policies that transfer purchasing power from rich to poor, Hum argues convincingly that the economic theories and complicated econometric analyses employed tend to exclude the beneficiaries of tax-transfer programmes from the public debate and discussion.

I argue in this comment that, although Hum is probably right about the effects of economic discourse in this area, he could have added an important comment about the economic analysis itself. It is that the bulk of the claims that economists make about the *equality–efficiency trade-off*, the *efficiency costs* of tax-transfer schemes and the *excess burden of taxation* are based on flawed welfare economics. In addition, I claim that a reasonable policy discussion needs an explicit ethical stance such as utilitarianism, and that a thicker theory of the good than the preference view usually taken by economists would be a useful expansion of utilitarian ethics.

When discussing the consequences of tax-transfer schemes such as the negative income tax, ordinary people focus their attention on incentive effects — changes in work effort, saving and investment — but economists typically use want-regarding ethical principles based on preferences, and they provide no room for Calvinistic beliefs in the value of work and thrift. Economists argue, instead, that the 'distortions' of income-based tax-transfer schemes interfere with the economy's ability to provide people with what they want, and they call the consequences of this interference an efficiency loss.

The ethical principle that most economists use is based on the idea of Pareto-optimality or Pareto-efficiency (the two expressions are used inter-changeably). A state of affairs is Pareto-efficient if and only if it is impossible to make anyone better off without making someone else worse off. [1] There are always many Pareto-efficient states, however, and the differences among them concern the distribution of consumption across the population, a phenomenon on which Paretian value-judgements are silent.

A simple example will illustrate. Suppose that a fixed quantity of a single good — yams, say — is to be distributed to a number of selfish adults. Pareto-efficiency requires only that all of the yams must be handed out: *every* way of distributing them is Pareto-efficient. Now suppose that the pre-tax amount and distribution of yams is determined by land ownership (I assume that no-one works in this simple economy). Suppose further, that a government that wants to change the distribution of yams is constrained to leave the ownership of land unchanged. If a government programme transfers yams from rich to poor, there is no efficiency loss as long as none are wasted in the process. If, for example, the tax-transfer scheme is costless — no yams are used up by it — all the distributions of yams corresponding to the original Pareto-efficient distributions can be achieved through the tax-transfer scheme. If, however, some yams are needlessly wasted in the process, fewer yams are given out than could be and there is an efficiency loss — everyone could be made better off by distributing the wasted yams.

Now suppose that a *necessary* part of the tax-transfer scheme is that some resources — yams — are used up in the tax-transfer process. Even if this resource cost is kept to a minimum, it is tempting to conclude, as many economists do, that the reduction in the total number of yams consumed represents an efficiency loss. But this claim requires the possibility, in the post tax-transfer state of affairs, of making at least one person better off without making anyone else worse off. If the resource use of the tax-transfer scheme is minimized, the only way that it could be done is to redistribute consumption in another way. The only possibility in my simple example is to change the pattern of land ownership, and that is not possible. It follows that there is *no* efficiency loss: it is impossible to make anyone better off in the post tax-transfer situation without making someone else worse off.

Welfare economists distinguish between cases in which governments are free from constraints and cases in which policies such as changes in ownership of factors of production cannot be made by calling Pareto-efficiency *first-best* in the unconstrained environment and *second-best* when constraints limit the set of feasible options. *All* real-world tax-transfer efficiency problems fall into the second-best category.

Although the identification of the necessary costs of taxes and transfers in the yam economy as an efficiency loss is an obvious confusion, the discussion of real tax-transfer policies — at least in its standard form — enshrines that error. When most economists discuss efficiency costs, they assert that, if redistribution could have been done by *non-distorting* taxes and transfers, then everyone could be made better off in the post-tax situation. Given the models that these economists work with, this is true, but the claim rests on the assumption that these non-distorting taxes and transfers are feasible, and that assumption is, in general, false.

The non-distorting taxes and transfers economists discuss are called *lump-sum*: they are not based on economic variables such as income or wealth but rather depend on non-economic variables — age and race are examples. These taxes avoid the incentive effects that standard taxes contain. It is not possible for people to change their age or race, but it is possible for them to change their incomes — by adjusting work effort. If it were possible to change the distribution of purchasing power by using lump-sum taxes and transfers, then schemes such as income taxes or the negative income tax would be associated with efficiency losses: it would be possible to make someone better off in the post-tax situation without harming anyone else.

Two conditions are necessary for valid efficiency-loss claims: first, the tax-transfer scheme must not be lump-sum (the negative income tax is not), and second, it must be possible — through an alternative scheme such as lump-sum taxes and transfers — to make at least one person better off without making anyone else worse off. But lump-sum taxes and transfers are, in fact, politically and administratively unfeasible, and even if they could be used, they cannot redistribute income from rich to poor in the same way that conventional tax-transfer policies can. Even if, for example, members of one racial group are economically disadvantaged, on average, lump-sum transfers to them must be the same for all, providing equal benefits to rich and poor members of the group, and the requisite lump-sum taxes on the rest of the population must similarly affect rich and poor members of the advantaged group equally. It follows that, in virtually any post tax-transfer state achieved by conventional policies, it is impossible to use feasible lump-sum taxes and transfers to make some people better off without making others worse off. Therefore, virtually all income-based tax-transfer policies involve *no* efficiency loss at all.[2] In addition, just as in the yams example, Paretian welfare economics is silent when it comes to choosing among the many distributionally different alternatives. This does not mean that (second-best) Pareto-efficiency considerations are useless, but it does mean that they are not adequate for policy decisions.

Given this, an alternative to the narrow ethical view of Paretianism must be found. An obvious and simple candidate is utilitarianism — it has been used by a few economists in discussing these issues (see, for example, Mirrlees 1971). It is able to choose among the many Pareto-optima, and the ethical view that it represents is easily understood by all participants in the policy discussion. In addition, when used in economic models of tax-transfer policies, sense can be made of the trade-off between the consequences of incentive effects and the gains in distributive justice.

It is easy, however, to object to the economist's preference-based utilitarianism. It ignores aspects of the good life — both economic and non-economic — that are of obvious importance. But utilitarian arguments are flexible: there are many varieties other than preference-utilitarianism. An obvious alternative is one that incorporates a thicker theory of the good; attempts at such accounts can be found in Griffin (1986) and in Drover and Kerans (*supra*).

But utilitarianism also has advantages over the many 'non-welfarist' ethical theories that are popular at the moment. It permits everyone's interests to receive equal consideration in policy discussions, independently of age, sex, disability, participation in claimsmaking groups, and so on. And when resources to satisfy competing claims are scarce, or when the claims of different groups conflict, it is capable of assigning priorities. In addition, utilitarianism — suitably extended — permits us to extend our notion of justice and the common good to population questions (Blackorby and Donaldson 1984). This is an important advantage over competing principles of justice in a world where population growth is the most important environmental problem.

Alternatives to utilitarianism and other welfarist moral theories such as the 'claimsmaking' theory of Drover and Kerans face other difficulties as well. Some individuals — children, the mentally disabled, wrongly convicted prisoners, people with serious chronic illnesses — are almost never part of claimsmaking groups. Their interests may be given some consideration if members of these groups are sufficiently altruistic, but altruism is a shaky foundation for rights. In addition, the focus on groups of people and the extension of some aspects of well-being to them has real difficulties. Groups of people are not natural categories. Am I, for example, a propertied white male or a handicapped musician? In my society, I am classified as and encouraged to align my identity to the former; handicapped musicians exist, of course, but they do not constitute a social group. This means that the division of ourselves into social groups is itself part of the social reality we are concerned with. Attempts to change that reality will, in general, change the structure of social groups as well.

Welfarist ethical theories such as utilitarianism are concerned with what Griffin (1986) calls prudential value — the value of a life to the particular individual who is living it. If, as Drover and Kerans claim, groups are more than the sum of their parts, then group welfare cannot be entirely prudential — there is no individual person who lives the group's life. Rather it must be some sort of objective or perfectionist welfare (see Sumner 1992).

None of these quibbles should be taken as an argument against a thicker theory of the good than the preference view of standard welfare economics. A reasonable welfarist moral position, whether it is the utilitarian one or a variant that is concerned with inequality of well-being, must have an explicit link to prudential value. Economists have some reasons on their side, to be sure, for their simple practice; individuals have more information about their own needs and well-being than governments do, and the liberal theory of the state enjoins governments to be neutral toward alternative views of the good (well-being). But in a world of asymmetric information and preference change through advertising, policies that protect people from the harm that unregulated markets can do are needed, and economists could profitably expand the preference theory of the good that they now use almost universally. The contributions of Drover and Kerans and Griffin could prove to be helpful in extending welfare economics in this direction.

In addition, if economists are to contribute to a solution of the problems of exclusion from policy debates that Hum discusses, it is critically important that they abandon the mendacity and obfuscation that so much of their Paretian arguments contain. The alternative is to move toward a policy debate that is based on explicitly stated social ethics. Only in such a setting can productive debate, open to the full participation of everyone affected, take place.

Notes

1   Children are usually ignored in this exercise by treating households as individual — a practice which, although convenient, is hard to justify.
2   It is theoretically possible for an efficiency loss to occur if taxes are high enough so that small increases reduce revenue and therefore, the well-being of the poor as well as the rich. Studies have shown that this is not a practical problem.

COMMENT ON LUSTIGER-THALER AND SHRAGGE

Alan Scott

Lustiger-Thaler and Shragge's core argument is that 'the manner in which social movements frame and interpret needs is critical to the elaboration of any future democratic design of the welfare state.' Their analysis takes three concepts — need, social movement, and the welfare state — and focuses attention on the complex ways in which these are linked. The authors are dissatisfied with accounts which reduce social movements either to political entities which can be absorbed into the state, or purely cultural phenomena locked within civil society.

In their view, a social movement is both a medium through which needs are constituted and articulated, and a mechanism for transmitting these needs to the state which to varying degrees either acknowledges or ignores them. Following Agnes Heller, they argue that the 'pluralistic state can never be the source of the elaboration of new systems of needs'. The state, at least in liberal democracies, must interact with those agencies in which needs are formed and articulated if it is to govern effectively. The state's reaction to social movement demands will in turn influence the formation of needs and this will shape the course of future collective action. Lustiger-Thaler and Shragge are thus thinking through these relations temporally — diachronically.

This analysis is very fruitful, and the single critical import of my comments is to persuade them to push the implications further. I will suggest that the conceptual apparatus they employ to develop their argument must not be reified if the implications of their analysis are to be worked through.

To develop their argument Lustiger-Thaler and Shragge employ two conceptual tools: (i) *parallel agency* and (ii) the distinction between *rights* and *counter-rights*. By *parallel agency* they mean the ways in which social movements act to *either* gain access to political processes by framing their demands in terms of rights (PA1) *or* challenge those political decision-making processes (PA2). In this second case, demands are framed not merely in terms of rights but also in terms of counter-rights. The prime concern of their paper is with the counter-rights which challenge the principles underlying decision-making in 'liberal' states, the most basic of which is a hierarchy of need based upon property and commodity relations.

While the concepts of parallel agency and rights/counter-rights in some way re-express more familiar distinctions drawn between demands for outcomes and demands for participation (Habermas 1975), or between negotiable and non-negotiable demands (Touraine 1981), or between instrumental and expressive strategies (Rucht 1990), it seems to me to have two advantages: (i) in some of the above cases the activities of social movements are polarized to an extent which limits the sociological (as opposed to normative) utility of the concepts (eg. Habermas); (ii) in other cases, for example Touraine, these distinctions are drawn primarily in order to periodize social movements into 'old' and 'new'. In contrast, Lustiger-Thaler and Shragge locate social movements on the boundary between state and civil society.

The fuller import of this framework becomes apparent in their analysis of Alternative Service Organizations (ASOs) and Community Economic Development (CED). On the account offered here, ASOs and CED demand the following:

(i) resources from the (local) state; (ii) sufficient autonomy from their state patron to develop innovative, and more democratic organizational forms and modes of operation. These two demands — for participation and self-determination — broadly echo the distinction between PA1 and PA2. In addition, the ASOs and CED are credited with evolving a model of welfare provision and economic assistance which is an alternative to the individualized and property/commodity-based model implicit in the *liberal welfare state*. In this way they challenge the distinction between public and private and they frame counter-rights.

Two aspects of this case study are of particular interest for social movement and welfare state theory and raise issues of general interpretation.

The first is the relationship between the two central demands made by the ASOs and CED. My main residual worry about the concepts of parallel agency and counter-rights is that if we treat these distinctions as absolute they are being asked to do too much work. In this case they would appear to play two overlapping but not entirely compatible roles; one analytical, the other normative. Insofar as parallel agency and counter-rights are to play a normative role in the argument, they must be treated as qualitative and categorical distinctions. Where the concepts of parallel agency and counter-rights serve to demarcate clearly actions/demands which are innovative and located within the social movement sector from those which are conventional and located within the state, this serves the normative function of ascribing a generally positive value to the former, and a generally negative value to the latter.

However, analytically and sociologically it seems to me that these concepts would be of more use were they to be treated as ideal types and as variable over time; specifically in the course of the development of a social movement and its relation to the state. Treating the distinctions as categorical, I would suggest, drives the argument back into the division between political and cultural interpretations of social movements which Lustiger-Thaler and Shragge clearly, and rightly, want to overcome.

Treating the distinctions as fixed would also imply an interpretation of the ASOs and CED as representing a generalizable alternative social model. But can a political project so radically different from that of the liberal welfare state remain an alternative system of welfare provision and participation? Or would such an alternative in effect imply such a radical transformation of general social relations that we could no longer talk of a welfare state in any recognizable sense? On Lustiger-Thaler and Shragge's account it would seem that the social movements they are analysing are themselves caught between these two projects: a revisionist one and the demand, or at least the implicit demand, for a wider social transformation. The distinction between PA1 and PA2 may thus overlap with the familiar disjunction between ideology and practical action.

Lustiger-Thaler and Shragge are fully aware of the complexities of the relationship between the two types of demands — for resources and autonomy — and the ambiguity of the status of the ASOs and CED which are situated somewhere between government agency and social movement. What might the complexities of these relationships mean for our understanding of liberal welfare states and social movements?

The second aspect is the relationship between the ASOs/CED and the local state. Were the actions of the local state simply determined by its 'liberal' political philosophy it could not recognize the need to interact with innovative and challenging bodies. Chris Pickvance, in a critique of Castells, pointed out that the state can be and often is innovative in its interactions with social movements (Pickvance 1976).

I think the case of the ASOs and CED provides an example of such innovation. As Lustiger-Thaler and Shragge point out, notwithstanding the inherent conflicts between the local state and the ASOs and CED, the latter are partly financed and sponsored by the former.

This has an important implication for the analysis. We must recognize that the state is in a sense creating for itself an interlocutor within civil society. In other words, at some level the liberal welfare state must (at least occasionally) recognize the limits of a property- and commodity-based hierarchy of needs and of the system of welfare provision. It is thus the local state itself that is contributing to the production of counter-rights which challenge the state's own basic working principles. Perhaps one could further argue that, given the historical role of collective action in forming the welfare state (cf. Esping-Andersen 1990), this communication regarding new systems of needs from civil society to the state has always been a precondition for the development of any form of welfare provision.

This is not at all to dispute that the CED and ASOs are sources of innovation, but I would argue that a too rigidly drawn distinction between PA1 and PA2, and between rights and counter-rights oversimplifies the source and location of such innovation: innovative citizens vs. conservative state bodies. Too strict a distinction between rights and counter-rights, and the assumption that innovation springs exclusively from citizens acting against the state obscures the fact that just as collective action produces knowledge about the entry of social movements into the polity, so too does the interaction between the state and social movements produce knowledge for the state about new systems of needs. Likewise, the contestation of liberal and individualizing assumptions in the delivery of welfare outputs is a precondition for, and not merely the outcome of, communication between the state and civil society in the form of collective action.

Insofar as the interaction between local state and social movements produces innovative forms of welfare development and delivery it represents a model which can be imitated elsewhere in such a way as to increase democratic participation in the welfare state. But, given the mutual dependence of local state and social movement, the claims based upon counter-rights in this case cannot be thought of as offering an autonomous and generalizable alternative to the 'liberal welfare state' whose product it in some ways is.

But the solution to these interpretative difficulties seems to me to be already at hand in Lustiger-Thaler and Shragge's analysis. A dynamic analysis of the relationship between need, collective action and the state leads us to relativize the distinctions between PA1 and PA2, and rights and counter-rights. Such an analysis would also need to demonstrate the fluidity of the relationship between PA1 and PA2 and how, depending on the reaction of the state, counter-rights can be transformed into rights. By treating the relationship between PA1 and PA2 as fluid rather than ascribing them to distinct political philosophies, we can begin to theorize the vacillation between innovation and consolidation of both social movements *and* the local state in such a way that the latter is not simply viewed as the captive of a 'liberal' political framework. We may then start to analyse the developmental, and often cyclic, character of social movements (see, for example, Offe 1990), and understand how states and social movements mutually influence and are dependent upon each other. I interpret Lustiger-Thaler and Shragge's analysis as attempting to open up these questions for a general theory of welfare states and collective action.

COMMENT ON JORDAN

Allan Moscovitch

First a personal note. Although I have continued to be an academic, for the last several years I have in fact been spending much of my time involved in the implementation of policy proposals in Ontario as the Chair of the Advisory Group on New Social Assistance Legislation, 1990–92. I have also been involved in the administration of local social welfare services as a director of research and planning in regional government, 1988–89.

The Practice of Resistance

Bill Jordan's chapter presents an attempt to combine a self-reflexive examination of personal experience as a worker and as a member of a claimsmaking organization with the results of a research project of several years' duration. In doing so, his chapter focuses attention not on the larger philosophical questions which relate to the nature of claimsmaking and the nature of the claim but on the interaction between claimant and worker, from which will come the adjudication of the claim. The title of the work refers us to the 'weapons of the weak' because its purpose is to focus on the methods which are used by the weak, by the relatively powerless, to cajole the more powerful into giving their circumstances as positive a review as possible. His experience as a social worker, activist and researcher led him to recognize the 'artful practices' adopted by clients to achieve recognition of their claims.

Jordan's work suggests the need to understand the practical administrative interactional level of claimsmaking. As he notes, as a young worker his work was in a sense being directed by clients who understood how to employ his earnestness. This activity led him to gain some consciousness of the actual interactional processes at work.

What is the actual content of artful practices of resistance? As Jordan notes, they vary from rhetorical flourishes, to a knowledge of the rules which is at least the match of the most experienced workers. They go further, however, encompassing a series of activities which claimants recognize as the means of survival in a system which neither provides them with enough to establish a decent standard of poverty nor with a legitimate means of bridging the gap between financial dependency on the state and a job which pays enough to improve the standard provided by the state.

What is at issue here is the continuing dominance of the principle of *less eligibility* in the conditions of eligibility for minimum income social welfare programmes. Claimants are forced to find means to supplement their incomes without informing the administrator, because the less eligibility conditions would cause them to lose at least as much as they would gain and possibly more. Such practices are part of the game of resistance, of survival in a system which is geared not to the support of the autonomy of the person but to their stigmatization and punishment for the crime of being poor.

Mr Bow does not report his income derived from the sale of rabbits caught by his dogs. He argues that since the funds earned simply pay for the cost of the dogs' upkeep then there really is no harm done and certainly no reason to report it.

Considerations on What Clients Must Do

Interactions — the term presupposes more than one party. What I wish I could see here is the complement — the views of the workers with responsibility for adjudicating claims. To what extent have they too, like the young Bill Jordan, become aware of the artful practices, and what view do they take of these practices? Why do they tolerate these practices, if they do? How do these interactive practices influence their adjudication?

Workers too, like the clients, must often work by the book, and are guided by a framework within which they must frame their response. As a social work educator I know well the people who have been and will be the workers who must do the adjudicating. In relation to the clients they are clearly agents of power. They are employed to work with and within a stated set of rules which define the conditions of an acceptable claim.

Graduates wishing to work in an empowering way with clients must also learn artful practices of their own as well as those of the clients if they are to assist as much as possible and at the same time continue to survive in the job. They in turn attempt to frame acceptable claims, finding ways to provide the benefits available despite the limits which may have been put on them administratively.

As a senior administrator, where I worked with a group of similarly committed managerial staff, my task was to employ a language and a methodology which would permit me to support and encourage front-line staff to develop a client-centred approach. At the same time my task was to find a language to explain to politicians and the public why it was that the cost of social assistance was rising and how we were competently spending their funds. My point is that in some sense artful practices occur at different points in the same process of claimsmaking and it would be interesting to comprehend how administrators too employ their own set of artful practices.

It is my recent experience of the issue raised by Mr Bow that activist clients have a very clear idea of the acceptable and the unacceptable. Admittedly their views may be cultural or it may be, as Jordan notes, that they are temporally specific and related to contemporary dominant ideology. But they would, like Mr Bow, not be happy to know of people whose claims were wholly or largely fraudulent because of the level of their other income. They are sensitive to the publicly expressed views that large numbers of recipients are committing fraud and they would not want to see further publicity about individual claimants whose claims are dishonest. At a more visceral level, they believe, even if the public is not always in agreement, that they are deserving, that they meet the conditions. Income security is, in their view, for those who need it not for those who have jobs and are simply supplementing their income. It is certainly not for people who have submitted several claims in different names and in different cities.

My last point here concerns the choice of interview material. Mr Bow is a married man with a spouse and children. He appears, for want of additional information, to be the classic male employable. I do not know the British minimum income programme well enough to know if he is representative of the majority of claimants. In Canada he would not be. At present a claimant is equally likely to be a person with a disability, a single parent, frequently a woman, or a person who is unemployed, many of whom are young and single, with few skills and little education. Do resistance practices vary by the individual and the social conditions of the claimant? Does the extent to which claimants are trapped in poverty vary? I am inclined to think so. I would encourage Jordan to examine the resistance practices of a wider range of claimants.

Dissent, Dignity and Social Justice

The artful dialogues and methods of survival are about obtaining a measure of dignity in a world which claimants find treats them with disdain. Jordan reminds us that rather than challenging the nature of power, claimants join in and reinforce the practices of domination because their stake in the world rests on their relations of domination and subordination. They do so however by stressing that power holders have duties and obligations which they must live up to.

It is indignities which, Jordan notes, most move people to resistance. This is consistent with the work of James Scott (1985) who provided some inspiration for this understanding of welfare claiming. The transcripts from two interviews illustrate this attitude on the part of two working men. And while I think this approach is important in understanding the substance of claimsmaking, the research would be richer with consideration of the practice of a broader range of the subordinated.

My own recent work as Chair of the Advisory Group on New Social Assistance Legislation confirms the essential point that is made here. In order to have the direct input of a wide range of recipients of a minimum income programme, we hired a staff member who had been a leader in a recipients' rights organization to help organize and conduct a series of focus groups with recipients from across the province. The groups were conducted in confidence with the transcripts available only to this staff member and to two other staff members who worked with her. They produced a report that summarizes the results of extensive discussion with more than 400 consumers.[1]

What was interesting was the result that the single most important issue for those participating was the lack of dignity afforded them as welfare claimants. They found the practices of claiming to be too often humiliating, evidence of the extent to which we should be careful to understand that meeting human needs is not simply about state policy at high levels. It is very much about the administrative practices which guide interaction as well as the interaction itself. It is a most powerful confirmation of the observations of Scott and Jordan.

Women and the Practice of Resistance

So far I have refrained from commenting on two sections of the paper which present material drawn from interviews with higher-income households. This material is woven into the text to illustrate the interactional relations of resistance in a different context, that of higher-income women, all of whom have assumed primary responsibility for childcare and domestic work.

The results appear to indicate that 'in public accounts of their lives, they choose not to challenge the dominant order, but to seek a measure of autonomy and opportunistic gain within it.' (*supra* p.215). There are several difficulties I have with this and other material presented later. First comes my own sense of insecurity in commenting on material in an area with which I have considerably less familiarity. That being said I wondered whether in fact there were 'artful practices' that the research had missed. In their relations in the household, did these women truly do all of the childcare and domestic tasks or did they have methods of ensuring that their spouses did undertake some of this work? What were the dialogues used, like the clients of the young Bill Jordan social worker? To what extent as the paper hints, did the gender and the methodology of the research play a role in the results? As the paper notes the stories he was told as an activist, as a social worker and as a researcher are not necessarily the same as the ones told at the pub, the laundromat or at the office, in the park or at morning coffee with friends.

Conclusion

This is a work rich in nuance and observation which gave me reason to reflect on my own experience and provided me with the benefit of the experience of the author and of those whom he interviewed. It provides an important reminder to us that the framing of claims is not an abstract nor a monolithic process. It is one which must be understood at least as much at the interactional level as at the level of public discourse and state policy.

Notes
1. The final report of the Advisory Group on New Social Assistance Legislation is titled *Time for Action* (Ministry of Community and Social Services, Government of Ontario, 1992). See *Speaking Out: Final Report* for the results of dialogue with social assistance consumers in the province of Ontario.

COMMENT ON RISTOCK

Deborah Stienstra

Feminists have often offered alternative models of political action and political theory based in an understanding of the interconnection between political practice and theory. Janice Ristock's chapter does just this. It offers an alternative way of theorizing social service practice located in the experiences of feminist social service collectives. Ristock also proposes that a model based in the experiences of these collectives may foster the work of the collectives themselves and of other alternative groups who oppose the dominant values and approaches within society.

Ristock suggests that using the standpoint of feminist experience in social service collectives, such as rape crisis or sexual assault centres, can provide examples of how some activists attempt to deal with the tensions between providing services and promoting social change. She offers a theoretical framework of helping to explore the tensions these feminist collectives face in their day-to-day work. The tensions are evident in two poles of political practice: the traditional social service model and a feminist approach to services. She argues that feminist collectives are pulled in both directions; although their goal is to provide services based in the feminist ideal, they are challenged and limited in providing these services by the traditional social services structures which value service over activism, justice over caring, power over empowerment, direction over choice and access over survival.

One of Ristock's contributions in this chapter is to identify an alternative model for providing care based in examples of feminist practice. The richness of this chapter is found in the examples from Ristock's research in feminist collectives in Canada. Using this research she builds a model of an ideal feminist practice based on empowering staff and service recipients; offering care and support to co-workers and clients; valuing choice for workers and service users; and recognizing that feminist activity is often one of survival. She does not leave the model at the ideal, she recognizes that feminist collectives live with the tensions of trying to mainstream, or respond within the confines of the existing system based in the traditional values, and trying to disengage, or organize separate services based on feminist goals.

The strength of working from the standpoint of feminist practices also leads to one of the weaknesses of this chapter. Ristock is quite explicit that her goal is to understand feminist collectives and their social context for providing help. She does this extremely well. But she contrasts this with the ideal of the traditional system and its values from the vantage-point of feminist practices and experiences. Her analysis of the traditional model often falls into stereotypical characterizations of the values of that model. For example, in opposition to the feminist ideal of empowerment, she portrays the traditional one as power 'found in hierarchies where it is centralized and often oppressive because it remains with a select few.' (*supra* p.226). As a political scientist, I am perhaps overly fond of analysing the concept of power, although as a feminist I am more comfortable with the value of empowerment. In spite of this, I would suggest that power is a more complex value than that defined by Ristock, in both traditional social service structure and in society. Power cannot simply be seen as power-over another person or 'might makes right' evident in centralized hierarchies or used by experts with the discretion to choose who is needy enough to receive welfare. It is also having the resources to be able to act. Both the bureaucrats and the experts have the necessary resources to act. One could also argue they have been empowered, but by this point the line between the two values becomes hazy. Using a limited understanding of power allows us to see only two positions in the social relations: those who have power and those who don't or, as Ristock notes, 'The world of power-over relations has been identified by feminists as conceptualizing women as "other" and creating separateness and powerlessness.' (*supra* p.226). Jordan reminds us (*supra*) that the 'weak' or those without power can use their resources to act and resist in ways that we may least expect and thus are not necessarily victimized by their apparent lack of power. Clearly, as well, not all the bureaucrats within the social service system are powerful. They too have constraints that shape their ability to act, even though from the point of view of claimsmakers they may appear very powerful. This tendency towards narrowing the scope of the ideal of the traditional is seen again in the word-pair of *survival* and *access*. Ristock provides a good description of what survival means in the feminist approach (although I would be hard pressed to find many feminists who want to leave the ideal goal of feminist activism and service at survival) and offers an undifferentiated description of what access means in the traditional power structures.

The two poles, feminist and traditional, offered in Ristock's theory of helping are attempts to define two differing ideals of political practice and ideology. But even with this caveat, the two poles and Ristock's discussion of how feminist collectives deal with the tensions of working between poles reflect a more normative assumption. While Ristock suggests that these are opposing albeit attracting poles in political practice, in her theoretical model they remain opposing and mutually repelling alternatives. For example, in the section on the ethics of care and justice she argues that our society, and the traditional social service structure, 'emphasizes a normatively male ethic of justice with a focus on autonomy and separation' (*supra* p. 227), but also underscores that the feminist approach includes caregiving and relating to others as its primary elements. She concedes that these are universal experiences and thus care should not be seen as the exclusive domain of women nor justice the domain of men, but suggests that, in practice, feminist collectives offer alternatives based on caring. She offers no attempt to see how both ethics are evident in both political practices nor does she suggest that the ethic of justice is one that should be included in feminist practice. It seems to me that the ideal for feminist practice is one which balances both care and justice, rather than calling for one or the other.

Ristock is careful to suggest throughout the chapter that these poles must be identified as ideals and that we all have multiple, contradictory, and continually changing places along the continuum. She also argues that feminists should be wary of being pulled to one extreme or the other since a goal of feminist political practice is to maintain a balance between the two poles. Indeed, Adamson et al., who developed the disengagement/mainstreaming model, argue,

> Making change, then, is a question not of choosing between these two approaches, but of reconciling them. Feminists must maintain the integrity of their overall vision of change, yet reach and influence the majority of women who are necessarily focused on the specific concerns of their own lives. (1988 p.179)

The theoretical model Ristock offers is successful in identifying those forces which pull at feminist social service collectives and may be useful in identifying the forces that other alternative groups may experience. But it is less successful in drawing out the contradictions within or between these poles. With Ristock's model of opposing ideals set in stark contrast, we are left convinced that we should recognize our multiple, contrasting and changing positions in the continuum, but not finding theoretical tools to enable us to identify these. This is reinforced by the often limited portrayal of the traditional values in the model.

Ristock's vision, and it is one that I share, is a world that has been and is being transformed by feminist activism and service. Her model of helping based in the experiences of feminist social service collectives is a useful reminder of the tensions and constraints that feminists who work for social change and provide service deal with in their work. My hope is that this theory will be further developed so that we can see the contradictions within as well as between poles in order to enable activists and service providers to target areas for change within and outside the existing social service systems.

Bibliography

Abbott, E. and K. Bompas (1943) *The Woman Citizen and Social Security*, London: Mrs Bompass

Abercombie, Nicolas et al. (1986) *The Sovereign Individuals of Capitalism*, London: Allen & Unwin

Acosta, F. (1987) 'De l'événement à l'infraction: le processus de mise en forme pénale', *Déviance et Société* **XI** (1) pp.1–40

Acosta, F. (1981) 'A propos des illégalismes privilégiés: réflexions conceptuels et mise en contexte', *Criminologie* **XXI** (1) pp.7–34

Adamson, N., L. Briskin and M. McPhail (1988) *Feminist Organizing For Change: the contemporary women's movement in Canada*, Toronto: Oxford University Press

Alber, J., G. Esping-Andersen, and L. Rainwater (1987) 'Studying the welfare state: issues and queries', in M. Dierkes, H. Weiler and A. Antal (eds) *Comparative Policy Research*, Aldershot: Gower

Alexander, Larry and Maimon Schwarzchild (1987) 'Liberalism, Neutrality, and Equality of Welfare vs. Equality of Resources', *Philosophy and Public Affairs* **16**

Allen, A. (1987) *Uneasy Access: Privacy for Women in a Free Society*, Totowa, New Jersey: Rowman & Littlefield

Amariglio, Jack L. (1988) 'The body, economic discourse, and power: an economist's introduction to Foucault', *History of Political Economy* **20** (4)

Andrews, Geoff (ed.) (1991) *Citizenship*, London: Lawrence & Wishart

Arneson, Richard (1990) 'Liberalism, Distributive Subjectivism, and Equal Opportunity for Welfare', *Philosophy and Public Affairs* **19**

Arneson, Richard (1989) 'Equality and Equal Opportunity for Welfare', *Philosophical Studies* **56**

Arneson, Richard (1987) 'Meaningful Work and Market Socialism', *Ethics* **97**

Arrighi, Giovanni, Terrence Hopkins and Immanuel Wallerstien (1989) *Antisystemic Movements*, London: Verso

Atkinson, A.B. and J.E. Stiglitz (1980) *Lectures on Public Economics*, New York: McGraw-Hill

Bach, Michael (1992) *Methodological Issues in Developing a Conceptual Framework of Social Well-Being*, Toronto: Roeher Institute

Baines, C. (1991) 'The Professions And An Ethic Of Care', in C. Baines, P. Evans and S. Neysmith (eds) *Women's Caring: Feminist Perspectives on Social Welfare*, Toronto: McClelland & Stewart

Baker, John (1987) *Arguing for Equality*, London: Verso

Balbo, L. (1991) 'Cittadini, cittadini dimezzati, non-cittadini', *Inchiesta* **90**

Ballard, Charles L. (1988) 'The Marginal Efficiency Cost of Redistribution', *American Economic Review* **78**(5)

Banting, Keith (1987) *The Welfare State and Canadian Federalism*, Montreal: McGill-Queen's

Baratta, A. (1991) 'Les fonctions instrumentales et les fonctions symboliques du droit pénal', *Déviance et Société* **XV**(1) pp.1–25

Barbalet, J.M. (1988) *Citizenship*, Milton Keynes: Open University Press

Baron, R. and D. Byrne (1987) *Social Psychology: Understanding Human Interaction*, Boston: Allyn & Bacon

Barr, Nicholas (1992) 'Economic Theory and the Welfare State', *Journal of Economic Literature* **30** (2)

Barry, Norman (1990) *Welfare*, Milton Keynes: Open University Press

Barsh, Russel Lawrence and James Youngblood Henderson (1982) 'Aboriginal rights, treaty rights, and human rights: Indian tribes and "Constitutional Renewal"', *Journal of Canadian Studies* **17** (2)

Bartky, Sandra Lee (1990) *Femininity and Domination: Studies in the Phenomenology of Oppression*, New York: Routledge

Basilevsky, Alexander and Derek Hum (1984) *Experimental Social Programs and Analytic Methods: An Evaluation of the U.S. Income Maintenance Projects*, New York: Academic Press, Inc.

Baudrillard, Jean (1981) *For a Critique of the Political Economy of the Sign* (Translation by Charles Levin), St. Louis: Telos Press

Bauman, Zygmunt (1992) *Intimations of Post-Modernity*, London: Routledge

Baumol, William. J. (1986) *Superfairness*, Cambridge: MIT Press

Beenstock, M. and Associates (1987) *Work Welfare and Taxation: A Study of Labour Supply Incentives in the UK*, London: Allen & Unwin

Belisle, C. et B. Schiele (dir.) (1984a) *Les savoirs dans les pratiques quotidiennes: recherches sur les représentations*, Paris: Editions du CNRS

Belisle, C. et B. Schiele (dir.) (1984b) 'Les représentations', numéro spécial de la revue *Communication/Information* **VI** (2–3)

Benhabib, Seyla (1991) 'Feminism and Postmodernism: An Uneasy Alliance', *Praxis International* **11** (2) pp.139–49

Benhabib, Seyla (1990) 'Afterword: Communicative Ethics and Current Controversies in Practical Philosophy', in Fred Dahlmayr and Seyla Benhabib (eds) *The Communicative Thics Controversy*, Cambridge: MIT Press

Benhabib, Seyla (1989) 'Liberal Dialogue Versus a Critical Theory of Discursive Legitimation', in Nancy Rosenblum (ed.) *Liberalism and the Moral Life*, Cambridge: Harvard University Press

Benhabib, Seyla (1988) 'Autonomy, Modernity and Community: Communitarianism and Critical Social Theory in Dialogue', in A. Honneth et al. (ed.) *Zwischenbetrachtungen im Prozess der Aufklärung*, Frankfurt: Suhrkamp

Benhabib, Seyla (1986a) *Critique, Norm, and Utopia: A Study of the Foundations of Critical Theory*, New York: Columbia University Press

Benhabib, Seyla (1986b) 'The Generalized and the Concrete Other: The Kohlberg-Gilligan Controversy and Feminist Theory', *Praxis International* **5**(4) pp.402–424

Benhabib, Seyla (1982) 'The methodological illusions of modern political theory: the case of Rawls and Habermas', *Neue Hefte für Philosophie* **21** pp.47–74

Benhabib, Seyla and Drucilla Cornell (eds) (1987) *Feminism as Critique*, Minneapolis, MN: University of Minnesota Press

Benjamin, Jessica (1988) *The Bonds of Love: Psychoanalysis, Feminism, and the Problem of Domination*. New York: Pantheon

Benn, S.I. and R.S. Peters (1959) *Social Principles and the Democratic State*, London: Allen & Unwin

Bennett, John (1985) 'Ethics and Markets', *Philosophy and Public Affairs* **14**

Bentham, Jeremy (1982) *An Introduction to the Principles of Morals and Legislation*, London: Athlone Press

Beveridge, W. (1942) *Social Insurance and Allied Services*, London: HMSO, Cmnd 6404

Black, D. (1970) 'Production of Crime Rates', *American Sociological Review* **35** pp.733–48

Blackorby, Charles, and David Donaldson (1984) 'Social criteria for evaluating population change,' *Journal of Public Economics* **25** pp.13–33

Bloch, E. (1959) *Le principe esperence*, Paris: Gallimard

Block, Fred (1987) *Revising State Theory: Essays in Politics and Postindustrialism*, Philadelphia: Temple

Blomqvist, A.G. (1985) 'Political Economy of the Canadian Welfare State', in David Laidler (ed.) *Approaches to Economic Well-Being*, Toronto: University of Toronto Press

Borella, François (1991) 'Nationalité et citoyenneté' in D. Colas et al., *Citoyenneté et nationalité*, Paris: Presses Universitaires de France

Boswell, J. (1990) *Community and the Economy*, London: Routledge

Bottomley, K. and C. Coleman (1981) *Understanding Crime Rates: police and public roles in the production of official statistics*, Aldershot: Gower

Bradach, J. and R. Eccles (1989) 'Price, authority and trust: from ideal types to plural forms', in G. Thompson et al. (eds) *Markets, Hierarchies and Networks: The Coordination of Social Life*, London: Sage

Braybrooke, D. (1987) *Meeting Needs*, Princeton: Princeton University Press

Breton, Gilles and Jane Jenson (1992) 'Les Enjeux actuels de la citoyenneté', paper presented to the Canadian Political Science Association, Charlottetown, June

Breton, Gilles and Jane Jenson (1991) 'La Nouvelle dualité canadienne: L'Entente de Libre-Echange et l'après-Meech' in L. Balthazar et al. (eds.), *Le Québec et la restructuration du Canada*, Sillery, Que: Eds du Septention

Breuilly, John (1982) *Nationalism and the State*, NY: St Martin's

Briskin, L. (1991) 'Feminist Practice: a new approach to evaluating feminist strategy' in J. Wine and J. Ristock (eds) *Women and Social Change: Feminist Activism in Canada*, Toronto: James Lorimer

Brodeur, J.-P.(1988) 'Justice pénale et privatisation', in G. Boismenu and J.-J. Gleizal (eds) *Les mécanismes de régulation sociale: la justice, l'administration, la police*, Montreal: Boréal/Presses universitaires de Lyon, pp.183–231

Brodie, Janine (1985) *Women and Politics in Canada*, Toronto: McGraw-Hill Ryerson Limited

Brody, H. (1987) *Stories of Sickness*. New Haven: Yale University Press

Broome, John (1991)*Weighing Goods*, Oxford: Basil Blackwell

Brown, R. (1988) *Group Processes: Dynamics within and between groups*, New York: Basil Blackwell

Browning, Edgar K. and William R. Johnson (1984) 'The Trade Off Between Equality and Efficiency', *Journal of Political Economy* **92** (2)

Bruyn S. (ed.) (1987) *Beyond the State and the Market*, Philadelphia: Temple University Press

Buchanan, Allen (1984) 'The Right to a Decent Minimum of Health Care', *Philosophy and Public Affairs* **13**

Calabresi, G. and Ph. Bobbit (1968) *Tragic Choices*, New York: Norton

Cameron, David (1974) *Nationalism, Self-Determination and the Quebec Question*, Toronto: Macmillan

Cammack, P.(1989) *New Institutionalist Approaches to Macro-Social Analysis*, Manchester Papers in Politics, Manchester University

Canada (1985) *Report of the Royal Commission on the Economic Union and Development Prospects for Canada*, Ottawa: Minister of Supply and Services

Carens, Joseph (1981) *Equality, Moral Incentives, and the Market*, Chicago: University of Chicago Press

Cassell, Eric J. (1991) 'Recognizing Suffering', *Hastings Centre Report* **21** (3) pp.24–31

Castan, N. (1983) 'La justice en question à la fin de l'Ancien Régime', *Déviance et Société* **VII** (1) pp.23–34

Castan, N. (1980) *Justice et répression en Languedoc à l'époque des Lumières*, Paris: Flammarion

Castel R. (1992) 'De l'exclusion comme état à la vulnerabilité comme processus', in J. Affichard et J.B. de Foucauld (eds) *Justice sociale et inegalités*, Paris: Editions Esprit

Castoriadis, Cornelius (1984) *The Crossroads in the Labyrinth*, Sussex: Harvester Press

Chartrand, Paul (1991) '"Terms of Division": Problems of "Outside-Naming" for Aboriginal People in Canada', *The Journal of Indigenous Studies* **2** (2)

Chichilnisky, Graciela (1982) *Basic Needs and the North/South Debate* New York: Institute for World Order. World Order Models Project. Working Paper Number twenty-one

Chodorow, Nancy (1978) *The Reproduction of Mothering: Psychoanalysis and the Sociology of Gender*, Berkeley: University of California Press

Cicourel, A. (1968) *The Social Organisation of Juvenile Justice*, New York: Heinemann

Cicourel, A. and J. Kitsuse (1963) 'A Note on the Uses of Official Statistics', *Social Problems* **11** pp.131–9

Code, Lorraine (1993) 'Taking Subjectivity into Account', in Linda Alcoff and Elizabeth Potter (eds) *Feminist Epistemologies*, New York: Routledge

Cohen, G. A. (1989) 'On the Currency of Egalitarian Justice', *Ethics* **99**

Cohen, G. A. (1986) 'Self-ownership, World Ownership, and Equality: Part II', *Social Philosophy and Policy* **33**

Cohen, Jean (1985) 'Strategy or Identity: New Theoretical Paradigms and Contemporary Social Movements', *Social Research* **52** (4) pp.663–716

Cohen, Jean (1982) *Class and Civil Society*, Amherst: University of Massachussets Press

Cohen, Jean and Andrew Arato (1984) 'Social Movements, Civil Society and the Problem of Sovereignty', *Praxis International* **4**

Connell, R. W. (1987) *Gender and Power*, Stanford: Stanford University Press

Coote, A. (1992) *The Welfare of Citizens*, London: Institute of Public Policy Research

Courchene, Thomas (1980) 'Towards a Protected Society: The Politicization of Economic Life', *Canadian Journal of Economics* **12** (4)

Crozier, M. (1987) *Etat Modest, Etat Moderne. Stratégie pour un Autre Changement*, Paris: Fayard

Cuff, E.C. (1980) 'Some Issues in Studying the Problem of Versions in Everyday Situations', Department of Sociology, Manchester University, Occasional Paper No.3

Culyer, A.J.(1973) *The Economics of Social Policy*, London: Martin Robertson

Dawe, Alan (1978) 'Theories of Social Action', in Tom Bottomore and Robert Nisbet (ed.) *A History of Sociological Analysis*, London: Heinemann

de Beauvoir, Simone (1974 [1949]) *The Second Sex*. Translated by H.M. Parshley. New York: Vintage Books

de Leonardis, O. (1992) 'Justice as a Social Process: Rights, Differences and Capabilities', Inter-University Course of Dubrovnik, Ischia, April (Revised version of: 'Diritti, differenze, Capacità', *Democrazia e Diritto* **5–6**

de Leonardis, O. (1990) *Il terzo escluso*, Milano: Feltrinelli de Leonardis O., D. Mauri and F. Rotelli (1986) 'Deinstitutionalization, another way: The Italian mental health reform', *Health Promotion* **2**

De Marneffe, Peter (1990) 'Liberalism, Liberty, and Neutrality', *Philosophy and Public Affairs* **19**

Debuyst, C. (1985) *Modèle éthologique et criminologie*, Brussels: Mardaga

Delmas-Marty, Mireille (1992) *Les grands systèmes de politique criminelle*, Paris: Presses Universitaires de France

Dempsey, John J. (1981) *The Family and Public Policy*, Baltimore: Paul Barookes

Dickson, James and Bob Russell (ed.) (1986) *Family, Economy and State*, Toronto: Garamond Press

Didion, Joan (1979) *The White Album*, New York: Simon and Schuster

Donolo, C. e F. Fichera (1988) *Le vie dell'innovazione*, Feltrinelli: Milano

Douglas, M. (1986) *How Institutions Think*, Syracuse: Syracuse Univ. Press

Doyal, Len and Ian Gough (1991) *A Theory of Human Need*, London: Macmillan

Doyal, Len and Ian Gough (1984) 'A theory of human needs', *Critical Social Policy* **10** pp.6–38

Drover, Glenn and Patrick Kerans (1993) 'Toward a Theory of Social Welfare' *Canadian Review of Social Policy*

Durkheim, Emile (1898) 'Individualism and the Intellectuals', *Reveu Bleu*, 4th Series, No.10, pp.7–13

Durkheim, Emile (1933[1893]) *The Division of Labour in Society*, New York: Free Press

Dworkin, Ronald (1987) 'What is Equality? The Place of Liberty', *Iowa Law Review* **72**

Dworkin, Ronald (1985) *A Matter of Principle*, Cambridge: Cambridge University Press

Dworkin, Ronald (1983) 'What Liberalism Isn't', *New York Review of Books* **20** January

Dworkin, Ronald (1981a) 'What is Equality?, Part 1: Equality of Resources', *Philosophy & Public Affairs* **10**

Dworkin, Ronald (1981b) 'What is Equality?, Part 2: Equality of Resources', *Philosophy & Public Affairs* **10**

Dworkin, Ronald (1977) *Taking Rights Seriously*, Cambridge: Harvard Unversity Press

Eichler, Margrit (1983) *Families in Canada Today*, Toronto: Gage

Elliot, Carl (1991) 'Literature and psychiatry' *Current Opinion in Psychiatry* **4** pp.753–7

Elster, Jon (1992) *Local Justice*, Cambridge: Cambridge Univ. Press

Elster, Jon (1990) 'Local Justice', *Archives Européennes de Sociologie* **XXXI** pp.117–40

Elster, Jon (1988) 'Is There A Right To Work?', in Amy Gutman (ed.) *Democracy and the Welfare State*, Princeton: Princeton University Press

Elster, Jon (1985) *Making Sense of Marx*, Cambridge: Cambridge University Press

Epstein, S., G. Russell and L. Silvern (1988) 'Structure and ideology in shelters for battered women', *American Journal of Community Psychology* **16** pp.345–67

Esping-Andersen, Gösta (1990) *The Three Worlds of Welfare Capitalism*, Princeton: Princeton University Press

Esping-Andersen, Gösta (1985) *Politics Against Markets*, Cambridge: Cambridge University Press

Etzioni, A. (1988) *The Moral Dimension: Towards a New Economics*, New York: Free Press

Eyerman, Ron and Andrew Jamison (1991) *Social Movements : A Cognitive Approach*, Cambridge: Polity

Fanon, Franz (1967) *Black Skins, White Masks*, New York: Grove

Faugeron, Cl. (1991) 'La production de l'ordre et le contrôle pénal: bilan de la recherche en France depuis 1980', *Déviance et Société* **XV**(1) pp.51–91

Faugeron, Cl. (1978) 'Du simple au complexe: les représentations sociales de la justice pénale', *Déviance et Société* **II**(4) pp.411–32

Faugeron, Cl. et Ph. Robert (1976) 'Les représentations sociales de la justice pénale', *Cahiers internationaux de sociologie* **61** pp.342–66

Fay, Brian (1987) *Critical Social Science: Liberation and Its Limits*, Cambridge: Polity

Feher, Ferenz and Agnes Heller (1977) 'Forms of Equality', *Telos* **32** pp.6–25

Feinberg, Joel (1980) *Rights, Justice, and the Bounds of Liberty*, Princeton: Princeton University Press

Ferard, M.L. and N.K. Hunnybun (1962) *The Caseworker's Use of Relationship*, London: Tavistock

Ferguson, K. (1984) *The Feminist Case Against Bureaucracy*, Philadelphia: Temple University Press

Finch, Janet (1989) *Family Obligations and Social Change*, Oxford/Cambridge: Polity Press/Blackwell

Finch, Janet (1984) '"It's Great to Have Someone to Talk To": The Ethics and Politics of Interviewing Women', in C. Bell and H. Roberts (eds) *Social Researching: Politics, Problems and Practice*, London: Routledge & Kegan Paul

Finch, Janet and David Morgan (1991) 'Marriage in the 1980's: A New Sense of Realism?', in D. Clarke (ed.) *Marriage, Domestic Life and Social Change*, London: Routledge pp.55–80

Fischer, Lorenzo (1976) *Besogni, Consumi e Pratiche Sociali*, Torino: Edizioni Giappichelli

Fishkin, James (1983) *Justice, Equal Opportunity, and the Family*, New Haven: Yale University Press

Flew, Anthony (1981) *The Politics of Procrustes: Contradictions of enforced equality*, Buffalo: Prometheus

Foucault, Michel (1980) *The History of Sexuality*, New York: Vintage Press

Foucault, Michel (1977) *Discipline and Punish: The Birth of a Prison*, New York: Vintage Press

Foucault, Michel (1972) *The Archeology of Knowledge*, New York: Pantheon

Fraser, Nancy (1989) *Unruly Practices: Power, Discourse and Gender in Contemporary Social Theory*, Minneapolis: University of Minnesota Press

Fraser, Nancy and Linda Gordon (forthcoming) 'A Genealogy of "Dependency": A Keyword of the US Welfare State', *Signs*

Freeman, J. (1977) 'Crises and conflicts in social movement organizations', *Chrysalis* **5** pp.43–51

Freeman, J. (1973) 'The Tyranny of Structurelessness', in A. Koedt, E. Levine and A. Rapone (eds) *Radical Feminism*, New York: Quadrangle

Freire, Paolo (1973) *Education for Critical Consciousness*, New York: Seabury

Freire, Paolo (1972) *Pedagogy of the Oppressed*, New York: Seabury

Fried, Charles (1978) *Right and Wrong*, Cambridge: Harvard University Press

Fuss, D. (1989) *Essentially Speaking: feminism, nature and difference*, New York: Routledge

Gagnon, Alain-G and Mary Beth Montcalm (1990) *Quebec: Beyond the Quiet Revolution*, Toronto: Nelson

Gallio, G. (ed.)(1991) *Nell' impresa sociale*, Trieste: Edizioni E

Galtung, Johan (1980) 'The Basic Needs Approach', in Katrin Lederer (ed.) *Human Needs*, Cambridge, Mass.: Oelgeschlager, Gunn & Hain

Gamble, A. (1988) *The Free Economy and the Strong State*, London: Macmillan

Garfinkel, Harold (1967) *Studies in Ethnomethodology*, Englewood Cliffs, N.J.: Prentice Hall

Gaylin, William et al. (1978) *Doing Good: The Limits of Benevolence*, New York: Pantheon

Geertz, Clifford (1973) *The Interpretation of Cultures*, London: Hutchinson

Geras, Norman (1985) 'The Controversy about Marx and Justice' *New Left Review* **150**

Geras, Norman (1983) *Marx and Human Nature: Refutation of a Legend*, London: Verso

Gewirth, Alan (1977) *Reason and Morality*, Chicago: University of Chicago Press

Giddens, Anthony (1990) *The Consequences of Modernity*, Stanford: Stanford University Press

Giddens, Anthony (1984) *The Constitution of Society: Outline of the Theory of Structuration*, Berkeley and Los Angeles: University of California Press

Giddens, Anthony (1981) *A Contemporary Critique of Historical Materialism: Vol. 1 Power, Property and the State*, Berkeley and Los Angeles: University of California Press

Giddens, Anthony (1979) *Central Problems in Social Theory: Action, structure and contradiction in social analysis*, Berkeley and Los Angeles: University of California Press

Gilligan, Carol (1982) *In A Different Voice*, Cambridge: Harvard University Press

Gilligan, Carol and J. Attanucci (1988) 'Two Moral Orientations' in Gilligan, Ward and Taylor (eds) *Mapping the Moral Domain*, Cambridge: Harvard University Press

Goffman, Erving (1969) *Interaction Ritual*, New York: Doubleday Anchor

Goffman, Erving (1961) *Asylums: Essays on the Social Situation of Mental Patients and Other Inmates*, Garden City, N.J.: Doubleday

Goffman, Erving (1959) *The Presentation of the Self in Everyday Life*, New York: Doubleday Anchor

Goffman, Erving (1955) 'On Face-Work: An Analysis of the Ritual Elements in Social Interaction', *Psychiatry* **18** (3) pp.213–31

Goldberg, David Theo (ed.) (1990) *Anatomy of Racism*, Minneapolis: University of Minnesota Press

Goldberg, E.M. (1963) 'The Function and Use of Relationship in Psychiatric Social Work', in *Relationship in Casework*, London: Association of Psychiatric Social Workers

Goodin, Robert (1988) *Reasons for Welfare: the Political Theory of the Welfare State*, Princeton: Princeton University Press

Gordon, Linda (forthcoming) 'Social insurance and public assistance: the influence of gender in welfare thought in the United States, 1890–1935', *American Historical Review*

Gorz, A. (1988) *Métamorphoses du travail*, Paris: Galilée

Gorz, A. (1982) *Farewell to the Working Class: An Essay on Post-Industrial Socialism*, London: Pluto

Gough, I. (1992) 'Economic institutions and the satisfaction of human needs', unpublished paper

Gough, I. (1979) *The Political Economy of the Welfare State*, London: Macmillan

Gould, Carol (1988) *Rethinking democracy: Freedom and social cooperation in politics, economy and society*, Cambridge: Cambridge University Press

Gray, John (n.d.) *The Moral Foundations of Market Institutions*

Gray, John (1984) *Hayek on Liberty*, Oxford: Basil Blackwell

Green, Hazel (1985) *Informal Carers: A study*, London: OPCS/HMSO

Greenberg, David H. and Marvin B. Mandell (1991) 'Research Utilization in Policymaking: A Tale of Two Series (of Social Experiments)', *Journal of Policy Analysis and Management* **10** (4)

Greenberg, E. (1986) *Workplace Democracy: The Political Effects of Participation*, Boston: Cornell University Press

Greenberg, Valerie D. (1989) 'The "Uneven Mirrors" of Art and Science: Kunert and Eischer', *Mosaic* 22

Griffin, James (1986) *Well-Being: Its meaning, measurement and moral importance*, Oxford: Clarendon Press

Gronemeyer, Marianne (1988) *Die Macht der Bedürfnisse: Reflexionen über ein Phantom*, Reinbek: Rowohlt TB

Günther, Klaus (1989) 'Ein normativer Begriff der Kohärenz für eine Theorie der juristischen Argumentation', *Rechtstheorie* 20 pp.163–90

Günther, Klaus (1988) *Der Sinn für Angemessenheit: Anwendungsdiskurse in Moral und Recht*, Frankfurt: Suhrkamp

Guntrip, Harry (1971) *Psychoanalytic Theory, Therapy, and the Self*, New York: Basic Books

Gusfield, J. (1981) *The Culture of Public Problems: Drinking-Driving and the Symbolic Order*, Chicago: University of Chicago Press

Gutmann, Amy (1980) *Liberal equality*, Cambridge: Cambridge University Press

Gutting, Gary (1989) *Michel Foucault's Archaeology of Scientific Reason*, Cambridge: Cambridge University Press

Habermas, Jürgen (1992) *Autonomy and Solidarity: Interviews with Jürgen Habermas*, Peter Dews (ed.) London: Verso

Habermas, Jürgen (1990) *Moral Consciousness and Communicative Action*, Cambridge: MIT Press

Habermas, Jürgen (1987) *The Theory of Communicative Action: Volume 2: Lifeworld and System: A Critique of Functionalist Reason*, Boston: Beacon Press

Habermas, Jürgen (1975) *Legitimation Crisis*, Boston: Beacon Press

Hahn, F. H. (1973) 'On Optimum Taxation', *Journal of Economic Theory* 6

Hahnel, Robin and Michael Albert (1990) *Quiet Revolution in Welfare Economics*, Princeton: Princeton University Press

Hall, P. (1986) *Governing the Economy*, Cambridge: Polity

Hall, Stuart and David Held (1989) 'Citizens and Citizenship', in Stuart Hall and Martin Jacques (eds) *New Times*, London: Lawrence & Wishart

Haraway, Donna (1991) *Simians, Cyborgs, and Women: The Reinvention of Nature*. New York: Routledge

Harding, Sandra (1986) *The Science Question in Feminism*, Ithaca: Cornell University Press

Hassard, John and Denis Pym (1990) *The Theory of Philosophy of Organisations*, London: Routledge

Hayek, Friedrich A. von (1960) *The Constitution of Liberty*, Chicago: University of Chicago Press

Heilbroner, Robert (1986) *The Essential Adam Smith*, London: Norton

Heilbrun, Carolyn (1988) *Writing a Woman's Life*, New York: Ballantine

Heller, Agnes (1988) 'On Formal Democracy', in J. Keane (ed.) *Civil Society and the State*, London: Verso

Heller, Agnes (1985) *The Power of Shame: A Rational Perspective*, London: Routledge & Kegan Paul

Heller, Agnes (1984) *Radical Philosophy*, Oxford: Basil Blackwell

Heller, Agnes (1976) *The Theory of Need in Marx*, New York: St. Martin's Press

Herzlich, C. (1972) 'La représentation sociale', in S. Moscovici (dir.) *Introduction à la psychologie sociale*, vol. I Paris: Larousse, pp.303–25

Hewitt, M. (1992) *Welfare, Ideology and Need*, Sussex: Harvester

Hill, Michael and Glen Bramley (1986) *Analysing Social Policy*, London: Basil Blackwell

Hirschman, A. (1985), 'Against Parsimony: three easy ways of complicating some categories of economic discourse', *Economics and Philosophy* 1

Hodgson, G. (1988) *Economics and Institutions*, Cambridge: Polity

Hodgson, G. (1984) *The Democratic Economy*, Harmondsworth: Pelican

Hollander, Samuel (1987) *Classical Economics*, Oxford: Basil Blackwell

Honneth, Axel (1990) 'Integrität und Missachtung: Grundmotive einer Moral der Anerkennung', *Merkur* 501 pp.1043–54

Honneth, Axel and Hans Joas (1988) *Social Action and Human Nature*, Cambridge: Cambridge University Press

Hooker, M.B. (1975) *Legal Pluralism: An Introduction to Colonial and Neo-Colonial Laws*, Oxford: Clarendon Press

hooks, bell (1991) *Yearning: race, gender, and cultural politics*, Toronto: Between the Lines

Hughes, Kenneth (1986) *Signs of Literature: Language, Ideology and the Literary Text*, Vancouver: Talonbooks

Hum, Derek and Wayne Simpson (1991) *Income Maintenance, Work Effort, and the Canadian Mincome Experiment*, Ottawa: Economic Council of Canada

Inman, Robert P. (1985) 'Markets, Government and the "New" Political Economy', in Alan Auerbach and Martin Feldstein (eds) *Handbook of Public Economics*, Amsterdam: Elsevier Science Publishers

Jacobs, Lesley A. (forthcoming) 'Equity and Opportunity', in Pierre-François Gingras, (ed.) *Gender and Politics in Contemporary Canada*, Ottawa: University of Ottawa Press

Jacobs, Lesley A. (1993a) *Rights and Deprivation*, Oxford: Oxford University Press

Jacobs, Lesley A. (1993b) 'The Enabling Model of Rights', *Political Studies* 41

Jenson, Jane (1992) 'Citizenship and Equity: Variations Across Time and In Space', in J. Hiebert (ed.) *Political Ethics: A Canadian Perspective*, vol. 12 of the Research Studies of the Royal Commission on Electoral Reform and Party Financing, Toronto: Dundurn Press

Jenson, Jane (1991) 'All the World's a Stage: Ideas, Spaces and Time in Canadian Political Economy', *Studies in Political Economy* 36

Jenson, Jane (1990) 'Representations in Crisis: The Roots of Canada's Permeable Fordism', *Canadian Journal of Political Science* **XXIII** (4)

Jenson, Jane (1989a) '"Different" but not "exceptional": Canada's Permeable Fordism', *Canadian Journal of Sociology and Anthropology* 26 (1)

Jenson, Jane (1989b) 'Paradigms and Political Discourse: Protective Legislation in France and the United States Before 1914', *Canadian Journal of Political Science* **XXII** (2)

Jenson, Jane (1986) 'Gender and Reproduction: Or, Babies and the State', *Studies in Political Economy* 20

Jenson, Jane and Rianne Mahon (1992) 'Representing Solidarity: Class, Gender and the Crisis of Social Democratic Sweden', paper presented to the 8th International Conference of Europeanists, Chicago, March

Jessop, Bob (1982) *The Capitalist State: Marxist Theories and Methods*, Oxford: Martin Robertson

Jhappan, Radha (1992) 'A Global Community? Supranational Strategies of Canada's Aboriginal Peoples', paper presented to the Canadian Political Science Association, Charlottetown, June

Jodelet, D. (ed.) (1989) *Les représentations sociales*, Paris: Presses universitaires de France

Jordan, Bill (1992) 'The Politics of Citizen's Income', *Basic Income Research Group Bulletin*, 15 pp.15–17

Jordan, Bill (1991) 'Efficiency, justice and the obligations of citizenship; the basic income approach'. Paper to Anglo-German Social Policy conference, Nottingham

Jordan, Bill (1990) *Social Work in an Unjust Society*, Hemel Hempstead: Harvester Wheatsheaf

Jordan, Bill (1989) *The Common Good: Citizenship, Morality and Self-Interest*, Oxford: Blackwell

Jordan, Bill (1973) *Paupers: The Making of the New Claiming Class*, Routledge & Kegan Paul

Jordan, Bill, Simon James, Helen Kay and Marcus Redley (1992) *Trapped in Poverty? Labour-Market Decisions in Low-Income Households*, London: Routledge

Jordan, Bill, Marcus Redley and Simon James (forthcoming) *Putting the Family First*

Jordan, Judith, Alexandra Kaplan, Jean Baker Miller, Irene Stiver and Janet Surrey (eds) (1991) *Women's Growth in Connection: Writing From the Stone Center*, New York: The Guildford Press

Jordan, William (1972) *The Social Worker in Family Situations*, London: Routledge & Kegan Paul

Jordan, William (1970) *Client-Worker Transactions*, London: Routledge & Kegan Paul

Kamerman, Sheila B. and Alfred J. Kahn (1981) *Child Care, Family Benefits, and Working Parents*, New York: Columbia University Press

Kaplan, A. (1991) 'The "Self-in Relation": Implications for Depression in Women', in Jordon, Kaplan, Miller, Stiver and Surrey (eds) *Women's Growth in Connection*, New York: The Guildford Press

Katz, D. and R. L. Kahn (1978) *The Social Psychology of Organization*, New York: Wiley

Katzenstein, P. (1985) *Small States in World Markets*, Ithaca: Cornell University Press

Kearney, Richard (1988) *The Wake of Imagination: Toward a Postmodern Culture*, Minneapolis: University of Minnesota Press

Kerans, Patrick (1993) 'Are There Universal Human Needs? A Review of Len Doyal and Ian Gough, *A Theory of Human Need*', *Canadian Review of Social Policy*

Kerans, Patrick (1991) 'Welfare and Need', paper presented to the Fifth Conference of Social Welfare Policy, Bishop's University, Lennoxville, Quebec, August

Kingdom, Elizabeth F. (1991) *What's Wrong With Rights? Problems for Feminist Politics of Law*, Edinburgh: Edinburgh University Press

Kohli, Atul (1987) *The State and Poverty in India: the Politics of Reform*, Cambridge: Cambridge University Press

Korpi, W. (1983) *The Democratic Class Struggle*, London: Routledge

Kristeva, Julia (1980) *Desire in Language: A Semiotic Approach to Literature and Art*, Translated by Thomas Gora, Alice Jardine, and Leon S. Roudiez. New York: Columbia University Press

Kritzman, Lawrence, D. (1988) *Michel Foucault: Politics, Philosophy and Culture (1977–1984)*, New York: Routledge

Kymlicka, Will (1991) 'Liberalism and the Politicization of Ethnicity', *The Canadian Journal of Law and Jurisprudence* IV (2)

Kymlicka, Will (1990) *Contemporary Political Philosophy: An Introduction*, Oxford: Clarendon Press

Kymlicka, Will (1989a) 'Liberal Individualism and Liberal Neutrality', *Ethics* 99

Kymlicka, Will (1989b) *Liberalism, Community, and Culture*, Oxford: Clarendon Press

Laclau, Ernesto and Chantal Mouffe (1985) *Hegemony and Socialist Strategy: Towards a Radical Democratic Politics*, London: Verso

Land, Hilary and Hilary Rose (1985) 'Compulsory altruism for some or an altruistic society for all', in P. Bean, J. Ferris and D. Whynes (eds) *In Defence of Welfare*, London: Tavistock

Lascoumes, P. (1986) *Les affaires ou l'art de l'ombre: les délinquances économiques et financières et leur contrôle*, Paris: Le Centurion

Lascoumes, P. (1985) 'La place du pénal dans le règlementation différentiel des conflits', *L'Année sociologique* **35** pp.153–165

Lascoumes, P., P. Poncela and P. Lenoel (1989) *Au nom de l'ordre: Histoire politique du code*, Paris: Hachette

Lea, J and J. Young (1986) *Losing the Fight against Crime*, London: Blackwell

Lea, J and J. Young (1984) *What is to be Done about Law and Order?*, Harmondsworth: Penguin

Leander, Karen (n.d.) 'Beyond criminology: Getting to know women in a Swedish prison', unpublished paper, Centre for Women's Studies, Stockholm University

Leboeuf, M.-E. (1990) 'La construction sociale des lois criminelles: l'expérience canadienne concernant l'ivresse au volant', *Déviance et Société* **XIV** (4) pp.395–420

Lévy, R. (1985) 'Police et sociologie pénale en France', *L'Année sociologique* **35** pp.61–82

LEWRG (1980) London Edinburgh Weekend Return Group, *In and Against the State*, London: Verso

Lie, J. (1991) 'Embedding Polanyi's market society', *Sociological Perspectives* **34** (2) pp.219–35

Lipietz, Alain (1989) *Choisir l'audace*, Paris: La Découverte

Lister, Ruth (1990a) 'Women, Economic Dependency and Citizenship', *Journal of Social Policy* **19** (4) pp.445–67

Lister, Ruth (1990b) *The exclusive society: citizenship and the poor*, London: Child Poverty Action Group

Long, David (1992) 'Culture, Ideology, and Militancy: The Movement of Native Indians in Canada, 1969–91', in W. E. Carroll (ed.) *Organising Dissent: Contemporary Social Movements in Theory and Practice*, Toronto: Garamond

Lorraine, Tamsin (1990) *Gender, Identity and the Production of Meaning*, Boulder, Col.: Westview Press

Luke, Timothy (1990) *Social Theory and Modernity*, London: Sage

Maas, Henry (1984) *People and Contexts: Social Development from Birth to Old Age*, Englewood Cliffs, N.J.: Prentice-Hall

MacIntyre, Alisdair (1983) *After Virtue*, Notre Dame: University of Notre Dame Press

Mack, Eric (1988) 'Liberalism, Neutrality, and Rights', in R. Pennock and John Chapman (eds) *NOMOS XXX: Religion, Morality and the Law*, New York: New York University Press

MacKinnon, C. (1989) *Toward a Feminist Theory of the State*, Cambridge: Harvard University Press

Macpherson, C.B. (1973) *Democratic Theory: Essays in Retrieval*, Oxford: Clarendon

Mallmann, Carlos (1980) 'Society, Needs, and Rights: a Systemic Approach', in Katrin Lederer (ed.) *Human Needs*, Cambridge, Mass.: Oelgeschlager, Gunn & Hain

Mannheim, V.K. (1956) *Idéologie et Utopie*, Paris: M. Rivière

Mansbridge, Jane (ed.) (1990) *Beyond Self-Interest*, Chicago: University of Chicago Press

Mansbridge, J.J. (1973) 'Time, emotion and inequality: Three problems of participatory groups', *The Journal of Applied Behavioural Science* **9** pp.351–68

March, J. and J. Olsen (1984) 'The new institutionalism: organisational factors in political life', *American Journal of Political Science* **78** pp.734–49

Marcuse, Herbert (1964) *One-Dimensional Man: Studies in the Etiology of Advanced Industrial Society*, Boston: Beacon

Mardaga, (1990) *Acteur social et délinquance: une grille de lecture du système de justice pénal*, Brussels: Mardaga

Markus, G. (1981) 'Planning the crisis: some remarks on the economic system of Soviet-type societies', *Praxis International* 3

Marshall, T.H. (1965 [1949]) 'Citizenship and Social Class', in *Class, Citizenship and Social Development*, New York: Anchor

Marshall, T.H. (1963 [1949]) 'Citizenship and Social Class', in *Sociology at the Crossroads*, London: Heinemann

Masson, J. Mousaieff (1984) *The Assault on Truth: Freud's Suppression of the Seduction Theory*, New York: Farrar, Straus & Giroux

Mathiesen, Thomas (1965) *The Defenses of the Weak: A Sociological Study of a Norwegian Correctional Institution*, London: Tavistock

Matthews, R. and J. Young (eds) (1986) *Confronting Crime*, Beverley Hills: Sage

McCloskey, Donald (1986) *The Rhetoric of Economics*, Madison: University of Wisconsin Press

McLaughlin, Eithne (1992) 'Equal Opportunities, Community Care and the Invalid Care Allowance since 1986' Paper presented to the Social Policy Association Annual Conference, University of Nottingham

Mead, George Herbert (1964 [1949]) *On Social Psychology*, Edited by Anselm Straus. Chicago: The University of Chicago Press

Mead, Lawrence (1985) *Beyond Entitlement: The Social Obligations of Citizenship*, New York: Free Press

Meade, J. (1989) *Agathotopia: the Economics of Partnership*, Milano: Feltrinelli

Melucci, Alberto (1989) *Nomads of the Present*, London: Hutchinson Radius

Melucci, Alberto (1985) 'The Symbolic Challenge of Contemporary Movements', *Social Reserach 52 (4), pp.789–816*

Melucci, Alberto (1983) 'Mouvements sociaux, mouvements post-politiques', and 'Partir des conflits pour analyser les mouvements sociaux', *Revue internationale d'action communautaire*, automne

Michels, R. (1962 [1915]) *Political Parties: A Sociological Study of the Oligarchic Tendencies of Modern Democracy*, New York: Collier

Miles, S.H. (1990) 'The Case: A Story Found and Lost', *Second Opinion* 15 pp.55–9

Miller, David (1989) *Market, State and Community: Theoretical Foundations of Market Socialism*, Oxford: Clarendon Press

Miller, David (1976) *Social Justice*, Oxford: Clarendon

Miller, Jean Baker (1986) *Toward a New Psychology of Women*, Boston: Beacon Press

Minow, Martha (1990) *Making All the Difference*, Cornell: Cornell University Press

Mirrlees, James (1971) 'An exploration in the theory of optimum income taxation,' *Review of Economic Studies* 38 pp.175–208

Mishra, Ramesh (1984) *The Welfare State in Crisis: Social Thought and Social Change*, Brighton: Wheatsheaf

Molyneux, Maxine (1985) 'Mobilization without Emancipation? Women's Interests, the State and Revolution in Nicaragua', *Feminist Studies* 11 pp.227–54

Moon, Donald (1988) 'The Moral Basis of the Welfare State', in Amy Gutman (ed.) *Democracy and the Welfare State*, Princeton: Princeton University Press

Morgen S. (1983) 'Towards a politics of "feelings" : beyond the dialectic of thought and action', *Women's Studies* 10 pp.203–23

Morley, R. and A. Mullender (1992) 'Hype or Hope? The importation of pro-arrest policies and batterers' programmes from North America to Britain as key measures for preventing violence against women in the home', *International Journal of Law and the Family* **6** pp.265–88

Moroney, R. M. (1976) *The Family and the State*, London: Longman

Moscovici, S. (1976) 'La psychologie des représentations sociales', *Revue européenne de science sociales* **XIV** (38–9) pp.409–16

Mulkay, Michael and Jonathan Potter (1985) 'Scientists' Interview Talk: Interviews as a Technique for Revealing Participants' Interpretive Practices', in M. Brenner, J. Brown and D. Canter (eds) *The Research Interview: Uses and Approaches*, New York: Academic Press pp.247–71

Murray, Charles (1989) *In Pursuit of Happiness and Good Government*, New York: Touchstone Books

Murray, Charles (1984) *Losing Ground: American Social Policy 1950–1980*. New York: Basic Books

Myles, John (1988) 'Decline or Impasse? The Current State of the Welfare State', *Studies in Political Economy* **26**

Nancy, Jean Luc (1991) *The Inoperative Community*, Minneapolis: University of Minnesota Press

Nash, June C. (1989) *From Tank Town to High Tech: The Clash of Community and Industrial Cycles*, Albany, NY: State University of New York Press

Negt, O. (1988) *Lavoro e tempo*, Roma: Edizioni Lavoro

Nelson, B. (1984) 'Women's poverty and women's citizenship: some political consequences of economic marginality', *Signs* **10**

Nelson, Robert H. (1991) *Reaching for Heaven on Earth: The Theological Meaning of Economics*, Savage, Md.: Rowman & Littlefield

Nemmi, Max (1991) 'Le "dés" accord du Lac Meech et la construction de l'imaginaire symbolique des Québécois', in L. Balthazar et al. (eds) *Le Québec et la restructuration du Canada*, Sillery, Que: Eds du Septention

Neysmith, S. (1991) 'From Community Care to a Social Model of Care', in C. Baines, P. Evans and S. Neysmith (eds) *Women's Caring: Feminist Perspectives on Social Welfare*, Toronto: McClelland & Stewart

Novak, Michael et al. (1987) *The New Consensus on the Family and Welfare: A Community of Self-Reliance*, Washington: American Enterprise Institute for Public Policy Research

Nozick, R. (1974) *Anarchy, State and Utopia*, Oxford: Blackwell

O'Donnell, A. T. (1989) 'The Neutrality of the Market', in Robert Goodin and Andrew Reeve (eds) *Liberal Neutrality*, London: Routledge

O'Sullivan, L. (1976) 'Organizing for Impact', *Quest* **3** pp.69–80

Oakley, Anne (1974) *The Sociology of Housework*, New York: Pantheon

Offe, Claus (1990) 'Reflections on the Institutional Self-transformation of Movement Politics: A Tentative Stage Model', in Russell J. Dalton and Manfried Kuechler (eds) *Challenging the Political Order: New Social and Political Movements in Western Democracies*, Cambridge: Polity Press, pp.232–50

Offe, Claus (1987) 'Challenging the boundaries of institutional politics: social movements since the 1960s', in Charles S. Maier (ed.) *Changing boundaries of the political: Essays on the evolving balance between the state and society, public and private in Europe*, Cambridge: Cambridge University Press

Offe, Claus (1984) *Contradictions of the Welfare State*, Cambridge: MIT Press

Offe, Claus (1974) 'Structural Problems of the Capitalist State', in Klaus von Beyme (ed.) *German Political Studies*, vol.1 London: Sage

Offe, Claus and Ulrich K. Preuss (1991) 'Democratic Institutions and Moral Resources', in David Held (ed.) *Political Theory Today*, Stanford: Stanford University Press

Oldfield, Adrian (1990) *Citizenship and Community: Civic Republicanism and the Modern World*, London: Routledge

Olson, Mancur (1982) *Rise and Decline of Nations*, New Haven: Yale University Press

Omi, Michael and Howard Winant (1986) *Racial Formation in the United States: From the 1960s to the 1980s*, New York: Routledge & Kegan Paul

Ontario, *Speaking Out: Final Report*, The Advisory Group on New Social Assistance Legislation, Ministry of Community and Social Services, Government of Ontario

Ontario, *Time for Action*. The Final Report of the Advisory Group on New Social Assistance Legislation, Ministry of Community and Social Services, Government of Ontario

Parker, Hermione (1989) *Instead of the Dole: An Enquiry into the Integration of the Tax and Benefit Systems*, London: Routledge

Parkin, Frank (1979) *Class Inequality and Political Order*, London: Paladin

Pascall, G. (1986) *Social Policy: A feminist analysis*, London: Tavistock

Pateman, C. (1989) *The Disorder of Women*, Chicago: Polity Press

Pavlich, George (1992) 'Mediating Disputes: The Regulatory Logic of Government Through Pastoral Power', University of British Columbia: Ph.D. Thesis

Peffer, R. G. (1990) *Marxism, Morality, and Social Justice*, Princeton: Princeton University Press

Penz, Peter (1990) 'Basic Human Needs and Social Efficiency', Paper to Conference on Socio-Economics, Washington

Penz, Peter (1987) 'Normative Issues in Social Needs Assessment: A Theoretical Overview', Faculty of Environmental Studies, York University

Penz, Peter (1986) *Consumer Sovereignty and Human Interests*, Cambridge: Cambridge University Press

Pepinsky, H. (1976) 'Police patrolmen's offense-reporting behaviour', *Journal of Research in Crime and Delinquency* 13 pp.33–47

Phillips, Anne (1991) *Engendering Democracy*, Cambridge: Polity Press

Pickvance, Chris (1976) 'On the Study of Urban Social Movements', in C. Pickvance (ed.) *Urban Sociology: Critical Essays*, London: Tavistock

Pinker, Robert (1979) *The idea of welfare*, London: Heinemann

Pinker, Robert (1971) *Social Theory and Social Policy*, London: Heinemann

Pires, A. et J. Roberts, (1992) 'Le renvoi et la classification des infractions d'agression sexuelle', *Criminologie* XXV (1) pp.27–63

Pitch, T.(1989) *Responsabilità limitate*, Milano: Feltrinelli

Pitch, T. (1985) 'Critical Criminology, the Construction of Social Problems and the Question of Rape', *International Journal of the Sociology of Law* 13 pp.35–46

Plant, Raymond (1991a) *Modern Political Thought*, Oxford: Basil Blackwell

Plant, Raymond (1991b) 'Citizenship and Civilizing Processes: A Political Science Perspective', in B. S. Turner (ed.) *Citizenship, Civil Society and Social Cohesion*, Swindon: ESRC

Plant, Raymond (1988) *Citizenship, Rights and Socialism*, London: Fabian Society (Fabian tracts; 531)

Plant, Raymond (1982) *Hegel*, Oxford: Basil Blackwell

Plant, Raymond, H. Lesser and P. Taylor-Gooby (1980) *Political Philosophy and Social Welfare*, London: Routledge & Kegan Paul

Pogge, T. (1989) *Realizing Rawls*, Ithaca: Cornell University Press

Polanyi, Karl (1957 [1944]) *The Great Transformation*, Beacon Press

Popkin, Samuel L. (1979) *The Rational Peasant: The Political Economy of Rural Vietnam*, Chicago: Chicago University Press

Powell, W. (1990) 'Neither market nor hierarchy: network forms of organisation', in G. Thompson et al. (eds) *Markets, Hierarchies and Networks*, London: Sage

Powell, David M. (1986) 'Managing Organizational Problems in Alternative Service Organizations', *Administration in Social Work* **10** (3) pp.56–62

Préteceille, Edmond (1975) 'Besoins sociaux et socialisation de la consommation', *La Pensée* **180** pp.22–60

Préteceille, Edmond and Jean-Pierre Terrail (1985) *Capitalism, Consumption and Needs*, Oxford: Basil Blackwell

Putterman, L. (1990) *Division of Labor and Welfare: An Introduction to Economic Systems*, Oxford: Oxford University Press

Raphael, D.D. (1990) *Problems of Political Philosophy*, London: Macmillan

Rasmussen, David M. (1990) *Reading Habermas*, Oxford: Blackwell

Rawls, Anne Warfield (1989) 'Language, Self and Social Order: A Reformulation of Goffman and Sacks', *Human Studies* **12** pp.147–72

Rawls, Anne Warfield (1987) 'The Interaction Order *Sui Generis*: Goffman's Contribution to the Social Theory', *Sociological Theory* **5** pp.136–49

Rawls, John (1988) 'The Priority of Right and Ideas of the Good', *Philosophy and Public Affairs* **17**

Rawls, John (1987) 'The Idea of an Overlapping Consensus', *Oxford Journal of Legal Studies* **7**

Rawls, John (1982a) 'The Basic Liberties and Their Priority', *The Tanner Lectures on Human Values III*, Cambridge: Cambridge University Press

Rawls, John (1982b) 'Social Unity and Primary Goods', in Amartya Sen and Bernard Williams (eds) *Utilitarianism and Beyond*, Cambridge: Cambridge University Press

Rawls, John (1971) *A Theory of Justice*, Cambridge: Harvard University Press

Raz, Joseph (1989) 'Facing Up: A Reply', *Southern California Law Review* **62**

Raz, Joseph (1986) *The Morality of Freedom*, Oxford: Clarendon Press

Redley, Marcus (1991) 'Interview Moments: How is it that Some Respondents Appear to have more Personality than Others?' Paper given to the 13th Discourse Analysis Workshop. Exeter University, September

Reich, Robert B. (1991) 'The REAL Economy', *The Atlantic Monthly* February, pp.35–52

Reisman, D.A. (1976) *Adam Smith's Sociological Economics*, London: Croom Helm

Repucci, N.D., (1973) 'The social psychology of institutional change: General principles for intervention', *American Journal of Community Psychology* **1** pp.330–41

Revue internationale d'action communautaire (1983) automne

Ridington, J. (1982) 'Providing Services the Feminist Way', in M. Fitzgerald, C. Guberman and M. Wolfe (eds) *Still Ain't Satisfied: Canadian Feminism Today*, Toronto: Women's Press

Riger, S. (1984) 'Vehicles For Empowerment: The Case of Feminist Movement Organizations', in J. Rappaport, C. Swift and R. Hess (eds) *Studies In Empowerment*, New York: Hawthorne Press

Rioux, Marcia and Cameron Crawford (1990) 'Poverty and Disability' *Canadian Journal of Mental Health* **9** (2)

Rist, G. (1980) 'Basic questions about basic human needs', in K.Lederer (ed.) *Human Needs*, Oelgeschlager, Gunn & Hain

Ristock, J.L. (1991) 'Feminist Collectives: The struggles and contradictions in our quest for a "uniquely feminist structure"', in J. Wine and J.L. Ristock (eds) *Women and Social Change: Feminist Activism in Canada*, Toronto: James Lorimer

Ristock, J.L. (1990) 'Canadian Feminist Social Services Agencies: Caring and Contradictions', in L. Albrecht and R. Brewer (eds) *Bridges of Power: Women's Multicultural Alliances*, Philadelphia: New Society Publishers

Ristock, J.L. (1989) 'Feminist Social Service Collectives in Canada — a viable force or a contradiction?' Unpublished Doctoral Dissertation. University of Toronto

Ristock, J. L. (1987) 'Working Together for Empowerment', *Canadian Women's Studies* **8** (4) pp.74–6

Robert, Ph. (1990) 'L'Utilisation du concept d'acteur social dans l'étude du crime', in *Acteur social et délinquance*, Brussels: Mardaga

Robert, Ph. (1985) 'Insécurité, opinion publique et politique criminelle', *L'Année sociologique* **35** pp.199–231

Robert, Ph. et Cl. Faugeron (1978) *La Justice et son public: les représentations sociales du système pénal*, Masson/Médecine et Hygiène

Roderick, Rick (1986) *Habermas and the Foundations of Critical Theory*, New York: St. Martin's Press

Roemer, John (1992) 'The Morality and Efficiency of Market Socialism', *Ethics* **102**

Roemer, John (1989) *Free to Lose: An Introduction to Marxist Economic Philosophy*, London: Radius

Rogowski, Ronald (1985) 'Conclusion', in E. A. Tiryakian and R. Rogowski (eds) *New Nationalisms of the Developed West: Toward Explanation*, Boston: Allen & Unwin

Rosch, E. and B. B. Lloyd (eds) (1978) *Cognition and Categorization*, Hillsdale, N.J.: Erlbaum

Ross. D. (ed.) (1956) *Aristotle's Metaphysics*, London: Dent

Ross, David and Richard Shillington (1989) *The Canadian Fact Book on Poverty*, Ottawa: Canadian Council on Social Development

Rucht, Dieter (1990) 'The Strategies and Action Repertoires of New Movements', in Russell J. Dalton and Manfred Kuechler (eds) *Challenging the Political Order: New Social and Political Movements in Western Democracies*, Cambridge: Polity Press, pp.156–78

Rueschemeyer, D. and P. Evans (1985) 'The state and economic transformation', in P. Evans et al. (eds) *Bringing the State Back In*, Cambridge: Cambridge University Press

Sachs, Wolfgang (ed.) (1992) *The Development Dictionary: A Guide to Knowledge as Power*, London: Zed Books

Said, Edward (1978) *Orientalism*, New York: Pantheon

Saint-Amand, Néré and Huguette Clavette (1992) *Entraide et Débrouillardise sociale chez des personnes aux prises avec des problèmes psychiatriques: Importance pour la formation professionelle*, Ottawa: Canadian Council for Social Development

Sandbrook, Richard (1982) *The Politics of Basic Needs: Urban Aspects of Assaulting Poverty in Africa*, Toronto: University of Toronto Press

Sandel, M. (1982) *Liberalism and the Limits of Justice*, Cambridge: Cambridge University Press

Sartre, Jean-Paul (1976) *Critique of Dialectical Reason*, London: New Left Books

Scales, Ann (1986) 'The Emergence of Feminist Jurisiprudence: An Essay', *Yale Law Review* **95**

Scanlon, Thomas (1988) 'The Significance of Choice', *The Tanner Lectures on Human Values VIII*, Cambridge: Cambridge University Press

Scanlon, Thomas (1975) 'Preference and Urgency', *Journal of Philosophy* **72**

Schumpeter, J. (1976) *Capitalism, Socialism and Democracy*, Allen & Unwin

Scott, Alan (1990) *Ideology and the New Social Movements*, London: Unwin Hyman

Scott, James C. (1990) *Domination and the Arts of Resistance: Hidden Transcripts*, New Haven: Yale University Press

Scott, James C. (1985) *Weapons of The Weak: Everyday Forms of Peasant Resistance*, New Haven: Yale University Press

Scott, Joan (1987) 'Re-writing History', in M.R. Higonnet, J. Jenson, S. Michel and M. Weitz (eds) *Behind the Lines: Gender and the Two World Wars*, New Haven: Yale University Press

Sen, A. (1988) 'Che cosa significa la povertà in una metropoli industriale avanzata', Conferenza internazionale del Progetto Milano, Milano: IRER

Sen, Amartya, (1987a) *The Standard of Living*, Cambridge: Cambridge University Press

Sen, Amartya (1987b) 'Equality of What?', in Sterling M. Mcmurrin (ed.) *Liberty, Equality and Law*, Cambridge: Cambridge University Press

Sen, Amartya (1987c) *On Ethics and Economics*, Oxford: Basil Blackwell

Sen, Amartya (1985a) *Commodities and Capabilities*, Amsterdam: Elsevier

Sen, Amartya (1985b) 'Rights and Capabilities', in T. Honderich (ed.), *Morality and Objectivity*, London: Routledge

Sen, Amartya (1984) *Resources, Values and Development*, Oxford: Blackwell

Sen, Amartya (1982a) *Choice, Welfare, and Measurement*, Oxford: Basil Blackwell

Sen, Amartya (1982b) 'Rights and Agency', *Philosophy and Public Affairs* **10**

Sen, Amartya (1979) 'Welfarism and Utilitarianism', *Journal of Philosophy* **76** pp.463–88

Sen, Amartya (1977) 'Rationals Fools: a Critique of the Behavioural Foundations of Economic Theory', *Philosophy and Public Affairs* **6**

Sen, Amartya (1970) 'The Impossibility of a Paretian Liberal', *Journal of Political Economy* **78**

Sen, Amartya and Bernard Williams (eds) (1982) *Utilitarianism and Beyond*, Cambridge: Cambridge University Press

Sennett, Richard and Jonathan Cobb (1972) *The Hidden Injuries of Class*, New York: Knopf

Shearing, C. and P. Stenning (1987) *Private Policing*, Beverley Hills: Sage

Shragge, Eric (1990) 'Community-Based Practice: Political Alternatives or New State Forms?', in Linda Davies and Eric Shragge (eds) *Bureaucracy and Community*, Montreal/New York: Black Rose Books

Silverman, David (1989) 'Telling Convincing Stories: A Plea for Cautious Positivism', in B. Glassner and J.D. Moreno (eds) *The Qualitative-Quantitative Distinction in the Social Sciences*, Dordrecht: Kluwer pp.57–77

Silverman, David (1985) *Qualitative Methodology and Sociology*, Aldershot: Gower

Simeon, Richard and Ian Robinson (1990) *State, Society and the Development of Canadian Federalism*, Toronto: University of Toronto Press

Skocpol, T. (1985) 'Bringing the state back in: strategies of analysis in current research', in P. Evans et al. (eds) *Bringing the State Back In*, Cambridge: Cambridge University Press

Smith, Adam (1976) *The Theory of Moral Sentiments*, Oxford: Clarendon Press

Smith, Dorothy E. (1990) *The Conceptual Practices of Power: A Feminist Sociology of Knowledge*. Toronto: University of Toronto Press

Smith, Dorothy E. (1987) *The Everyday World as Problematic: A Feminist Sociology*, Toronto: University of Toronto Press

Smith, G. (1980) *Social Need: Policy, Practice and Research*, London: Routledge & Kegan Paul

Soper, Kate (1990) *Troubled Pleasures*, London: Verso

Soper, Kate (1986) *Humanism and Anti-Humanism*, London: Hutchinson

Soper, Kate (1985) 'Re-thinking Ourselves', in Dan Smith and E.P. Thompson (eds) *Prospectus for a Habitable Planet*, Harmondsworth: Penguin

Soper, Kate (1981) *On Human Needs*. Sussex: Harvester Press

SPARC et al. (1993) 'Well-Being: A Literature Review and Conceptual Paper', Toronto: Ontario Premier's Council on Health, Well-Being and Social Justice

Springborg, Patricia (1981) *The Problem of Human Needs and the Critique of Civilization*, London: Allen & Unwin

Staggenborg, S. (1989) 'Stability and Innovation in the Women's Movement: a comparison of two movement organizations', *Social Problems* **36**(1) pp.75–90

Steele, Shelby (1992) 'The New Sovereignty: Grievance Groups have become nations unto themselves', *Harper's Magazine*, July

Stiglitz, Joseph (1985) 'Pareto Efficient and Optimal Taxation and the New New Welfare Economics', in Alan Auerbach and Martin Feldstein (eds) *Handbook of Public Economics*, Amsterdam: Elsevier

Streeck, W. and P. Schmitter (1985) 'Community, market, state – and associations?', in W. Streeck and P.Schmitter (eds) *Private Interest Government: Beyond Market and State*, London: Sage

Strümpel, B. and J. Scholz (1987) 'The comparative study of the economy: dimensions, methods and results', in M. Dierkes et al. (eds) *Comparative Policy Research*, Aldershot: Gower

Stuart, Charles (1984) 'Welfare Cost per Dollar of Additional Tax Revenue in the United States', *American Economic Review* **74** (3)

Sumner, L.W. (1992) 'Two Theories of the Good', *Social Philosophy and Policy* **9** pp.1–14

Tajfel, H. (1982) *Social Identity and Intergroup Relations*, Cambridge: Cambridge University Press

Tajfel, H. (1981) *Human Groups and Social Categories*, Cambridge: Cambridge University Press

Taylor, Charles (1991) *The Malaise of Modernity*, Concord, Ontario: Anansi Press

Taylor, Charles (1989) *Sources of the Self: The Making of the Modern Identity*, Cambridge: Harvard University Press

Taylor, Charles (1985) *Philosophy and the Human Sciences: Philosophical Papers 2*, Cambridge: Cambridge University Press

Taylor, Charles (1979) *Hegel and Modern Society*, Cambridge: Cambridge University Press

Taylor-Gooby, Peter (1991) 'Scrounging, moral hazard and unwaged work: citizenship and human need.' Paper presented at Social Policy Association conference, University of Nottingham

Theweleit, Klaus (1987) *Male Fantasies*. Translated by Stephen Conway. Minneapolis: University of Minnesota Press

Thompson, G. et al. (eds) (1991) *Markets, Hierarchies and Networks: The Coordination of Social Life*, London: Sage

Thompson, John B. (1990) *Ideology and Modern Culture*, Cambridge: Polity Press

Thompson, John B. (1985) *Studies in the Theory of Ideology*, Berkeley: University of California Press

Tilly, Charles (1981) 'Introduction', in Lousie Tilly and Charles Tilly (eds) *Class, Conflict and Collective Action*, Beverley Hills: Sage

Tilly, Charles (1978) *From Mobilization to Revolution*, Reading Mass.: Addison-Wesley

Tiryakian, Edward A. (1985) 'Introduction', in E. A. Tiryakian and R. Rogowski (eds) *New Nationalisms of the Developed West: Toward Explanation*, Boston: Allen and Unwin

Tobin, J. (1973) 'On Limiting the Domain of Inequality', in E. S. Phelps (ed.) *Economic Justice*, Harmondsworth: Penguin Books

Torjman, Sherri (1988) *Income Insecurity: The Disability Income System in Canada*, Toronto: The G. Allan Roeher Institute

Toronto Rape Crisis Centre, Working-Class Caucus (1988) 'Around The Kitchen Table', *Fireweed* Winter/Spring

Touraine, Alain (1985) 'An Introduction to the Study of Social Movements', *Social Research* 52(4) pp.749–87

Touraine, A. (1984) *Le retour de l'acteur*, Paris: Fayard

Touraine, Alain (1981) *The Voice and the Eye: an Analysis of Social Movements*, Cambridge: Cambridge University Press

Travers, Andrew (forthcoming) 'Strangers to Themselves: How Interactants Are Other than They Are', *British Journal of Sociology*

Travers, Andrew (1992) 'The Experience of Self: Looping the Loop in Face-to-Face Interaction', Department of Sociology, Exeter University

Tronto, J. (1987) 'Beyond Gender Difference to a Theory of Care', *Signs: Journal of Women in Culture and Society* 12 (4)

Turnaturi, G. (1990) *Associati per amore*, Milano: Feltrinelli

Turner, B. (ed.) (1991) *Citizenship, Civil Society and Social Cohesion*, Swindon: Economic and Social Research Council

Turner, B. (1990) 'Outline of a theory of citizenship', *Sociology* 24 (2) pp.189–217

Turner, John C. (1987) *Rediscovering the Social Group*, Oxford: Basil Blackwell

Turner, John C. and Howard Giles (1981) *Intergroup Behaviour*, Oxford: Basil Blackwell

Unger, Roberto M. (1987) *False Necessity: Anti-Necessitarian Social Theory in the Service of Radical Democracy*, Cambridge: Cambridge University Press

Unger, Roberto M. (1986) *The Critical Legal Studies Movement*, Cambridge: Harvard University Press

Ungerson, Clare (1992) 'Payment for caring – mapping a territory', Paper for the Social Policy Association Annual Conference, University of Nottingham

Ungerson, Clare (1987) *Policy is Personal: Sex, Gender and Informal Care*, London: Tavistock

Valverde, Mariana (1991) 'As if subjects existed: analysing social discourses', *Canadian Review of Sociology & Anthropology* 28 (2) pp.173–87

Van der Veen, R. and P. van Parijs (1987) 'A capitalist road to communism', *Theory and Society* 15

Varian, Hal R. (1984) *Microeconomic Analysis*, Second ed., New York: W.W. Norton

Varian, Hal (1975) 'Distributive Justice, Welfare Economics, and the Theory of Fairness', *Philosophy and Public Affairs* 4

Vickers, J. M. (1991) 'Bending the Iron Law of Oligarchy: debates on the feminization of organization and the political process in the English Canadian women's movement, 1970–1988', in J. Wine and J.L. Ristock (eds) *Women and Social Change: Feminist Activism in Canada*, Toronto: James Lorimer

Walby, Sylvia (1990) *Theorising Patriarchy*, Oxford: Blackwell

Waldron, Jeremy (1989) 'Autonomy and Perfectionism in Raz's *Morality of Freedom*', *Southern California Law Review* 62

Walker, Gillian (1993) 'The Conceptual Politics of Struggle: Wife Battering, the Women's Movement and the State', in Patricia Connelly and Pat Armstrong (ed) *Action: Studies in Political Economy*, Toronto: Canadian Scholars Press

Walker, Gillian (1990) *Family Violence and the Women's Movement: the conceptual politics of struggle*, Toronto: University of Toronto Press

Walzer, Michael (1992) 'Exclusion, Unjustice, and the Democratic State', in *Colloque: Justice sociale et inégalites*, Paris: Commissariat Général du Plan, November

Walzer, Michael (1987) *Interpretation and Social Criticism*, Cambridge: Harvard University Press

Walzer, Michael (1983) *Spheres of Justice: A Defense of Pluralism and Justice*, New York: Basic Books

Weale, Albert (1983) *Political Theory and Social Policy*, London: Macmillan

Weale, Albert (1978) *Equality and Social Policy*, London: Routledge & Kegan Paul

Weber, Max (1968) *Economy and Society*, New York: Bedminster

Weedon, C. (1987) *Feminist Practice and Poststructuralist Theory*, Oxford: Basil Blackwell

Weir, M., A. Orloff and T. Skocpol, (1988) 'Understanding American social politics', in M. Weir et al. (eds) *The Politics of Social Security in the United States*, Chicago: University of Chicago Press

Wellmer, Albrecht (1991) *The Persistence of Modernity: Essays on Aesthetics, Ethics, and Postmodernism*, Cambridge: MIT Press

Wellmer, Albrecht (1990) 'Practical Philosophy and the Theory of Society: On the Problem of the Normative Foundations of a Critical Social Science', in Seyla Benhabib and Fred Dallmayr (eds) *The Communicative Ethics Controversy*, Cambridge: MIT Press pp.293–329

Wiggins, David (1987) *Needs, Values, Truth: Essays in the Philosophy of Value*, Aristotelian Society Series. Volume 6. Oxford: Basil Blackwell

Wiggins, David (1985) 'The Claims of Need', in Ted Honderich (ed.) *Morality and Objectivity*, London: Routledge & Kegan Paul

Williams, Bernard (1985) *Ethics and the Limits of Philosophy*, Cambridge: Harvard University Press

Wilson, Elizabeth (1977) *Women and the Welfare State*, London: Tavistock

Withorn, A. (1984) 'For better and for worse: social relations among women in the welfare state', *Radical America* **18** pp.37–47

Wolfe, A. (1991) 'Market, state and society as codes of moral obligation', in M. Mendell and D. Salee (eds) *The Legacy of Karl Polanyi*, London: Macmillan

Wolfensburger, W. (1972) *Normalization: the principle of normalization in human services*, Downsview: National Institute on Mental Retardation

Wood, Allen (1986) 'Marx and Equality', in John Roemer (ed.) *Analytical Marxism*, Cambridge: Cambridge University Press

Young Iris Marion (1990a) *Justice and the Politics of Difference*, Princeton: Princeton University Press

Young, Iris Marion (1990b) 'The Ideal of Community and the Politics of Difference', in L. E. Nicholson (ed.) *Feminism/Postmodernism*, New York: Routledge

Young, Iris Marion (1989) 'Polity and Group Difference: A Critique of the Ideal of Universal Citizenship', *Ethics* **99**

Zaretsky, Eli (1986) *Capitalism, The Family, and Personal Life*, New York: Harper & Row

Zauberman, R. (1991) 'Victimes en France: des positions, intérêts et stratégies diverses', *Déviance et Société* **XV** (1) pp.27–49

Zauberman, R. (1985) 'Les victimes: étude du crime ou sociologie du pénal?', *L'Année sociologique* **35** pp.31–59

Zimmerman, M. (1990) 'Taking Aim on Empowerment Research: On the Distinction Between Individual and Psychological Conceptions', *American Journal of Community Psychology* **18** (1) pp.169–77

Zofel, A. (1985) 'Feminist Consciousness vs. Profit — an unsolvable contradiction?', *Women's Studies International Forum* **8** pp.25–28

Index